Marketing and Big Data Analytics in Tourism and Events

Tareq Nael Hashem
Applied Science Private University, Jordan

Ahmad Albattat
Management and Science University, Malaysia

Marco Valeri
Niccolò Cusano University, Italy

Anukrati Sharma
University of Kota, India

IGI Global
PUBLISHER of TIMELY KNOWLEDGE

A volume in the Advances in Marketing, Customer Relationship Management, and E-Services (AMCRMES) Book Series

Published in the United States of America by
IGI Global
Business Science Reference (an imprint of IGI Global)
701 E. Chocolate Avenue
Hershey PA, USA 17033
Tel: 717-533-8845
Fax: 717-533-8661
E-mail: cust@igi-global.com
Web site: http://www.igi-global.com

Library of Congress Cataloging-in-Publication Data

CIP Pending
ISBN: 979-8-3693-3310-5
EISBN: 979-8-3693-3311-2

This book is published in the IGI Global book series Advances in Marketing, Customer Relationship Management, and E-Services (AMCRMES) (ISSN: 2327-5502; eISSN: 2327-5529)

British Cataloguing in Publication Data
A Cataloguing in Publication record for this book is available from the British Library.

All work contributed to this book is new, previously-unpublished material.
The views expressed in this book are those of the authors, but not necessarily of the publisher.

For electronic access to this publication, please contact: eresources@igi-global.com.

Advances in Marketing, Customer Relationship Management, and E-Services (AMCRMES) Book Series

ISSN:2327-5502
EISSN:2327-5529

Editor-in-Chief: Eldon Y. Li, National Chengchi University, Taiwan & California Polytechnic State University, USA

MISSION

Business processes, services, and communications are important factors in the management of good customer relationship, which is the foundation of any well organized business. Technology continues to play a vital role in the organization and automation of business processes for marketing, sales, and customer service. These features aid in the attraction of new clients and maintaining existing relationships.

The Advances in Marketing, Customer Relationship Management, and E-Services (AMCRMES) Book Series

addresses success factors for customer relationship management, marketing, and electronic services and its performance outcomes. This collection of reference source covers aspects of consumer behavior and marketing business strategies aiming towards researchers, scholars, and practitioners in the fields of marketing management.

COVERAGE

- Electronic Services
- CRM and customer trust
- Cases on Electronic Services
- Mobile CRM
- Cases on CRM Implementation
- Web Mining and Marketing
- B2B marketing
- Text Mining and Marketing
- E-Service Innovation
- Customer Retention

IGI Global is currently accepting manuscripts for publication within this series. To submit a proposal for a volume in this series, please contact our Acquisition Editors at Acquisitions@igi-global.com or visit: http://www.igi-global.com/publish/.

The Advances in Marketing, Customer Relationship Management, and E-Services (AMCRMES) Book Series (ISSN 2327-5502) is published by IGI Global, 701 E. Chocolate Avenue, Hershey, PA 17033-1240, USA, www.igi-global.com. This series is composed of titles available for purchase individually; each title is edited to be contextually exclusive from any other title within the series. For pricing and ordering information please visit http://www.igi-global.com/book-series/advances-marketing-customer-relationship-management/37150. Postmaster: Send all address changes to above address.

Titles in this Series

For a list of additional titles in this series, please visit:
http://www.igi-global.com/book-series/advances-marketing-customer-relationship-management/37150

Impact of Teleworking and Remote Work on Business Productivity, Retention, Advancement, and Bottom Line
Harish Chandra Chandan (Independent Researcher, USA)
Business Science Reference • © 2024 • 311pp • H/C (ISBN: 9798369313145) • US $290.00

AI-Driven Marketing Research and Data Analytics
Reason Masengu (Middle East College, Oman) Option Takunda Chiwaridzo (University of Science and Technology Beijing, Beijing, China) Mercy Dube (Midlands State University, Zimbabwe) and Benson Ruzive (Modern College of Business and Science, Oman)
Business Science Reference • © 2024 • 490pp • H/C (ISBN: 9798369321652) • US $290.00

Marketing Innovation Strategies and Consumer Behavior
Belem Barbosa (University of Porto, Portugal)
Business Science Reference • © 2024 • 469pp • H/C (ISBN: 9798369341957) • US $325.00

Corporate Governance and CSR Strategies for Sustainability
Maja Pucelj (Faculty of Organisation Studies, University of Novo Mesto, Slovenia) and Rado Bohinc (Scientific Research Centre Koper, Slovenia)
Information Science Reference • © 2024 • 368pp • H/C (ISBN: 9798369358634) • US $290.00

Balancing Automation and Human Interaction in Modern Marketing
Arjun J. Nair (St. Lawrence College, Canada) Sridhar Manohar (Chitkara Business School, Chitkara University, India) Amit Mittal (Chitkara Business School, Chitkara University, India) and Wasim Ahmed (University of Hull, UK)
Business Science Reference • © 2024 • 326pp • H/C (ISBN: 9798369322765) • US $290.00

Building Strong Brands and Engaging Customers With Sound
Minna-Maarit Jaskari (School of Marketing and Communication, University of Vaasa, Finland)
Business Science Reference • © 2024 • 267pp • H/C (ISBN: 9798369307786) • US $265.00

For an entire list of titles in this series, please visit:
http://www.igi-global.com/book-series/advances-marketing-customer-relationship-management/37150

IGI Global
PUBLISHER of TIMELY KNOWLEDGE

701 East Chocolate Avenue, Hershey, PA 17033, USA
Tel: 717-533-8845 x100 • Fax: 717-533-8661
E-Mail: cust@igi-global.com • www.igi-global.com

Table of Contents

Detailed Table of Contents

In the realm of travel, a silent revolution is unfolding, driven by artificial intelligence (AI). Tailored experiences powered by AI are tangible, with data analytics crafting bespoke itineraries and recommendations fueled by natural language processing and simplifying planning and navigation. AI optimizes transportation, refining traffic control and route planning for convenience. Augmented reality adds immersive layers to traveler experiences. AI plays a pivotal role in sustainability, regulating visitor flows and energy usage. Real-time data analysis aids crisis management, ensuring safety and industry resilience. AI systems, standalone or integrated, encompass recommendation engines, personalization algorithms, conversational interfaces, predictive tools, language translation software, and intelligent destination mapping. Smart destinations integrate these technologies with social and organizational elements. AI empowers travelers with personalized options and enables companies to tailor experiences.

In an age marked by an abundance of information, the tourism industry grapples with the task of effectively reaching and engaging potential visitors. This study explores the transformative potential of big data analytics (BDA) in reshaping strategies for marketing touristic destinations, emphasizing a more personalized and efficient approach. It thoroughly examines BDA's pivotal role in revolutionizing destination promotion in the digital era, highlighting the importance of data-driven decision-making for impactful campaigns. The chapter also addresses challenges and ethical considerations associated with utilizing extensive data for tourism promotion. This contribution is significant for industry practitioners, policymakers, and researchers interested in leveraging BDA for sustainable and impactful tourism growth.

The integration of MKIS and BDA, along with data fusion techniques, can lead to more targeted and effective marketing strategies for touristic destinations. This can result in better customer satisfaction, increased visitor numbers, and higher revenue for the destinations. By leveraging data fusion, touristic destinations can gain a deeper understanding of tourists' preferences and behaviors. This understanding can enable them to provide personalized and tailored experiences, leading to higher visitor satisfaction and loyalty. The chapter aims to shed light on the integration of MKIS and BDA in the marketing of touristic destinations and highlight the potential of data fusion for destination success. By bridging the gap between traditional marketing information systems and the advanced analytics capabilities of big data, this chapter seeks to empower touristic destinations with actionable insights for effective marketing strategies and improved visitor experiences.

For effective strategic planning and focused marketing campaigns, it is essential to understand the museum's target audience and how cultural tourism can influence sports tourism. The study aims to investigate the satisfaction and experience of international visitors to the Museum of Futebol Clube do Porto and their profiles. The TripAdvisor reviews were considered to gather information on the Museum of Futebol Clube do Porto's target audience using a business intelligence tool to process, analyze, and draw conclusions from the data. Insights regarding the geographic and gender distribution of reviewers and their overall evaluations of the museum were discovered by analysing TripAdvisor reviews.

In today's dynamic and competitive business environment, marketing intelligence systems (MIS) are vital tools that empower organizations to understand the market, monitor competitors, identify trends, evaluate performance, and make informed decisions, ultimately contributing to effective marketing strategies, enhanced customer experiences, and sustainable business growth. This chapter discusses the impact of MIS in the tourism industry. It explains how the integration of data and advanced technologies allows these systems to provide insights that can sharpen a tourism organization's competitive edge. The chapter outlines the key components of MIS—data collection, analysis, and decision support—and their role in driving strategic marketing decisions. It also examines how these systems enhance customer segmentation, campaign personalization, pricing, and customer relations, with real-world examples underscoring their efficacy. Challenges of implementation are acknowledged, with the chapter concluding on the need for ongoing innovation and future research in this area.

This chapter proposes to explore the intersection of virtual reality (VR), augmented reality (AR), data analytics, and marketing in the context of the tourism and events industry. As technology continues to advance, organizations within this sector are seeking innovative and transformative ways to engage and attract tourists and event attendees. VR and AR have emerged as powerful tools for creating immersive experiences, while data analytics provides insights into consumer behavior and preferences. This chapter will examine how these technologies can be integrated into marketing strategies to enhance engagement, visitor experiences, and decision-making processes. By discussing real-world case studies, ethical considerations, and future trends, this chapter aims to provide a comprehensive overview of the subject and offer practical insights for professionals and researchers in the field.

Hemant Gupta, Alliance University, India
Anand Kumar Sonkar, Dhirendra Mahila P.G. College, India

Medical tourism is known as a phenomenon where millions of patients a year from all over the world travel across international destinations in order to obtain various forms of healthcare. Most of these patients are known to travel from developed countries to developing countries, looking for highly invasive medical treatments to lesser invasive and recreational medical treatment. The main objective of this research is to try and understand the importance of marketing medical tourism in India. This research mandated registering the observations of the medical tourists from Gulf countries to find answers to how the attitudes and behaviors of patients towards the concept of medical tourism influence their decision to become a medical tourist. The authors interviewed patients from the UAE through questionnaires that address the objective of the research. The authors noted that the primary drivers of medical tourism to India are the country's highly skilled medical professionals, as well as its extensive medical facilities and reasonably priced treatments.

Dwijendra Nath Dwivedi, Krakow University of Economics, Poland
Ghanashyama Mahanty, Department of Analytical and Applied Economics, Utkal University, Bhubaneswar, India
Shafik Khashouf, University of Liverpool, UK

Travel and tourism represent a multifaceted sector, with the customer's journey from departure to return encompassing myriad interactions. A deeper comprehension of these interactions allows for enhanced planning aimed at enriching the customer's experience. The integration of advanced data analytics has significantly advanced the focus on customer needs within the travel and tourism industry. In this specific study, data analytics is applied to tailor experiences for visitors to an amusement park, using a comprehensive dataset from a fictional park to explore how variables such as age, group makeup, admission time, ride preferences, and eating habits can enhance the visitor experience. The findings offer valuable insights into visitor behaviors, facilitating the customization of services. For instance, age-related data informs the imposition of ride restrictions, while data on arrival and departure times aid in refining park operations and managing crowds more effectively.

Preface

Marketing and Big Data Analytics in Tourism and Events delves into the dynamic intersection of marketing information systems (MkIS) and big data analytics (BDA) within the realm of promoting touristic destinations.

The advent of artificial intelligence (AI) has profoundly impacted MkIS, catalyzing a paradigm shift in marketing practices. AI innovations have empowered marketers with tools to enhance customer experiences, optimize digital marketing endeavors, and deploy chatbots for seamless consumer engagement across temporal boundaries.

Furthermore, AI-driven advancements have ushered in a new era of big data analysis, redefining the possibilities of predictive analytics. By harnessing intelligent algorithms such as machine learning, deep learning, and neural network analysis, organizations can extract actionable insights from vast datasets, thereby driving strategic decision-making and fostering competitive advantages.

Throughout this book, Editors invite academicians, practitioners, industry players, postgraduate students, and researchers to explore the multifaceted dimensions of MkIS-BDA integration in the context of tourism and events. Whether you seek theoretical frameworks, practical case studies, or emerging trends, this compilation endeavors to provide valuable perspectives and stimulate intellectual discourse in this burgeoning field.

Editors extend our gratitude to all the contributors whose expertise and dedication have enriched this volume. May this book serve as a beacon for navigating the evolving landscape of marketing and big data analytics in the dynamic domain of tourism and events.

ORGANIZATION OF THE BOOK

The book collects 13 chapters. These chapters present a comprehensive exploration of the transformative intersection between technology and tourism marketing. The Authors shed light on the future trajectory of artificial intelligence (AI), big data analytics (BDA), and marketing information systems (MKIS) within the dynamic landscape of tourism and events.

Chapter 1, "A Future Look at Artificial Intelligence in the World of Tourism: Exploring the Future of AI in Tourism," sets the stage for our inquiry into the evolving role of AI in shaping travel experiences. Authored by Saba Farheen N S and colleagues from RV College of Engineering, India, this chapter forecasts the profound impact of AI on tourism, from personalized recommendations to sustainable destination management. By examining AI's integration across various touchpoints, the chapter provides valuable insights into how AI empowers both travelers and tourism companies.

Chapter 2, "Bridging the Digital Divide: Unleashing the Power of Big Data Analytics for Touristic Destination Promotion," authored by Hebat Allah Gaafar and Bassam Al-Romeedy from the Faculty of Tourism and Hotels, Egypt, delves into the transformative potential of big data analytics in revolutionizing destination promotion strategies. Through an exploration of data-driven decision-making and personalized marketing approaches, this chapter elucidates the pivotal role of BDA in shaping the future of tourism marketing.

Chapter 3, "Data Fusion for Destination Success: Exploring the Integration of MKIS and BDA in Marketing Touristic Destinations," authored by Hebat Allah Gaafar and Bassam Al-Romeedy, extends the discourse by highlighting the synergistic benefits of integrating MKIS and BDA. By leveraging data fusion techniques, this chapter demonstrates how touristic destinations can enhance visitor satisfaction and loyalty through personalized experiences, underlining the importance of strategic integration for destination success.

Chapter 4, "Exploring the Consumer Profile of the Museum of Futebol Clube do Porto Through Online Reviews: A Study Using TripAdvisor Data," by Raquel Martins and Célia Ramos from the University of Algarve, Portugal, provides a nuanced understanding of target audiences in cultural tourism, utilizing TripAdvisor data to uncover insights into visitor profiles and satisfaction levels, thus informing strategic planning for cultural destinations.

Chapter 5, "From Insight to Advantage Harnessing the Potential of Marketing Intelligence Systems in Tourism," authored by Bassam Al-Romeedy and Tareq Hashem, explores the pivotal role of Marketing Intelligence Systems (MIS) in driving strategic marketing decisions and enhancing customer experiences within the tourism industry. By analyzing the components and real-world applications of MIS, this chapter underscores their significance in maintaining a competitive edge.

Chapter 6, "Leveraging Virtual Reality (VR) and Augmented Reality (AR) for Enhanced Tourism and Event Marketing: A Data-Driven Approach," authored by Krishna Khanal from Westcliff University, USA, examines the integration of VR, AR, and data analytics in transforming tourism and event marketing strategies.

Through case studies and future trends, this chapter provides practical insights into harnessing immersive technologies for engaging and attracting visitors.

Chapter 7, "Marketing Strategies for Medical Tourism in India Amongst Gulf Countries: An Empirical Study," by Hemant Gupta and Anand Sonkar, offers empirical insights into the marketing dynamics of medical tourism in India, particularly among Gulf countries. Through interviews and questionnaires, the chapter uncovers the factors driving medical tourists' decisions and underscores India's appeal as a medical tourism destination.

Chapter 8, "Personalization of Travel Experiences Through Data Analytics: A Case Study in Amusement Parks," authored by Dwijendra Nath Dwivedi from Krakow University of Economics, explores the application of data analytics in tailoring visitor experiences within amusement parks. By analyzing visitor data, this chapter elucidates how personalized services can enhance visitor satisfaction and operational efficiency.

Chapter 9, "Techniques and Tools for Big Data Analytics in the Tourism Sector," authored by Bhupender Dighliya from Starex University, India, offers a comprehensive overview of cutting-edge analytics methodologies tailored to address the unique challenges and opportunities within the tourism sector. Through real-world case studies, this chapter illustrates the practical application of these techniques in optimizing resource allocation and predicting travel trends.

Chapter 10, "Tomorrow's Travel Companion: The Role of Artificial Intelligence in Shaping the Future of Tourism," by Bassam Al-Romeedy, examines the transformative potential of AI in various facets of the tourism industry. Through an exploration of applications, advantages, and challenges, this chapter offers recommendations for industry stakeholders on maximizing the benefits of AI in shaping a sustainable and resilient tourism future.

Chapter 11, "Unlocking the Power of Data- Exploring the Dynamic Role of MKIS in Revolutionizing Tourism Marketing," by Bassam Al-Romeedy, highlights the instrumental role of Marketing Knowledge and Information Systems (MKIS) in driving strategic marketing decisions and enhancing visitor experiences within the tourism industry. By exploring the strategic application of MKIS, this chapter enriches the existing literature in the field.

Chapter 12, "Utilizing Marketing Information Systems and Big Data Analytics in Promoting Tourism Destinations: MKIS and BDA in Tourism Destination Marketing," by Saba Farheen N S, Goutham Bhandari, Lalshawala Abdulmatin, and Gaurav Makhija from RV College of Engineering, India, explores the integration of MKIS and BDA in the context of tourism destination marketing. Through a theoretical framework and review of tools and technologies, this chapter provides insights into leveraging data-centric methodologies for effective destination promotion.

Chapter 13, "Utilization of Marketing Information Systems in the Tourism Marketing Sector," by Tahreer M. Abu Hmeidan, examines Marketing Information Systems (MKIS) crucial significance in tourism. Given the rapid changes in the tourism industry due to technological breakthroughs and evolving consumer behaviours, marketing professionals must prioritize efficiently using Management Information Systems (MIS).

Collectively, these chapters offer a panoramic view of the evolving landscape of technology-driven tourism marketing, providing valuable insights and practical guidance for industry practitioners, policymakers, researchers, and students alike.

IN CONCLUSION

As we draw the curtains on this meticulously crafted volume, it's important to reflect on the wealth of insights and perspectives shared by our esteemed contributors. Through a multidisciplinary lens, the book has navigated the intricate nexus of technology and tourism marketing, exploring the transformative potential of artificial intelligence (AI), big data analytics (BDA), and marketing information systems (MKIS) in shaping the future of the tourism industry.

From forecasting the impact of AI on travel experiences to unraveling the power of big data analytics in destination promotion, each chapter has contributed to a deeper understanding of how technology is reshaping the tourism landscape. Through empirical studies, theoretical frameworks, and real-world case analyses, our contributors have illuminated the opportunities and challenges inherent in leveraging technology for strategic decision-making, customer engagement, and sustainable growth.

At the heart of exploration lies a recognition of the dynamic interplay between innovation and adaptation. As the tourism industry continues to evolve in response to changing consumer preferences, market dynamics, and technological advancements, it becomes increasingly imperative for industry stakeholders to embrace innovation and harness the power of data-driven insights.

Editors are humbled by the depth of knowledge and expertise demonstrated by our contributors, whose dedication has enriched this volume. It is fervent hope that this collection serves as a valuable resource for industry practitioners, policymakers, researchers, and students, inspiring further inquiry and innovation in the dynamic realm of technology-driven tourism marketing.

In closing, Editors extend heartfelt gratitude to all those who have contributed to this endeavor, and invite readers to embark on their own journeys of exploration and discovery in the ever-evolving landscape of tourism and events marketing.

Tareq Nael Hashem
Applied Science Private University, Jordan

Ahmad Albattat
Management and Science University, Malaysia

Marco Valeri
Niccolò Cusano University, Italy

Anukrati Sharma
University of Kota, India

Chapter 1
A Future Look at Artificial Intelligence in the World of Tourism

N. S. Saba Farheen
RV College of Engineering, India

V. Dheeraj
RV College of Engineering, India

Chethan S. Badiger
RV College of Engineering, India

Sindhu R. Rajendran
RV College of Engineering, India

Lalith Kishore
RV College of Engineering, India

ABSTRACT

In the realm of travel, a silent revolution is unfolding, driven by artificial intelligence (AI). Tailored experiences powered by AI are tangible, with data analytics crafting bespoke itineraries and recommendations fueled by natural language processing and simplifying planning and navigation. AI optimizes transportation, refining traffic control and route planning for convenience. Augmented reality adds immersive layers to traveler experiences. AI plays a pivotal role in sustainability, regulating visitor flows and energy usage. Real-time data analysis aids crisis management, ensuring safety and industry resilience. AI systems, standalone or integrated, encompass recommendation engines, personalization algorithms, conversational interfaces, predictive tools, language translation software, and intelligent destination mapping. Smart destinations integrate these technologies with social and organizational elements. AI empowers travelers with personalized options and enables companies to tailor experiences.

DOI: 10.4018/979-8-3693-3310-5.ch001

1. INTRODUCTION TO ARTIFICIAL INTELLIGENCE AND TOURISM

Artificial intelligence (AI) is transforming the travel sector by altering the manner individuals perceive the globe. Personalized travel experiences fueled by AI are already a reality. Data analysis is employed to craft bespoke itineraries and recommendations. Natural language processing-driven virtual travel assistants facilitate planning and navigation. AI enhances transportation, upgrading traffic control and route planning for more convenient travel. AI-guided augmented and virtual reality adds immersive layers to traveler experiences. The ethical ramifications are substantial and demand the judicious utilization of AI to address privacy and cultural concerns. AI assumes the forefront in sustainability, managing visitor flows and energy consumption. AI's real-time data analysis aids crisis management by ensuring traveler safety and industry resilience. AI systems in the tourism sector can be standalone or incorporated into existing applications and systems. These systems include recommender tools, personalization methodologies, conversational interfaces (chatbots and voice aides), forecasting utilities, language translation software, and intelligent travel destinations (Bulchand-Gidumal, 2020). It is crucial to acknowledge that visitors will typically interact with technologies integrating several of these systems. A visitor might converse with a robot encompassing a conversational interface, recommender tool, personalization approach, or autonomous agent, depending on requirements. A voice aide or chatbot may conduct the user's conversation. As elucidated later in this section, smart destinations are ecosystems established where these cutting-edge technologies are implemented alongside other social and organizational elements.

The development of AI in the travel and tourism sector (Bowen & Morosan, 2018) necessitates research in multiple domains. Contemplating the use of robots in tourism and hospitality, firstly, customers must embrace AI systems. Secondly, AI poses a greater peril by replacing humans in the future, impacting the economics of the travel and tourism sector. This chapter also pinpointed another quartet of questions: Firstly, the impacts of AI on marketing and operations must be scrutinized; secondly, the working dynamics of the travel and tourism industry should be transformed in areas like product development and packet composition; thirdly, sustainability may be affected by AI; and, finally, research is required on amalgamating data from diverse sources (European Commission, 2017) with information generated during travel and tourism activities to comprehend customer profiles and behavior. Nevertheless, AI's future in tourism is promising. On the one hand, there is an upbeat outlook where society can address primary issues with AI. Connectivity implementation will enable AI system deployment, privacy concerns resolution, and worker-AI system collaboration. AI, a collection of technologies, will enhance the tourism experience for all involved parties. From the customer's standpoint, AI will expedite travel planning, reduce transaction costs, and offer a fully personalized itinerary. On the flip side, a less optimistic perspective envisions job displacement and the loss of hospitality. Machines may be obligatory, not optional, in certain environments, leading to equipment and robots that may not be optimized. Technology replacing people may not lower costs for consumers, who could experience a diminished overall experience. Data security and privacy remain uncertain. Tourists and workers may find collaboration with AI systems challenging, and companies may not be adequately prepared for AI system utilization.

2. THE TOURISM INDUSTRY: PAST VS. PRESENT VS. FUTURE

The United Nations Global Tourism Organization (UNWTO) (Grosz et al., 2015) initiated an initiative in 2005 to generate a consistent lexicon of terms for tourism because there are numerous explanations for the sector. It supplies the ensuing interpretation of tourism:

Tourism is a societal, cultural, and economic occurrence that involves the migration of individuals to nations or locations beyond their accustomed surroundings for personal or business/professional intentions. These individuals are termed guests (which could be either travelers or excursionists; inhabitants or non-residents) and tourism is associated with their pursuits, certain of which signify tourism spending (Bullinger et al., 2009).

Adding to the concept of tourism, "someone who travels at least 80 km from his or her home for at least 24 hours, for business or leisure or other reasons" is a widely accepted definition of a tourist. One can differentiate tourism into the following three categories:

- Domestic travel - travel made by citizens of the same nation only within that nation.
- Inbound - visitors who are not citizens of a particular nation
- Outbound travelers - citizens of one nation visiting another

Tourism can also be classified based on the purpose and the goals of the individual or the group:

- Cultural tourism
- Eco tourism
- Adventure tourism:
- Wildlife tourism
- Scientific tourism

- Food tourism

There have always been a multitude of reasons why people have relocated. Early explorers mostly traveled for religious purposes or to engage in commerce, fight battles, and conquer new territories. the religious journey or trip to carry out rituals to pray to gods, deities, or other holy forces to satisfy wishes, cleanse the body, or advance one's material or spiritual well-being. As physicians promoted the health benefits of mineral water in the middle of the seventeenth century, pilgrimages and trips to natural springs or spas became more and more common. They quickly developed into significant hubs for gentry or aristocratic gatherings.

Leisure travel began in the nineteenth century (Brynjolfsson & McAfee, 2011), and at the start of that century, tourism as a vocation was established. The history of the tourist industry begins with the transportation revolution (ETB, 2017) that took place concurrently with World War II. Travel was once considered a luxury only accessible to the wealthy due to the exorbitant expense of transportation. Nowadays, tourism is a thriving business that is highly accessible to the average person.

In this current era, the tourism industry is widespread and covers almost all domains, tourism in the past was an opportunity given only to a few, but it is not the case right now. These days everyone has access to basic resources such as travel, food, accommodation, etc which are the necessities for tourism and can be found in every corner of the world. There are industries built around these resources that give a boost to tourism and its related activities. People have different needs when it comes to tourism, may it be adventure or a relaxed vacation, these needs or goals of people give rise to multiple trends in tourism.

Responsible and Sustainable Tourism - Tourists are becoming more interested in eco-friendly and sustainable travel alternatives that minimize their influence on the environment and help local communities.

Technology Integration - Using smartphone applications, augmented reality, and virtual reality to improve the whole trip experience, from planning to exploring, has become more popular.

Travel with Experience - To fully immerse themselves in local cultures and lives, travelers were shifting away from standard tourist sites in search of real and one-of-a-kind experiences.

Health-Related Travel - Well-being tourism has increased as a result of people's rising interest in health and wellbeing. Destinations that provided fitness activities, spa getaways, and overall experiences related to well-being were sought after by travelers.

Leisure Travel - Leisure, or the combining of business and leisure travel, was growing in popularity as professionals extended their business travels to include leisure travel.

Local and Hyper-Local Exploration - To promote local businesses and lessen their carbon impact, travelers have been shown a preference for discovering surrounding locations or their own countries.

Customization and Personalization - In response to individual preferences and interests, travel services and platforms have provided more personalized and custom experiences.

Gastronomic Tourism - Travelers were increasingly incorporating local cuisines into their trips and looking for distinctive gastronomic experiences.

These trends continue to evolve and the tourism industry is evolving with it new technologies and inventions are being introduced in the tourism world to make it more and more economical and the need to provide "THE BEST EXPERIENCE" is given the utmost importance.

In the future, vacationers will be accustomed to technology and will be heavily reliant on it, they will also be drawn towards uncommon and new attractions, and themic restaurants, tourists will be heavily reliant on their smartphones, the next phase after this will be reliant on Internet Of Things (IoT) and AI, there is more emphasis on developing apps or devices with these technologies embedded in them, making the tourist more addicted to digital aid. This can also be used to give them a personalized feel and provide features that help them to decide every step they take from lodging to restaurant comparison, best way of transport from palace A to B, as well as attractions between the journeys. The tourists will get information on everything that can be conceivable but there needs to be a way in which this enormous amount of data can be sifted (Benckendorff et al., 2019), organized, rated, and recommended to the target audience, here is where AI comes into the picture the extensive amount of data and the analytical system needs to be enhanced, this is where big tech giants such as Google, Baidu, Alibaba, Amazon, WeChat, Meta etc, come into the picture and will be the major players in the tourism industry in the future (Basiri et al., 2018).

The various technologies such as:

- Gates will be replaced with facial recognition on the fly, enabling unrestricted human mobility.
- Share our cloud-based profile with all border authorities run by foreign governments.
- Security X-rays will be exchanged throughout nations so that one can be screened on the flight.
- Passing through a single tunnel that simultaneously scans, sprays, and sniffs you and your luggage
- Big hotels will hire autonomous, programmable pods to get guests home quickly.

- Virtual reality travel experiences will be accessible in real-time.

The traveler will have a better experience thanks to all of these, and there will always be a need for these technologies to go further.

3. COLLABORATION BETWEEN AI WITH THE EXISTING BUSINESS MODELS

This section of the chapter will elaborate on the usage of AI technology in the current tourism business models, how and where it has been implemented, and where it can be used to improve the tourism experience and provide a comfortable travel experience. The current trends of the tourism industry ranging from online websites, apps, and even the locally available tours and travel enterprises depend on these services but they too at times collaborate with a certain industry such as travel, booking of flights/busses, leasing/renting of cars/cabs. Another service that they focus on is accommodation, assisting in choosing the best (within the budget of the tourist) hotel/resort to stay, and making a list of must-visit places or attractions for a given destination. They may also at times provide a guide to aid the traveler with all these services. These services often come in packages including all of the above and the tourist has a choice of picking whichever he or she finds to be convenient and ticking all their checkboxes of the trip. This style of "packaged" type of tour (House of Lords, 2017) is the most common in the current tourism industry, even though these are customizable they are a little restrictive, the tourist always has to stick to the little box of services that the enterprise offers, their freedom is compromised this is what needs to be solved and one of the possible solution for this being AI is the main focus in this chapter, how and where AI can be used, to give more freedom for the traveler and increasing their chooses while providing them with a wonderful and amazing experience.

The very initial place where AI can be implemented is the current excursions and journeys industry, AI can be utilized along with substantial data to bring more choices onto the table, this also aids in enhancing the customizability of the current "packages" Trend. In the travel and traveler sector, AI technologies can be incorporated into already-existing applications and systems or utilized independently. These systems encompass prognostication tools, self-sufficient agents, conversational systems (chatbots and voice aides), suggestion systems, personalization systems and approaches, and language applications for translation and intelligent travel locations. It is crucial to observe that, even though one scrutinizes each system independently, visitors commonly engage with technology that incorporates many systems. A visitor could talk with a robot that incorporates a conversational system, a recommender system, a personalization method, or an independent agent, depending on the needs. The user's discussion may be aided by a voice aid or chatbot. Intelligent destinations are the ecosystems developed in locations where these cutting-edge technologies are executed with additional organizational and societal elements.

The link between the AI systems and applications that are looked at here and the IT underpinnings of AI that were reviewed in the previous part is depicted in Figure 1.

Figure 1. Impact of artificial intelligence in tourism

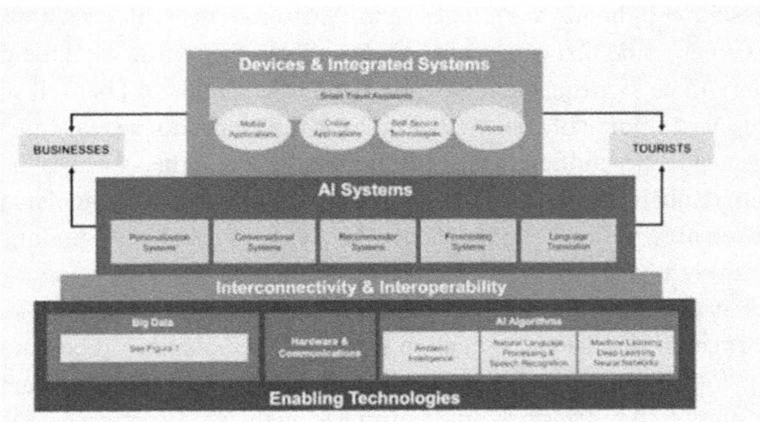

The objective of recommender systems is to supply travelers with choices based on their preferences. With online environments providing consumers exponentially more choices, the utilization of recommender systems in the tourist sector has escalated in significance. Ordinarily, recommender systems offer suggestions on the optimal choices by contrasting the characteristics of the available options with user profiles. Through the utilization of customization strategies, consumers are endeavored to acquire information that is tailored to their preferences and constraints. Consequently, businesses are transitioning from marketing to many to marketing to one using personalization approaches. Vast quantities of user behavior data are required for personalization approaches to establish a fitting profile.

Utilizing historical and contextual data, forecasting is a procedure that generates future predictions based on current patterns. It is employed in a broad array of industries and commercial contexts to enlighten decisions that require predicting future events. AI algorithms are exceedingly well suited for forecasting, particularly in the context of massive data. The five varieties of artificial intelligence (AI) methods for forecasting include fuzzy time series, support vector machines (SVMs) (Gov.uk, 2017), ANNs, gray theory, and rough sets approach. Forecasting has numerous applications in the tourism sector, encompassing comprehending visitor demand, formulating marketing strategies, allocating financial resources and human resources, detecting restaurant frauds, and aiding with facility and maintenance needs.

4. PERSONAL AI ASSISTANCE AND BIG DATA

In this section, the emphasis lay in highlighting the efficacy of personal AI—artificial intelligence that could be seamlessly incorporated into present-day portable devices, encompassing cellphones, earphones, and electronic wearables such as watches personal helper/guide that can guide one throughout the tour is what the giant tech companies will be focusing on in the future, these AI guides will be well versed and trained on a vast amount of content that is already present and the real-time data that is being generated by millions of people around the world this is where the concept of Big data (Buhalis & Leung, 2018) comes into picture. These big data analytics when backed up within AI can potentially be a system capable of guiding a tourist in every corner of the world. AI personal assistance in tourism content enhances the travel experience through personalized trip planning, booking assistance, local information provision, navigation guidance, personalized recommendations for dining and activities, real-time weather updates, safety information, and 24/7 customer support. It utilizes machine learning to analyze user preferences, historical data, and current trends, offering tailored suggestions for destinations, itineraries, accommodations, and activities. Additionally, AI can assist with language translation, provide augmented reality guides, and offer emergency assistance, contributing to a seamless and enjoyable travel experience.

One of the primary IT pillars of synthetic intelligence is extensive information since it provides the input necessary for AI systems to learn, identify, and understand behavioral patterns, and generate insights. One description of extensive information is a sequence of exceedingly massive datasets that are generated rapidly, from a variety of sources, and include a diversity of data kinds (Agarwal, 2002). Four Vs are commonly employed to characterize extensive information: volume, velocity, variety, and veracity (Bulchand-Gidumal, 2020).

The surroundings and the traveler are the two primary sources of extensive information in the tourism industry. Weather details, incidents occurring at the destination, and real-time data from sensors, the Internet of Things (IoT), and transactions are all procured from the surroundings. There are five ways that travelers may contribute data before, during, and after their journey: wearables, biometric and emotional data, offline and online activities, and user-generated content (UGC). Users use the internet to search for and reserve services both before and during their trip, leaving a digital trail that may be trailed. Along the journey, users also leave offline traces (such as movements, bookings, and consumption), which are picked up by several technologies, including GPS, mobile roaming, Bluetooth device data, Internet of Things, and point-of-service (PoS) devices. Additionally, users' biometric and emotional data can be automatically collected during the journey (e.g., facial recognition, thermal imaging). Similarly, data from wearables (such as smartwatches, activity trackers, and clothes) may also be gathered while traveling, contingent on the user granting access. Lastly, both during and after the journey, UGC is produced. Online reviews, social media comments, and publicly shared images and videos are instances of this type of material. Before user-generated material can be efficiently utilized by analysts and researchers, AI processing is required. Artificial intelligence may assist in the processing of sentiment analysis in textual data as well as the analysis and labeling of user-shared images, audio files, and videos (e.g., location, participants, sentiments).

By providing algorithms that utilize the data substantially more information, these methods significantly enhance UGC as a data origin. These data origins can be amalgamated to formulate a user profile. The user's requirements can then be accommodated in product and service suggestions made using this profile. Figure 2 contains a recapitulation of all the data origins and data creation processes indicated for the particular scenario of hospitality.

The data gathering pre- and post-journey, the encounters throughout the tour, and the environmental data will be employed as input for the prospective vacationers; more about these will be expounded in the approaching sections.

Applications of virtual personal assistants as travel consultants provide businesses a competitive edge, but they also pose a risk to the careers of travel consultants. A robot could never be able to match the expertise of a specialized travel agent, according to Jacks (2017), who believes that "the real threat of Artificial Intelligence is on the budget travel agents who specialize in cheap deals to the clients focus on tailor-made bookings." The whole human lexicon cannot be replaced by the existing Natural Language Processing (NPL) integrated virtual personal assistant, despite the fact that it generates a personalized tale. NLP, according to ITB Berlin (2017), is the capacity of computers to analyze phrases in a natural language like English, which calls for the knowledge of ontology (meaning of terminology particular to certain disciplines, like travel) and taxonomy (hierarchy).

Except for the fact that a human could never identify and bring to light underlying causes with such speed and precision, the VPA does not currently have the empirical taxonomy and ontology needed to build an accurate cultural lexicon with the proper speed and precision. Despite its lack of linguistic accuracy and speed, conversing with VPA is identical to speaking with a human. Asserting that word-of-mouth is one of the most important factors for a hotel's future, along with guest satisfaction and guest retention through word-of-mouth advertising, other tourism organizations prefer to invest in human empirical taxonomy and ontology rather than VPAs. In this sense, the demand from tourists allows them to base their travel plans on the firsthand accounts of friends and family. Decisions made by consumers' friends, family, and other acquaintances make up their consumer demand. As a result, firms that specialize in travel counseling make similar investments in expanding their businesses through client testimonials.

Figure 2. Data generation and use in hospitality

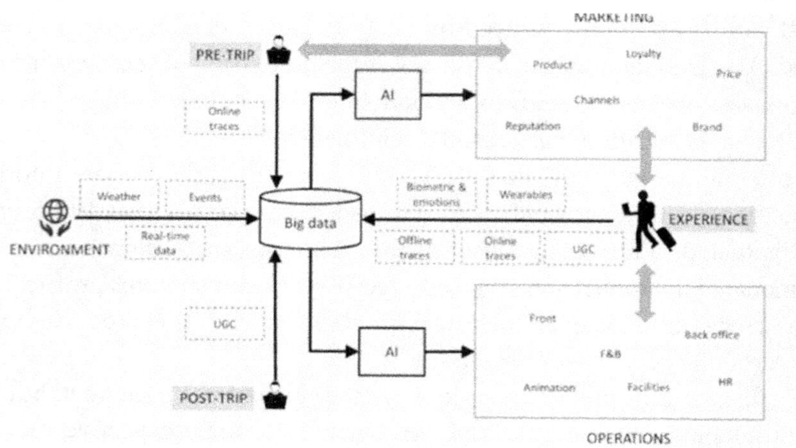

5. AI IN PRE-TOURISM

Artificial Intelligence plays an important role before people start their tour. AI technologies are being used to give personalized user experiences and offer individualized services. All of these are based on the customers' preferences and requirements. New AI models come every day with very niche use cases. Some of them like trippplanner.ai (Bulchand-Gidumal, 2020), roam around (Bullinger et al., 2009), etc., are very useful in planning the trip and making the itinerary.

Some of the potential applications of AI before people start their tour are:

Personalized Offers: Customers' online activity like social media interactions, website visits, cookies, bookmarked websites, etc. can be analyzed and with this data, the AI model can create personalized travel offers. The models will check their interests and pass conduct to do the same.

Chatbots and Virtual Assistants: A lot of travel platforms use chatbots to help customers in making pre-purchase decisions. They do this by providing customers with custom packages and offers. Virtual assistants like Amazon Alexa, Apple

Siri, and Google Assistant can help humans complete tasks using voice, graphic, or text input.

Micro-Targeted Marketing Campaigns: AI tools such as predictive analytics, deep learning, and machine learning can be used to assess customers' behavior offline and online. Using this data it creates micro-targeted marketing campaigns. This course of action gives added value to customers using personalized offers based on their choice.

Predictive Management and Forecasting: Artificial Intelligence models can be used for predictive management and forecasting within the hospitality and tourism industry. It helps in creating learning advisory situational systems. These systems can quickly respond to changing business conditions. It can also offer options for overcoming emerging negative economic scenarios.

Neural Network Analysis and Intelligent Management: The use of AI in combination with neural network analysis helps in the identification of explicit and hidden dependencies in the data and models of economic behaviors, It can also help in detecting unexpected or implied changes.

Agent technology and Neural Agents: AI technologies, such as neural agents are used for the analysis and estimation of economic information, demand forecast, and identification of non-standard economic situations or risks. Neutral agents help in the prediction and analysis of critical conditions of the economic system. This helps in manage and prevent negative impacts of the same.

The tourism industry is also trying to keep up: the Hilton hotel chain has launched an online concierge, Facebook is analyzing data to offer users accommodation options through contextual advertising, and Booking.com has introduced a booking service Experience that helps tourists organize leisure time and buy tickets using AI without queues in popular world capitals using a QR code.

When a customer chooses a package tour, he or she relies on three components: affordable price, assortment, and convenience. Many times, a person has to spend a lot of days finding the perfect option. According to the authors' data, a tourist spends an average of 5 to 7 sessions on the websites of online travel agencies to choose a trip. In this situation, personalized algorithms that analyze behavioral data on the platform can be very useful. For example, how many times he or she returned to the website. After gathering all the information about the user, the service offers the most suitable options. OTAs can also send travelers personalized offers of any travel arrangements based on an analysis of a customer's profile, preferences, and even location data. A large number of OTAs and travel platforms use chatbots to help the customer make a pre-purchase. It provides them with several packages and offers.

For example, suppose one wants to travel to another country, say India, they first need to buy tickets to where they would like to visit. Suppose they visit Delhi, then they would need to book plane tickets, for many websites need to be checked as ticket prices keep varying. This tiring job can be made simple by using AI chatbots, they will scavenge the web and provide a list of all airline tickets. They can also be filtered based on cost and ticket type (First Class, Second Class, coach). This is way better than manually checking all the websites on the World Wide Web! Once the plane tickets are booked, maybe you would want to plan the places you would like to visit. Delhi is the capital city of India and has many places to visit like the Red Fort, India Gate, Humayun's Tomb, Qutub Minar, Hauz Khas Village, etc., One can ask the AI to make an itinerary for them with the timings and it will do that for you as well. Yes, there are many itineraries available online but again this reduces time.

Now that both the plane tickets are booked and the itinerary done you would need a place to stay over because it won't be a one-day trip for sure. It's always better to book a place before the trip begins. This is for safety and it costs less to do this than renting it on the spot. AI again helps here! Just like how it can sort plane tickets with filters, there are AI models that can do the same for hotel rooms too! It can filter rooms based on price, location, hotel rating, etc., This just shows how helpful AI is if used in the right manner.

6. AI DURING TOURISM

In the previous chapter, the exploration was centered on how AI assists individuals before embarking on journeys to foreign countries. In the current chapter, the focus shifts to examining its role in aiding travelers during their tours.

Recall the example of traveling to Delhi taken in the previous chapter. Now after reaching the airport, there is a need to book a cab or rent a car to go to the hotel room. The 2 major taxi providers in India- Ola and Uber, use AI in multiple ways.

Take the example of Ola, one of The Largest Ride-Hailing Indian Companies in The World. The rise of Ola started when it acquired a Bangalore-based artificial intelligence startup called "Pickup.ai".

Ola has millions of bytes of data consisting of their drivers, customers, vehicles, etc., It also has information about every single trip that takes place. Ola has insights into the time and day of booking, pickup and drop locations, location of nearby taxis and autos, etc., It has collected data from approximately nine lakh cabs on the road which helps them create accurate scenarios of traffic around the road. This data is used to create an estimated time of arrival which is shown to the users during their travel too!

In recent years Ola launched the "Guardian". It is an AI model that provides real-time ride-monitoring features. It is available in more than 17 cities in India. The Guardian uses real-time data collected from rides to spontaneously detect irregular activities by drivers. It also includes prolonged stopping and unexpected route deviations by drivers. In the end, these activities are sent to Ola's 24/7 safety team which takes a look at this problem, analyzes the situation, and does a custom check on the passengers to check if they are safe. Ola's Guardian Is Purely Built on Artificial Intelligence and Machine Learning which helps it to learn from continuously coming data and to find instant solutions.

These are all the features of AI in enhance user experience while traveling in taxis:

Intelligent Route Optimization: Route optimization has to be on point. This is very important as route optimization can lower fuel costs by up to 20%. It also helps reduce the travel time and enhances user experience. AI algorithms can be used to analyze several data points including historical traffic patterns, real-time road conditions, and more to provide optimal routes for travel.

Personalized Recommendations: As customers, one would expect the brand to understand our needs. AI can help in this too, all the personal data of the customer will be stored in the database and can be accessed and analyzed to provide the best possible custom routes and destinations. It can also be integrated with the itinerary and help make travel much smoother. It can also help in choosing preferred drivers.

Better Safety Features: Safety is very important. AI-powered taxi apps use advanced technologies like Natural Language Processing (NLP) and computer vision to ensure safe rides. Emergencies like reckless driving behavior, sudden breaks, and near-miss accidents can be detected. Real-time alerts about hazards like heavy rain, construction zones, and icy roads can be sent to the driver and passengers too.

Predictive Pricing: Before the user finalized the ride, they saw various options at different prices. The pricing is calculated based on various factors, some of which include traffic patterns, demand and supply of drivers, and external events.

Integrated Payment Systems: Many payment methods like credit cards, digital wallets, and mobile payment systems like UPI are safely combined on these apps via algorithms. This gives the users quick and easy ways to pay for their rides. By examining customer preferences, transaction history, and real-time data, artificial intelligence (AI) may adjust payment options, enhance transaction security, and provide a faultless payment experience.

Real-Time Traffic Updates: Artificial Intelligence (AI) can predict traffic conditions, congestion, and likely delays along certain routes using machine learning techniques. To give real-time traffic updates, taxi booking software employs artificial intelligence (AI) to gather and analyze enormous amounts of data from several sources, such as GPS signals, traffic cameras, and historical traffic trends.

Smart Assistance: Functions like voice-activated bookings, real-time journey tracking, and automatic price calculation are some utilities offered by AI tools within the app. Virtual assistants and AI-powered chatbots help smooth the process even more.

Accurate ETAs (Estimated Time of Arrival): Accurate ETA is a very crucial parameter. Traditional taxi services usually struggle with factors like unpredictable traffic conditions, inefficient routing, and lack of real-time data. Businesses may now provide their consumers with an exact projected time of arrival thanks to AI algorithms. One of the most cherished aspects of the app is its ability to tell users exactly when their transport will arrive at their house so they can make plans appropriately.

The prospect of AI in tourism presents vast potential, transforming the sector by offering customized, effective, and engaging experiences for travelers. From AI-powered suggestion systems and anticipatory analytics to the incorporation of extensive data and the Internet of Things (IoT), progress in technology is restructuring how businesses address individual inclinations, amplify decision-making procedures, and boost general customer contentment. Despite enduring difficulties like moral reflections and plausible employment substitution, the probable advantages in the form of efficient operations, upgraded sustainability, and heightened safety establish AI as a pivotal contributor in molding the forthcoming panorama of the tourism sector.

7. CONCLUSION

In the above sections, its seen what AI in tourism is, its advantages, and how helpful it is in real-time. The integration of artificial intelligence has revolutionized the industry and has made many changes that are of great use to us. The traditional tourism model has transformed into a more dynamic, customized, and data-driven model. Artificial Intelligence has significantly influenced the evolution of the tourism industry in multiple ways. Its collusion with existing business models has increased operational productivity, customer support, and critical decision-making. Big Data and personal AI assistants have been vital in this transformation, providing tailor-made experiences and insights that were unimaginable in the past. It is part of all stages of tourism starting from pre-tourism stages which involve planning and booking to during-tourism stages such as navigation, exploration, recommendations, and real-time help. AI will drive innovation and promote growth in the industry. Various initiative steps can be taken to promote the usage of AI by tourism agencies such as encouraging collaboration amidst corporations providing AI solutions and travel agencies, and fostering partnerships that facilitate the development and utilization of tailored AI solutions to address specific challenges encountered by the industry. Cooperative efforts and joint ventures can accelerate the adoption of AI-driven solutions. The potential of AI in tourism is huge and largely untapped and promises exciting opportunities for both businesses and tourists alike. By extending incentives and support for the integration of AI, governments and business associations may play a pivotal role. For enterprises investing in AI technologies, this might encompass grants, tax refunds, or monetary incentives. The tourism industry will cultivate an inventive culture if favorable regulations are instituted. As people continue to explore and understand this potential, it is important to also consider ethical implications and strive for a future where AI in tourism is used responsibly and sustainably.

8. FUTURE SCOPE

The future of Artificial Intelligence in tourism shimmers with possibilities as vast as the uncharted landscapes awaiting exploration. It can be seen how it has transformed the tourist's journey, from creating beautifully hand-crafted itineraries with AI companions to optimizing logistics with smart cityscapes. The best part is that one can custom-design AI from scratch and use it for anything. One can also create maps with places people generally would want to visit and make them so realistic that with a touch they can virtually visit the place, and learn about its history and culture without even visiting setting foot there. Real-time accessibility tools can be woven into the fabric of travel, which will cater to any explorer's needs and preferences. One very important aspect is also about environmental considerations. AI holds the key to sustainable tourism practices. Management of resources like water and energy can be done optimally in hotels and famous tourist attractions. Smart transportation networks can even help visualize how many people are traveling in a route and our routes can be adjusted to minimize environmental impact. Endangered ecosystems like the Nilgiris of Southern India, The Sundarbans, The Himalayas, and The Amazon rainforest can be protected by analyzing travel patterns and suggesting responsible travel practices. But, ethical concerns always exist. Data privacy is very important in today's world. One must be wary of algorithmic bias and ensure that Artificial Intelligence augments the human connection and doesn't end up replacing it altogether. Responsible development and transparent communication are significant. Looking at all this one can see how beneficial AI can be if used in the right way. The future of AI in tourism is not a predetermined script, it is a collaborative story waiting to be written.

REFERENCES

Aarts, E., & Wichert, R. (2009). Ambient intelligence. In H. J. Bullinger (Ed.), *Technology guide* (pp. 244–249). Springer. doi:10.1007/978-3-540-88546-7_47

Agarwal, S. (2002). Restructuring seaside tourism: The resort lifecycle. *Annals of Tourism Research*, *29*(1), 25–55. doi:10.1016/S0160-7383(01)00002-0

Basiri, A., Amirian, P., Winstanley, A., & Moore, T. (2018). Making tourist guidance systems more intelligent, adaptive, and personalized using crowd-sourced movement data. *Journal of Ambient Intelligence and Humanized Computing*, *9*(2), 413–427. doi:10.1007/s12652-017-0550-0

Benckendorff, P. J., Xiang, Z., & Sheldon, P. J. (2019). *Tourism information technology*. CABI. doi:10.1079/9781786393432.0000

Bowen, J., & Morosan, C. (2018). Beware the hospitality industry: The robots are coming. *Worldwide Hospitality and Tourism Themes*, *10*(6), 726–733. doi:10.1108/WHATT-07-2018-0045

Brynjolfsson, E., & McAfee, A. (2011). *Race against the machine: How the digital revolution is accelerating innovation, driving productivity, and irreversibly transforming employment and the economy*. Digital Frontier Press.

Buhalis, D., & Leung, R. (2018). Smart hospitality—Interconnectivity and interoperability towards an ecosystem. *International Journal of Hospitality Management*, *71*, 41–50. doi:10.1016/j.ijhm.2017.11.011

Bulchand-Gidumal, J. (2020). *Impact of Artificial Intelligence in Travel*. Tourism, and Hospitality., doi:10.1007/978-3-030-05324-6_110-1

ETB. (2017). Virgin Holidays launches AI technology for holidaymakers. *ETB Travel News*, 5–7.

European Commission. (2017). *Digital Transformation*. Retrieved July 5, 2017, from https://ec.europa.eu/growth/industry/digital-transformation_en

Gov.uk. (2017). *Robotics and AI: apply in the Industrial Strategy Challenge Fund*. Retrieved from https://www.gov.uk/government/news/robotics-and-ai-apply-in-The-industrial-strategy-challenge-fund

Grosz, B. J., Altman, R., Horvitz, E., Mackworth, A., Mitchell, T., Mulligan, D., & Shoham, Y. (2015). *Artificial Intelligence and Life in 2030*. Retrieved from https://ai100.stanford.edu/sites/default/files/ai_100_report_0831fnl.pdf

House of Lords. (2017). *Brexit: trade in non- financial services*. European Union Committee. Retrieved from https://publications.parliament.uk/pa/ld201617/ldselect/ldeucom/135/135.pdf

Chapter 2
Bridging the Digital Divide:
Unleashing the Power of Big Data Analytics for Touristic Destination Promotion

Hebat Allah Ali Gaafar
https://orcid.org/0000-0001-8214-4451
Faculty of Tourism and Hotels, Egypt

Bassam Samir Al-Romeedy
Faculty of Tourism and Hotels, Egypt

ABSTRACT

In an age marked by an abundance of information, the tourism industry grapples with the task of effectively reaching and engaging potential visitors. This study explores the transformative potential of big data analytics (BDA) in reshaping strategies for marketing touristic destinations, emphasizing a more personalized and efficient approach. It thoroughly examines BDA's pivotal role in revolutionizing destination promotion in the digital era, highlighting the importance of data-driven decision-making for impactful campaigns. The chapter also addresses challenges and ethical considerations associated with utilizing extensive data for tourism promotion. This contribution is significant for industry practitioners, policymakers, and researchers interested in leveraging BDA for sustainable and impactful tourism growth.

DOI: 10.4018/979-8-3693-3310-5.ch002

INTRODUCTION

In the contemporary era of technology, big data analytics (BDA) has emerged as a valuable asset for businesses across diverse industries, tourism being no exception. However, a digital divide exists, with certain tourist destinations yet to fully leverage the potential of BDA in their promotional endeavors. Tourist destinations inherently possess an extensive reservoir of data encompassing website analytics, social media interactions, customer feedback, booking patterns, and more. By embracing BDA techniques, destinations can adeptly collect, process, and analyze this wealth of information. BDA empowers destinations to extract actionable insights from the data, unveiling trends, patterns, and customer preferences that can serve as the foundation for more targeted and impactful promotional strategies (Egger, 2022; Mohamed & Al-Azab, 2021).

Big Data Analytics (BDA) equips tourist destinations with the capability to gain profound insights into customer behavior. By analyzing data from various touchpoints, destinations can grasp customer preferences, interests, and the elements shaping their decision-making process. BDA streamlines the identification of crucial customer segments, allowing destinations to tailor their promotional initiatives for specific target audiences. This understanding of customer behavior empowers destinations to fashion personalized marketing messages, curate bespoke experiences, and optimize the allocation of resources (Xiang & Fesenmaier, 2017; Farahat, 2023).

Crucially, a key advantage of BDA lies in its ability to facilitate real-time monitoring and responsiveness. By continuously analyzing data, tourist destinations can stay abreast of market trends, gauge customer sentiment, and track competitor activities. Real-time monitoring empowers destinations to promptly recognize emerging opportunities or challenges, fostering agile decision-making and adjustments as required (Ankam, 2016; Ragab, 2017).

Utilizing BDA, tourist destinations can conduct agile testing and real-time optimization of their promotional campaigns. Employing methods like A/B testing and multivariate testing, destinations can experiment with different versions of marketing messages, landing pages, visuals, and calls to action. Real-time BDA provides instant feedback on campaign performance, allowing destinations to recognize successful strategies and make immediate adjustments to enhance their promotional efforts (Alani et al., 2018; Aktaş et al., 2022).

Eliminating the digital gap and adopting BDA is crucial for tourist destinations seeking success in an era dominated by data. By tapping into the potential of data, understanding customer behavior, implementing real-time monitoring, personalizing marketing campaigns, optimizing marketing channels, and making informed decisions, destinations can fully capitalize on the advantages of BDA in their promotional strategies. The incorporation of BDA in promoting tourist destinations can lead to increased marketing effectiveness, improved customer satisfaction, and sustainable growth in the dynamic and competitive tourism market (Sedkaoui, 2018; Agrawal et al., 2022; Horng et al., 2022).

This chapter explores the potential of BDA in addressing the digital gap and transforming the promotion of tourist destinations. It conducts an in-depth review of academic research, industry reports, and case studies to gain insights into the current landscape of touristic destination promotion, the role of BDA, and the challenges associated with bridging the digital divide. The chapter underscores the importance of data collection and integration, customer segmentation, personalized marketing approaches, real-time insights, data-driven decision-making, trend prediction, campaign optimization, and collaborative partnerships. By adopting BDA, tourist destinations can enhance their promotional strategies, elevate customer satisfaction, and achieve sustainable growth in the highly competitive tourism industry.

The aim of this chapter is to explore various facets related to BDA and its influence on the promotion of tourist destinations. Firstly, it endeavors to deepen our understanding of the role BDA plays in promoting these destinations. Secondly, it investigates the potential of BDA in overcoming the digital gap and reshaping promotional strategies in the tourism industry. Thirdly, it scrutinizes how BDA facilitates the process of data collection and integration, allowing destinations to obtain comprehensive insights, implement customer segmentation, and formulate personalized marketing approaches. Fourthly, the chapter underscores the importance of real-time insights and adaptable strategies in effectively responding to evolving customer preferences and market dynamics. Fifthly, it illustrates the value of predictive analytics and forecasting in optimizing promotional efforts. To achieve these objectives, the chapter conducts a thorough literature review and aims to establish a framework outlining the key components and strategies for leveraging BDA in the promotion of tourist destinations.

Big Data Analytics (BDA) in Tourism

BDA encompasses the collection, processing, and analysis of extensive and intricate datasets to unveil patterns, trends, and insights crucial for decision-making processes. Within the tourism sector, BDA has become highly significant, given the substantial data generated by travelers, online platforms, and various stakeholders in tourism-related activities (Egger, 2022; Mohamed & Al-Azab, 2021). Its pivotal role in the tourism industry lies in furnishing valuable insights that influence tourism strategies and destination promotional endeavors. The surge in digital platforms and the prevalence of online travel services contribute to the generation of massive datasets, including details about traveler behavior, preferences, booking patterns, and feedback. BDA empowers destination marketers to effectively harness this data, extracting actionable insights that drive informed decision-making (Kulkarni et al., 2016; Ragab, 2017).

The significance of data-driven insights in shaping tourism strategies and destination promotion has grown substantially for several reasons (Mariani et al., 2021). Firstly, in a fiercely competitive tourism environment, grasping traveler behavior and preferences is crucial for destinations seeking to distinguish themselves and provide distinctive experiences. BDA facilitates the identification of emerging trends, market segments, and visitor preferences, assisting destinations in customizing their offerings and promotional initiatives accordingly (Aggarwal et al., 2018; Mandal, 2018).

Secondly, insights derived from data empower destinations to enhance the efficiency of their marketing initiatives and allocate resources with precision. Through the analysis of data related to visitor demographics, expenditure patterns, and source markets, destinations can pinpoint the most lucrative segments to target and allocate their promotional budgets accordingly. This focused approach guarantees that marketing campaigns reach the intended audience, leading to increased conversion rates and a more favorable return on investment (Wong, 2016; Mohamed & Al-Azab, 2021).

Thirdly, the utilization of BDA empowers destinations to actively monitor and assess the real-time impact of their promotional endeavors. Through the analysis of data encompassing website traffic, social media interactions, and online bookings, destinations can gauge the effectiveness of their marketing campaigns and promptly implement necessary adjustments. This iterative approach fosters continuous improvement, ensuring that marketing strategies stay pertinent and adaptable to evolving market dynamics (Mehta, 2017; Ragab, 2017).

Moreover, BDA aids destinations in securing a competitive advantage by offering insights into visitor satisfaction levels and conducting sentiment analysis (Stylos et al., 2021). Through the analysis of feedback gathered from online review platforms, social media mentions, and customer surveys, destinations can pinpoint areas for enhancement, address customer concerns, and elevate the overall visitor experience (Chang et al., 2019). This data-driven approach cultivates customer loyalty and positive word-of-mouth, thereby contributing to the enduring success of destination promotion endeavors (Pyne et al., 2016; Dewnarain et al., 2019).

BDA has become a pivotal instrument in the tourism sector, furnishing invaluable insights that influence tourism strategies and destination promotion (Mariani et al., 2021). Through the analysis of extensive and intricate datasets, destinations can gain insights into traveler behavior, preferences, and emerging trends, allowing them to customize their offerings, optimize marketing endeavors, and enrich the overall visitor experience. The escalating significance of data-driven insights underscores the imperative for destination marketers to adopt BDA and harness its potential in an environment characterized by growing competition and abundant data (Amankwah-Amoah & Adomako, 2019; Walkowiak, 2016).

Harnessing the BDA in the Tourism Industry

Data Collection and Integration

Effectively utilizing the potential of BDA in the tourism sector demands a thorough strategy for collecting and integrating data. To leverage the myriad sources of available data, destination marketers and stakeholders must explore diverse channels such as social media platforms, travel websites, mobile apps, geolocation data, booking platforms, and Internet of Things (IoT) devices (Dey et al., 2018; Mohamed & Al-Azab, 2021).

Data collection methods in tourism can include (Farahat, 2023; Ragab, 2017; Mohamed & Al-Azab, 2021):

1. Social Media Monitoring: Social media platforms like Facebook, Twitter, Instagram, and TripAdvisor present an abundance of user-generated content that holds value in comprehending traveler preferences, sentiment, and behavior. Destinations can gather data on visitor experiences and opinions by monitoring relevant hashtags, mentions, and reviews.
2. Web Scraping: Travel websites and online booking platforms encompass a wealth of data, covering details on accommodations, flights, attractions, and reviews. Utilizing web scraping techniques allows the extraction of data from these sources, which can then be aggregated for analysis.
3. Mobile Apps and IoT Devices: Mobile applications and Internet of Things (IoT) devices, including wearables and smart devices, produce data related to traveler movements, activities, and preferences. Harnessing these sources provides destinations with valuable insights into visitor behaviors, location-based trends, and personalized recommendations.
4. Surveys and Feedback: Conventional approaches such as surveys and feedback forms remain valuable sources of data. Destinations can directly obtain information from visitors through online surveys, on-site feedback mechanisms, or post-visit questionnaires, gathering insights into visitor satisfaction, preferences, and motivations.

To amalgamate data collected from diverse sources, it is crucial to institute data management systems and frameworks. This process entails cleaning, transforming, and organizing the data to guarantee consistency and usability. Techniques like data warehousing, data lakes, and Extract, Transform, Load (ETL) processes can be utilized to merge distinct datasets into a unified and easily accessible format.

Understanding Customer Behavior

BDA is pivotal in comprehending customer behavior in the tourism sector, leveraging extensive data from platforms, booking systems, social media, and feedback. This analysis reveals valuable insights into how customers engage with tourism services, identifying trends, preferences, and travel decisions. Destinations utilize this information to customize offerings, develop attractions, and enhance infrastructure, catering to customer demands. Moreover, granular analysis of customer demographics and interests enables personalized recommendations and targeted marketing, significantly enhancing customer satisfaction through tailored suggestions aligned with individual preferences (Hwang & Chen, 2017; Mohamed & Al-Azab, 2021).

BDA provides destinations with valuable insights into customer sentiment and feedback through the examination of online reviews, social media mentions, and surveys. This aids in understanding customer satisfaction, pinpointing improvement areas, and addressing issues promptly. The feedback-driven approach allows destinations to enhance services, make data-informed decisions, and provide outstanding customer experiences (Chaudhary & Alam, 2022; Farahat, 2023). Additionally, BDA facilitates the prediction of customer behavior and trends using predictive modeling, enabling destinations to forecast travel patterns, demand fluctuations, and emerging market segments. This proactive strategy ensures destinations stay ahead in market trends and meet evolving customer expectations (Ghavami, 2019; Ragab, 2017).

Real-Time Monitoring and Adaptation

BDA is crucial for real-time monitoring and adaptation in the dynamic tourism industry. Real-time monitoring involves continuous analysis of data streams, particularly from social media and online platforms, providing immediate insights into customer sentiments and emerging trends. This enables quick decision-making and issue resolution (Moreira et al., 2018; Aktaş et al., 2022). Additionally, Big Data drives real-time adaptation, as seen in dynamic pricing strategies that adjust rates based on demand fluctuations, optimizing revenue. This approach enhances competitiveness by aligning prices with market dynamics, ensuring businesses stay responsive and profitable (Chen et al., 2021; Ahmed & Pathan, 2018).

Geolocation data is integral for real-time monitoring, enabling businesses to optimize traffic flow and manage crowds in tourist areas. This is particularly crucial for addressing over-tourism and preserving attractions' quality. Big Data's real-time monitoring is essential for predicting and managing disruptions caused by events like natural disasters or pandemics (Araz et al., 2021; Hassanien et al., 2020). By processing data from various sources, including weather forecasts and social media, BDA provides early warnings, facilitating swift decision-making. This agility in monitoring and adapting to real-time data offers a competitive edge in the unpredictable tourism industry, allowing businesses and destinations to enhance services, optimize operations, and stay resilient (Shah et al., 2019; Somani & Deka, 2017).

Personalized Marketing Campaigns

BDA is pivotal in crafting personalized marketing approaches for tourism destinations. Leveraging data from travelers, online platforms, and various stakeholders, BDA enables destinations to derive valuable insights for targeted campaigns, personalized recommendations, and tailored experiences across diverse traveler segments. BDA's capability to analyze extensive datasets aids in identifying patterns and trends in customer behavior, facilitating the segmentation of the customer base. This segmentation allows destinations to design personalized marketing campaigns that align with the unique needs and interests of various traveler segments, delivering messages and offers that resonate individually (Balas et al., 2019; Mohamed & Al-Azab, 2021).

Data-driven insights empower destinations to offer personalized recommendations by utilizing BDA techniques like collaborative filtering and recommendation algorithms. By analyzing customer preferences, browsing history, and previous bookings, destinations enhance customer satisfaction and conversion rates (Dartmann et al., 2019; Farahat, 2023). BDA enables tailored experiences for different traveler segments, leveraging data on behavior, feedback, and sentiment to customize offerings. Additionally, BDA facilitates the measurement and evaluation of personalized marketing impact, ensuring strategies remain relevant, responsive, and effective, ultimately increasing customer satisfaction and optimizing return on investment (Rejeb et al., 2020; Thomas et al., 2019).

Agile Campaign Testing and Optimization

BDA transforms marketing with agile campaign testing and optimization. Unlike linear traditional approaches, big data enables an agile methodology (Saggi & Jain, 2018). Destinations utilize advanced analytics to collect and analyze real-time data from customer interactions, social media, website traffic, and campaign metrics. This allows destinations to quickly assess campaign effectiveness, identify strengths and weaknesses, and make data-driven adjustments on the fly. This agile approach enhances campaign performance and responsiveness, ensuring marketing strategies align with dynamic market conditions and customer preferences (Jayaram et al., 2015; Sun, 2019).

Agile campaign testing, supported by BDA, involves continuous experimentation and iteration of marketing strategies. Destinations utilize techniques like A/B testing and multivariate testing to compare different campaign elements, identifying the most effective variations. BDA enables accurate measurement of campaign impact through key performance indicators, facilitating data-driven adjustments. This iterative process ensures ongoing refinement and optimization of marketing strategies based on real-time insights, enhancing overall campaign performance and return on investment (Liebowitz, 2020; Ragab, 2017). Additionally, BDA informs targeted and personalized marketing campaigns by understanding customer behavior and preferences, resulting in higher engagement and conversion rates (Jiwat & Zhang, 2022; Tyagi, 2021).

Optimizing Marketing Channels

BDA is instrumental in optimizing marketing channels in the tourism industry by strategically allocating resources and refining strategies. BDA assesses the effectiveness of various channels, analyzing customer interactions and engagement across platforms like social media, online travel agencies, search engines, and email marketing. This data-driven approach allows businesses to allocate budgets to the most effective channels, optimizing overall marketing strategies. BDA enables attribution modeling, providing insights into the customer journey and helping businesses focus on channels driving the most conversions while adjusting strategies for underperforming ones (Rahimi et al., 2020; Ragab, 2017).

BDA aids in audience segmentation, enabling businesses to tailor messages to different customer segments across channels. By understanding preferences and behaviors, marketers can create targeted and personalized campaigns. For example, if BDA shows higher engagement in a demographic on social media, efforts can be intensified in that channel for that segment. BDA also supports real-time monitoring, allowing businesses to adapt quickly to changing trends and behaviors, ensuring the marketing strategy aligns with the dynamic nature of the tourism industry (Alnoukari, 2022; Farahat, 2023).

Data-Driven Decision-Making

BDA is instrumental in driving data-driven decision-making in diverse sectors, including tourism. Leveraging extensive data from customer interactions, market trends, social media, and operational systems, destinations utilize BDA to extract valuable insights for informed decisions. This approach involves employing advanced analytics algorithms to identify influential factors in business performance, customer behavior, and market dynamics. The obtained insights empower destinations to make precise predictions, evaluate risks, and recognize opportunities for growth and enhancement (Aroraa et al., 2022; Mohamed & Al-Azab, 2021).

BDA excels in swiftly processing vast datasets, enabling destinations to monitor real-time data and swiftly respond to market shifts. This adaptability empowers destinations to make agile decisions, adjusting pricing, optimizing campaigns, and improving operational efficiency to meet dynamic demands (Ikegwu et al., 2022; Khan et al., 2021). Furthermore, big data's integration of diverse data sources provides a comprehensive view of operations, customer preferences, and market trends. This holistic perspective unveils correlations and dependencies, enhancing decision-making accuracy. Additionally, data-driven decision-making supports personalized offerings by segmenting audiences, understanding preferences, and tailoring products and experiences, fostering heightened customer satisfaction, engagement, and loyalty (Santos & Costa, 2022; Farahat, 2023).

Dynamic Pricing and Offers

BDA is instrumental in implementing dynamic pricing strategies in the tourism industry. This approach involves real-time adjustments to prices based on factors like demand, seasonality, and competitor pricing. BDA enables businesses to analyze extensive datasets, including historical booking patterns and market trends, to identify optimal pricing for maximizing revenue (Sedkaoui, 2018; Ragab, 2017). It also helps businesses recognize patterns in customer behavior, allowing strategic pricing adjustments during peak demand periods (Mariani & Wamba, 2020). BDA's continuous monitoring of competitor pricing and market conditions enables businesses to stay agile and competitively price their offerings. The real-time insights ensure adaptive responses to changes in the market landscape and competitor strategies (Farahat, 2023; Liebowitz, 2020).

BDA enhances dynamic pricing by enabling personalized strategies. Businesses use BDA to analyze individual customer preferences, booking histories, and responses to tailor pricing and incentives. For instance, identifying customer segments that respond well to discounts allows businesses to customize promotions effectively. BDA's predictive analytics supports forecasting future demand, helping adjust pricing strategies based on historical data patterns and external factors. This proactive approach allows businesses to capture demand surges by strategically setting prices or lowering them during anticipated low-demand periods (Chaudhary & Alam, 2022; Mohamed & Al-Azab, 2021).

Predictive Modeling and Forecasting

BDA plays a vital role in predictive modeling and forecasting for the tourism industry. It enables businesses to anticipate future trends, optimize operations, and make strategic decisions based on real-time analysis of vast datasets (Hofmann & Rutschmann, 2018). Leveraging machine learning algorithms and statistical models, BDA extracts meaningful patterns from historical data, forming the foundation for predictive models. These models forecast aspects such as demand fluctuations, customer behaviors, and market trends, empowering businesses to adapt proactively. Predictive modeling helps anticipate changes in customer preferences, enabling businesses to optimize marketing strategies and allocate resources effectively (Bharadiya, 2023).

BDA is pivotal in demand forecasting, enabling businesses to adapt their offerings based on anticipated demand fluctuations. Through the analysis of booking patterns, historical visitation data, and external factors like events or holidays, BDA facilitates data-driven decisions for optimizing pricing, inventory, and marketing strategies (Popovič et al., 2018; Egger, 2022). Additionally, BDA supports operational optimization by forecasting peak visitor times, allowing strategic allocation of staff, crowd management, and improved overall visitor experiences. The personalization capabilities of BDA enhance predictive modeling effectiveness, enabling businesses to tailor marketing strategies based on individual customer preferences and behaviors, leading to more personalized and targeted offers (Mohammed et al., 2020; Pyne et al., 2016).

Location-Based Targeting

BDA is pivotal for location-based targeting in the tourism industry, utilizing vast location data from sources like mobile devices and social media check-ins. This strategy involves tailoring marketing messages, offers, and experiences to individuals based on their geographic location. Destinations leverage BDA to understand customer movement patterns and behavior in different areas, allowing for targeted marketing campaigns. By analyzing location data alongside other customer information, destinations create personalized marketing strategies for diverse locations, enhancing customer engagement and increasing the likelihood of conversion through tailored messages and offers (Egger, 2022; Mohamed & Al-Azab, 2021).

BDA enhances location-based targeting by identifying high-value locations and micro-markets. It enables destinations to pinpoint areas with a high concentration of potential customers or significant revenue, aiding effective resource allocation and targeted marketing efforts for optimal return on investment. Beyond marketing, BDA extends to customer experience and operations in tourism. Destinations leverage location data to personalize on-site experiences with location-specific recommendations, promotions, and services. Additionally, in operations, location data analysis optimizes transportation routes, crowd management, and resource allocation through real-time location information (Farahat, 2023; Moreira et al., 2018; Chaudhary & Alam, 2022).

Media Listening and Influencer Marketing

BDA is integral to media listening and influencer marketing in tourism. By monitoring and analyzing online conversations and sentiments on various platforms, destinations gain insights into customer perceptions and preferences. Media listening, utilizing BDA, enables destinations to manage their brand reputation, identify areas for improvement, and enhance offerings. Additionally, it assists in influencer marketing by identifying influencers aligned with brand values, relevant audiences, and high engagement. Destinations leverage data-driven insights to make informed decisions when selecting and partnering with influencers for effective marketing campaigns (Mohamed et al., 2022).

BDA supports destinations in evaluating influencer marketing impact by tracking key metrics like reach, engagement, conversions, and sentiment analysis. Destinations utilize data-driven insights to assess the ROI of influencer campaigns, refine messaging, and allocate resources efficiently. Furthermore, BDA helps destinations identify emerging trends and insights in their industry by monitoring online conversations. This proactive approach allows destinations to adapt marketing strategies, stay competitive, and create innovative offerings aligned with evolving customer preferences and emerging market segments (Gupta et al., 2021; Mohamed & Al-Azab, 2021; Ragab, 2017).

Performance Measurement and Optimization

BDA is pivotal for performance measurement and optimization in the tourism sector. BDA processes large datasets, including key performance indicators (KPIs) like website traffic, bookings, customer satisfaction, and revenue. This comprehensive analysis provides businesses with a holistic view, offering data-driven insights for identifying strengths and areas of improvement (Liebowitz, 2020; Farahat, 2023). Real-time performance monitoring through BDA allows prompt responses to market changes and customer behaviors, enhancing adaptability and overall performance in the dynamic tourism landscape (Mohamed et al., 2022).

BDA not only aids in performance measurement but also supports predictive analytics for anticipating future trends and customer behaviors. This forward-looking approach enables proactive planning and strategic decision-making (Talwar et al.,

2021; Moreira et al., 2018). BDA is instrumental in optimizing performance by refining strategies based on insights, streamlining processes, and enhancing user experiences. The personalization capabilities of BDA contribute to performance optimization by tailoring offerings to individual customer preferences, fostering satisfaction, loyalty, and improved overall performance (Côrte-Real et al., 2019; Webber & Zheng, 2020).

Collaborative Partnerships and Data Sharing

BDA is pivotal in promoting collaborative partnerships and data sharing across stakeholders in the tourism industry. It enables entities like destinations, hotels, airlines, and agencies to collectively share and analyze data, leading to a more comprehensive understanding of the tourism ecosystem. Collaborative data sharing allows pooling of resources, combining expertise, and deriving insights that contribute to better decision-making and strategy formulation. BDA facilitates the integration of diverse datasets, unveiling valuable patterns and trends that emerge when multiple data sources are combined, enhancing the development of targeted marketing campaigns and personalized experiences (Liebowitz, 2020; Khan et al., 2021; Mohamed & Al-Azab, 2021).

BDA not only supports collaborative partnerships and data sharing in the tourism industry but also fosters the creation of data-driven solutions and innovations. Stakeholders, by sharing data and expertise, can collectively develop predictive models, forecasting tools, and intelligent systems that improve operational efficiency, customer experiences, and industry competitiveness. This collaborative innovation allows stakeholders to stay ahead in technology and industry trends (Hassanien et al., 2020; Alnoukari, 2022; Mohamed et al., 2022). Moreover, BDA contributes to the sustainability and resilience of the tourism sector by facilitating collaborative efforts in sharing data on environmental impacts, resource consumption, and sustainable practices. This collective approach encourages knowledge sharing, best practices, and innovative solutions to address common challenges like climate change, overtourism, and resource management (Agrawal et al., 2022; Egger, 2022).

Optimizing Destination Marketing

BDA has transformed destination marketing by leveraging vast amounts of traveler-generated data. Analyzing data from diverse sources like social media, search engines, booking systems, and reviews, destinations gain insights into traveler behavior and preferences. This knowledge helps identify popular destinations and activities, allowing targeted marketing. BDA facilitates personalized campaigns by analyzing customer demographics and behaviors, enhancing engagement, and fostering customer loyalty. With data-driven strategies, destinations can optimize marketing efforts, tailoring messages to specific audience segments, improving satisfaction, and increasing the likelihood of conversions (Mohamed & Al-Azab, 2021; Mohamed et al., 2022).

BDA enhances destination marketing by providing real-time evaluation of key performance indicators (KPIs) such as website traffic and social media engagement. Destinations can optimize strategies based on performance insights, allocate budgets effectively, and identify emerging market trends. BDA enables the prediction of future travel trends through predictive analytics, allowing destinations to forecast demand, optimize pricing, and plan marketing campaigns proactively. This proactive approach positions destinations to adapt to evolving traveler needs and capitalize on emerging opportunities in the tourism industry (Farahat, 2023).

BDA Challenges and Ethical Considerations

BDA encounters several challenges in the tourism sector that necessitate attention to ensure the responsible and ethical utilization of visitor information (Egger, 2022; Mohamed & Al-Azab, 2021). One significant challenge pertains to data privacy. The collection and analysis of extensive data volumes in BDA raise apprehensions regarding the confidentiality of visitor information. It is imperative for destinations and stakeholders to comply with data protection regulations and acquire appropriate consent from visitors before engaging in data collection. The implementation of robust data privacy policies and secure data management practices plays a crucial role in safeguarding visitor information and upholding trust (Pyne et al., 2016; Moreira et al., 2018; Mohamed & Al-Azab, 2021).

Security issues also emerge in the context of big data in tourism. The extensive volume and diversity of data expose it to potential security breaches and cyber threats. Destinations are required to allocate resources to robust cybersecurity measures aimed at safeguarding visitor data from unauthorized access, hacking attempts, and data breaches. The implementation of encryption technologies, access controls, and regular security audits stands as essential in mitigating these risks and maintaining the integrity and confidentiality of visitor information (Chaudhary & Alam, 2022; Alani et al., 2018; Farahat, 2023).

Data accuracy presents another challenge in the realm of BDA. Extensive datasets may include incomplete, inconsistent, or inaccurate information, potentially resulting in flawed analyses and misguided insights. To tackle this challenge, destinations must prioritize data quality by incorporating processes such as data cleansing, validation, and verification. The establishment of data governance frameworks and the implementation of measures for data quality control are imperative to guarantee the accuracy and reliability of the data utilized for analysis (Farahat, 2023; Liebowitz, 2020; Hassanien et al., 2020).

Ethical considerations become significant when incorporating visitor information into destination promotion. It is imperative to uphold visitor privacy and employ data in an ethical and responsible manner. Destinations ought to maintain transparency regarding the collected data, its intended purpose, and the methods of utilization. Additionally, visitors should be given choices to control and manage their data, including options to opt-out or request the deletion of their information. Adhering to ethical guidelines and industry best practices is essential to preserve visitor trust and guarantee the responsible utilization of visitor information (Mohamed & Al-Azab, 2021; Farahat, 2023).

FUTURE TRENDS AND RECOMMENDATIONS

Effectively harnessing BDA for destination promotion while addressing challenges and ensuring ethical practices requires practical implications for stakeholders, tourism boards, and policymakers.

As for stakeholders, they should enhance data collection across touchpoints and invest in analytical capabilities to process diverse data sources. Utilizing tools like data visualization, machine learning, and predictive modeling can reveal valuable insights, informing decision-making and targeted marketing. Personalization of the visitor experience, driven by data analysis, boosts satisfaction and loyalty. Exploration of emerging analytics techniques, like machine learning and natural language processing, is recommended for uncovering hidden patterns and predicting trends. Investment in analytics talent and technologies is vital to leverage these advanced techniques effectively.

Stakeholders should invest in robust data infrastructure and build organizational data capabilities for effective BDA. Collaboration with technology providers and research institutions can provide access to expertise and tools. Regular assessment of BDA initiatives is crucial, involving monitoring key performance indicators and collecting visitor feedback for continuous improvement. Ensuring data quality through validation processes and adherence to standards is essential for accurate insights and informed decision-making, preventing potential bias. High data quality standards empower stakeholders to make informed decisions and avoid misleading outcomes. Similarly, stakeholders should embrace a data-driven decision-making culture, where insights from BDA are integrated into the decision-making processes. This involves using data to support strategic planning, marketing campaigns, product development, and resource allocation. Data-driven decision making helps stakeholders stay agile, responsive to visitor needs, and competitive in the market.

Regrading the tourism boards, collaboration is crucial for effective BDA in destination promotion, involving tourism boards, businesses, and academia. Encouraging data sharing and collaboration enhances the integration of diverse datasets for more comprehensive insights. Establishing data-sharing agreements, ensuring privacy, and promoting open data initiatives facilitate collaboration. BDA aids tourism boards in destination management by identifying overcrowded areas, peak seasons, and infrastructure gaps, informing decisions on resource allocation, crowd management, and sustainable tourism development. As well, tourism boards can educate stakeholders on BDA benefits and ethics while leveraging it to enhance destination branding. Analyzing visitor data helps identify target markets and preferences, enabling targeted marketing campaigns for improved effectiveness. BDA supports tourism boards in implementing sustainable practices by analyzing visitor behavior and environmental impacts. It aids in waste management, energy efficiency, and community engagement. Additionally, BDA helps tourism boards gain insights into visitor experiences by analyzing feedback, sentiment, and social media conversations, guiding improvements in infrastructure and services for enhanced satisfaction.

Regarding the policymakers, they need to enforce stringent data privacy and security measures, promoting encryption, access controls, and regular audits to safeguard visitor information. They should collaborate with tourism boards to establish robust data governance frameworks that prioritize privacy, security, and ethics, ensuring compliance with regulations. Regular audits are essential to maintain data quality, accuracy, and ethical practices. Further, policymakers can develop ethical guidelines for BDA in tourism. These guidelines should outline best practices for data collection, analysis, and use, emphasizing fairness, transparency, and accountability. Policymakers should also encourage stakeholders to conduct regular audits and assessments to ensure compliance with ethical guidelines. Policymakers can promote data sharing and collaboration among stakeholders by creating incentives and platforms that facilitate data exchange. Encouraging partnerships between tourism organizations, research institutions, and technology providers can foster innovation, knowledge sharing, and the development of data-driven solutions for destination promotion. There is also need to support initiatives that promote skills development and training in data analytics and BDA. This includes investing in educational programs, workshops, and certifications to equip tourism professionals with the necessary skills to leverage BDA effectively. By nurturing a skilled workforce, policymakers can ensure the sustainable adoption and utilization of BDA in the tourism industry.

CONCLUSION

The study underscores the significant potential of employing BDA in touristic destination promotion within the tourism industry. By tapping into extensive data generated by travelers, businesses, and online platforms, destination marketers can glean valuable insights to shape effective promotional strategies and improve the visitor experience. BDA empowers marketers to comprehend traveler preferences, behavior patterns, and emerging trends in unprecedented detail. This knowledge enables tailored promotional efforts, personalized recommendations, and the creation of unique, resonant experiences. Additionally, BDA aids in identifying untapped market segments, discovering growth opportunities, and optimizing resource allocation for sustainable tourism development. Real-time monitoring allows marketers to evaluate campaign effectiveness, facilitating prompt adjustments for continuous improvement in the dynamic tourism landscape. Despite its potential, challenges such as data privacy concerns, data quality, and the need for skilled professionals must be addressed through collaborative efforts among destination marketing organizations, policymakers, and industry stakeholders. Embracing BDA can revolutionize touristic destination promotion, driving sustainable tourism growth, enhancing visitor satisfaction, and contributing to overall destination success, provided it is guided by ethical and responsible practices.

REFERENCES

Aggarwal, J., Bhatnagar, V., & Mishra, D. (2018). *Big data analytics*. Springer Singapore. doi:10.1007/978-981-10-6620-7

Agrawal, R., Wankhede, V., Kumar, A., Luthra, S., & Huisingh, D. (2022). Big data analytics and sustainable tourism: A comprehensive review and network based analysis for potential future research. *International Journal of Information Management Data Insights*, *2*(2), 100122. doi:10.1016/j.jjimei.2022.100122

Ahmed, M., & Pathan, A. (2018). *Data analytics: concepts, techniques, and applications*. Crc Press. doi:10.1201/9780429446177

Aktaş, E., Kurgun, A., Ozeren, E., & Kucukaltan, B. (2022). Real-Time Data Analysis (RTDA) and Proposed Innovative Business Models: A Conceptual Study of the Tourism Industry. *International Journal of Organizational Leadership, 11*, 4-20.

Alani, M., Tawfik, M., Saeed, M., & Anya, O. (2018). *Applications of Big Data Analytics- Trends, Issues, and Challenges*. Springer. doi:10.1007/978-3-319-76472-6

Alnoukari, M. (2022). From business intelligence to big data: The power of analytics. In Research Anthology on Big Data Analytics, Architectures, and Applications (pp. 823-841). IGI Global.

Amankwah-Amoah, J., & Adomako, S. (2019). Big data analytics and business failures in data-Rich environments: An organizing framework. *Computers in Industry*, *105*, 204–212. doi:10.1016/j.compind.2018.12.015

Ankam, V. (2016). *Big data analytics*. Packt Publishing Ltd.

Araz, O., Choi, T., Olson, D., & Salman, F. (2020). Role of analytics for operational risk management in the era of big data. *Decision Sciences*, *51*(6), 1320–1346. doi:10.1111/deci.12451

Aroraa, G., Lele, C., & Jindal, M. (2022). *Data Analytics: Principles, Tools, and Practices: A Complete Guide for Advanced Data Analytics Using the Latest Trends, Tools, and Technologies (English Edition)*. BPB Publications.

Balas, V., Solanki, V., Kumar, R., & Khari, M. (2019). *Internet of things and big data analytics for smart generation* (Vol. 154). Springer. doi:10.1007/978-3-030-04203-5

Bharadiya, J. (2023). Machine learning and AI in business intelligence: Trends and opportunities. *International Journal of Computer*, *48*(1), 123–134.

Chang, Y., Ku, C., & Chen, C. (2019). Social media analytics: Extracting and visualizing Hilton hotel ratings and reviews from TripAdvisor. *International Journal of Information Management*, *48*, 263–279. doi:10.1016/j.ijinfomgt.2017.11.001

Chaudhary, K., & Alam, M. (2022). *Big data analytics: applications in business and marketing*. Auerbach Publications. doi:10.1201/9781003307761

Chen, L., Yang, Y., & Xu, Q. (2021). Retail dynamic pricing strategy design considering the fluctuations in day-ahead market using integrated demand response. *International Journal of Electrical Power & Energy Systems*, *130*, 106983. doi:10.1016/j.ijepes.2021.106983

Côrte-Real, N., Ruivo, P., Oliveira, T., & Popovič, A. (2019). Unlocking the drivers of big data analytics value in firms. *Journal of Business Research*, *97*, 160–173. doi:10.1016/j.jbusres.2018.12.072

Dartmann, G., Song, H., & Schmeink, A. (2019). *Big data analytics for cyber-physical systems: machine learning for the internet of things*. Elsevier.

Dewnarain, S., Ramkissoon, H., & Mavondo, F. (2019). Social customer relationship management: An integrated conceptual framework. *Journal of Hospitality Marketing & Management, 28*(2), 172–188. doi:10.1080/19368623.2018.1516588

Dey, N., Hassanien, A., Bhatt, C., Ashour, A., & Satapathy, S. (2018). *Internet of things and big data analytics toward next-generation intelligence*. Springer. doi:10.1007/978-3-319-60435-0

Egger, R. (2022). *Applied Data Science in Tourism*. Springer International Publishing. doi:10.1007/978-3-030-88389-8

Farahat, E. (2023). *Applications of artificial intelligence as a marketing tool and their impact on the competitiveness of the Egyptian tourist destination* (Doctoral Dissertation, Minia University).

Ghavami, P. (2019). *Big data analytics methods: analytics techniques in data mining, deep learning and natural language processing*. Walter de Gruyter GmbH & Co KG. doi:10.1515/9781547401567

Gupta, S., Justy, T., Kamboj, S., Kumar, A., & Kristoffersen, E. (2021). Big data and firm marketing performance: Findings from knowledge-based view. *Technological Forecasting and Social Change, 171*, 120986. doi:10.1016/j.techfore.2021.120986

Hassanien, A., Dey, N., & Elghamrawy, S. (2020). Big data analytics and artificial intelligence against COVID-19. Springer Nature.

Hofmann, E., & Rutschmann, E. (2018). Big data analytics and demand forecasting in supply chains: A conceptual analysis. *International Journal of Logistics Management, 29*(2), 739–766. doi:10.1108/IJLM-04-2017-0088

Horng, J., Liu, C., Chou, S., Yu, T., & Hu, D. (2022). Role of big data capabilities in enhancing competitive advantage and performance in the hospitality sector: Knowledge-based dynamic capabilities view. *Journal of Hospitality and Tourism Management, 51*, 22–38. doi:10.1016/j.jhtm.2022.02.026

Hwang, K., & Chen, M. (2017). *Big-data analytics for cloud, IoT and cognitive computing*. John Wiley & Sons.

Ikegwu, A., Nweke, H., Anikwe, C., Alo, U., & Okonkwo, O. (2022). Big data analytics for data-driven industry: A review of data sources, tools, challenges, solutions, and research directions. *Cluster Computing, 25*(5), 3343–3387. doi:10.1007/s10586-022-03568-5

Jayaram, D., Manrai, A., & Manrai, L. (2015). Effective use of marketing technology in Eastern Europe: Web analytics, social media, customer analytics, digital campaigns and mobile applications. *Journal of Economics, Finance and Administrative Science*, *20*(39), 118–132. doi:10.1016/j.jefas.2015.07.001

Jiwat, R., & Zhang, Z. (2022). Adopting big data analytics (BDA) in business-to-business (B2B) organizations–Development of a model of needs. *Journal of Engineering and Technology Management*, *63*, 101676. doi:10.1016/j.jengtecman.2022.101676

Khan, M., Algarni, F., & Quasim, M. (2021). *Smart Cities: A Data Analytics Perspective*. Springer International Publishing. doi:10.1007/978-3-030-60922-1

Kulkarni, P., Joshi, S., & Brown, M. (2016). *Big data analytics*. PHI Learning Pvt. Ltd.

Liebowitz, J. (2020). *Data analytics and AI*. CRC Press. doi:10.1201/9781003019855

Mandal, S. (2018). Exploring the influence of big data analytics management capabilities on sustainable tourism supply chain performance: The moderating role of technology orientation. *Journal of Travel & Tourism Marketing*, *35*(8), 1104–1118. doi:10.1080/10548408.2018.1476302

Mariani, M., Bresciani, S., & Dagnino, G. (2021). The competitive productivity (CP) of tourism destinations: An integrative conceptual framework and a reflection on big data and analytics. *International Journal of Contemporary Hospitality Management*, *33*(9), 2970–3002. doi:10.1108/IJCHM-09-2020-1102

Mariani, M., & Wamba, S. (2020). Exploring how consumer goods companies innovate in the digital age: The role of big data analytics companies. *Journal of Business Research*, *121*, 338–352. doi:10.1016/j.jbusres.2020.09.012

Mehta, R. (2017). *Big Data Analytics with Java*. Packt Publishing Ltd.

Mohamed, H., & Al-Azab, M. (2021). Big Data Analytics in Airlines: Opportunities and Challenges. *Journal of Association of Arab Universities for Tourism and Hospitality*, *21*(4), 77–112.

Mohamed, M., Farahat, E., & Al-Romeedy, B. (2022). The Mediating Role of Marketing Effectiveness in the Relationship between Artificial Intelligence and Destination Competitiveness. *Minia Journal of Tourism and Hospitality Research*, *14*(1), 113–129.

Mohammed, S., Arabnia, H., Qu, X., Zhang, D., Kim, T., & Zhao, J. (2020). IEEE access special section editorial: Big data technology and applications in intelligent transportation. *IEEE Access : Practical Innovations, Open Solutions*, *8*, 201331–201344. doi:10.1109/ACCESS.2020.3035440

Moreira, J., Carvalho, A., & Horvath, T. (2018). *A general introduction to data analytics*. John Wiley & Sons. doi:10.1002/9781119296294

Popovič, A., Hackney, R., Tassabehji, R., & Castelli, M. (2018). The impact of big data analytics on firms' high value business performance. *Information Systems Frontiers*, *20*(2), 209–222. doi:10.1007/s10796-016-9720-4

Pyne, S., Rao, B., & Rao, S. (2016). *Big data analytics: Methods and applications*. Springer.

Ragab, A. (2017). The Behavioural Intention of Adopting Big Data Analytics in the Tourism Sector: An Empirical Investigation in Egypt. *Minia Journal of Tourism and Hospitality Research MJTHR*, *2*(2), 1–19. doi:10.21608/mjthr.2017.139608

Rahimi, I., Gandomi, A., Fong, S., & Ülkü, M. (2020). *Big data analytics in supply chain management: Theory and applications*. CRC Press.

Rejeb, A., Rejeb, K., & Keogh, J. (2020). Potential of big data for marketing: A literature review. *Management Research and Practice*, *12*(3), 60–73.

Saggi, M., & Jain, S. (2018). A survey towards an integration of big data analytics to big insights for value-creation. *Information Processing & Management*, *54*(5), 758–790. doi:10.1016/j.ipm.2018.01.010

Santos, M., & Costa, C. (2022). *Big data: concepts, warehousing, and analytics*. CRC Press.

Sedkaoui, S. (2018). *Data analytics and big data*. John Wiley & Sons. doi:10.1002/9781119528043

Sedkaoui, S. (Ed.). (2018). *Big data analytics for entrepreneurial success*. IGI Global.

Shah, S., Seker, D., Rathore, M., Hameed, S., Yahia, S., & Draheim, D. (2019). Towards disaster resilient smart cities: Can internet of things and big data analytics be the game changers? *IEEE Access : Practical Innovations, Open Solutions*, *7*, 91885–91903. doi:10.1109/ACCESS.2019.2928233

Somani, A., & Deka, G. (2017). *Big data analytics: Tools and technology for effective planning*. CRC Press. doi:10.1201/b21822

Stylos, N., Zwiegelaar, J., & Buhalis, D. (2021). Big data empowered agility for dynamic, volatile, and time-sensitive service industries: The case of tourism sector. *International Journal of Contemporary Hospitality Management*, *33*(3), 1015–1036. doi:10.1108/IJCHM-07-2020-0644

Sun, Z. (2019). Intelligent big data analytics: a managerial perspective. In *Managerial Perspectives on Intelligent Big Data Analytics* (pp. 1–19). IGI Global. doi:10.4018/978-1-5225-7277-0.ch001

Talwar, S., Kaur, P., Fosso Wamba, S., & Dhir, A. (2021). Big Data in operations and supply chain management: A systematic literature review and future research agenda. *International Journal of Production Research*, *59*(11), 3509–3534. doi:10.1080/00207543.2020.1868599

Thomas, J., Karagoz, P., Ahamed, B., & Vasant, P. (2019). *Deep learning techniques and optimization strategies in big data analytics*. IGI Global.

Tyagi, A. (2021). *Data Science and Data Analytics: Opportunities and Challenges*. CRC Press. doi:10.1201/9781003111290

Walkowiak, S. (2016). *Big Data analytics with R*. Packt Publishing Ltd.

Webber, K., & Zheng, H. (2020). *Big data on campus: Data analytics and decision making in higher education*. Johns Hopkins University Press. doi:10.1353/book.78960

Wong, K. (2016). *Big data analytics in genomics*. Springer. doi:10.1007/978-3-319-41279-5

Xiang, Z., & Fesenmaier, D. (2017). *Analytics in smart tourism design: concepts and methods*. Springer International Publishing Switzerland. doi:10.1007/978-3-319-44263-1

Chapter 3
Data Fusion for Destination Success:
Exploring the Integration of MKIS and BDA in Marketing Touristic Destinations

Hebat Allah Ali Gaafar
https://orcid.org/0000-0001-8214-4451
Faculty of Tourism and Hotels, Egypt

Bassam Samir Al-Romeedy
Faculty of Tourism and Hotels, Egypt

ABSTRACT

The integration of MKIS and BDA, along with data fusion techniques, can lead to more targeted and effective marketing strategies for touristic destinations. This can result in better customer satisfaction, increased visitor numbers, and higher revenue for the destinations. By leveraging data fusion, touristic destinations can gain a deeper understanding of tourists' preferences and behaviors. This understanding can enable them to provide personalized and tailored experiences, leading to higher visitor satisfaction and loyalty. The chapter aims to shed light on the integration of MKIS and BDA in the marketing of touristic destinations and highlight the potential of data fusion for destination success. By bridging the gap between traditional marketing information systems and the advanced analytics capabilities of big data, this chapter seeks to empower touristic destinations with actionable insights for effective marketing strategies and improved visitor experiences.

DOI: 10.4018/979-8-3693-3310-5.ch003

INTRODUCTION

The marketing of tourist destinations plays a crucial role in the economic development of diverse countries and regions. To attract and keep visitors, these destinations must efficiently showcase their appeal. In the digital age, the abundance of data and advancements in data analytics provides an opportunity for tourist destinations to gain valuable insights into tourists' preferences, behaviors, and patterns. This, consequently, empowers them to formulate precise marketing strategies and improve the overall tourist experience (Telfer & Sharpley, 2015).

In the realm of marketing, Marketing Information Systems (MKIS) play a crucial role by facilitating the collection, organization, analysis, and dissemination of marketing information. They offer valuable insights into market trends, customer preferences, and competitors' activities, thereby supporting the decision-making process (Tsiakis, 2015; Erevelles et al., 2016). Big Data Analytics (BDA) involves extracting valuable insights from extensive and intricate datasets (Belhadi et al., 2019). In today's digital landscape, tourist destinations have unprecedented access to an abundant volume of data generated by tourists through various online platforms and social media channels (Ferrer-Rosell et al., 2023). The integration of MKIS and BDA empowers tourist destinations to gain a comprehensive understanding of tourists' preferences, behaviors, and patterns. With this knowledge, destinations can craft targeted marketing campaigns tailored to specific customer segments. Instead of employing a generic approach, destinations can optimize their marketing resources by focusing on segments more likely to positively respond to their offerings. This targeted approach ensures efficient allocation of resources, preventing wastage on marketing efforts that may have limited impact (Ferrer-Rosell et al., 2023; Stylos et al., 2021; Kachniewska, 2021).

Through data fusion, tourist destinations can create personalized marketing messages customized to the preferences and behaviors of individual tourists. By analyzing data from MKIS and BDA sources, destinations can discern specific interests, demographics, and purchasing patterns of tourists. Leveraging this information, personalized marketing messages can be crafted to resonate with each individual. Personalization fosters greater engagement, enhances customer satisfaction, and boosts conversion rates. By allocating resources to personalized marketing efforts, destinations can maximize the returns on their marketing investments (Chandra et al., 2022; Miah et al., 2017).

Moreover, by integrating MKIS and BDA, destinations can scrutinize customer behaviors and activities across various touchpoints. Through monitoring and analyzing interactions like website visits, social media engagements, and transaction histories, destinations can create comprehensive customer profiles that encompass individual behaviors, preferences, and purchase patterns. This analysis of customer behavior facilitates the identification of customer segments that share similar behaviors, enabling destinations to target them with personalized marketing messages and tailored offerings (Kushwaha et al., 2021; Rosário & Dias, 2023).

The aim of this chapter is to scrutinize the amalgamation of MKIS and BDA in the marketing of touristic destinations and evaluate the influence of data fusion on destination success. Data fusion involves the integration of data from diverse sources to create a unified and comprehensive perspective of the phenomenon under study. By merging data from MKIS and BDA, touristic destinations can attain an extensive understanding of tourists' preferences, behaviors, and patterns, thereby capitalizing on the advantages of a holistic approach. The chapter's objectives are as follows: 1) examining the potential benefits of integrating MKIS and BDA in the marketing of touristic destinations, 2) identifying data fusion techniques and methodologies for merging and analyzing data from MKIS and BDA sources, 3) assessing the challenges and limitations associated with integrating MKIS and BDA in the context of touristic destinations, and 4) offering recommendations and insights for touristic destinations on leveraging data fusion to enhance marketing strategies and achieve destination success.

This chapter aims to contribute to the growing domain of destination marketing by investigating the integration of MKIS and BDA and exploring the possibilities of data fusion. The outcomes of the study have the capacity to aid touristic destinations in enhancing their marketing strategies, optimizing resource allocation, and ultimately providing more personalized and engaging experiences to tourists.

MKIS and BDA Integration

MKIS pertain to the technological framework and instruments facilitating the gathering, storage, retrieval, analysis, and distribution of marketing information within an organizational context. MKIS includes diverse elements like databases, software applications, data mining methodologies, and communication networks. In the realm of tourism marketing, its central function is to streamline the handling of marketing information, empowering stakeholders to make well-informed decisions and craft specific marketing strategies (Kinyua, 2020).

Conversely, BDA is the procedure of examining extensive and intricate datasets, commonly referred to as big data, to unveil patterns, correlations, and insights that can guide decision-making. BDA incorporates the utilization of sophisticated analytics techniques, such as machine learning, predictive modeling, and data visualization, to extract valuable insights from vast datasets. In the sphere of tourism marketing, BDA assumes a pivotal role in scrutinizing diverse data sources, encompassing customer behavior data, social media data, online reviews, and booking data, fostering a comprehensive comprehension of customer preferences, market trends, and competitive dynamics (Egger, 2022; Mohamed & Al-Azab, 2021).

The fusion of MKIS with BDA in marketing creates a symbiotic relationship, enhancing the capabilities of both systems and equipping stakeholders with advanced insights for decision-making. This integration facilitates a thorough analysis of extensive MKIS-acquired data using cutting-edge analytics, revealing intricate patterns and correlations. Stakeholders can capitalize on this unified approach to devise personalized marketing strategies, segmenting target audiences based on customer data to enhance communication effectiveness. Moreover, the real-time monitoring capabilities inherent in MKIS and BDA integration empower stakeholders to remain agile, responding promptly to evolving market dynamics and trends. In essence, this integration leverages technology and advanced analytics to deepen the understanding of customer preferences, pinpoint trends, and navigate the dynamic terrain of the competitive tourism industry (Juska, 2021; Morales-Serazzi et al., 2023; Stienmetz et al., 2022).

Reasons of Integrating MKIS With BDA

The integration of MKIS with BDA presents numerous compelling reasons and advantages. By merging the infrastructure capabilities of MKIS, which facilitate data collection, storage, and analysis, with the advanced analytics techniques of BDA, stakeholders can elevate data-driven decision-making, personalization, and campaign effectiveness.

Data Volume and Complexity

The tourism sector produces extensive data from diverse channels such as customer interactions, online bookings, social media, and market research. Conventional data processing approaches frequently struggle to cope with the extensive volume and intricacy of this data. The integration of MKIS with BDA empowers stakeholders to proficiently handle and analyze extensive and varied datasets, allowing them to extract valuable insights and make informed, data-driven decisions (Mohamed & Al-Azab, 2021; Awan et al., 2021).

Deeper Customer Understanding

MKIS establishes the groundwork for collecting and preserving customer information, encompassing demographics, preferences, and purchase history. Yet, deriving significant insights from this data necessitates the application of advanced analytics techniques. BDA empowers stakeholders to conduct in-depth analysis of customer data, unveiling patterns, trends, and correlations that provide a more profound comprehension of customer behavior, preferences, and motivations. This heightened understanding enables destination marketers to design precise marketing campaigns and provide personalized experiences (Maheshwari et al., 2021; Shmueli et al., 2017).

Real-time Insights

Tourism marketing operates in a constantly changing environment where market trends, customer preferences, and competitive dynamics evolve swiftly. The integration of MKIS with BDA equips stakeholders with the ability to access real-time insights from diverse data sources. BDA techniques can analyze streams of real-time data, including social media discussions, website interactions, and location data, providing updated information on customer sentiment, emerging trends, and competitive activities. These real-time insights empower destination marketers to respond swiftly, make informed decisions, and adjust their marketing strategies promptly (Benckendorff et al., 2019; Ikegwu et al., 2022).

Competitive Advantage

In the fiercely competitive tourism industry, securing a competitive advantage is imperative. The integration of MKIS with BDA enables stakeholders to harness data as a strategic asset. Through the analysis of market trends, customer behavior, and competitor activities, destination marketers can pinpoint opportunities, foresee market shifts, and devise innovative marketing strategies. The capacity to make decisions driven by data and maintain a leading position in the market provides destination marketers with a competitive edge in attracting and retaining customers (Rosário & Dias, 2023; Spiller, 2020).

Improved Decision-Making

The integration of MKIS with BDA establishes a robust basis for decision-making rooted in data. BDA techniques excel at analyzing intricate datasets, revealing concealed patterns and insights, and producing actionable recommendations. Armed with these insights, destination marketers can make well-informed decisions regarding product development, pricing strategies, marketing campaigns, and improvements to the customer experience. Relying on data-driven decision-making diminishes dependence on intuition and speculation, ultimately contributing to more effective and successful marketing initiatives (Ikegwu et al., 2022; Luca & Bazerman, 2021).

Enhanced Customer Engagement

The amalgamation of MKIS with BDA empowers destination marketers to interact with customers on a more personalized and focused level. Through BDA techniques, customer data can be analyzed to comprehend preferences, interests, and behavioral patterns. Armed with this understanding, marketers can craft customized marketing messages, offers, and recommendations tailored to individual customers or specific segments. The delivery of personalized experiences enables destination marketers to elevate customer engagement, cultivate loyalty, and encourage repeat visits (Hofmann & Rutschmann, 2018; Rather & Hollebeek, 2020).

Improved Marketing Efficiency

The fusion of MKIS with BDA holds the potential to enhance marketing efficiency and streamline resource allocation. Utilizing BDA techniques for data analysis allows for the identification of the most impactful marketing channels, campaigns, and messaging, thereby optimizing marketing endeavors. With a clear understanding of which initiatives generate the highest return on investment, destination marketers can allocate resources more judiciously, minimizing unnecessary expenses and ultimately improving overall marketing efficiency (Mukhopadhyay et al., 2024; Wörndl et al., 2021).

Uncovering Hidden Insights

MKIS accumulates diverse data, encompassing customer interactions, booking history, and market research. However, deriving meaningful insights from this data is a complex task without advanced analytics capabilities. BDA techniques empower stakeholders to scrutinize data, revealing concealed insights, patterns, and correlations that might elude initial observation. These revelations can unveil fresh market opportunities, customer preferences, and emerging trends, providing destination marketers with the knowledge to make informed decisions and devise innovative marketing strategies (Aggarwal et al., 2023; ZareRavasan, 2023).

Targeted Marketing Campaigns

Combining MKIS with BDA facilitates the development of precisely targeted marketing campaigns. Through BDA techniques, customer data can be analyzed and the target audience segmented based on diverse criteria like demographics, behavior, and preferences. This segmentation empowers destination marketers to customize their marketing initiatives for specific customer segments, providing messages and offers that align with their interests and needs. Targeted campaigns are more likely to succeed, capturing the attention and interest of the intended audience (Ram & Zhang, 2022; Gupta et al., 2021).

Personalized Customer Experiences

Customization is a pivotal factor in fostering customer satisfaction and loyalty. Through the integration of MKIS with BDA, destination marketers can provide personalized customer experiences across different touchpoints throughout the customer journey. BDA techniques enable the analysis of customer data to comprehend individual preferences and behaviors, facilitating the customization of services, suggestions, and interactions. Tailored experiences generate a sense of exclusivity, making customers feel appreciated and elevating their overall satisfaction, thereby increasing the likelihood of recommending the destination to others (Keskin et al., 2024; Ding et al., 2024; Lehrer et al., 2018).

MKIS and BDA Integration Strategies

The integration of MKIS and BDA in marketing touristic destinations necessitates the adoption of efficient strategies and frameworks that facilitate smooth operation and seamless data integration.

Data Integration Techniques

Data integration stands as a crucial phase in the amalgamation of MKIS and BDA systems. This process entails the merging and unifying of data from diverse origins to form a comprehensive and cohesive dataset. Techniques involved in data integration encompass tasks such as data cleaning, data transformation, and data consolidation. These methodologies guarantee that information from MKIS and BDA sources is harmonized, standardized, and interoperable, thereby facilitating a comprehensive understanding of the marketing data. Common data integration techniques include data mapping, schema alignment, and data format conversion (Wang et al., 2023; Pesonen & Neidhardt, 2019; Avazpour et al., 2019).

Interoperability

Interoperability plays a crucial role in the seamless integration of MKIS and BDA systems, emphasizing the facilitation of smooth communication and data interchange among diverse systems and technologies. Achieving interoperability requires the establishment of shared standards, protocols, and formats that simplify the exchange and interpretation of data. This involves the adoption of industry-standard data formats like XML or JSON, the implementation of standardized APIs, and adherence to common data modeling practices. Through ensuring interoperability, marketers can effectively integrate MKIS and BDA systems, allowing for the fluid flow of data and insights throughout the entire ecosystem (Maroufkhani et al., 2020; Noura et al., 2019; Neidhardt & Wörndl, 2020).

Systems Compatibility

Ensuring systems compatibility is essential for the smooth operation of MKIS and BDA systems. This entails guaranteeing that various systems and technologies utilized in marketing touristic destinations can function together seamlessly. Achieving compatibility involves considerations at different levels, including hardware, software, and data formats. This can be accomplished through meticulous system design, the selection of compatible software solutions, and verifying that the hardware infrastructure aligns with integration requirements. By addressing systems compatibility, marketers can sidestep technical challenges and facilitate a seamless exchange and analysis of data (Wamba et al., 2017; Borgogno & Colangelo, 2019).

Unified Data Architecture

A consolidated data architecture serves as the foundation for amalgamating MKIS and BDA systems. This entails creating a cohesive and scalable infrastructure that supports the collection, storage, processing, and analysis of data. A unified data architecture commonly incorporates elements like data warehouses, data lakes, data marts, and analytical tools. These components enable the aggregation and integration of data from MKIS and BDA sources, fostering data-driven decision-making and the formulation of effective marketing strategies (Ferrer-Rosell et al., 2023; Stienmetz et al., 2022; Gorelik, 2019).

Real-time Data Processing

The significance of real-time data processing is growing in the context of marketing touristic destinations. This practice entails the analysis of data as it is generated, empowering marketers to swiftly adapt to evolving market conditions and customer behaviors. Frameworks for real-time data processing, such as Apache Kafka or Apache Flink, facilitate the ingestion, processing, and analysis of streaming data from diverse sources. By integrating real-time data processing capabilities, marketers can promptly extract insights from MKIS and BDA systems, facilitating agile decision-making and the implementation of personalized marketing strategies (Zhang & Dong, 2021; Saxena & Gupta, 2017).

Data Governance and Privacy

Effective data governance and privacy strategies are imperative in the integration of MKIS and BDA systems. Marketers need to uphold data governance principles, define data ownership, implement access controls, and ensure compliance with pertinent regulations, such as GDPR (General Data Protection Regulation). To safeguard customer data and instill trust, data privacy measures, including anonymization and encryption, should be incorporated. By giving precedence to data governance and privacy considerations, marketers can establish a trustworthy foundation and ensure the responsible utilization of data in marketing touristic destinations (Mikalef et al., 2020; Abd Razak et al., 2020).

Utilizing these strategies and frameworks allows marketers to integrate MKIS and BDA systems seamlessly in marketing touristic destinations. This integration facilitates the extraction of valuable insights, refines decision-making processes, and augments marketing effectiveness. Ultimately, the integration of MKIS and BDA systems empowers marketers to provide targeted, personalized experiences to tourists, contributing to success in the competitive tourism industry.

Data Fusion Techniques

The integration of MKIS and BDA relies heavily on the application of data fusion techniques and methodologies. These approaches are instrumental in merging and analyzing data from diverse sources within integrated MKIS-BDA systems. The primary goal is to amalgamate data originating from various MKIS and BDA sources, striving to achieve a comprehensive and unified perspective on the data (Zhang et al., 2018; Vosgien, 2015).

Data Integration

Data integration encompasses the merging of data from various sources to form a unified dataset. This process guarantees the harmonious and consistent combination of data from MKIS and BDA sources. Data integration may include tasks such as aligning data schemas, resolving format disparities, and standardizing variables across different datasets (Dhayne et al., 2019; Doan et al., 2012).

Data Cleaning and Preprocessing

Data cleaning and preprocessing methods are employed to eradicate inconsistencies, errors, and redundancies in the data. This process includes tasks such as eliminating duplicate records, addressing missing values, and handling outliers. By upholding data quality, these techniques contribute to the precision and dependability of the fused data (García et al., 2015; Gudivada et al., 2017).

Entity Resolution

Entity resolution, also recognized as record linkage or deduplication, involves recognizing and consolidating records that pertain to the same entity across diverse datasets. This process aids in eliminating duplicates and forming a unified representation for each entity. Entity resolution techniques may employ different matching algorithms, including deterministic matching, probabilistic matching, or approaches based on machine learning (Azeroual et al., 2022; Kooli et al., 2018).

Data Transformation and Mapping

Data transformation and mapping methods are utilized to align data representations and guarantee consistency among various datasets. This process entails associating data attributes with a standardized schema, regularizing variable formats, and converting data into a uniform and coherent structure. The application of data transformation and mapping facilitates the smooth integration and analysis of data from various sources (St-Jean et al., 2020; Kohler et al., 2023).

Semantic Integration

Semantic integration concentrates on harmonizing the meaning and semantics of data from diverse sources. This process includes creating relationships, mappings, and ontologies that capture conceptual similarities and connections among data elements. Through aligning semantics, semantic integration facilitates a more profound comprehension and analysis of the fused data (Pfaff et al., 2018; Mountantonakis & Tzitzikas, 2019).

Contextual and Temporal Integration

Contextual and temporal integration methods take into account contextual factors and time dependencies linked to the data. These methods capture situational context, including aspects like location, time of day, or user behavior, and integrate it into the consolidated dataset. Contextual and temporal integration improves the relevance and accuracy of the analysis by considering dynamic factors that impact data interpretation (McDonald, 2014; Janssen et al., 2017).

The Impact of Data Fusion on Touristic Destination Success

Data fusion plays a pivotal role in the prosperity of touristic destinations. Through the integration and amalgamation of data from diverse sources, including MKIS, BDA, and other pertinent data streams, touristic destinations can access valuable insights and base their decisions on data-driven approaches.

Comprehensive Understanding of Visitors

Data fusion enables touristic destinations to achieve an in-depth comprehension of their visitors. Through the integration of data from various sources like hotel bookings, transportation records, social media interactions, and survey responses, destinations can construct a holistic profile of their visitors. This profile encompasses demographic details, preferences, behaviors, travel patterns, and interests. Armed with this comprehensive understanding, destinations can customize their offerings, refine marketing strategies, and enhance experiences to cater to the specific needs and desires of their target audience (Mariani et al., 2021; Salas-Olmedo et al., 2018).

Personalized Marketing and Experiences

Through data fusion, touristic destinations can provide exceptionally personalized marketing messages and experiences. By amalgamating data related to visitor preferences, past behaviors, and engagement patterns, destinations can segment their audience and devise targeted campaigns. For instance, if a destination is aware that a specific visitor has an affinity for adventure sports and gourmet dining, they can customize their marketing messages and suggest particular activities and restaurants that resonate with those preferences. This personalized approach elevates visitor satisfaction, boosts engagement, and cultivates a positive perception of the destination (Del Vecchio et al., 2018; Villamediana-Pedrosa et al., 2020).

Improved Operational Efficiency

Data fusion empowers touristic destinations to enhance their operations and streamline resource allocation. Through the integration of data from diverse operational systems, encompassing visitor traffic, crowd management, and resource utilization, destinations gain insights into patterns, trends, and bottlenecks. This knowledge enables destinations to make informed decisions based on data, subsequently enhancing operational efficiency. For instance, if data fusion reveals peak visitor traffic at certain attractions or facilities during specific times, destinations can strategically allocate resources to ensure a seamless visitor experience and optimize capacity utilization (Li et al., 2017; Mohamed et al., 2020; Haque et al., 2022).

Proactive Decision-Making

Data fusion provides touristic destinations with the capability to make informed and proactive decisions. Through the real-time consolidation and analysis of data from various sources, destinations can discern emerging trends, predict visitor demand, and foresee shifts in the market. This proactive decision-making approach enables destinations to stay ahead of the competition, seize opportunities, and address potential challenges. For example, if data fusion highlights a growing interest in sustainable travel practices, a destination can proactively develop eco-friendly initiatives and promote them to attract environmentally conscious visitors (Stylos et al., 2021; Gajdošík, 2019; Bharadiya, 2023).

Enhanced Visitor Experience

Data fusion enhances the visitor experience at touristic destinations by integrating data from diverse touchpoints. Destinations can attain a comprehensive view of the visitor journey, pinpoint areas for enhancement, and ensure continuous improvement. For instance, through the analysis of visitor feedback, social media sentiment, and on-site interactions, destinations can identify pain points, address concerns, and elevate the overall experience. This iterative improvement, guided by data insights, contributes to a positive and memorable visitor experience, fostering increased satisfaction, positive reviews, and repeat visits (Mariani et al., 2021; Villaespesa & Álvarez, 2020).

Sustainable Growth and Competitive Advantage

Data fusion is integral to fostering sustainable growth and securing a competitive advantage for touristic destinations. Through the utilization of integrated data, destinations can discern market trends, comprehend visitor demands, and formulate innovative strategies. This data-centric approach empowers destinations to craft distinctive value propositions, stand out from competitors, and capture a more significant portion of the tourism market. Additionally, data fusion aids destinations in gauging the effectiveness of their marketing endeavors, refining resource allocation, and optimizing revenue generation, thereby contributing to enduring success and sustainability (Rasoolimanesh et al., 2023; Rehman et al., 2016).

Data fusion serves as a transformative force in the prosperity of touristic destinations. Through the integration and analysis of diverse data sources, destinations attain a holistic comprehension of visitors. This, in turn, enables the delivery of personalized marketing and experiences, optimization of operational efficiency, proactive decision-making, enhancement of the visitor experience, and attainment of sustainable growth. Data fusion empowers destinations to adapt, innovate, and flourish within the fiercely competitive tourism landscape, paving the way for their enduring success.

Challenges of Integrating MKIS and BDA

The integration of MKIS and BDA within touristic destinations presents a complex undertaking. Despite the considerable potential for enhancing marketing strategies and decision-making in the tourism sector through the amalgamation of these technologies, there are various challenges that require careful consideration.

Data Quality and Integration

A key hurdle lies in guaranteeing the quality and seamless integration of data originating from diverse sources. Big data analytics heavily depends on extensive datasets sourced from various outlets, encompassing customer details, social media inputs, online reviews, and operational data. The integration of these datasets while upholding accuracy and uniformity poses a notable challenge (Fillinger et al., 2019; Jimenez-Marquez et al., 2019).

Privacy and Security

The rising prominence of big data analytics accentuates the significance of privacy and security considerations. Tourism destinations amass extensive customer data, encompassing personal details and travel preferences. Ensuring the protection of this sensitive information and adhering to pertinent privacy regulations, such as GDPR (General Data Protection Regulation), presents a multifaceted challenge (Abba Ari et al., 2024; Ferrer-Rosell et al., 2023).

Data Governance

Implementing robust data governance practices is pivotal for the integration of MKIS and BDA. This entails delineating data ownership, establishing access controls, formulating data sharing protocols, and setting data quality standards. Inadequate data governance may lead to data silos, discrepancies, and hindered collaboration among diverse stakeholders (Ladley, 2019).

Technical Infrastructure and Expertise

Deploying MKIS and BDA necessitates sturdy technical infrastructure and proficient personnel. Touristic destinations might be required to invest in high-performance computing, storage systems, and analytical tools capable of managing substantial data volumes. Furthermore, the demand for data scientists and analysts proficient in extracting insights from the data and translating them into actionable marketing strategies is essential (Mach-Król, 2019; Marr, 2017).

Ethical Considerations

Employing big data analytics in tourism destinations gives rise to ethical considerations. For instance, apprehensions may emerge regarding personalized marketing campaigns that potentially exploit customer data or issues associated with algorithmic bias. It is imperative to conduct data analytics in an ethical and responsible manner, emphasizing transparency, fairness, and the preservation of individual privacy (Reif & Schmücker, 2020; Rubel & Jones, 2016).

CONCLUSION AND RECOMMENDATIONS

Enhancing the integration of MKIS and BDA in tourism demands meticulous planning and strategic execution. Stakeholders need to explicitly outline the marketing goals they intend to accomplish through the integration of MKIS and BDA. Whether the focus is on refining customer segmentation, personalization, campaign efficacy, or enhancing visitor experience, establishing clear objectives will steer the integration process and guarantee coherence with overarching marketing strategies.

Identifying pertinent data sources that offer valuable insights for tourism marketing is imperative for stakeholders. These sources encompass customer databases, social media platforms, website analytics, online booking systems, and data from third-party providers. A comprehensive comprehension of available data sources aids stakeholders in crafting an integration strategy that captures the most pertinent and actionable data for analysis. Likewise, emphasizing data quality is paramount for conducting meaningful analysis and deriving actionable insights. Stakeholders should prioritize data quality and allocate resources to data integration processes, ensuring the precision and reliability of information. Implementing robust data governance practices becomes instrumental in upholding data integrity throughout the integration process.

Stakeholders ought to allocate resources to develop the essential data analytics capabilities for proficiently analyzing integrated data. This could entail recruiting data scientists, data analysts, or collaborating with external specialists proficient in data analytics. Strategic investment in appropriate tools, technologies, and expertise empowers stakeholders to extract valuable insights and make informed, data-driven marketing decisions. In addition, delving into advanced analytics techniques like machine learning, predictive modeling, and sentiment analysis can unveil concealed patterns and trends within the integrated data. This approach enables stakeholders to attain more profound customer insights, enhance personalized marketing efforts, and refine marketing campaigns using predictive analytics.

Prioritizing data security and privacy is imperative throughout the integration process. Stakeholders must enforce strong data protection measures to secure customer information and adhere to pertinent data protection regulations. Formulating protocols for data access, sharing, and anonymization is essential for upholding customer trust and mitigating privacy risks. As well, stakeholders should monitor key performance indicators (KPIs) associated with marketing goals and conduct regular assessments of the integrated MKIS and BDA's effectiveness. This iterative process enables adjustments and enhancements, ultimately yielding improved marketing outcomes.

REFERENCES

Abba Ari, A., Ngangmo, O., Titouna, C., Thiare, O., Mohamadou, A., & Gueroui, A. (2024). Enabling privacy and security in Cloud of Things: Architecture, applications, security & privacy challenges. *Applied Computing and Informatics*, *20*(1/2), 119–141. doi:10.1016/j.aci.2019.11.005

Abd Razak, S., Nazari, N., & Al-Dhaqm, A. (2020). Data anonymization using pseudonym system to preserve data privacy. *IEEE Access : Practical Innovations, Open Solutions*, *8*, 43256–43264. doi:10.1109/ACCESS.2020.2977117

Aggarwal, K., Khoa, B., Sagar, K., Agrawal, R., Dhingra, M., Dhingra, J., & R, L. K. (2023). Marketing information system based on unsupervised visual data to manage transportation industry using signal processing. *Expert Systems: International Journal of Knowledge Engineering and Neural Networks*, e13384. Advance online publication. doi:10.1111/exsy.13384

Avazpour, I., Grundy, J., & Zhu, L. (2019). Engineering complex data integration, harmonization and visualization systems. *Journal of Industrial Information Integration*, *16*, 100103. doi:10.1016/j.jii.2019.08.001

Awan, U., Shamim, S., Khan, Z., Zia, N., Shariq, S., & Khan, M. (2021). Big data analytics capability and decision-making: The role of data-driven insight on circular economy performance. *Technological Forecasting and Social Change*, *168*, 120766. doi:10.1016/j.techfore.2021.120766

Azeroual, O., Jha, M., Nikiforova, A., Sha, K., Alsmirat, M., & Jha, S. (2022). A record linkage-based data deduplication framework with datacleaner extension. *Multimodal Technologies and Interaction*, *6*(4), 27. doi:10.3390/mti6040027

Belhadi, A., Zkik, K., Cherrafi, A., & Sha'ri, M. (2019). Understanding big data analytics for manufacturing processes: Insights from literature review and multiple case studies. *Computers & Industrial Engineering*, *137*, 106099. doi:10.1016/j.cie.2019.106099

Benckendorff, P., Xiang, Z., & Sheldon, P. (2019). *Tourism information technology*. Cabi. doi:10.1079/9781786393432.0000

Bharadiya, J. (2023). Machine learning and AI in business intelligence: Trends and opportunities. *International Journal of Computer*, *48*(1), 123–134.

Borgogno, O., & Colangelo, G. (2019). Data sharing and interoperability: Fostering innovation and competition through APIs. *Computer Law & Security Report*, *35*(5), 105314. doi:10.1016/j.clsr.2019.03.008

Chandra, S., Verma, S., Lim, W., Kumar, S., & Donthu, N. (2022). Personalization in personalized marketing: Trends and ways forward. *Psychology and Marketing*, *39*(8), 1529–1562. doi:10.1002/mar.21670

Del Vecchio, P., Mele, G., Ndou, V., & Secundo, G. (2018). Creating value from social big data: Implications for smart tourism destinations. *Information Processing & Management*, *54*(5), 847–860. doi:10.1016/j.ipm.2017.10.006

Dhayne, H., Haque, R., Kilany, R., & Taher, Y. (2019). In search of big medical data integration solutions-a comprehensive survey. *IEEE Access : Practical Innovations, Open Solutions*, *7*, 91265–91290. doi:10.1109/ACCESS.2019.2927491

Ding, K., Gong, X., Huang, T., & Choo, W. (2024). Recommend or not: A comparative analysis of customer reviews to uncover factors influencing explicit online recommendation behavior in peer-to-peer accommodation. *European Research on Management and Business Economics, 30*(1), 100236. doi:10.1016/j.iedeen.2023.100236

Doan, A., Halevy, A., & Ives, Z. (2012). *Principles of data integration*. Elsevier.

Egger, R. (2022). *Applied Data Science in Tourism*. Springer International Publishing. doi:10.1007/978-3-030-88389-8

Erevelles, S., Fukawa, N., & Swayne, L. (2016). Big Data consumer analytics and the transformation of marketing. *Journal of Business Research, 69*(2), 897–904. doi:10.1016/j.jbusres.2015.07.001

Ferrer-Rosell, B., Massimo, D., & Berezina, K. (2023). *Information and Communication Technologies in Tourism 2023: Proceedings of the ENTER 2023 eTourism Conference, January 18-20, 2023*. Springer Nature. 10.1007/978-3-031-25752-0

Fillinger, S., de la Garza, L., Peltzer, A., Kohlbacher, O., & Nahnsen, S. (2019). Challenges of big data integration in the life sciences. *Analytical and Bioanalytical Chemistry, 411*(26), 6791–6800. doi:10.1007/s00216-019-02074-9 PMID:31463515

Gajdošík, T. (2019). Big data analytics in smart tourism destinations. A new tool for destination management organizations? In *Smart Tourism as a Driver for Culture and Sustainability: Fifth International Conference IACuDiT, Athens 2018* (pp. 15-33). Springer International Publishing.

García, S., Luengo, J., & Herrera, F. (2015). *Data preprocessing in data mining* (Vol. 72). Springer International Publishing. doi:10.1007/978-3-319-10247-4

Gorelik, A. (2019). *The enterprise big data lake: Delivering the promise of big data and data science*. O'Reilly Media.

Gudivada, V., Apon, A., & Ding, J. (2017). Data quality considerations for big data and machine learning: Going beyond data cleaning and transformations. *International Journal on Advances in Software, 10*(1), 1–20.

Gupta, S., Justy, T., Kamboj, S., Kumar, A., & Kristoffersen, E. (2021). Big data and firm marketing performance: Findings from knowledge-based view. *Technological Forecasting and Social Change, 171*, 120986. doi:10.1016/j.techfore.2021.120986

Haque, A., Bhushan, B., & Dhiman, G. (2022). Conceptualizing smart city applications: Requirements, architecture, security issues, and emerging trends. *Expert Systems: International Journal of Knowledge Engineering and Neural Networks, 39*(5), e12753. doi:10.1111/exsy.12753

Hofmann, E., & Rutschmann, E. (2018). Big data analytics and demand forecasting in supply chains: A conceptual analysis. *International Journal of Logistics Management, 29*(2), 739–766. doi:10.1108/IJLM-04-2017-0088

Ikegwu, A., Nweke, H., Anikwe, C., Alo, U., & Okonkwo, O. (2022). Big data analytics for data-driven industry: A review of data sources, tools, challenges, solutions, and research directions. *Cluster Computing, 25*(5), 3343–3387. doi:10.1007/s10586-022-03568-5

Janssen, M., Van Der Voort, H., & Wahyudi, A. (2017). Factors influencing big data decision-making quality. *Journal of Business Research, 70*, 338–345. doi:10.1016/j.jbusres.2016.08.007

Jimenez-Marquez, J., Gonzalez-Carrasco, I., Lopez-Cuadrado, J., & Ruiz-Mezcua, B. (2019). Towards a big data framework for analyzing social media content. *International Journal of Information Management, 44*, 1–12. doi:10.1016/j.ijinfomgt.2018.09.003

Juska, J. (2021). *Integrated marketing communication: advertising and promotion in a digital world.* Routledge. doi:10.4324/9780367443382

Kachniewska, M. (2021). *Smart Tourism: Towards the Concept of a Data-Based Travel Experience. In Handbook of Sustainable Development and Leisure Services.* Springer.

Keskin, E., Aktaş, F., Yayla, Ö., & Dedeoğlu, B. (2024). The importance of nostalgic emotions and memorable tourism experience in the cultural experience. *Journal of Quality Assurance in Hospitality & Tourism, 25*(1), 1–21. doi:10.1080/1528008X.2022.2097976

Kinyua, D. (2020). *Effect of Marketing Information Systems on Competitive Advantage of Ict Application Service Providers in Nairobi County* (Doctoral dissertation, University of Nairobi).

Kohler, S., Boscá, D., Kärcher, F., Haarbrandt, B., Prinz, M., Marschollek, M., & Eils, R. (2023). Eos and OMOCL: Towards a seamless integration of openEHR records into the OMOP Common Data Model. *Journal of Biomedical Informatics, 144*, 104437. doi:10.1016/j.jbi.2023.104437 PMID:37442314

Kooli, N., Allesiardo, R., & Pigneul, E. (2018). Deep learning based approach for entity resolution in databases. In *Asian conference on intelligent information and database systems* (pp. 3-12). Cham: Springer International Publishing. 10.1007/978-3-319-75420-8_1

Kushwaha, A., Kumar, P., & Kar, A. (2021). What impacts customer experience for B2B enterprises on using AI-enabled chatbots? Insights from Big data analytics. *Industrial Marketing Management*, *98*, 207–221. doi:10.1016/j.indmarman.2021.08.011

Ladley, J. (2019). *Data governance: How to design, deploy, and sustain an effective data governance program*. Academic Press.

Lehrer, C., Wieneke, A., Vom Brocke, J., Jung, R., & Seidel, S. (2018). How big data analytics enables service innovation: Materiality, affordance, and the individualization of service. *Journal of Management Information Systems*, *35*(2), 424–460. doi:10.1080/07421222.2018.1451953

Li, Y., Hu, C., Huang, C., & Duan, L. (2017). The concept of smart tourism in the context of tourism information services. *Tourism Management*, *58*, 293–300. doi:10.1016/j.tourman.2016.03.014

Luca, M., & Bazerman, M. (2021). *The power of experiments: Decision making in a data-driven world*. Mit Press.

Mach-Król, M. (2019). Requirements for temporal BDA implementation methodology in organizations. *Informatyka Ekonomiczna*, *1*(51), 44–54. doi:10.15611/ie.2019.1.04

Maheshwari, S., Gautam, P., & Jaggi, C. (2021). Role of Big Data Analytics in supply chain management: Current trends and future perspectives. *International Journal of Production Research*, *59*(6), 1875–1900. doi:10.1080/00207543.2020.1793011

Mariani, M., Bresciani, S., & Dagnino, G. (2021). The competitive productivity (CP) of tourism destinations: An integrative conceptual framework and a reflection on big data and analytics. *International Journal of Contemporary Hospitality Management*, *33*(9), 2970–3002. doi:10.1108/IJCHM-09-2020-1102

Maroufkhani, P., Tseng, M., Iranmanesh, M., Ismail, W., & Khalid, H. (2020). Big data analytics adoption: Determinants and performances among small to medium-sized enterprises. *International Journal of Information Management*, *54*, 102190. doi:10.1016/j.ijinfomgt.2020.102190

Marr, B. (2017). *Data strategy: How to profit from a world of big data, analytics and the internet of things*. Kogan Page Publishers.

McDonald, A. (2014). *Improving Driver Drowsiness Detection through Temporal, Contextual, and Hierarchical Modeling* (Doctoral dissertation, The University of Wisconsin-Madison).

Miah, S., Vu, H., Gammack, J., & McGrath, M. (2017). A big data analytics method for tourist behaviour analysis. *Information & Management, 54*(6), 771–785. doi:10.1016/j.im.2016.11.011

Mikalef, P., Boura, M., Lekakos, G., & Krogstie, J. (2020). The role of information governance in big data analytics driven innovation. *Information & Management, 57*(7), 103361. doi:10.1016/j.im.2020.103361

Mohamed, H., & Al-Azab, M. (2021). Big Data Analytics in Airlines: Opportunities and Challenges. *Journal of Association of Arab Universities for Tourism and Hospitality, 21*(4), 77–112.

Mohamed, N., Al-Jaroodi, J., Jawhar, I., Idries, A., & Mohammed, F. (2020). Unmanned aerial vehicles applications in future smart cities. *Technological Forecasting and Social Change, 153*, 119293. doi:10.1016/j.techfore.2018.05.004

Morales-Serazzi, M., González-Benito, Ó., & Martos-Partal, M. (2023). A new perspective of BDA and information quality from final users of information: A multiple study approach. *International Journal of Information Management, 73*, 102683. doi:10.1016/j.ijinfomgt.2023.102683

Mountantonakis, M., & Tzitzikas, Y. (2019). Large-scale semantic integration of linked data: A survey. *ACM Computing Surveys, 52*(5), 1–40. doi:10.1145/3345551

Mukhopadhyay, S., Singh, R., & Jain, T. (2024). Developing big data enabled Marketing 4.0 framework. *International Journal of Information Management Data Insights, 4*(1), 100214. doi:10.1016/j.jjimei.2024.100214

Neidhardt, J., & Wörndl, W. (2020). *Information and Communication Technologies in Tourism 2020*. Springer International Publishing. doi:10.1007/978-3-030-36737-4

Noura, M., Atiquzzaman, M., & Gaedke, M. (2019). Interoperability in internet of things: Taxonomies and open challenges. *Mobile Networks and Applications, 24*(3), 796–809. doi:10.1007/s11036-018-1089-9

Pesonen, J., & Neidhardt, J. (2019). Information and communication technologies in tourism 2019. In *Proceedings of the International Conference*. Springer International Publishing. 10.1007/978-3-030-05940-8

Pfaff, M., Neubig, S., & Krcmar, H. (2018). Ontology for semantic data integration in the domain of IT benchmarking. *Journal on Data Semantics*, *7*(1), 29–46. doi:10.1007/s13740-017-0084-9 PMID:29497460

Ram, J., & Zhang, Z. (2022). Examining the needs to adopt big data analytics in B2B organizations: Development of propositions and model of needs. *Journal of Business and Industrial Marketing*, *37*(4), 790–809. doi:10.1108/JBIM-10-2020-0464

Rasoolimanesh, S., Ramakrishna, S., Hall, C., Esfandiar, K., & Seyfi, S. (2023). A systematic scoping review of sustainable tourism indicators in relation to the sustainable development goals. *Journal of Sustainable Tourism*, *31*(7), 1497–1517. doi:10.1080/09669582.2020.1775621

Rather, R., & Hollebeek, L. (2020). *Experiential marketing for tourism destinations. In The Routledge handbook of tourism experience management and marketing*. Routledge.

Rehman, M., Chang, V., Batool, A., & Wah, T. (2016). Big data reduction framework for value creation in sustainable enterprises. *International Journal of Information Management*, *36*(6), 917–928. doi:10.1016/j.ijinfomgt.2016.05.013

Reif, J., & Schmücker, D. (2020). Exploring new ways of visitor tracking using big data sources: Opportunities and limits of passive mobile data for tourism. *Journal of Destination Marketing & Management*, *18*, 100481. doi:10.1016/j.jdmm.2020.100481

Rosário, A., & Dias, J. (2023). How has data-driven marketing evolved: Challenges and opportunities with emerging technologies. *International Journal of Information Management Data Insights*, *3*(2), 100203. doi:10.1016/j.jjimei.2023.100203

Rubel, A., & Jones, K. (2016). Student privacy in learning analytics: An information ethics perspective. *The Information Society*, *32*(2), 143–159. doi:10.1080/01972243.2016.1130502

Salas-Olmedo, M., Moya-Gómez, B., García-Palomares, J., & Gutiérrez, J. (2018). Tourists' digital footprint in cities: Comparing Big Data sources. *Tourism Management*, *66*, 13–25. doi:10.1016/j.tourman.2017.11.001

Saxena, S., & Gupta, S. (2017). *Practical real-time data processing and analytics: distributed computing and event processing using Apache Spark, Flink, Storm, and Kafka*. Packt Publishing Ltd.

Shmueli, G., Bruce, P., Yahav, I., Patel, N., & Lichtendahl, K. Jr. (2017). *Data mining for business analytics: concepts, techniques, and applications in R*. John Wiley & Sons.

Spiller, L. (2020). Direct, digital & data-driven marketing. *Sage (Atlanta, Ga.)*.

St-Jean, S., Viergever, M., & Leemans, A. (2020). Harmonization of diffusion MRI data sets with adaptive dictionary learning. *Human Brain Mapping*, *41*(16), 4478–4499. doi:10.1002/hbm.25117 PMID:32851729

Stienmetz, J., Ferrer-Rosell, B., & Massimo, D. (2022). *Information and Communication Technologies in Tourism 2022: Proceedings of the ENTER 2022 ETourism Conference, January 11-14, 2022*. Springer Nature. 10.1007/978-3-030-94751-4

Stylos, N., Zwiegelaar, J., & Buhalis, D. (2021). Big data empowered agility for dynamic, volatile, and time-sensitive service industries: The case of tourism sector. *International Journal of Contemporary Hospitality Management*, *33*(3), 1015–1036. doi:10.1108/IJCHM-07-2020-0644

Telfer, D., & Sharpley, R. (2015). *Tourism and development in the developing world*. Routledge. doi:10.4324/9781315686196

Tsiakis, T. (2015). *Trends and innovations in marketing information systems*. IGI Global. doi:10.4018/978-1-4666-8459-1

Villaespesa, E., & Álvarez, A. (2020). Visitor journey mapping at the Museo Nacional Thyssen-Bornemisza: Bringing cross-departmental collaboration to build a holistic and integrated visitor experience. *Museum Management and Curatorship*, *35*(2), 125–142. doi:10.1080/09647775.2019.1638821

Villamediana-Pedrosa, J., Vila-Lopez, N., & Küster-Boluda, I. (2020). Predictors of tourist engagement: Travel motives and tourism destination profiles. *Journal of Destination Marketing & Management*, *16*, 100412. doi:10.1016/j.jdmm.2020.100412

Vosgien, T. (2015). *Model-based system engineering enabling design-analysis data integration in digital design environments: application to collaborative aeronautics simulation-based design process and turbojet integration studies* (Doctoral dissertation, Ecole Centrale Paris).

Wamba, S., Gunasekaran, A., Akter, S., Ren, S., Dubey, R., & Childe, S. (2017). Big data analytics and firm performance: Effects of dynamic capabilities. *Journal of Business Research*, *70*, 356–365. doi:10.1016/j.jbusres.2016.08.009

Wang, F., Iyamu, T., Phillips-Wren, G., & Forrest, J. (2023). BDAS-EPM: An Integrated Evolution Process Model for Big Data Analytics Systems. In *Development Methodologies for Big Data Analytics Systems: Plan-driven, Agile, Hybrid, Lightweight Approaches* (pp. 187–203). Springer International Publishing.

Wörndl, W., Koo, C., & Stienmetz, J. (2021). *Information and Communication Technologies in Tourism 2021: Proceedings of the ENTER 2021 eTourism Conference, January 19–22, 2021*. Springer Nature. 10.1007/978-3-030-65785-7

ZareRavasan, A. (2023). Boosting innovation performance through big data analytics: An empirical investigation on the role of firm agility. *Journal of Information Science*, *49*(5), 1293–1308. doi:10.1177/01655515211047425

Zhang, J., & Dong, L. (2021). Image monitoring and management of hot tourism destination based on data mining technology in big data environment. *Microprocessors and Microsystems*, *80*, 103515. doi:10.1016/j.micpro.2020.103515

Zhang, L., Xie, Y., Xidao, L., & Zhang, X. (2018). Multi-source heterogeneous data fusion. In *2018 International conference on artificial intelligence and big data (ICAIBD)* (pp. 47-51). IEEE.

Chapter 4
Exploring the Consumer Profile of the Museum of Futebol Clube do Porto Through Online Reviews:
A Study Using TripAdvisor Data

Raquel Alexandra Carvalho Martins
University of Algarve, Portugal

Célia M. Q. Ramos
https://orcid.org/0000-0002-3413-4897
Univeristy of Algarve, Portugal

ABSTRACT

For effective strategic planning and focused marketing campaigns, it is essential to understand the museum's target audience and how cultural tourism can influence sports tourism. The study aims to investigate the satisfaction and experience of international visitors to the Museum of Futebol Clube do Porto and their profiles. The TripAdvisor reviews were considered to gather information on the Museum of Futebol Clube do Porto's target audience using a business intelligence tool to process, analyze, and draw conclusions from the data. Insights regarding the geographic and gender distribution of reviewers and their overall evaluations of the museum were discovered by analysing TripAdvisor reviews.

DOI: 10.4018/979-8-3693-3310-5.ch004

INTRODUCTION

In addition to becoming a more popular leisure activity for a broader social class, sports have become more widespread (Ito & Higham, 2020). It is one of the most common leisure activities in the modern world, along with tourism. Football has become a significant tourism focus, especially in big cities (Edensor et al., 2021).

Sports tourism is one of the most vibrant subsectors of the tourism industry. Sports-related travel is thought to account for 15% to 30% of all international tourism receipts, and the expectation for the industry's growth in the coming years points to a continued rise in these journeys (Vehmas, 2010).

Sport may be a major cultural tourist attraction (Kusnoto et al., 2024) since it gives travellers a unique insight into a particular location's customs, history, and character (Wong et al., 2020). Sports-related activities and events are frequently intricately woven into local culture, and they can give tourists a rich and genuine experience that captures the essence and character of the host town. In the modern world, sport plays a significant socio-cultural function that extends to the tourism industry. Sports tourism can, therefore, be viewed as a distinct phenomenon of contemporary society, reflecting current trends, desires, and lifestyles like the pursuit of intense emotions or leading an active lifestyle (Malchrowicz-Mosko & Munsters, 2018).

Sports tourism can take one of two fundamental forms: active or passive (Kuchkarova, 2023; Ritchie & Adair, 2002; Terzić et al., 2021). Active sport tourism involves participating physically in competitions to practice sports, while passive sport tourism involves going to attractions and watching sporting activities (Woodham, 2017).

Travel involving participating in or watching sporting events or activities is referred to as sport tourism (Dixon et al., 2023; Gibson, 2003; Smith & Stewart, 2007). The most precise and thorough definition of sport tourism was provided by Gibson in 1998: "Leisure-based travel that takes individuals temporarily outside of their home communities to participate in physical activities, to watch physical activities, or to venerate attractions associated with physical activities" (Gibson, 1998, p. 10).

This can be attending professional or recreational sporting events, participating in athletic camps or clinics, engaging in extreme sports like bungee jumping, skiing, or surfing, or even visiting sports halls of fame and museums. Visits to famous stadiums or sports museums are becoming increasingly popular (Jeong & Kim, 2020).

Sports tourism involves cultural excursions centred on the sport, allowing visitors to learn about the sport's material, intangible, and non-material heritage (Malchrowicz-Mosko & Munsters, 2018).

Against this background, this work aims to identify the consumer profile of the Museum of Futebol Clube do Porto through the analysis of online reviews obtained from TripAdvisor. As a case study will be considered, the Museu do Futebol Clube do Porto, which originated in a professional football team called Futebol Clube do Porto (FCP), is situated in Porto, Portugal. António Nicolau d'Almeida, a well-known businessman and sports fan, created it on September 28, 1893 (FC Porto, 2024a). One of the top football teams in Portugal (Vieira & Simões, 2024), FCP has a long and illustrious history of local and international triumphs (FC Porto, 2024a). TripAdvisor is a website built on the premise that tourists rely on the reviews of other travellers to plan their journeys, or at the very least, can be suitably helped by them. TripAdvisor has 25 million monthly visitors, 10 million travel reviews and opinions contributed by 5 million registered members (TripAdvisor, 2023).

The study aims to look into the profile and level of satisfaction of foreign visitors to the Museum of Futebol Clube do Porto. The study's contributions include the knowledge that visitors to the Museum have come from five continents and that men make up the bulk of visitors, but women also make up a sizable portion of the tourist base. Couples from the United Kingdom are among the other guests.

This work is divided into four sections without considering the present introduction. The first section presents a bibliographic review of sport and cultural tourism in the context of museum activity, considering the Futebol Clube do Porto and the Museum of this football team. The second section shows the methodology considered in this study, which will consider the environment proportionated by a Business intelligence tool. The third presents the results, highlights their insights, and complements them with a brief discussion.

SPORTS TOURISM

Sports tourism is extremely popular worldwide (Zarotis, 2019), inspiring locations and travel businesses to develop and market additional goods and services related to this market. Establishing alliances and collaborations between the public and private sectors to comprehend and meet the expectations and needs of tourists and residents is a challenge for practitioners and anybody interested in sport tourism (Abatecola et al., 2020).

Destination marketers must determine the roles that sport plays in drawing tourists to the destination as well as how each sport element interacts with other attractions and activities at the destination to shape the tourist's overall experience in order to capitalize on sport's contribution to the destination's mix of attractions (Harrison-Hill & Chalip, 2005; Liberato et al., 2019).

According to Semedo (2015), sports tourism entails travelling for leisurely activities, such as participating in various physical activities, attending sporting events, or visiting attractions with a sporting theme (King et al., 2021).

Sports tourism is viewed as a booming niche sector from the standpoint of the travel and tourism industry since it frequently draws more expensive visitors who are ready to pay more for specialized experiences. As a result, many tourist locations are investing in the construction of sports infrastructure and facilities and in marketing initiatives that draw attention to their sporting attractions among prospective visitors (King et al., 2021). Sport can be a helpful strategy for improving some tourists' quality of experience when visiting a place (Harrison-Hill & Chalip, 2005; Jeong & Kim, 2020; Kusunah & Wahyudin, 2024).

Since sport is viewed as both a practice and a spectacle, sports tourism also reveals two types. In terms of this concept, tourists who participate in sports and those who watch sports as spectators are both included (Ito & Higham, 2020; King et al., 2021). Live coverage of sporting events has been sparked by some more alluring and competitive comparisons, such as the Olympic

Games, Formula 1, Football World, or bicycle races. Therefore, these large-scale performances become a new type of economically significant activity in the nation where they are produced (Thomson et al., 2021; Tomlinson & Young, 2006).

Other attractions, tourism-sports facilities, stadiums, museums, theme parks, and tourist-sports events cover significant athletic events that mobilize a large number of spectators, participants, and organizers inserted in the context of sports tourism (Pereira, 2016).

Multipurpose tourism sports facilities that can accommodate many sports and activities have become increasingly popular in recent years. These facilities frequently combine indoor and outdoor spaces, providing guests various experiences and activities. By drawing more tourists and presenting a wider variety of activities, they also frequently have a more significant economic influence on the neighbourhoods.

Cultural Tourism in the Context of Museum Activity

Travelling to experience a region's cultural legacy, including its customs, history, arts, and architecture, is known as cultural tourism (Smith, 2015). Since museums are frequently the central repositories of a region's cultural heritage, they play a significant role in cultural tourism. Cultural tourism has become a significant economic activity in places where the conventional production sector is worsening.

The primary goal of most museums is to preserve these aspects for future generations while educating visitors about the history, culture, and natural heritage of a given city, region, or nation (Allam et al., 2023; Pekarik, 2003).

By developing initiatives supporting cultural-tourism dynamics of cultural, social, and environmental exchange and projecting the territories by promoting our heritage and museums, museums have transformed into assets for protecting heritage.

According to Pekarik (2003), the presence of a museum typically denotes the existence of something meaningful and worthwhile that can be shared with the general public. Pekarik (2003) has stated that the primary function of museums should be to preserve cultural heritage and draw in more visitors.

From the very young to the very old, and in various groups, including families, friends, schools, and couples, a wide range of people attend museums. Museums engage visitors in several ways by telling tales about the objects they house and their research. Museums are distinctive learning environments frequently called "free-choice" learning environments (Doring, 2007; Falk & Dierking, 2000; Takata & Hallman, 2021).

The museums must comprehend why visitors travel to draw in cultural tourists. Only some people are interested in culture, just as not every cultural product is eager, prepared, or competent to draw tourists. Many tourism surveys have yet to consider the various levels of consumer motivation for cultural tourism which exist in reality. Tourists partially inspired by culture are included in the broadest definition of cultural tourism (Lord, 2002; Petroman, 2021; Richards, 2021).

Museums are organizations that keep and interpret artefacts with significant cultural, historical, and scientific value. They allow visitors to discover a region's past and present and the various cultural and social settings that have shaped it. By drawing tourists and creating income, cultural tourism in the context of museum activity can considerably boost a region's economy. Additionally, it can encourage a more profound knowledge of and respect for a region's cultural heritage, which can aid in maintaining and conserving its cultural assets.

Ramshaw and Gammon (2005; 2017) contend that a collection of sporting locations and events has historical elements, such as history, memories, architecture, or something similar. Sports heritage attractions can deliver new and different forms of revenue for sports organizations and destinations and provide distinctive and meaningful experiences of place for tourists (Chang et al., 2022). These attractions go beyond simply offering a singular tourist attraction for both ardent fans and casual observers, as well as creating a channel for disseminating and interpreting the sports cultures and the sporting past, such as Futebol Clube do Porto.

Futebol Clube do Porto

The Portuguese sports organization Futebol Clube do Porto (FCP) is well-versed in and actively participates in various sports besides football, including handball, basketball, billiards, boxing, cycling, adapted sports, hockey, rollerblading, and swimming. Some of them, and as a result of their accomplishments, give the club a booster of remarkable dimension for professional competitive sport (Magalhães, 2010).

FCP is a professional football club based in Porto, Portugal. Founded in 1893, it is one of the oldest and most successful clubs in Portuguese football history. The team plays their home matches at the Estádio do Dragão, which has a seating capacity of over 50,000 spectators (FC Porto, 2024b).

"The Dragão has a capacity for 50,033 spectators and is endowed with unique features that, enriched by the placement of green spaces and the restructuring of the roads annexed to the sports, residential and commercial complex, materialize a new centrality in Porto. The Dragão asserts itself as the city and region's sporting and cultural reference point" (FC Porto, 2024b).

The club has a solid fan base and is widely regarded as one of the "Big Three" football clubs in Portugal, alongside Benfica and Sporting Clube of Portugal. During the first decades of the twentieth century, this club experienced significant growth as a recreational organization and opened its doors to numerous other sports alongside football, transforming itself into a club accessible to people from all socioeconomic levels and without gender-specific restrictions (Magalhães et al., 2017).

Overall, Futebol Clube do Porto is a highly regarded and prosperous football team with an illustrious past and a promising future. It is a vital institution for the people of Porto and all of Portugal. It is a fundamental component of Portuguese football culture. The FC Porto Museum, one of the most well-known landmarks in Porto, serves as a tool to expand the city's tourist and cultural offerings and reflects FC Porto's social role as an essential institution for the growth of the neighbourhood5, the city, region, and nation (Magalhães et al., 2017).

Museum of Futebol Clube do Porto

The Museu do Futebol Clube do Porto was established and officially opened on September 28, 2013, and it welcomed visitors on October 26 of the same year (FC Porto, 2024b). The exhibits cover the club's history, from its early beginnings in the late 19th century to its modern-day successes. Visitors can see various trophies won by the club over the years, including the UEFA Champions League and the Europa League titles, as well as other domestic and international trophies (Liberato et al., 2020).

The FC Porto Museum invites any interested parties to visit and learn more about the club's history, its stories, the Estádio do Dragão, and participate in activities that the Museum sponsors. Supporters and fans of other sports can learn about, engage with, and feel the entirety of the club's universe at the Museum. As a result, the location provides guided and orientated tours in various languages, including English, Spanish, French, and German (FC Porto, 2024a).

The "Tunnel of Champions," a recreation of the illustrious tunnel players pass through before entering the field, is one of the Museum's centrepieces. Visitors will have an emotive and immersive experience thanks to the tunnel's presentation of the club's most memorable achievements. A section of the Museum is devoted to the club's supporters, exhibiting the distinctive and fervent fandom of FC Porto. This section contains a variety of artefacts and memorabilia that illustrate the close bond between the club and its followers, including scarves, flags, and images (FC Porto, 2024).

The Museum employs an innovative expository language and a robust technological dynamic with access to technological resources, allowing it to express the love of football through its various identity representations connected to the club's history and the memories of its fans. It regularly turns to new technologies to communicate and disseminate information on historical events, current affairs, and the appearances of public people (Magalhães et al., 2017).

Since its debut in 2013, the Museum of Futebol Clube do Porto has won numerous honours and recognitions (FC Porto, 2024a). Several of the prestigious honor's include:

- The Museum was nominated in 2015 for the coveted European Museum of the Year Award, honouring excellence in museums throughout Europe (FC Porto, 2024a).
- Portuguese Museum of the Year: In 2014, only one year after it opened, the Museum received the Portuguese Museum of the Year award. This prize honours Portugal's top museums for their outstanding display designs, educational initiatives, and conservation activities. This nomination undoubtedly aided the growth of the Museum, the expansion of international tourism in Portugal, particularly in the city of Porto, and the Museum's recognition (Magalhães et al., 2017).
- The Museum has repeatedly been awarded the TripAdvisor Certificate of Excellence, honouring establishments that frequently obtain customer reviews. The Museum was also noted for being a vital hub of Porto's cultural attractions, establishing itself in the tourist industry by securing the top spot on the TripAdvisor tourist network among the options for museums across the north zone visit to Portugal. This method is an outstanding way of promoting the Museum because visitors to the Museum can rate their experience in terms of space with a score that is near the maximum (FC Porto, 2024a).
- Best Sports institution in Europe: The European Museum Academy named this institution the Best Sports Museum in Europe for 2019. The Museum's dedication to quality in exhibition design, visitor engagement, and educational programming is honoured by this award (FC Porto, 2024a).

Overall, the Museum of Futebol Clube do Porto has won praise for its unique method of presenting the background and traditions of one of Portugal's most illustrious football clubs. Its numerous honours and recognitions attest to its significance as a cultural landmark and a must-see location for Porto tourists and football fans (FC Porto, 2024a).

METHODOLOGY

The study aims to investigate the satisfaction and experience of international visitors to the Museum of Futebol Clube do Porto and their personal characteristics. Data accessibility, data collecting speed, and non-intrusiveness with human subjects are all benefits of researching internet evaluations (Taecharungroj & Mathayomchan, 2019).

The methodological approach used in this study involves gathering data (reviews) from TripAdvisor about the Museum of Futebol Clube do Porto, followed by processing and analyzing the data using Business Intelligence tools, more specifically for Power BI from Microsoft, in order to conclude, considering a methodology as proposed by El-Masri et al. (2017).

The source considered for spontaneous visitor comments and reviews was TripAdvisor, which offers precise information about visitors' experiences that standard interviews may miss (Xin et al., 2023). Visitors prefer digital evaluations because of their usability, accessibility, immediacy, freedom of speech, and integration with current communication channels, according to research by Winter (2018).

The data was transformed using an Excel tool, facilitating the identification of invalid values and repeated responses, which were subsequently removed. Additionally, nine columns were created to organize the data, encompassing the following variables: Review Rating, Published Date, Title, Full Text, Author City, Author Country, Author Name (optional), Author Age (optional), and Author Gender (optional). This process allowed for a structured and organized dataset for further analysis.

Upon completion of the transformation process, the data were exported to the Power BI tool. In Power BI, comprehensive graphs and interactive dashboards were meticulously prepared, enabling in-depth data analysis. This step facilitated the visualization and exploration of the dataset, providing valuable insights and facilitating the interpretation of the findings.

RESULTS

Sample Characterization

TripAdvisor is an online community where travellers may post reviews, ratings, and personal accounts to help other people plan their travels with more knowledge (Edensor et al., 2021). Conducting a comprehensive analysis of visitor genres is of utmost importance in understanding the dynamics of museum attendance. It is a fascinating avenue of study to explore the prevalence of different genres among museum visitors and the diverse perspectives they bring regarding their experiences within the museum setting (Ito & Higham, 2020).

A fundamental discovery was made after a thorough investigation of the dataset in Power BI using a ring chart display. It became clear that males make up the bulk of respondents who took part in TripAdvisor reviews of the museum. Male respondents comprised 52.53%, 46.46% female, and the rest were couples of all international tourists who contributed their insightful opinions.

Understanding which countries are the primary source of visitors allows researchers to identify trends, preferences, and factors that attract individuals from different geographic backgrounds.

By leveraging a map visualization and a ring chart, a comprehensive analysis of the geographic distribution of online reviewers was conducted. This analysis unveiled a notable finding: the United Kingdom emerged as the predominant source of respondents among foreign tourists who have visited and reviewed the museum on TripAdvisor. Specifically, visitors from the United Kingdom accounted for 30.30% of the total foreign tourists who shared their experiences, as illustrated in Figure 1. However, it is worth highlighting that the museum has garnered attention from individuals hailing from diverse continents across the globe.

We can gain important insights into the various ideas and impressions visitors state by examining the significance of geographic distribution and gender in connection to online evaluations. This knowledge guides the creation of focused tactics to improve visitor satisfaction, engagement, and overall museum experience.

Figure 1. Countries of the authors that reviewed the museum (Own elaboration)

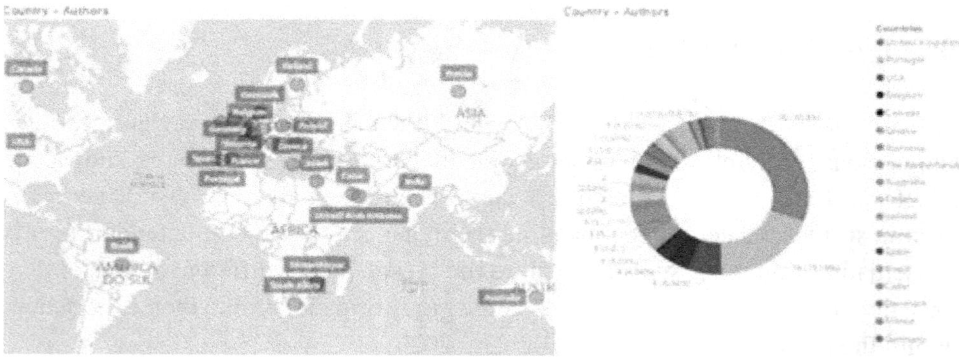

A comprehensive analysis was conducted using various visualizations, including a map to display the countries, a ring chart to represent the genders, a bar chart to showcase the reviews, and a bar column chart to depict the countries connected to the genres. Most respondents originated from Europe, as shown by the map visualization in Figure 2.

Figure 2. Dashboard of the countries, gender, and reviews from the authors reviewers (Own elaboration)

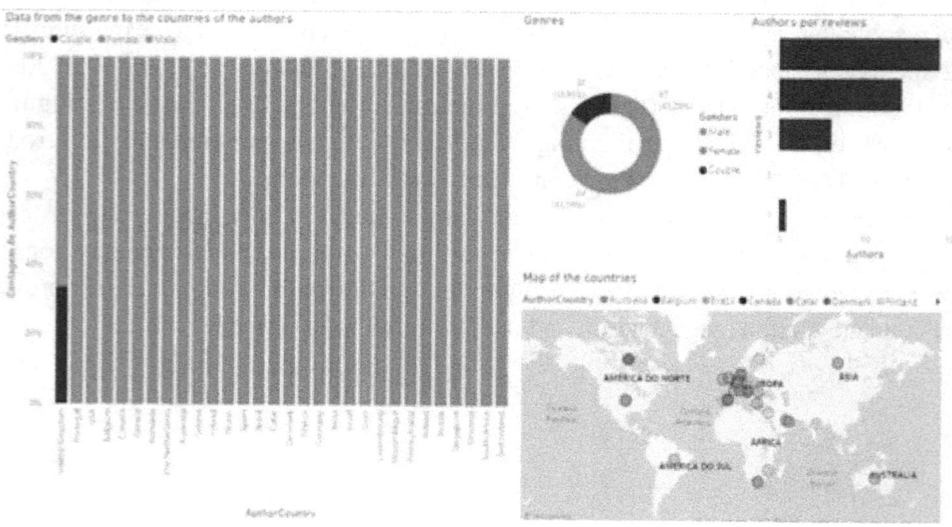

The ring chart revealed that male reviewers predominated among the respondents. The bar chart showcased that the most awarded rating was 5, indicating high reviewer satisfaction. The bar column chart provided insights into the connection between countries and genres. It facilitated the understanding of which genres were more prevalent among visitors from different countries, providing a deeper perspective on the diverse interests and preferences of the museum's international audience, as shown in Figure 2.

A notable observation emerges from the analysis: the respondents exclusively comprise males in a minimum of nine countries. This indicates a gender imbalance among the reviewers in these regions. Furthermore, the rating chart reveals that a significant proportion, 80.00% precisely, of male respondents awarded the highest rating of "5" to the Museum of Futebol Clube do Porto. Notably, no male reviewer rated the museum below "3". These findings underscore the dominant presence of male voices in the reviews and highlight their positive inclination towards the museum, as shown in Figure 3.

Figure 3. Dashboard of the countries by male gender authors reviewers (Own elaboration)

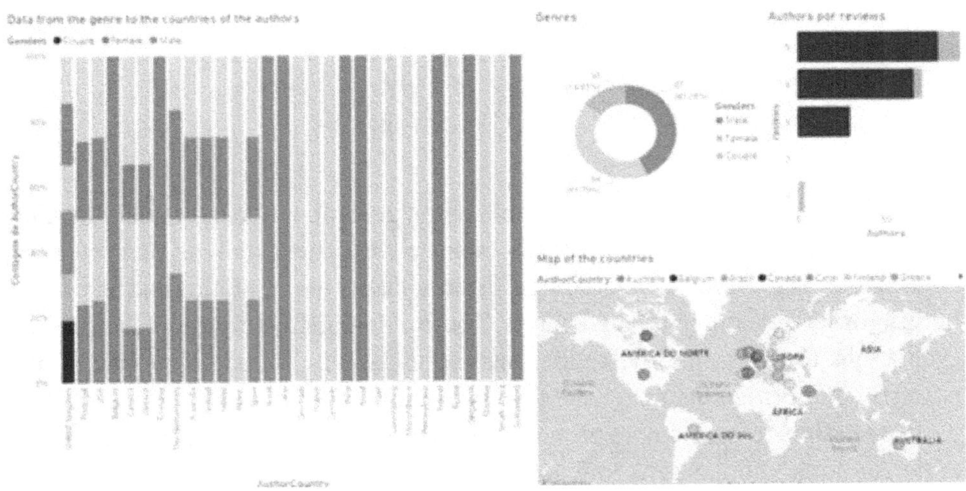

A noteworthy observation arises from the analysis: female respondents are exclusively represented in eleven countries, although in smaller numbers than male respondents. Additionally, it is worth mentioning that the lone individual who rated the museum with a score of "1" is female. However, it is noteworthy that most female respondents, precisely 72 individuals, awarded the museum the highest rating of "5" stars. These findings shed light on female voices in the reviews, highlighting their varied perspectives and overall positive assessment of the museum.

Figure 4. Dashboard of the countries by female gender authors reviewers (Own elaboration)

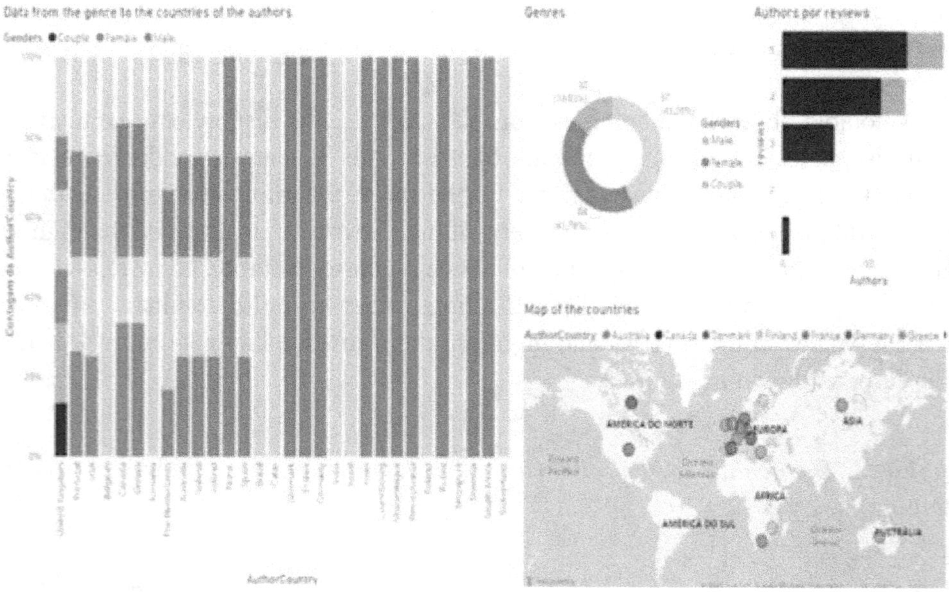

DISCUSSION

Since TripAdvisor reviews are accessible to the general public, potential travellers can access and consider other people's perspectives before making their own trip plans. This user-generated material significantly shapes the reputation and perception of different travel companies and places. Tourists frequently rely upon TripAdvisor evaluations to determine the caliber and dependability of lodgings, making it a powerful platform in the travel and tourism sector.

It is possible to gain a more profound knowledge of the demographics and tastes of the museum's audience by looking at different visitor genres. We can learn more about what draws people from varied backgrounds and interests by determining the genres most frequently represented among visitors; in the Museum of Futebol Clube do Porto case, the most frequent are male.

By analyzing the two different genres, we can know essential details about the advantages and disadvantages of museums from many viewpoints. This knowledge can aid in creating focused tactics to improve visitor satisfaction, engagement, and overall museum experience.

Examining the geographic distribution of online reviewers provides invaluable insights into the museum's international appeal and the countries that contribute the most to its visitor base. Moreover, studying the diverse opinions of reviewers from different countries offers a nuanced understanding of the museum's perception and impact across various cultural contexts.

One of the primary objectives of this study was to identify the consumer profile of the Museum of Futebol Clube do Porto through the analysis of online reviews obtained from TripAdvisor. However, it is essential to acknowledge the challenges faced during the research process due to the absence of open-ended questionnaires specifically designed for the museum's visitors. As a result, obtaining a comprehensive understanding of the museum's clientele proved to be complicated.

As the main contributions from the study, it can be concluded that the museum has had visitors from five continents, that the majority of visitors are male, but there are also many female visitors. There are also visitors, couples who come from the United Kingdom.

The limitations in gathering direct feedback from the museum's visitors hindered the ability to capture essential demographic and psychographic information that would contribute to a more detailed consumer profile. The absence of structured questionnaires restricted the examination of factors such as age, occupation, interests, and motivations, which would have provided valuable insights into the characteristics and preferences of the museum's visitors.

Despite these challenges, this study made valuable use of TripAdvisor reviews as a proxy for understanding the perceptions and experiences of visitors. By leveraging these online reviews, insights were gleaned regarding the geographic distribution, gender distribution, and overall ratings provided by reviewers. While these findings offer some understanding of the consumer base, they represent a partial view without the ability to delve deeper into the specific consumer profiles.

ACKNOWLEDGMENT

This paper is financed by National Funds provided by FCT Foundation for Science and Technology through project UIDB/04020/2020 and with DOI 10.54499/UIDB/04020/2020 (https://doi.org/10.54499/UIDB/04020/2020).

REFERENCES

Abatecola, G., Mari, M., & Poggesi, S. (2020). How can virtuous real estate public-private partnerships be developed? Towards a co-evolutionary perspective. *Cities (London, England)*, *107*, 102896. doi:10.1016/j.cities.2020.102896

Allam, Z., Cheshmehzangi, A., & Jones, D. S. (2023). Urban Consumerism and Colonial Structures of Mercantilism. In *Climate and Social Justice: The Political Economy of Urban Resilience and Mercantilism* (pp. 43–60). Springer Nature Singapore. doi:10.1007/978-981-99-6624-0_3

Chang, M. X., Choong, Y. O., Ng, L. P., & Seow, A. N. (2022). The importance of support for sport tourism development among local residents: The mediating role of the perceived impacts of sport tourism. *Leisure Studies*, *41*(3), 420–436. doi:10.1080/02614367.2021.2011950

Dixon, A. W., Henry, M., & Martinez, J. M. (2023). Assessing the economic impact of sport tourists' expenditures related to a university's baseball season attendance. *Journal of Issues in Intercollegiate Athletics*, *6*(1), 2.

Doering, Z. D. (2007). Strangers, guests, or clients? Visitor experiences in museums. In *Museum Management and Marketing* (pp. 331–344). Routledge.

Edensor, T., Millington, S., Steadman, C., & Taecharungroj, V. (2021). Towards a comprehensive understanding of football stadium tourism. *Journal of Sport & Tourism*, *25*(3), 217–235. doi:10.1080/14775085.2021.1884589

El-Masri, M., Altrabsheh, N., Mansour, H., & Ramsay, A. (2017). A web-based tool for Arabic sentiment analysis. *Procedia Computer Science*, *117*, 38–45. doi:10.1016/j.procs.2017.10.092

Falk, J., & Dierking, L. (2000). *Learning from Museums: Visitor Experiences and the Making of Meaning*. AltaMira Press.

Gibson, H. (1998). Sport tourism: A critical analysis of research. *Sport Management Review*, *1*(1), 45–76. doi:10.1016/S1441-3523(98)70099-3

Gibson, H. J. (2003). Sport tourism: An introduction to the special issue. *Journal of Sport Management*, *17*(3), 205–213. doi:10.1123/jsm.17.3.205

Harrison-Hill, T., & Chalip, L. (2005). Marketing Sport Tourism: Creating Synergy between Sport and Destination. *Sport in Society*, *8*(2), 302–320. doi:10.1080/17430430500102150

Ito, E., & Higham, J. (2020). Supplemental tourism activities: A conceptual framework to maximise sport tourism benefits and opportunities. *Journal of Sport & Tourism*, *24*(4), 269–284. doi:10.1080/14775085.2020.1850322

Jeong, Y., & Kim, S. (2020). A study of event quality, destination image, perceived value, tourist satisfaction, and destination loyalty among sport tourists. *Asia Pacific Journal of Marketing and Logistics*, *32*(4), 940–960. doi:10.1108/APJML-02-2019-0101

King, K., Shipway, R., Lee, I. S., & Brown, G. (2021). Proximate tourists and major sport events in everyday leisure spaces. In *Tourism Spaces* (pp. 112–130). Routledge. doi:10.4324/9781003152453-6

Kuchkarova, G. (2023). Concept of Active (Active) and Passive (Inactive) Tourism. *Science and Innovation*, *2*(C12), 60–64.

Kusnoto, Y., Supriatna, N., Wiyanarti, E., & Hasan, S. H. (2024). Trend and visualizing of historical tourism in education research during last twenty years: A bibliometric review and analysis. *Journal of Hospitality, Leisure, Sport and Tourism Education*, *34*, 100477. doi:10.1016/j.jhlste.2023.100477

Kusumah, E. P., & Wahyudin, N. (2024). Sporting event quality: Destination image, tourist satisfaction, and destination loyalty. *Event Management*, *28*(1), 59–74. doi: 10.3727/152599523X16896548396824

Liberato, D., Moreira, C., & Liberato, P. (2019). Sports tourism in Oporto as a destination: the influence of FC Porto Football Club. In *33rd IBIMA Conference Proceedings: Vision 2020: Sustainable Economic Development and Application of Innovation Management* (pp. 6007-6021). International Business Information Management Association (IBIMA).

Liberato, P., Liberato, D., Sousa, B., & Malheiro, A. (2020, October). Sports tourism and sports events as a Niche market in Oporto as a tourism destination. In *International Conference on Tourism, Technology and Systems* (pp. 610-623). Singapore: Springer Singapore.

Lord, B. (2002). Cultural Tourism and Museums. *Cultural Resources Planning and Management In*, *c*, 1–12.

Magalhães, M., Horta, P., Valente, L., & Costa, J. (2017). Sports museums as part of the touristic and cultural itineraries: The case of FC Porto and the Dragão stadium. *Worldwide Hospitality and Tourism Themes*, *9*(6), 669–674. doi:10.1108/WHATT-09-2017-0048

Magalhães, P. (2010). Percepções e Práticas de Responsabilidade Social Empresarial no Futebol Profissional Português: O Caso dos Três Grandes. Projeto de Mestrado. ISCTE Business School. Instituto Universitário de Lisboa, Lisboa.

Malchrowicz-Mosko, E., & Munsters, W. (2018). Sport tourism: A growth market considered from a cultural perspective. Ido Movement for Culture. *Journal of Martial Arts Anthropology*, *18*(4), 25–38. doi:10.14589/ido.18.4.4

Pekarik, A. (2003). Museum consumerism. *Curator (New York, N.Y.)*, *46*(1), 15–18. doi:10.1111/j.2151-6952.2003.tb00073.x

Pereira, M. (2016). *Dragon Force International Clinics – do Planeamento à Concretização de um Programa Internacional de Futebol.* Relatório de Mestrado. Faculdade de Desporto da Universidade do Porto.

Petroman, I. M., & Văduva, L. (2021). Forms of active tourism. *Quaestus*, (18), 271–279.

Porto, F. C. (2024a). Museu Futebol Clube do Porto. *Futebol Clube do Porto.* Available at: https://www.fcporto.pt/pt

Porto, F. C. (2024b). The Stadium. *Futebol Clube do Porto.* Available at: https://www.fcporto.pt/en/club/estadio-do-dragao

Ramshaw, G., & Gammon, S. (2005). More than just nostalgia? Exploring the heritage/sport tourism nexus. *Journal of Sport & Tourism*, *10*(4), 229–241. doi:10.1080/14775080600805416

Ramshaw, G., & Gammon, S. J. (2017). Towards a critical sport heritage: Implications for sport tourism. *Journal of Sport & Tourism*, *21*(2), 115–131. doi:10.1080/14775085.2016.1262275

Richards, G. (2021). *Rethinking cultural tourism.* Edward Elgar Publishing. doi:10.4337/9781789905441

Ritchie, B., & Adair, D. (2002). The growing recognition of sport tourism. *Current Issues in Tourism*, *5*(1), 1–6. doi:10.1080/13683500208667903

Semedo, M. (2015*). Avaliação do potencial do turismo marítimo desportivo em Cabo Verde: Uma análise a partir da população residente*. Dissertação de Mestrado. Escola Superior de Educação do Instituto Politécnico de Coimbra, Coimbra.

Smith, A. C., & Stewart, B. (2007). The travelling fan: Understanding the mechanisms of sport fan consumption in a sport tourism setting. *Journal of Sport & Tourism*, *12*(3-4), 155–181. doi:10.1080/14775080701736924

Smith, M. K. (2015). *Issues in cultural tourism studies.* Routledge. doi:10.4324/9781315767697

Taecharungroj, V., & Mathayomchan, B. (2019). Analysing TripAdvisor reviews of tourist attractions in Phuket, Thailand. *Tourism Management, 75*, 550–568. doi:10.1016/j.tourman.2019.06.020

Takata, K., & Hallmann, K. (2021). A systematic quantitative review of authenticity in sport tourism. *Journal of Sport & Tourism, 25*(1), 26–41. doi:10.1080/14775085.2021.1877564

Terzić, A., Demirović, D., Petrevska, B., & Limbert, W. (2021). Active sport tourism in Europe: Applying market segmentation model based on human values. *Journal of Hospitality & Tourism Research (Washington, D.C.), 45*(7), 1214–1236. doi:10.1177/1096348020926546

Thomson, A., Toohey, K., & Darcy, S. (2021). The political economy of mass sport participation legacies from large-scale sport events: A conceptual paper. *Journal of Sport Management, 35*(4), 352–363. doi:10.1123/jsm.2019-0166

Tomlinson, A., & Young, C. (Eds.). (2006). *National identity and global sports events: Culture, politics, and spectacle in the Olympics and the football World Cup*. Suny Press.

TripAdvisor. (2023). *TripAdvisor Fact Sheet.* TripAdvisor. Available at: https://www.tripadvisor.com/PressCenter-c4-Fact_Sheet.html

Vehmas, H. (2010). Rationale of active leisure: Understanding sport, tourism and leisure choices in the Finnish society. *Ido Movement for Culture, 10*, 121–127.

Vieira, T., & Simões, D. M. (2024). Virtues of Tribal Behaviour in Sport: The Case of Portuguese Football Brands. *International Journal of Marketing. Communication and New Media, 11*(21), 132–152.

Winter, M. (2018). Visitor perspectives on commenting in museums. *Museum Management and Curatorship, 33*(5), 484–505. doi:10.1080/09647775.2018.1496354

Wong, I. A., Ma, J., & Xiong, X. (2020). Touristic experience at a nomadic sporting event: Craving cultural connection, sacredness, authenticity, and nostalgia. *Journal of Hospitality and Tourism Management, 44*, 70–78. doi:10.1016/j.jhtm.2020.05.003

Woodham, A. (2017). Sport, history, and heritage: Studies in public representation. *International Journal of Heritage Studies, 23*(1), 74–75. doi:10.1080/13527258.2016.1218913

Xin, L., Qiao, G., Shao, Z., Jiang, T., Wen, C., Zhong, Y., & Li, Z. (2023). Understanding continuous sharing behavior of online travel community users: A case of TripAdvisor. *Journal of Tourism and Cultural Change*, *21*(3), 328–343. doi:10.1080/14766825.2023.2170239

Zarotis, G. (2019). Development of sports tourism. *International Journal of Humanities and Social Science Invention*, *8*(6), 1–7.

KEY TERMS AND DEFINITIONS

Business Intelligence: This results from information systems that combine data with analytical tools to provide information relevant to decision-making while seeking to improve the quality and availability of this information to decision-makers.

Cultural Heritage: This comprises physical artifacts and intangible attributes of a place or society that are inherited from past generations. Tangible heritage includes buildings, monuments, landscapes, books, works of art, and artifacts. Intangible heritage includes folklore, traditions, language, and knowledge.

Cultural Tourism: Type of tourism activity in which the visitor's essential motivation is to learn, discover, experience, and consume the tangible and intangible cultural attractions/products in a tourism destination, which can include heritage, gastronomy, sports among others destination cultural aspects.

Online Consumer Behavior: This is the focus of studies of consumers and the online processes they employ to choose, consume, and dispose of products and services.

Social Media: These aggregates of online communications channels can be considered tools that can be used to define new business models strategically, taking into consideration analyses of community user-generated content and information shared with other members of these online communities.

Sports Tourism: Refers to the visitors who visit a city or place to watch a sport event, or participate in the sports, the latter may also be called active sport tourism.

Tourism Experience: This is a set of activities in which individuals engage on their personal terms, such as pleasant and memorable places, allowing each tourist to build his or her own travel experiences so that these satisfy a wide range of personal needs, from pleasure to a search for meaning.

Tourism Industry: One of the largest industries in the world. It emerged to satisfy the human need to travel to and see different places as part of the service sector, including hospitality (e.g., accommodation, restaurants), transportation (e.g., airlines, car rental), travel facilitation and information (e.g., tour operators, tourist information centres), and attractions and entertainment (e.g., heritage sites and traditional and cultural events).

Chapter 5
From Insight to Advantage:
Harnessing the Potential of Marketing Intelligence Systems in Tourism

Bassam Samir Al-Romeedy
Faculty of Tourism and Hotels, Egypt

Tareq Hashem
https://orcid.org/0000-0001-9564-931X
Applied Science Private University, Jordan

ABSTRACT

In today's dynamic and competitive business environment, marketing intelligence systems (MIS) are vital tools that empower organizations to understand the market, monitor competitors, identify trends, evaluate performance, and make informed decisions, ultimately contributing to effective marketing strategies, enhanced customer experiences, and sustainable business growth. This chapter discusses the impact of MIS in the tourism industry. It explains how the integration of data and advanced technologies allows these systems to provide insights that can sharpen a tourism organization's competitive edge. The chapter outlines the key components of MIS—data collection, analysis, and decision support—and their role in driving strategic marketing decisions. It also examines how these systems enhance customer segmentation, campaign personalization, pricing, and customer relations, with real-world examples underscoring their efficacy. Challenges of implementation are acknowledged, with the chapter concluding on the need for ongoing innovation and future research in this area.

DOI: 10.4018/979-8-3693-3310-5.ch005

INTRODUCTION

In today's highly competitive and rapidly evolving tourism industry, staying ahead of the curve is crucial for businesses to thrive. The advent of technology has revolutionized the way organizations operate, and one such technological advancement that has gained significant attention is marketing intelligence systems (MIS). These systems have the potential to transform the tourism sector by providing valuable insights and enabling businesses to make data-driven decisions (Kotler et al., 2021).

MIS is designed to gather, analyze, and interpret vast amounts of data from various sources, including customer interactions, market trends, competitor activities, and social media. By harnessing the power of advanced analytics and machine learning algorithms, these systems can extract meaningful patterns and insights from the data, enabling businesses to gain a comprehensive understanding of their target audience, market dynamics, and emerging trends (Huang & Rust, 2021; Chintalapati & Pandey, 2022).

The tourism industry, with its diverse and ever-changing customer preferences, can greatly benefit from the implementation of MIS (Pencarelli, 2020). For tourism businesses, the ability to accurately anticipate customer needs, identify emerging travel trends, and tailor personalized experiences can lead to increased customer satisfaction and loyalty. Integrating MIS into the tourism industry offers numerous potential benefits for businesses. MIS enables businesses to gain a comprehensive understanding of their customers' preferences, behaviors, and demographics. By analyzing data from various sources, businesses can segment their customer base more effectively and tailor their marketing efforts to specific target segments. This allows for personalized messaging, offers, and experiences that resonate with customers, leading to increased engagement and conversion rates. With MIS, businesses can deliver highly personalized experiences to their customers. By leveraging data insights, businesses can understand individual preferences, anticipate needs, and offer customized recommendations and services. This level of personalization enhances customer satisfaction, fosters loyalty, and encourages repeat visits and positive word-of-mouth (Kotler et al., 2021; Farahat, 2023).

Likewise, MIS helps businesses analyze market trends, competitor pricing, and customer behavior to optimize their pricing strategies. By understanding price sensitivity, demand patterns, and competitive positioning, businesses can set optimal prices for their products or services. This ensures competitiveness in the market while maximizing profitability (Nagle & Muller, 2018). These potential benefits demonstrate how integrating MIS in the tourism industry can revolutionize marketing strategies, improve customer experiences, and drive business success in a highly competitive and evolving environment.

The primary objective of the chapter is to explore how MIS can be effectively integrated into marketing strategies within the tourism sector. It aims to identify the key benefits, challenges, and opportunities associated with the implementation of MIS in tourism businesses. The chapter also delves into the essential components of MIS, including data collection, data analysis, and data interpretation. It explores the various data sources utilized in MIS, such as customer feedback, social media platforms, market research reports, and competitor analysis. Besides, it highlights the potential benefits that tourism businesses can achieve by harnessing the power of MIS. These benefits may include improved customer targeting and segmentation, enhanced personalization, optimized pricing strategies, effective marketing campaign management, and improved customer satisfaction and loyalty.

Meanwhile, the chapter examines the latest trends and technologies related to MIS in the tourism industry. This may include the use of artificial intelligence, machine learning, predictive analytics, and sentiment analysis to gain deeper insights into customer behavior and preferences. With the increasing use of data in the tourism industry, the study also addresses the challenges associated with MIS implementation.

Overall, the chapter aims to provide a comprehensive understanding of how MIS can be harnessed to enhance and develop the tourism industry. By examining the potential benefits, challenges, and best practices, the chapter serves as a valuable resource for tourism industry professionals, researchers, and policymakers seeking to leverage the power of MIS to drive growth and innovation in the sector.

Marketing Intelligence Systems (MIS) in Tourism Industry

MIS is vital tools for collecting, analyzing, and leveraging data to support marketing decision-making and strategy formulation. These systems gather data from diverse sources like market research, customer feedback, competitor analysis, and industry reports, converting it into actionable insights for informed marketing initiatives (Verhoef et al., 2016). MIS plays a crucial role in helping organizations understand target markets, evaluate competition, recognize trends, monitor performance, and make data-driven decisions (Grandhi et al., 2021). Market understanding is a key aspect, enabling organizations to deeply comprehend their target markets by analyzing demographic data, consumer behavior, and market trends. Through market segmentation based on factors like age, gender, interests, and preferences, organizations can customize marketing efforts for specific customer segments, enhancing the effectiveness of campaigns and boosting customer engagement and conversion rates (Johnson et al., 2019; Kotler et al., 2021).

MIS plays a crucial role in competitive analysis, offering organizations insights into their competitors' strategies, activities, and performance. Through monitoring pricing strategies, promotional activities, and market positioning of competitors, organizations can pinpoint opportunities and potential threats. This information aids in developing competitive advantages, differentiating offerings, and adjusting marketing strategies for a competitive edge. MIS also assists in identifying market trends and consumer preferences by analyzing data on consumer behavior, social media trends, and industry reports. This knowledge enables organizations to adapt strategies and offerings to meet target audience needs, develop innovative products or services, and enhance competitiveness and market positioning (Hossain et al., 2022; Mohamed et al., 2022).

MIS has role in performance monitoring and evaluation, tracking key performance indicators (KPIs) like sales figures, customer satisfaction ratings, website traffic, and conversion rates. Continuous monitoring of these metrics allows organizations to gauge the effectiveness of their marketing activities and pinpoint areas for improvement. MIS supports strategic planning by providing valuable insights and data-driven recommendations, analyzing market data, consumer insights, and competitive environment. This enables organizations to develop informed marketing strategies, set realistic goals, identify growth opportunities, assess market potential, and make informed decisions regarding product development, market expansion, and resource allocation (Dam et al., 2019; Ghahremani-Nahr & Nozari, 2021).

Technologies of MIS

In the dynamic realm of the tourism industry, the integration of advanced technologies into MIS has proven pivotal in acquiring profound insights into customer behavior and preferences. Numerous state-of-the-art technologies are transforming the manner in which tourism businesses gather, analyze, and utilize data for strategic decision-making.

Artificial Intelligence (AI)

AI serves as a fundamental technology in MIS, allowing tourism businesses to automate and optimize diverse marketing processes. AI-driven chatbots and virtual assistants offer personalized customer support, addressing inquiries, and delivering real-time recommendations. AI algorithms analyze extensive customer data, revealing patterns, trends, and correlations, empowering businesses to make informed, data-driven marketing decisions (Mohamed et al., 2022).

Machine Learning (ML)

ML algorithms play a pivotal role in MIS, analyzing extensive datasets to derive valuable insights. These algorithms unveil concealed patterns and relationships within customer data, allowing businesses to segment their customer base, predict behavior, and tailor marketing campaigns. ML algorithms are also utilized to enhance pricing strategies, provide recommendations for products or services, and identify opportunities for cross-selling or upselling (Ghoshal et al., 2021).

Predictive Analytics

Predictive analytics, an integral aspect of MIS, leverages historical data and ML algorithms to foresee future outcomes. In the tourism sector, this approach proves valuable for predicting demand, refining inventory management, and anticipating customer preferences. Examining historical booking patterns, market trends, and external factors like events or holidays, predictive analytics empowers businesses to make informed decisions and strategically plan their marketing initiatives (Hofmann & Rutschmann, 2018; Kotler et al., 2021).

Sentiment Analysis

Sentiment analysis, or opinion mining, employs natural language processing (NLP) methods to scrutinize and comprehend customer sentiments derived from diverse sources like social media, online reviews, and customer feedback. Integration of sentiment analysis into MIS enables tourism businesses to glean valuable insights into customer perceptions, assess levels of customer satisfaction, and pinpoint potential issues or concerns. Armed with this information, businesses can customize their marketing messages, promptly address customer feedback, and elevate overall customer experiences (Naithani & Raiwani, 2023; Alshurideh et al., 2023).

Data Integration and Analytics Platforms

MIS depends on resilient data integration and analytics platforms that amalgamate data from various sources like customer databases, online booking systems, social media platforms, and marketing campaigns. Through these platforms, businesses can refine, process, and scrutinize data to extract meaningful insights. Advanced analytics tools and dashboards present visualizations and reports, streamlining data-driven decision-making and empowering marketers to track the real-time performance of marketing campaigns (Farahat, 2023).

Data Visualization

Data visualization tools play a crucial role in MIS, aiding marketers in comprehending and conveying intricate data insights efficiently. Through the presentation of data in visually engaging and interactive formats like charts, graphs, and maps, these tools enable marketers to swiftly comprehend trends, patterns, and correlations. This visual depiction of data eases the identification of actionable insights and facilitates the communication of these insights to stakeholders (Wirtz & Lovelock, 2021; Bharadiya, 2023).

In essence, the utilization of AI, ML, predictive analytics, sentiment analysis, data integration and analytics platforms, along with data visualization tools, constitutes the technological foundation of MIS in the tourism sector. These technologies empower businesses to enhance their comprehension of customer behavior and preferences, refine marketing strategies, and provide personalized experiences aligned with the changing needs of travelers.

MIS and Tourism Marketing Strategies

The tourism industry is highly competitive, and businesses need to understand their customers' preferences, market trends, and competition to stay ahead. MIS can provide valuable insights by analyzing large volumes of data, enabling businesses to make informed decisions, offer personalized experiences, and optimize marketing efforts. MIS is instrumental in shaping marketing strategies within the tourism sector. Through the utilization of data and insights, MIS empowers tourism businesses to craft focused, personalized, and impactful marketing campaigns. Various mechanisms highlight the influence of MIS on tourism marketing strategies.

Customer Segmentation and Targeting

MIS aids businesses in proficiently identifying and categorizing their customer base. Through the analysis of customer data encompassing demographics, preferences, behaviors, and past purchases, MIS facilitates the creation of customer segments characterized by specific traits. These segments become the focus of customized marketing messages and offers. For instance, a tourism business could utilize MIS to pinpoint adventure-seeking travelers, tailoring marketing campaigns to showcase adventure activities, outdoor experiences, or destinations known for adrenaline-pumping adventures (Markic & Tomic, 2010; Huang & Rust, 2021).

Personalization and Customization

MIS enables tourism businesses to individualize marketing messages and experiences for each customer. Through the utilization of customer data and insights, businesses can comprehend the preferences, past interactions, and specific interests of each customer. This knowledge empowers businesses to provide personalized recommendations, offers, and content across diverse marketing channels, including email campaigns, website personalization, and targeted advertisements. The implementation of personalization not only enhances customer engagement but also contributes to improved conversion rates and the cultivation of long-term loyalty (Kamel, 2023; El-Sherbiny, & Al-Romeedy, 2023).

Campaign Optimization and ROI

MIS empowers businesses to enhance the efficiency of their marketing campaigns and maximize return on investment (ROI). Through the analysis of campaign performance metrics, including click-through rates, conversion rates, and customer acquisition costs, businesses can pinpoint the most effective marketing channels, messages, and strategies. MIS facilitates the tracking and measurement of key performance indicators (KPIs), providing marketers with the insights needed to make data-driven decisions, allocate resources judiciously, and optimize marketing budgets for the greatest ROI (Al Khaldy et al., 2023).

Real-time Market Monitoring

MIS offers immediate monitoring of market trends, customer sentiments, and industry developments. This real-time information empowers tourism businesses to maintain agility and responsiveness to changes, allowing them to adapt their marketing strategies accordingly. For instance, in the event of a sudden trend, like a surge in eco-tourism, businesses can promptly recognize and capitalize on this opportunity by modifying their marketing messages, creating eco-friendly offerings, or establishing partnerships with sustainable travel organizations (Mandal, 2018; Alshurideh et al., 2023).

Customer Relationship Management (CRM)

MIS enhances the implementation of CRM strategies within the tourism sector. Through the integration of customer data from diverse touchpoints like bookings, interactions, and feedback, businesses can obtain a holistic understanding of each customer. This data empowers businesses to cultivate relationships, offer personalized experiences, and provide outstanding customer service. MIS streamlines the management of customer interactions, enables the tracking of customer journeys, and aids in identifying opportunities for upselling, cross-selling, or fostering repeat business (Al-Weshah, 2017; Ferrer-Rosell et al., 2023).

Content Strategy and Creation

MIS significantly influences the formulation of content strategies in tourism businesses. Through the analysis of customer data and insights, businesses can discern the content that resonates most with their target audience. MIS assists in identifying the most effective topics, formats, and channels for customer engagement. This knowledge empowers businesses to craft compelling and pertinent content, including blog posts, videos, social media campaigns, and interactive experiences, aligning with customer interests and preferences (Ahmed & Ganapathy, 2021; El-Sherbiny & Al-Romeedy, 2023).

Reputation Management

MIS plays a role in managing the reputation of tourism businesses. Through the monitoring of online reviews, social media mentions, and customer feedback, businesses can evaluate their brand reputation and customer sentiment. MIS assists in recognizing areas for improvement and responding promptly to negative feedback. Additionally, businesses can leverage positive experiences as testimonials or user-generated content to enhance their reputation. Efficient reputation management facilitated by MIS contributes to building trust, attracting new customers, and fostering loyalty (Christopher & Gaudenzi, 2009; Stienmetz et al., 2022; Farahat, 2023).

Multi-channel Marketing Integration

MIS streamlines the integration of marketing endeavors across diverse channels and touchpoints. Through amalgamating data from sources like website analytics, social media platforms, email campaigns, and offline interactions, businesses can attain a comprehensive perspective of customer interactions and preferences. MIS empowers businesses to provide uniform messaging and experiences across various channels, ensuring a smooth and unified customer journey. This integration augments brand recognition, customer engagement, and overall marketing effectiveness (Gao et al., 2020; Wörndl et al., 2021; Nguyen & Mogaji, 2023).

Trend Identification and Innovation

MIS assists tourism businesses in recognizing emerging trends and seizing opportunities for innovation. Through the analysis of market data, customer behavior, and industry insights, businesses can proactively adapt to evolving customer preferences, shifting market dynamics, and technological advancements. MIS empowers businesses to pinpoint new market segments, emerging destinations, or innovative service offerings. Utilizing these insights, businesses can craft inventive marketing strategies to remain competitive in the dynamically evolving tourism industry (Tsiakis, 2015).

Collaboration and Knowledge Sharing

MIS fosters collaboration and knowledge exchange among marketing teams within a tourism organization. By consolidating data, insights, and analytics in a centralized platform, MIS offers a shared space for teams to collaborate, exchange best practices, and synchronize their marketing endeavors. MIS facilitates the dissemination of customer insights, reports on campaign performance, and knowledge of market trends, nurturing a collaborative culture and allowing the organization to harness collective knowledge for enhanced marketing results (AL-Hashem, 2020; Ferrer-Rosell et al., 2023).

MIS, Competitor Analysis, and Market Insights

MIS plays a vital role in supporting competitor analysis and delivering market insights within the tourism industry. Through the utilization of diverse tools and methodologies, MIS empowers businesses to keep track of competitors, assess market trends, and pinpoint strategic opportunities.

Competitive Monitoring

MIS aids businesses in monitoring and overseeing the activities of their competitors, encompassing aspects like marketing campaigns, pricing strategies, product offerings, and customer reviews. This surveillance is facilitated through automated data collection tools, which extract information from competitor websites, social media platforms, industry publications, and other pertinent sources. Through ongoing competitor monitoring, MIS ensures that businesses remain abreast of shifts in the competitive terrain and helps identify opportunities for differentiation (Hussein, 2020; Neidhardt & Wörndl, 2020).

Market Trend Analysis

MIS gathers and evaluates data related to market trends, industry reports, customer preferences, and emerging technologies. This examination assists businesses in recognizing trends and changes in customer behavior, market requirements, and industry dynamics. MIS employs techniques like data mining, sentiment analysis, and text analytics to derive significant insights from extensive data sets. Armed with an understanding of market trends, businesses can adjust their strategies, create inventive offerings, and seize emerging opportunities (Thaduri, 2020; Ferrer-Rosell et al., 2023).

Benchmarking

MIS enables businesses to evaluate their performance against both competitors and industry benchmarks. Through the comparison of key performance indicators (KPIs) like market share, customer satisfaction, revenue growth, and online visibility, businesses can gauge their standing in the market. MIS offers insights into areas of excellence or areas where improvement is needed, allowing businesses to pinpoint opportunities for enhancement and establish performance targets (Albescu & Pugna, 2014; Pesonen & Neidhardt, 2019).

Competitive Intelligence Analysis

MIS facilitates thorough competitive intelligence analysis by consolidating data from diverse sources and conducting comprehensive evaluations. This process includes assessing competitors' strengths, weaknesses, market positioning, target segments, and marketing strategies. MIS assists businesses in recognizing their unique competitive advantages and areas for differentiation. Additionally, it empowers businesses to foresee competitors' actions, identify potential threats, and proactively respond to shifts in the market (Hussein, 2020; Stienmetz et al., 2022).

Social Media Listening

MIS incorporates tools for social media listening, actively monitoring conversations, mentions, and sentiments related to both competitors and the broader market. Through the analysis of social media data, businesses can glean valuable insights into customer perceptions, preferences, and needs. Social media listening aids businesses in identifying emerging trends, addressing customer concerns, and recognizing opportunities for engagement. Utilizing MIS, businesses can respond to customer feedback, resolve issues, and strategically leverage social media platforms for targeted marketing campaigns (Schweidel & Moe, 2014; Pesonen & Neidhardt, 2019).

Pricing and Revenue Management

MIS aids businesses in monitoring the pricing strategies of competitors and tracking fluctuations in market prices. Through the analysis of pricing data, businesses can discern trends, grasp the competitive environment, and make well-informed decisions regarding their own pricing strategies. Additionally, MIS supports revenue management by offering insights into the revenue generation tactics employed by competitors, including upselling, cross-selling, and promotional offers. Armed with this information, businesses can optimize their pricing and revenue strategies to stay competitive in the market (Wörndl et al., 2021; Farahat, 2023).

Search Engine Monitoring

MIS encompasses tools designed to oversee the online presence and visibility of competitors in search engines. Through the tracking of competitors' search engine rankings, businesses can glean insights into their digital marketing strategies and pinpoint opportunities for enhancing their own standings. MIS is instrumental in assisting businesses to identify keywords and search terms that contribute to driving traffic to competitors' websites, thereby enabling them to refine and optimize their own search engine optimization (SEO) efforts (Theodoridis & Gkikas, 2019; Neidhardt & Wörndl, 2020).

Advertising and Marketing Campaign Analysis

MIS empowers businesses to scrutinize the advertising and marketing campaigns of competitors, providing valuable insights into their messaging, targeting strategies, and media placement. Through the continuous monitoring of competitors' advertising expenditure, creative content, and campaign performance, businesses can discern effective marketing tactics and make informed adjustments to their own campaigns. This analytical approach aids businesses in maintaining competitiveness and ensuring that their marketing endeavors stand out in the dynamic environment of the tourism industry (Kietzmann et al., 2018; Huang & Rust, 2021; Stienmetz et al., 2022).

Destination Analysis

MIS facilitates the analysis of destinations by offering insights into the offerings, visitor demographics, and market positioning of competitors. This understanding of the strengths and weaknesses of rival tourism destinations enables businesses to pinpoint opportunities for differentiation or collaboration with industry stakeholders. Leveraging MIS for destination analysis empowers businesses to make well-informed decisions regarding product development, partnerships, and marketing strategies (Ferrer-Rosell et al., 2023; Farahat, 2023).

Emerging Technology and Innovation Tracking

MIS aids businesses in tracking emerging technologies and innovations within the tourism sector. Through the analysis of competitors' integration of new technologies, businesses can pinpoint opportunities to enhance their own offerings and improve customer experiences. Additionally, MIS ensures businesses stay informed about industry trends like virtual reality, artificial intelligence, and blockchain, enabling them to maintain a competitive edge in a dynamically evolving market (Jenster & Søilen, 2009; Pesonen & Neidhardt, 2019).

International and Global Market Insights

MIS offers businesses valuable insights into international and global tourism markets. Through the observation of competitors' endeavors in diverse regions and countries, businesses can pinpoint opportunities for expansion, partnerships, or collaborations. MIS aids businesses in comprehending the cultural intricacies, preferences, and regulations of various markets, empowering them to customize their marketing strategies and offerings to resonate with international audiences (Mandal, 2018; Thaichon & Quach, 2022).

Challenges of MIS

Introducing MIS in tourism businesses may pose several challenges, with some notable ones to consider. A primary hurdle involves the collection and integration of data from diverse sources. Tourism businesses amass extensive data through channels like online bookings, social media, customer feedback, and market research. However, the complexity arises in consolidating and integrating this data, given its varied formats and dispersed locations across different systems. Ensuring data quality and accuracy during the integration of disparate sources is essential for the efficacy of marketing intelligence (Thaichon & Quach, 2022; Alshurideh et al., 2023).

Additionally, in the tourism industry, companies are responsible for managing sensitive customer information, which includes personal details, payment data, and travel preferences. Complying with data protection regulations like the General Data Protection Regulation (GDPR) and ensuring the security of data pose significant challenges. To address these challenges, organizations must establish robust frameworks for data privacy, implement secure systems for data storage, and adopt strict access controls. These measures are essential in safeguarding customer data from breaches and unauthorized access (Georgiadis & Poels, 2021; Ferrer-Rosell et al., 2023).

Furthermore, the task of assembling and retaining a proficient team equipped with the requisite skills to manage MIS can be demanding. It necessitates expertise in data analysis, statistics, machine learning, and business intelligence to extract valuable insights from data. Given the high demand for data analytics talent and the constantly evolving nature of technology, recruiting and retaining skilled professionals in these domains can be challenging. To address this, organizations may need to invest in training programs or explore outsourcing options to bridge the skills gap. Moreover, the implementation of MIS typically necessitates a robust technological infrastructure, encompassing elements like data storage, processing capabilities, and analytics tools. Upgrading existing systems or adopting new technologies can pose complexities and come with considerable costs. Integration with current IT infrastructure, legacy systems, and third-party applications may also present challenges. Ensuring seamless interoperability and scalability of the MIS can be a substantial endeavor (Al-Romeedy, 2024a,b).

As well, the introduction of MIS requires organizational change and a shift in mindset. Employees must be willing to adapt to new procedures, tools, and data-driven decision-making approaches. Resistance to change and a lack of support from stakeholders can impede the successful implementation of MIS. To overcome these challenges, organizations should invest in change management strategies, effectively communicate the benefits to employees, and foster a data-driven culture. By doing so, they can achieve alignment and maximize the effectiveness of the system (Wörndl et al., 2021; Mohamed et al., 2022).

Although MIS offers access to vast amounts of data, the difficulty lies in converting this data into actionable insights. Extracting valuable insights from intricate datasets and translating them into actionable strategies can be a daunting task. It necessitates a profound understanding of the business, the capability to identify pertinent patterns and trends, and the expertise to derive insights that inform effective marketing decisions. Skills in data analysis, domain knowledge, and the ability to connect data insights with marketing strategies are vital in overcoming this challenge (Stienmetz et al., 2022; Thaichon & Quach, 2022).

Similarly, the tourism industry is characterized by its high dynamics, influenced by factors like shifting consumer preferences, evolving market trends, and disruptive technologies. To stay relevant, MIS must be able to keep up with these changes and offer real-time insights. Staying ahead of competitors necessitates ongoing monitoring, analysis, and adaptation. The challenge lies in ensuring that MIS is agile, flexible, and capable of capturing and analyzing data in real-time to effectively respond to the dynamic nature of the tourism industry (Thaichon & Quach, 2022; Farahat, 2023).

CONCLUSION AND IMPLICATIONS

To optimize the potential of MIS for tourism marketing, stakeholders need to take into account several practical implications. It is essential for stakeholders to ensure the comprehensive and relevant collection of data from various sources, including customer interactions, social media, website analytics, and booking systems. This data should be integrated into the MIS to provide a comprehensive understanding of customer behavior and preferences. Collaborating with technology partners and implementing robust data management strategies are critical to facilitate effective data collection and integration.

Stakeholders ought to allocate resources towards establishing a resilient technology infrastructure that can effectively support the implementation of MIS. This entails investing in suitable hardware, software, and networking capabilities capable of managing large datasets and facilitating real-time analytics. It is also crucial to ensure seamless integration with existing systems like customer relationship management (CRM) platforms to enable smooth data flow and achieve a unified view of customer information.

Moreover, it is imperative to make investments in talent development to fully capitalize on the potential of MIS. This involves recruiting professionals with specialized knowledge in data analysis, artificial intelligence (AI), and machine learning. Equally important is providing training to existing staff members on the proficient utilization of MIS tools and technologies. By fostering a data-driven culture within the organization, stakeholders can effectively harness the complete potential of MIS for tourism marketing.

Additionally, stakeholders should promote collaboration and cross-functional decision-making based on insights derived from MIS. By involving teams from marketing, sales, operations, and other relevant departments, stakeholders can collectively analyze the data and formulate strategies that align with business objectives. This collaborative approach ensures that MIS insights are leveraged throughout the organization, resulting in more impactful marketing initiatives.

Furthermore, stakeholders should consistently monitor the performance of marketing initiatives using insights from MIS. This includes tracking relevant key performance indicators (KPIs), analyzing trends, and identifying areas that require improvement. By utilizing real-time analytics and establishing feedback loops, stakeholders can optimize marketing campaigns, make necessary adjustments to strategies, and effectively adapt to evolving market dynamics.

Likewise, stakeholders need to give paramount importance to ethical considerations when employing MIS for tourism marketing. This entails adhering to data protection and privacy regulations, obtaining appropriate consent for data collection, and upholding transparency in data usage. Respecting customer privacy and responsibly utilizing data are vital in establishing trust and nurturing positive customer relationships.

Importantly, stakeholders should embrace an agile mindset and be receptive to adapting marketing strategies based on insights from MIS. The tourism industry is characterized by its dynamic nature, with market conditions changing rapidly. Through regular review and analysis of MIS data, stakeholders can identify emerging trends, customer preferences, and competitive threats. This empowers them to swiftly modify marketing strategies, seize opportunities, and maintain a competitive edge in the market. Additionally, stakeholders must prioritize the customer by placing them at the core of their marketing efforts. MIS offers valuable insights into customer behavior, preferences, and feedback. By harnessing these insights, stakeholders can develop personalized and targeted marketing campaigns, deliver exceptional customer experiences, and foster long-term customer loyalty.

MIS empowers stakeholders to engage in competitive analysis and assess their performance relative to industry peers. By monitoring competitor activities, analyzing market trends, and comparing key performance metrics, stakeholders can identify areas for improvement and capitalize on industry best practices. This enables them to maintain competitiveness and differentiate their marketing strategies within the bustling tourism market. Moreover, stakeholders should remain abreast of the latest advancements in MIS technologies and industry best practices. Embracing emerging trends and exploring innovative solutions allows stakeholders to unlock novel opportunities for tourism marketing. Regularly evaluating the efficacy of existing MIS tools and considering new technologies ensures that stakeholders remain at the forefront of marketing intelligence in the tourism industry.

REFERENCES

Ahmed, A., & Ganapathy, A. (2021). Creation of automated content with embedded artificial intelligence: A study on learning management system for educational entrepreneurship. *Academy of Entrepreneurship Journal, 27*(3), 1–10.

Al-Hashem, A. O. (2020). Mediation impact of marketing intelligence in the relationship between technology based knowledge sharing and product innovation. *TEM Journal, 9*(2), 688-693.

Al Khaldy, M., Al-Obaydi, B., & al Shari, A. (2023). The Impact of Predictive Analytics and AI on Digital Marketing Strategy and ROI. In *Conference on Sustainability and Cutting-Edge Business Technologies* (pp. 367-379). Cham: Springer Nature Switzerland. 10.1007/978-3-031-42455-7_31

Al-Romeedy, B. (2024a). AI and HRM in Tourism and Hospitality in Egypt: Inevitability, Impact and Future. In HRM, Artificial Intelligence and the Future of Work: Critical Insights from the Global South, Palgrave Macmillan.

Al-Romeedy, B. (2024b). HRM and Digital Leadership: Exploring the Mediating Role of Digital Talent and Digital Culture in Driving Innovative Performance in the Saudi Tourism and Hospitality Industry. In HRM, Artificial Intelligence and the Future of Work: Critical Insights from the Global South, Palgrave Macmillan.

Al-Weshah, G. A. (2017). Marketing intelligence and customer relationships: Empirical evidence from Jordanian banks. *Journal of Marketing Analytics*, *5*(3-4), 141–152. doi:10.1057/s41270-017-0021-7

Albescu, F., & Pugna, I. B. (2014). Marketing intelligence–the last frontier of business information technologies. *Romanian Journal of Marketing*, *3*, 55–68.

Alshurideh, M., Al Kurdi, B. H., Alzoubi, H. M., & Salloum, S. (Eds.). (2023). *The Effect of Information Technology on Business and Marketing Intelligence Systems* (Vol. 1056). Springer Nature. doi:10.1007/978-3-031-12382-5_140

Bharadiya, J. P. (2023). The role of machine learning in transforming business intelligence. *International Journal of Computing and Artificial Intelligence*, *4*(1), 16–24. doi:10.33545/27076571.2023.v4.i1a.60

Chintalapati, S., & Pandey, S. K. (2022). Artificial intelligence in marketing: A systematic literature review. *International Journal of Market Research*, *64*(1), 38–68. doi:10.1177/14707853211018428

Christopher, M., & Gaudenzi, B. (2009). Exploiting knowledge across networks through reputation management. *Industrial Marketing Management*, *38*(2), 191–197. doi:10.1016/j.indmarman.2008.12.014

Dam, N., Le Dinh, T., & Menvielle, W. (2019). Marketing intelligence from data mining perspective: A literature review. *International Journal of Innovation, Management and Technology*, *10*(5), 184–190. doi:10.18178/ijimt.2019.10.5.859

El-Sherbiny, M., & Al-Romeedy, B. (2023). Does loyalty moderate the impact of digital marketing on the purchase intention of customers in airlines? *Journal of the Faculty of Tourism and Hotels-University of Sadat City*, *7*(2), 1–16.

Farahat, E. (2023). *Applications of artificial intelligence as a marketing tool and their impact on the competitiveness of the Egyptian tourist destination* (Doctoral Dissertation, Minia University).

Ferrer-Rosell, B., Massimo, D., & Berezina, K. (2023). *Information and Communication Technologies in Tourism 2023: Proceedings of the ENTER 2023 eTourism Conference, January 18-20, 2023*. Springer Nature. 10.1007/978-3-031-25752-0

Gao, L., Melero, I., & Sese, F. J. (2020). Multichannel integration along the customer journey: A systematic review and research agenda. *Service Industries Journal, 40*(15-16), 1087–1118. doi:10.1080/02642069.2019.1652600

Georgiadis, G., & Poels, G. (2021). Enterprise architecture management as a solution for addressing general data protection regulation requirements in a big data context: A systematic mapping study. *Information Systems and e-Business Management, 19*(1), 313–362. doi:10.1007/s10257-020-00500-5

Ghahremani-Nahr, J., & Nozari, H. (2021). A Survey for Investigating Key Performance Indicators in Digital Marketing. *International Journal of Innovation in Marketing Elements, 1*(1), 1-6.

Ghoshal, A., Mookerjee, V. S., & Sarkar, S. (2021). Recommendations and cross-selling: Pricing strategies when personalizing firms cross-sell. *Journal of Management Information Systems, 38*(2), 430–456. doi:10.1080/07421222.2021.1912930

Grandhi, B., Patwa, N., & Saleem, K. (2021). Data-driven marketing for growth and profitability. *EuroMed Journal of Business, 16*(4), 381–398. doi:10.1108/EMJB-09-2018-0054

Hofmann, E., & Rutschmann, E. (2018). Big data analytics and demand forecasting in supply chains: A conceptual analysis. *International Journal of Logistics Management, 29*(2), 739–766. doi:10.1108/IJLM-04-2017-0088

Hossain, M. A., Agnihotri, R., Rushan, M. R. I., Rahman, M. S., & Sumi, S. F. (2022). Marketing analytics capability, artificial intelligence adoption, and firms' competitive advantage: Evidence from the manufacturing industry. *Industrial Marketing Management, 106*, 240–255. doi:10.1016/j.indmarman.2022.08.017

Huang, M. H., & Rust, R. T. (2021). A strategic framework for artificial intelligence in marketing. *Journal of the Academy of Marketing Science, 49*(1), 30–50. doi:10.1007/s11747-020-00749-9

Hussein, E. A. (2020). Marketing intelligence system and its impact in determining strategies of competitive positions. *Utopía y Praxis Latinoamericana, 25*(1), 530–544.

Jenster, P. V., & Søilen, K. S. (2009). *Market intelligence: building strategic insight*. Copenhagen Business School Press DK.

Johnson, D. S., Muzellec, L., Sihi, D., & Zahay, D. (2019). The marketing organization's journey to become data-driven. *Journal of Research in Interactive Marketing*, *13*(2), 162–178. doi:10.1108/JRIM-12-2018-0157

Kamel, M. A. (2023). Big data analytics and market performance: The roles of customization and personalization strategies and competitive intensity. *Journal of Enterprise Information Management*, *36*(6), 1727–1749. doi:10.1108/JEIM-04-2022-0114

Kietzmann, J., Paschen, J., & Treen, E. (2018). Artificial intelligence in advertising: How marketers can leverage artificial intelligence along the consumer journey. *Journal of Advertising Research*, *58*(3), 263–267. doi:10.2501/JAR-2018-035

Kotler, P., Kartajaya, H., & Setiawan, I. (2021). *Marketing 5.0: Technology for humanity*. John Wiley & Sons.

Mandal, P. C. (2018). Marketing information and marketing intelligence: Roles in generating customer insights. *International Journal of Business Forecasting and Marketing Intelligence*, *4*(3), 311–321. doi:10.1504/IJBFMI.2018.092786

Markic, B., & Tomic, D. (2010). Marketing intelligent system for customer segmentation. *Marketing Intelligent Systems Using Soft Computing: Managerial and Research Applications*, 79-111.

Mohamed, M., Farahat, E., & Al-Romeedy, B. (2022). The Mediating Role of Marketing Effectiveness in the Relationship between Artificial Intelligence and Destination Competitiveness. *Minia Journal of Tourism and Hospitality Research*, *14*(1), 113–129.

Nagle, T. T., & Muller, G. (2018). *The strategy and tactics of pricing*. Routledge.

Naithani, K., & Raiwani, Y. P. (2023). Realization of natural language processing and machine learning approaches for text-based sentiment analysis. *Expert Systems: International Journal of Knowledge Engineering and Neural Networks*, *40*(5), e13114. doi:10.1111/exsy.13114

Neidhardt, J., & Wörndl, W. (2020). *Information and Communication Technologies in Tourism 2020*. Springer International Publishing. doi:10.1007/978-3-030-36737-4

Nguyen, N. P., & Mogaji, E. (2023). Artificial intelligence for seamless experience across channels. In *Artificial Intelligence in Customer Service: The Next Frontier for Personalized Engagement* (pp. 181–203). Springer International Publishing. doi:10.1007/978-3-031-33898-4_8

Pencarelli, T. (2020). The digital revolution in the travel and tourism industry. *Information Technology & Tourism, 22*(3), 455–476. doi:10.1007/s40558-019-00160-3

Pesonen, J., & Neidhardt, J. (2019). Information and communication technologies in tourism 2019. In *Proceedings of the International Conference*. Springer International Publishing. 10.1007/978-3-030-05940-8

Schweidel, D. A., & Moe, W. W. (2014). Listening in on social media: A joint model of sentiment and venue format choice. *JMR, Journal of Marketing Research, 51*(4), 387–402. doi:10.1509/jmr.12.0424

Stienmetz, J., Ferrer-Rosell, B., & Massimo, D. (2022). *Information and Communication Technologies in Tourism 2022: Proceedings of the ENTER 2022 ETourism Conference, January 11-14, 2022*. Springer Nature. 10.1007/978-3-030-94751-4

Thaduri, U. R. (2020). Decision Intelligence in Business: A Tool for Quick and Accurate Marketing Analysis. *Asian Business Review, 10*(3), 193–200. doi:10.18034/abr.v10i3.670

Thaichon, P., & Quach, S. (Eds.). (2022). *Artificial Intelligence for Marketing Management*. Taylor & Francis. doi:10.4324/9781003280392

Theodoridis, P. K., & Gkikas, D. C. (2019). How artificial intelligence affects digital marketing. In Strategic Innovative Marketing and Tourism: 7th ICSIMAT, Athenian Riviera, Greece, 2018 (pp. 1319-1327). Springer International Publishing. doi:10.1007/978-3-030-12453-3_151

Tsiakis, T. (Ed.). (2015). *Trends and innovations in marketing information systems*. IGI Global. doi:10.4018/978-1-4666-8459-1

Verhoef, P. C., Kooge, E., & Walk, N. (2016). *Creating value with big data analytics: Making smarter marketing decisions*. Routledge. doi:10.4324/9781315734750

Wirtz, J., & Lovelock, C. (2021). *Services marketing: People, technology, strategy*. World Scientific. doi:10.1142/y0024

Wörndl, W., Koo, C., & Stienmetz, J. (2021). *Information and Communication Technologies in Tourism 2021: Proceedings of the ENTER 2021 eTourism Conference, January 19–22, 2021*. Springer Nature. 10.1007/978-3-030-65785-7

Chapter 6
Leveraging Virtual Reality (VR) and Augmented Reality (AR) for Enhanced Tourism and Event Marketing:
A Data-Driven Approach

Krishna Khanal
https://orcid.org/0009-0003-1369-0952
Westcliff University, USA

ABSTRACT

This chapter proposes to explore the intersection of virtual reality (VR), augmented reality (AR), data analytics, and marketing in the context of the tourism and events industry. As technology continues to advance, organizations within this sector are seeking innovative and transformative ways to engage and attract tourists and event attendees. VR and AR have emerged as powerful tools for creating immersive experiences, while data analytics provides insights into consumer behavior and preferences. This chapter will examine how these technologies can be integrated into marketing strategies to enhance engagement, visitor experiences, and decision-making processes. By discussing real-world case studies, ethical considerations, and future trends, this chapter aims to provide a comprehensive overview of the subject and offer practical insights for professionals and researchers in the field.

DOI: 10.4018/979-8-3693-3310-5.ch006

INTRODUCTION

In an era where technological innovation shapes every facet of human experience, the tourism and events industry stand at a pivotal juncture. The advent of Virtual Reality (VR) and Augmented Reality (AR) heralds a transformative epoch, not just in how destinations are promoted and experienced, but also in the very conception of what it means to travel or attend an event (Lee & Oh, 2022). VR operates within a completely artificial environment, offering a distinct and separate virtual world, while AR combines elements of both virtual and real-world environments (Guttentag, 2010; Jung et al., 2021). While AR and VR seem alike, they have key differences. AR enables interaction with the actual surroundings, requiring physical presence and movement. In contrast, VR is based entirely on a computer-generated virtual environment. This fundamental difference suggests that AR is better for augmenting and enriching the visitor's experience (Neuhofer et al., 2014). VR creates a world that only exists digitally, while AR adds digital elements to the real world around us (Kandaurova & Lee, 2019).

The surge in immersive technologies has not only redefined the boundaries of reality and virtuality but has also set a new benchmark in consumer engagement. In this milieu, the tourism and events sector, inherently experiential and sensory-driven, finds a fertile ground for innovation. By integrating VR and AR, this industry is not just enhancing the visitor experience but is also rewriting the paradigms of engagement, storytelling, and customer interaction. This integration can create experiences that feel real to our senses (Huisingh et al., 2016) and provide a way for old people to have travel-like experiences without facing the physical, mental, and financial challenges that real travel might involve (Fiocco et al., 2020). At the same time, with the emergence of metaverse, AR and VR is increasingly getting into our everyday experiences (Kraus et al., 2023). However, the integration of VR and AR into tourism and event marketing is not an isolated phenomenon. It is part and parcel of a broader, data-driven revolution that is reshaping the landscape of marketing and consumer analytics. The power of these technologies lies not just in their ability to create immersive experiences but also in their capacity to generate, collect, and analyze vast amounts of data on consumer behaviors, preferences, and interactions. This chapter, therefore, sets out to unravel the complex interplay between VR/AR and data analytics, underscoring how this synergy is crafting new pathways for personalized and impactful marketing strategies. As we delve deeper, we will explore how data gleaned from VR and AR experiences offers unparalleled insights into consumer psychology, enabling marketers to tailor experiences that resonate on a deeply personal level. This convergence of technology and data analytics is not just revolutionizing the way we market tourism and events; it is also setting new standards for what it means to understand and cater to the modern consumer.

Significance of VR, AR, and Data Analytics in Modern Tourism and Event Marketing

In the ever-evolving domain of modern marketing, Virtual Reality (VR) and Augmented Reality (AR) have emerged as game-changers, particularly in the realms of tourism and event marketing (Marasco et al., 2018). These technologies are not just tools; they are gateways to immersive worlds that offer novel and deeply engaging experiences to consumers (Tsai, 2020). These are innovative marketing tools to help promote local offerings and tourism destinations (Scholz & Smith, 2016). VR allows potential tourists to virtually visit destinations before they decide to travel, providing a sensory-rich preview of what awaits them. This not only fuels the wanderlust but also helps in making informed decisions. AR, on the other hand, enhances real-world experiences by overlaying digital information onto physical environments, offering a hybrid experience that enriches user interaction and engagement. For instance, AR can bring historical sites to life or provide interactive guides at events, thereby elevating the overall experience (Tscheu & Buhalis, 2016). These transformative technologies increase tourist experiences and also promote revisits (Lim et al., 2024). The significance of these technologies in modern marketing is profound – they are not just selling a destination or an event; they are selling an experience, an emotion, a promise of what could be.

Simultaneously, the role of data analytics in this context cannot be overstated. In a landscape inundated with choices, understanding consumer preferences, behaviors, and patterns through data becomes crucial. Data analytics enables marketers to gain insights into what experiences attract tourists, what keeps event attendees engaged, and what drives their decisions. This intelligence is invaluable in tailoring marketing strategies that are not just effective but also highly personalized. By analyzing data from VR and AR interactions, marketers can understand which aspects of an experience resonate most with users, allowing them to enhance and personalize their offerings continually. In this data-driven age, VR and AR are more than just experiential technologies; they are rich sources of consumer data (Olshannikova et al., 2012) that, when analyzed effectively, can transform the way tourism and event marketing strategies are crafted and executed. The integration of VR, AR, and data analytics is thus a powerful trifecta, reshaping the tourism and event marketing landscape into one that is more immersive, interactive, and informed.

Virtual Reality (VR) and Augmented Reality (AR) in Tourism and Events

The integration of Virtual Reality (VR) and Augmented Reality (AR) in tourism and events has marked a significant shift in how experiences are curated and delivered.

VR, with its ability to create entirely virtual environments, offers an unparalleled immersive experience. For the tourism sector, this means being able to transport potential travelers to distant locales, allowing them to wander through streets, explore landmarks, or even partake in activities that the destination offers, all from the comfort of their homes. This virtual exploration not only serves as a powerful marketing tool but also aids in decision-making, as it offers a tangible preview of the destination (Chung et al., 2018). In the context of events, VR can recreate entire venues or experiences, enabling remote attendance that feels almost as real as being physically present. This technology extends the reach of events far beyond physical boundaries, making them accessible to a global audience.

Augmented Reality (AR), on the other hand, adds a layer of digital enhancement to the real world, thus enriching the actual experience of a tourist or an attendee. In tourism, AR can bring to life historical tales at ancient ruins, provide real-time translation of signs, or offer contextual information about sights, all through the lens of a smartphone or AR glasses. This not only enhances the educational aspect of travel but also makes it more interactive and engaging. In events, AR can be used to provide interactive schedules, wayfinding solutions, and even personalized digital content that complements what is happening in the real world. This integration of digital and physical realms through AR transforms the way attendees interact with the event, ensuring a more engaging and memorable experience. Both VR and AR are thus pivotal in redefining the boundaries of what is possible in tourism and event marketing, offering experiences that are not only captivating but also deeply resonant with the modern consumer's desire for interactivity and immersion.

Exploring Current Applications and Use Cases of VR and AR in Tourism and Events

In the realm of tourism, VR and AR are being leveraged to create unprecedented interactive experiences (Raptis et al; 2018). A notable application of VR in tourism is virtual tours, which have become increasingly popular, especially in the wake of travel restrictions imposed by global events like the COVID-19 pandemic. Museums, historical sites, and even entire cities are now accessible virtually, offering a 360-degree exploration experience to potential visitors. This not only serves as an enticing preview but also aids in travel planning and accessibility for those unable to physically visit. In contrast, AR's applications in tourism often focus on enhancing the on-site experience. For example, AR apps can overlay historical information and reconstructions over ruins, providing a context-rich, engaging experience. Similarly, wildlife reserves and natural parks use AR to provide interactive educational content about flora and fauna, enriching visitor engagement and understanding.

The event industry, too, has witnessed a transformative impact due to VR and AR. Conferences, concerts, and exhibitions are now being hosted in virtual environments, providing an immersive experience that rivals physical attendance. VR enables attendees to navigate virtual spaces, interact with content, and network with others, breaking geographical barriers and expanding the event's reach. AR, on the other hand, is used to enhance physical events. For example, at trade shows, AR can bring products to life with 3D models and interactive features, allowing attendees to explore products in detail without physical constraints. Similarly, AR-enhanced navigation and information systems make event navigation more interactive and informative. These technologies not only enhance the user experience but also generate a wealth of data. By tracking user interactions and preferences in these virtual and augmented environments, organizers and marketers can gain valuable insights, enabling them to tailor future experiences more effectively, truly embodying the data-driven approach.

Discussing the Impact of Immersive Experiences on Consumer Engagement and Decision-Making

Immersive experiences created by VR and AR technologies have revolutionized consumer engagement in the tourism and event sectors. Through VR, potential tourists can be teleported to distant lands, walking through simulations of streets, landmarks, and experiences that are vivid and lifelike. This level of immersion creates a strong emotional connection, often influencing the decision-making process of the consumer. The ability to virtually experience a destination before physically visiting can significantly sway the decision to book a trip, as it reduces the uncertainty and hesitance associated with unfamiliar locations. In the context of events, VR's ability to replicate real-world experiences means attendees can feel as though they are part of an event without the constraints of physical presence, expanding the event's reach and making it accessible to a more diverse audience. This heightened level of engagement not only increases participation rates but also boosts the overall appeal and value of the event.

AR's impact, while different, is equally profound. By augmenting real-world experiences with digital information and interactions, AR enhances the on-site experience for tourists and event attendees. For instance, AR applications in museums or historical sites can bring stories and history to life, making the learning process more engaging and memorable. In events, AR can provide personalized experiences, like interactive agendas or location-based services, which cater to the individual preferences of attendees. This customization increases satisfaction and engagement, as attendees feel their experience is unique and tailored to their interests. Importantly, these immersive experiences generate a wealth of data on user interactions, preferences, and behaviors. By analyzing this data, organizations can gain insights into what aspects of the experience resonate most with consumers, allowing for more targeted and effective marketing strategies. This feedback loop, where immersive experiences inform data-driven decision-making, is crucial in understanding the evolving landscape of consumer engagement in tourism and events.

Data-Driven Insights in Tourism and Event Marketing

The advent of data analytics has been a pivotal development in understanding consumer behavior and trends, particularly in the context of tourism and event marketing (Saidali et al., 2019). In an industry where consumer preferences and expectations are constantly evolving, the ability to gather, analyze, and interpret data is invaluable. Data analytics offers a granular view of consumer behaviors, preferences, and patterns, enabling marketers to discern not just what consumers are doing, but why they are doing it (Aziz et al., 2023; Vasilopoulou, 2023). This understanding is crucial in an industry that thrives on delivering exceptional experiences. For instance, data gathered from VR and AR experiences can reveal how long a user engages with a particular virtual tour or how they interact with augmented information at an event. Such insights are critical in identifying consumer preferences and tailoring experiences to meet those expectations. Furthermore, data analytics helps in predicting future trends, enabling tourism and event marketers to stay ahead of the curve by adapting to changing consumer behaviors and preferences.

Data-driven decision-making has transformed the landscape of marketing strategies in the tourism and event sectors. By relying on data analytics, marketers can move beyond guesswork and intuition, making decisions based on concrete, actionable insights. This approach allows for more targeted marketing, where resources are allocated to strategies that are most likely to resonate with the intended audience. For example, data-driven insights can inform the development of VR and AR content, ensuring that these technologies are used in ways that are most appealing to consumers. This could mean focusing on certain types of virtual experiences or enhancing specific aspects of an AR application. Additionally, data analytics enables personalized marketing, which is particularly effective in the digital age. By understanding individual consumer behaviors and preferences, marketers can tailor their messaging and offerings to each consumer, significantly increasing engagement and conversion rates. This level of personalization not only enhances the consumer experience but also fosters loyalty and repeat engagement.

The integration of data analytics into VR and AR marketing strategies has led to enhanced marketing outcomes in tourism and event marketing. The insights derived from data analytics enable marketers to create more effective and efficient campaigns. For instance, by understanding the demographics, interests, and behaviors of their target audience, tourism marketers can create VR experiences that are more aligned with the expectations of potential visitors. In events, data analytics can be used to optimize the attendee experience, from personalized schedules to targeted networking opportunities. The effectiveness of these strategies can be measured and refined over time, leading to a continuous improvement loop. Moreover, data-driven strategies often result in a higher return on investment (ROI) as they are more focused and tailored to the audience. In a competitive industry, where consumer attention is a precious commodity, the ability to use data to create compelling, personalized experiences is a significant advantage.

Integration of VR/AR and Data Analytics

The synergy between VR/AR technologies and data analytics is a cornerstone of modern marketing in tourism and events. VR and AR create immersive experiences that engage users in ways traditional marketing cannot, while data analytics provides the insights needed to understand and enhance these interactions (Hirve & Reddy, 2023). This combination creates a powerful tool for marketers. For example, VR experiences can be analyzed to understand which elements users find most engaging, such as specific locations in a virtual tour or certain types of interactive content. Similarly, AR applications can provide data on how users interact with augmented elements in real-world settings. This data, when analyzed, offers valuable insights into user preferences and behaviors, enabling marketers to refine and optimize the VR and AR experiences. The synergy of these technologies also opens up opportunities for creating dynamic, responsive experiences that adapt to user interactions in real-time, offering a highly personalized experience.

Integrating VR/AR with data analytics presents both challenges and opportunities. One of the primary challenges is the technical complexity involved in creating high-quality, seamless VR and AR experiences that are also capable of gathering useful data. This requires a significant investment in technology and expertise. There is also the challenge of ensuring user privacy and data security, as these technologies often collect sensitive user data. On the opportunity side, integrating VR/AR with data analytics allows for a level of personalization and engagement that was previously unattainable. For tourism, this means being able to offer potential visitors a tailor-made virtual experience of a destination, increasing the likelihood of their actual visit. For events, this integration can transform how attendees interact with the event, offering personalized schedules, targeted networking opportunities, and interactive content that enhances their experience. These opportunities extend to creating more effective marketing campaigns and developing deeper insights into consumer behavior.

Data collection and analysis through VR/AR experiences are crucial for gaining insights into consumer behavior. In VR, data can be collected on user movements, gaze tracking (where users are looking), interaction patterns, and engagement duration. This data can reveal what aspects of a virtual experience are most engaging or where users may encounter issues. In AR, data can be gathered on how users interact with augmented elements, their movements in physical spaces, and the way they engage with overlay information. Analyzing this data requires sophisticated tools and techniques, such as machine learning algorithms that can identify patterns and preferences. By understanding these patterns, marketers can design VR/AR experiences that are more aligned with user interests, leading to higher engagement levels. Additionally, this data can be used to create predictive models that help in forecasting future consumer trends and preferences. The key lies in effectively integrating this wealth of data into the overall marketing strategy, ensuring that the insights gained are translated into actionable improvements in VR/AR experiences and broader marketing efforts.

Case Studies and Examples

Virtual Tourism Boost in Iceland: Iceland's tourism board implemented a VR campaign showcasing the country's breathtaking landscapes. By offering virtual tours of attractions like the Northern Lights and Reykjavík's landmarks, they provided potential tourists with a compelling preview of the Icelandic experience. Data collected from these VR tours revealed high engagement with natural sceneries, prompting the tourism board to focus their marketing on nature-based experiences. This campaign led to a significant increase in tourism inquiries and bookings, demonstrating the power of VR in enhancing destination appeal.

Augmented Reality at Historical Sites in Rome: Rome's tourism department introduced an AR app allowing visitors to see historical sites, like the Roman Forum, in their ancient glory. By pointing their devices at different ruins, visitors could view AR reconstructions of these sites. The app collected data on the most visited locations and user interactions, which helped in optimizing tour routes and improving informational content. This innovation not only enriched the visitor experience but also provided valuable insights into popular historical attractions, guiding future enhancements.

VR Conferences During the Pandemic: The shift to virtual events during the COVID-19 pandemic led to the rise of VR conferences. A notable example was a global tech conference that used VR to create a fully immersive event environment. Attendees from around the world could interact in a virtual space, attend talks, and network, replicating the physical conference experience. Data analytics played a crucial role in understanding attendee behavior, such as which sessions were most popular and how attendees interacted within the virtual space. These insights were invaluable for planning future events and tailoring content to audience preferences.

AR-Enhanced Music Festivals: A major music festival introduced an AR feature in its mobile app, allowing attendees to access interactive maps, view artist information, and even find friends in the crowd. The AR features provided a fun and practical enhancement to the festival experience. Data gathered from app usage, such as popular locations and peak usage times, informed logistical decisions and improved crowd management strategies in subsequent years.

Analyzing the Outcomes, Strategies, and Lessons Learned

Iceland's VR Tourism Campaign

Outcome: The campaign saw a notable increase in tourism interest and bookings, particularly towards the nature-centric experiences showcased in the VR tours.

Strategy: By using VR to immerse potential tourists in Iceland's unique landscapes, the campaign effectively captured the essence of the destination.

Lessons Learned: This case illustrates the effectiveness of VR in not only attracting interest but also in providing actionable insights into consumer preferences, guiding future marketing focus.

AR in Rome's Historical Sites

Outcome: Enhanced visitor engagement and satisfaction, with a subsequent increase in visitation rates to the featured sites.

Strategy: The use of AR to bring historical sites to life catered to the modern tourist's desire for interactive and educational experiences.

Lessons Learned: This example highlights the importance of blending technology with cultural heritage and the value of data in optimizing visitor experiences and managing tourist flows.

VR Conferences During the Pandemic

Outcome: High levels of participant engagement and positive feedback, demonstrating the viability of virtual conferences.

Strategy: Replicating a physical conference environment in VR allowed for a more natural and engaging form of remote interaction.

Lessons Learned: The success of this approach underlines the potential of VR in event management, particularly in ensuring continuity during disruptions like a pandemic. It also shows the importance of data in understanding attendee behavior in virtual environments.

AR-Enhanced Music Festival

Outcome: Improved attendee experience and more efficient crowd management.

Strategy: Integrating practical AR features into the festival's app provided both entertainment and utility, enhancing the overall festival experience.

Lessons Learned: This case demonstrates how AR can add value to event experiences and how data collected from such interactions can be instrumental in logistical planning and improving future events.

Ethical and Privacy Considerations

The utilization of VR and AR technologies in marketing inevitably involves the collection and analysis of consumer data, raising important ethical and privacy concerns. The immersive nature of these technologies means that they can collect a vast array of data, including personal preferences, behaviors, and even biometric data in some cases. This raises questions about the extent to which data collection is intrusive and how it is used. Consumers engaging with VR/AR experiences might not always be aware of the data being collected or how it might be used, potentially leading to breaches of privacy. Ethical considerations must also include the respect for user consent and the transparency of data usage. Companies using VR/AR technologies for marketing purposes need to establish clear guidelines on what data is collected, how it is stored, and who has access to it. Additionally, there should be a focus on ensuring that the data is used in ways that respect user privacy and do not manipulate consumer behavior unethically.

To navigate these concerns, it is vital to adhere to best practices and regulatory frameworks. This includes complying with data protection laws such as the General Data Protection Regulation (GDPR) in the European Union and similar regulations worldwide. Best practices involve obtaining explicit consent from users before collecting data, providing clear information about the data collection process, and ensuring the option for users to opt out. Data minimization principles should be applied, meaning only the data necessary for the intended purpose is collected. Furthermore, implementing robust cybersecurity measures is crucial to protect the data from breaches and unauthorized access. Regular audits and assessments of data practices can help in identifying potential risks and ensuring compliance with legal and ethical standards. It's also important to stay updated with evolving regulations and public sentiments around data privacy, as these can rapidly change, especially in the context of new technologies like VR and AR.

FUTURE TRENDS AND RESEARCH

The future of VR and AR in tourism and event marketing is poised for significant evolution, driven by technological advancements and changing consumer behaviors. We can expect to see a rise in the sophistication of VR and AR experiences, with more realistic and interactive features. This will likely include the integration of haptic feedback in VR, allowing users to 'feel' their virtual environment, thereby enhancing the immersive experience. AR is projected to become more seamless and intuitive, with advancements in wearable technology, like AR glasses, enabling more natural and unobtrusive interactions with digital content in real-world settings.

In terms of data analytics, the future holds a more nuanced and predictive approach to consumer behavior analysis. With the growing volume of data from VR and AR interactions, there will be a shift towards real-time data analysis and the use of AI and machine learning algorithms to predict consumer preferences and trends. This will allow for more dynamic and responsive marketing strategies that can adapt to consumer behavior in real-time.

The integration of VR/AR with other emerging technologies such as 5G, IoT (Internet of Things), and blockchain is also an anticipated trend. 5G will enhance the capabilities of VR/AR by enabling faster and more stable connections, essential for high-quality, real-time virtual experiences (Orlosky et al., 2017). IoT could lead to more personalized and context-aware AR experiences, while blockchain might offer new ways to secure and authenticate data transactions in VR/AR environments.

Suggesting Potential Areas for Future Research in This Dynamic Field

User Experience Optimization: Future research can delve into optimizing user experience in VR and AR, studying factors like immersion, usability, and interactivity. This includes understanding the psychological and physiological impacts of prolonged VR/AR usage.

Personalization Algorithms: Research into the development of sophisticated AI algorithms for personalizing VR and AR experiences based on real-time data analysis could be highly beneficial. This includes exploring adaptive content that changes based on user interactions and preferences.

Ethical and Privacy Challenges: As VR and AR technologies evolve, so do the ethical and privacy challenges associated with them. Future research should focus on developing frameworks and best practices for ethical data collection, user consent, and privacy protection in these immersive environments (Iqbal et al., 2023).

Cross-Technology Integration: Investigating how VR and AR can be effectively integrated with other technologies like AI, IoT, and 5G to create more comprehensive and seamless experiences is a potential research area (Torres Vega et al., 2020). This includes exploring the implications of these integrations for marketing effectiveness and consumer engagement.

Impact Measurement and ROI: Research into methodologies for measuring the impact of VR/AR marketing strategies and their return on investment (ROI) is crucial. This includes developing metrics and tools to assess the effectiveness of these technologies in driving consumer engagement and conversions.

Sustainable Practices in VR/AR: Exploring sustainable practices in the development and deployment of VR/AR technologies, particularly in light of environmental considerations and technological waste, is an area that warrants attention.

Cultural and Social Impacts: Investigating the cultural and social impacts of VR and AR in tourism and events, including how these technologies influence travel behavior, cultural understanding, and social interactions, is another key research area.

CONCLUSION

As we conclude this exploration into the realms of Virtual Reality (VR) and Augmented Reality (AR) within the context of tourism and event marketing, several key findings emerge. Firstly, VR and AR have shown themselves to be much more than mere technological novelties; they are powerful tools that can significantly enhance the marketing and experience of tourism and events. Through immersive virtual tours, interactive historical reconstructions, and engaging event experiences, these technologies have opened new avenues for consumer engagement and interaction.

Moreover, the integration of data analytics with VR and AR stands out as a critical factor in understanding consumer behavior and preferences. This data-driven approach enables a deeper, more nuanced understanding of what resonates with consumers, allowing for more effective and personalized marketing strategies. The case studies discussed illustrate not only the potential of these technologies but also the practical ways in which they are already transforming the industry.

Importantly, as we look towards the future, the fields of VR, AR, and data analytics are continuously evolving. Emerging trends such as increased realism in VR, more intuitive AR experiences, and the integration of these technologies with AI, IoT, and 5G, point to an even more interconnected and immersive future. Concurrently, the necessity to address ethical and privacy concerns in data collection and use becomes increasingly paramount. These areas not only offer opportunities for further research but also underline the importance of continual learning and adaptation for professionals in this sector.

To remain competitive and effective in the rapidly evolving landscape of tourism and event marketing, it is crucial to stay abreast of these technological advancements and understand how to leverage them effectively. Embracing a data-driven approach and integrating the latest in VR and AR technology will be key to crafting marketing strategies that are not only innovative but also deeply resonant with the modern consumer's expectations. As this chapter demonstrates, the fusion of technology, data, and creativity holds immense potential for the future of marketing in tourism and events, promising experiences that are more engaging, personalized, and impactful.

REFERENCES

Alkhamisi, A. O., & Monowar, M. M. (2013). Rise of Augmented Reality: Current and Future Application Areas. *International Journal of Internet and Distributed Systems*, *1*(4), 25–34. doi:10.4236/ijids.2013.14005

Aziz, F., Al Haque, T., Hossain, M. B., Rahman, A., & Siam, S. A. J. (2023). Customer Behavior Analysis Through Data Analytics in The Bangladeshi Retail Industry. *Malaysian E Commerce Journal*, *7*(2), 78–84. doi:10.26480/mecj.02.2023.90.96

Carlisle, S., Ivanov, S., & Dijkmans, C. (2023). The digital skills divide: Evidence from the European tourism industry. *J. Tour. Futures*, *9*(2), 240–266. doi:10.1108/JTF-07-2020-0114

Fiocco, A. J., Millett, G., D'Amico, D., Krieger, L., Sivashankar, Y., Lee, S. H., & Lachman, R. (2021). Virtual tourism for older adults living in residential care: A mixed-methods study. *PLoS One*, *16*(5), e0250761. doi:10.1371/journal.pone.0250761 PMID:34014948

Guttentag, D. A. (2010). Virtual reality: Applications and implications for tourism. *Tourism Management*, *31*(4), 637–651. doi:10.1016/j.tourman.2009.07.003

Hirve, S. A., & Pradeep Reddy, C. H. (2023). Improving big data analytics with interactive augmented reality. *International Journal of Information System Modeling and Design*, *13*(7), 19–29.

Huisingh, C., McGwin, G. Jr, & Owsley, C. (2016). Association of visual sensory function and higher-order visual proces- sing skills with incident driving cessation. *Clinical & Experimental Optometry*, *99*(5), 441–448. doi:10.1111/cxo.12404 PMID:27353969

Iqbal, M. Z., Xu, X., Nallur, V., Scanlon, M., & Campbell, A. G. (2023). Security, ethics and privacy issues in the remote extended reality for education. In Y. Cai, E. Mangina, & S. L. Goei (Eds.), *Mixed reality for education: Gaming media and social effects* (pp. 209–221). Springer. doi:10.1007/978-981-99-4958-8_16

Jung, T. & Han, D. I. (2014). Augmented Reality (AR) in Urban Heritage Tourism. *e-Review of Tourism Research,* (5), 1-5.

Jung, T. H., Bae, S., Moorhouse, N., & Kwon, O. (2021). The impact of user perceptions of AR on purchase intention of location-based AR navigation systems. *Journal of Retailing and Consumer Services, 61*, 102575. doi:10.1016/j.jretconser.2021.102575

Kandaurova, M., & Lee, S. H. M. (2019). The effects of virtual reality (VR) on charitable giving: The role of empathy, guilt, responsibility, and social exclusion. *Journal of Business Research, 100*, 571–580. doi:10.1016/j.jbusres.2018.10.027

Kounavis, C., Kasimati, A., & Zamani, E. (2012). Enhancing The Tourism Experience Through Mobile Augmented Reality: Challenges and prospects. *International Journal of Engineering Business Management, 4*, 1–6. doi:10.5772/51644

Kraus, S., Kumar, S., Lim, W. M., Kaur, J., Sharma, A., & Schiavone, F. (2023). From moon landing to metaverse: Tracing the evolution of Technological Forecasting and Social Change. *Technological Forecasting and Social Change, 189*, 122381. doi:10.1016/j.techfore.2023.122381

Lee, K., & Oh, S. (2022). The users' intention to participate in a VR/AR sports experience by applying the extended tech- nology acceptance Model (ETAM). *Health Care, 10*, 1117. PMID:35742168

Lim, W. M., Jasim, K. M., & Das, M. (2024). Augmented and virtual reality in hotels: Impact on tourist satisfaction and intention to stay and return. *International Journal of Hospitality Management, 116*, 116. doi:10.1016/j.ijhm.2023.103631

Marasco, A., Buonincontri, P., van Niekerk, M., Orlowski, M., & Okumus, F. (2018). Exploring the role of next-generation virtual technologies in destination marketing. *Journal of Destination Marketing & Management, 9*, 138–148. doi:10.1016/j.jdmm.2017.12.002

Neuhofer, B., Buhalis, D., & Ladkin, A. (2014). A typology of technology-enhanced tourism experiences. *International Journal of Tourism Research, 16*(4), 340–350. doi:10.1002/jtr.1958

Olshannikova, E., Ometov, A., Koucheryavy, Y., & Olsson, T. (2015). Visualizing Big Data with augmented and virtual reality: Challenges and research agenda. *Journal of Big Data, 2*(22), 1–27. doi:10.1186/s40537-015-0031-2

Orlosky, J., Kiyokawa, K., & Takemura, H. (2017). Virtual and Augmented Reality on the 5G Highway. *Journal of Information Processing, 25*(0), 133–141. doi:10.2197/ipsjjip.25.133

Raptis, G. E., Fidas, C., & Avouris, N. (2018). Effects of mixed reality on players' behaviour and immersion in a cultural tourism game: A cognitive processing perspective. *International Journal of Human-Computer Studies, 114*, 69–79. doi:10.1016/j.ijhcs.2018.02.003

Saidali, J., Rahich, H., Tabaa, Y., & Medouri, A. (2019). The combination between Big Data and Marketing Strategies to gain valuable Business Insights for better Production Success. *Procedia Manufacturing, 32*, 1017–1023. doi:10.1016/j.promfg.2019.02.316

Scholz, J., & Smith, A. N. (2016). Augmented reality: Designing immersive experiences that maximize consumer engagement. *Business Horizons, 59*(2), 149–161. doi:10.1016/j.bushor.2015.10.003

Torres Vega, M., Liaskos, C. K., Abadal, S., Papapetrou, E., Jain, A., Mouhouche, B., Kalem, G., Ergüt, S., Mach, M., Sabol, T., Cabellos-Aparicio, A., Grimm, C., De Turck, F., & Famaey, J. (2020). Immersive Interconnected Virtual and Augmented Reality: A 5G and IoT Perspective. *Journal of Network and Systems Management, 28*(4), 796–826. Advance online publication. doi:10.1007/s10922-020-09545-w

Tsai, S. P. (2020). Augmented reality enhancing place satisfaction for heritage tourism marketing. *Current Issues in Tourism, 23*(9), 1078–1083. doi:10.1080/13683500.2019.1598950

Tscheu, F., & Buhalis, D. (2016). Augmented reality at cultural heritage sites. In A. Inversini & R. Schegg (Eds.), *Information and communication technologies in tourism 2016* (pp. 607–619). Springer. doi:10.1007/978-3-319-28231-2_44

Vasilopoulou, Ch., Theodorakopoulos, L., & Giotopoulos, K. (2023). Big Data and Consumer Behavior: The Power and Pitfalls of Analytics in the Digital Age. *Technium Social Sciences Journal, 45*(7), 469–480. doi:10.47577/tssj.v45i1.9135

Weng, M. L., Mohamed Jasim, K., & Das, M. (2024). Augmented and virtual reality in hotels: Impact on tourist satisfaction and intention to stay and return. *International Journal of Hospitality Management, 116*, 103631. doi:10.1016/j.ijhm.2023.103631

Chapter 7
Marketing Strategies for Medical Tourism in India Amongst Gulf Countries:
An Empirical Study

Hemant Gupta
https://orcid.org/0000-0001-9553-6446
Alliance University, India

Anand Kumar Sonkar
Dhirendra Mahila P.G. College, India

ABSTRACT

Medical tourism is known as a phenomenon where millions of patients a year from all over the world travel across international destinations in order to obtain various forms of healthcare. Most of these patients are known to travel from developed countries to developing countries, looking for highly invasive medical treatments to lesser invasive and recreational medical treatment. The main objective of this research is to try and understand the importance of marketing medical tourism in India. This research mandated registering the observations of the medical tourists from Gulf countries to find answers to how the attitudes and behaviors of patients towards the concept of medical tourism influence their decision to become a medical tourist. The authors interviewed patients from the UAE through questionnaires that address the objective of the research. The authors noted that the primary drivers of medical tourism to India are the country's highly skilled medical professionals, as well as its extensive medical facilities and reasonably priced treatments.

DOI: 10.4018/979-8-3693-3310-5.ch007

INTRODUCTION

Over the past few decades, medical tourism (MT) has experienced tremendous growth. Many developing nations especially India in Asia, have benefited greatly from this, as there is travel for medical care between higher-income and lower- and middle-income nations (Behrmann, J., & Smith 2010). In this area, India has been making its own, unparalleled progress. India's health system has undergone a rapid transformation since the 1990s to address emerging health issues, and it is now the center of development. India has become a major player in the medical tourism sector thanks to its clinical and technical know-how, ability to meet international standards, and extremely affordable costs (Bagga T, Vishnoi SK, Jain S 2020).

However, the rapid changes in the local, national, and international environments make it difficult for stakeholders to strike a balance between opportunities and risks. The sector is exhibiting the effects of quick disruption and heightened competition. New opportunities are presented to service providers. Merely acknowledging this shift is insufficient. To lessen the effects of the paradigm shift, the government and businesspeople must learn how to handle disruption and modify their operating models holistically. It is essential to reflect and determine the resources and capabilities that stakeholders must recognize. This is essential to maintain the level of sophistication and expertise of India's medical tourism sector.

Important Concerns Facing the Indian Medical Tourism Sector

India has to carve out a niche for itself by utilising its current strengths and providing a distinctive value proposition, as other nations compete with one another for a larger share of the medical tourism market. Medical tourists can be broadly classified into three categories. foreign patients seeking medical care foreigners traveling for leisure and medical care Foreigners.

The following problems or obstacles must be overcome by India before it can develop into a popular travel destination with a strong medical tourism sector. They are as follows:

- Inadequate infrastructure, including inadequate power and water supplies, poor coordination, and a lack of connectivity.
- The majority of Indian hospitals also deal with foreign patients' lack of trust. The hospitals have seen a lack of proper hospitality services, uneven service pricing, unhygienic food handling, low hygiene awareness among medical attendants, and no industry standards.
- In order to encourage medical tourism in India, there are a few particular issues. These are: (a) providing Indian hospitals and service providers

with high-quality accreditations; (b) providing training and development to medical professionals, nurses, and paramedics; and (c) failing to adopt a customer-focused mind-set.

Table 1. Classification of the services available for Gulf countries

	Wellness tourism	Alternative systems of medicine	Cosmetic surgery	Advanced and life savings healthcare
Services offered	**Spas, Stress relief, rejuvenation centres**	**Ayurvedics, Siddha treatment for diseases e.g. Arthritis, Rheumatism**	**Dental Care, Plastic Surgery, Breast enhancement, Tummy reduction, Skin Treatment**	**Open transplants, cardio vascular surgery, Eye treatment, Hip Replacement, In vitrio fertilization**
Key Competitors	Thailand, South Africa	--	South Africa, Cuba, Thailand	Singapore, Jordan, Thailand
India's Strength	Low –Thailand has captured a significant share of the market	High-Kerala is popular for this service	Low –South Africa and Thailand leads in plastic surgery	High-India has strong image on medical tourism

Source: Authors creation

OBJECTIVES

This study looks at opportunities, highlights major issues, and develops appropriate plans of action for the growth of medical tourism in India. It is based on a survey of the literature, which includes articles from journals, websites, newspapers, and travel and tourism publications that provide information on medical tourism. This aids in the development of the marketing plans for medical travel to India. Understanding why some developing nations, like India, are more successful than others at promoting medical tourism is another goal of this research project. Stated differently, it also highlights India's comparative advantages over other nations.

This research aims to accomplish following goals: (1) to identify the factors influencing medical tourism through the existing literature; (2) to understand the competitive advantage of India, (3) to develop a framework for the development of medical tourism in a region.

REVIEW OF LITERATURE

The literature review includes a brief overview of the medical tourism sector, including its global trends, the state of the medical tourism sector in Asia and India at the moment, and the important aspects of medical tourism as reported in the literature.

Reputable market research databases estimate that the global medical tourism market will reach USD 273.7 billion by 2027, growing at a compound annual growth rate of 12.8% from its 2019 valuation of USD 104.7 billion (Chhabra A, Munjal M, Mishra PC, Singh K, Das D, Kuhar N 2021). Medical tourism is widely regarded as one of the sectors with the fastest current growth rates, despite the lack of a precise industry estimate. Trade economists have shown that this phenomenon has a significant effect on the world economy (Bookman M 2007). Leading nations offering healthcare services to patients from abroad include Singapore, India, Thailand, Brunei, Cuba, Hong Kong, Hungary, Israel, Jordan, Lithuania, Malaysia, the Philippines, and the United Arab Emirates (Heung V, Kucukusta D 2010).

According to the research, the largest percentage of foreign medical tourists in this region are from Thailand, Singapore, and India, followed by South Korea and Malaysia. Other quickly developing markets in this industry include Taiwan and the Philippines. Several private hospitals in this region are targeting the global market for medical travelers, as foreign patients account for one-third or more of their revenue. As a result, they have established a strong market position for themselves (Mooter 2017).

One of India's biggest and most intricate industries, healthcare is expected to generate USD 133.44 billion by 2020 (Pakholok 2020). In terms of both employment and revenue generation, the healthcare sector in India is growing rapidly. The medical tourism sector, which is supporting the level of improvements in care services in India, is providing additional impetus to this industry. India has grasped the opportunity presented by medical tourism and established itself as a major player in the industry, thanks to its highly competitive pricing, highly skilled medical staff, first-rate care, and accessibility to a variety of treatments (J 2013).

RESEARCH METHODOLOGY

To determine the variables influencing medical tourism in a given area, the research examines the body of existing literature. This paper's introduction contains a list of the conclusions drawn from the reviewed literature. The first step involved proposing a framework for the growth of medical tourism in a region based on the findings of the literature review and suggestions from the focus group. "Meeting or exceeding customer expectations, or as the difference between customer perception and expectations of service," is how Nitecki and Hernon (2000) defined service quality. The tool has been extensively utilized to evaluate the caliber of services in sectors like healthcare, retail, and hospitality (Ajam et al., 2014; Saleh & Ryan, 1991; Zhao et al., 2002). Therefore, it is defined as the discrepancy between the customer's perception of the service and his preconceived expectations in order to be quantitatively assessed. The comparison of expectations and actual performance is known as perception. When performance exceeds expectations and vice versa, it's a good sign of quality.

DATA ANALYSIS

The survey includes the responses of the 120 respondents through structured questionnaires and interviews, in which 09 were incomplete, 1 were not filled properly so, 110 responses were considered for further study.

Figure 1. Demographic gender in percentage

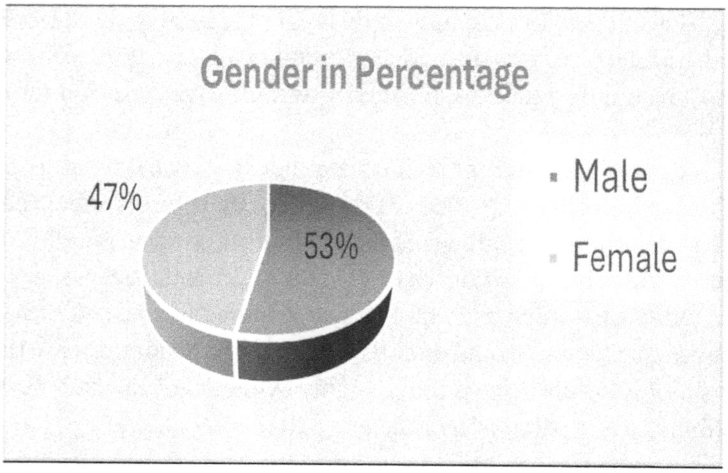

Figure 2. Age-wise distribution of the gulf countries patients

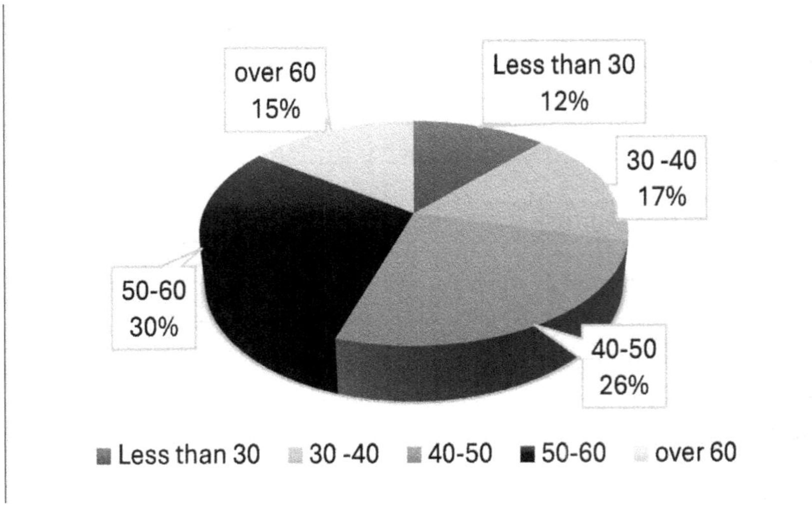

In Figure 2, it makes sense that the elderly were the ones using the services as medical tourists. About 56% of the respondents were between the ages of 40 and 60, and 29% were between the ages of up to 30.

Figure 3. Patients number details

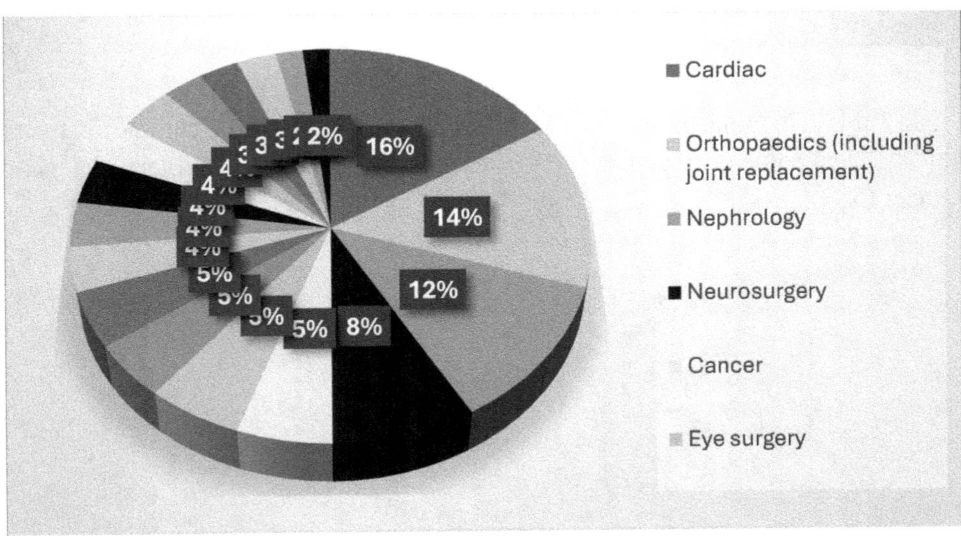

Table 2. Products and services offered by the Indian medical industry to Gulf countries

Medical Product / Services	Number	Percentage
Cardiac	18	30%
Orthopedics (including joint replacement)	15	14%
Nephrology	13	12%
Neurosurgery	9	8%
Cancer	6	5%
Eye surgery	6	5%
Regular check up	5	5%
ENT	5	5%
Seasonal disease	4	4%
Organ transplant	4	4%
Gastroenterology	4	4%
Dental	4	4%
Diabetes	4	4%
Tumour	3	3%
Gynae	3	3%
Urology	3	3%
Cosmetic	2	2%
IVF	2	2%
Total	110	

Source: Authors creation

In Table 2, In India, the most popular medical tourism product is cardiac treatment (30%). Then come orthopedics (14%), nephrology (12%), neurosurgery (8%), and cancer (5%).

Table 3. Treatment of gulf patients as per their nature

Treatment as per Age Group	Under 30		30-40		40-50		50-60	
	Nos.	%	Nos.	%	Nos.	%	Nos.	%
Cardiac	18	6.6	31	8.2	42	8.7	33	7
Orthopaedics	11	1.8	24	4.8	30	6	9	2.2
Neuro Surgery	8	1.6	20	4	22	4.4	7	1.4
Nephrology	8	1.6	18	4.6	24	4.8	6	1.2
Cancer	7	2.2	11	2.2	27	5.4	7	1.4
Others	28	5.6	35	7	28	5.6	11	2.2

Source: Authors creation

In the above Table 3, the most important product that patients of all ages seek out is cardiac care. Individuals between the ages of 40 and 60 are also pursuing orthopedic care. Along with rating their experience in relation to these five factors, the respondents were asked to assess the difference between "what they expected" and "what they got." Each time, the experience did not live up to the expectations.

Table 4. The relative importance of factors of concern (expectations) at the procedure stage

Factor	Mean (μ)	S.D. (σ)
Quality of treatment	4.25	0.46
Ease of access	4.17	1.14
Connectivity	4.10	1.88
Cost of treatment	4.05	0.71
Ease of purchase	3.54	0.70

In the above Table 4, As might be expected, respondents consistently ranked the quality of treatment as their top concern. Ease of access to the treatment process came next. But in these instances, there was the least difference between expectations and experience. The respondents were most offended by the total cost of care. Additionally, they felt uneasy about how simple it was to pay for the medical (and associated travel) services.

FINDINGS AND DISCUSSION

The study finds four key factors influencing the growth of medical tourism in the area based on the research. Through the focus group discussion, we were able to determine that the four most significant factors influencing the uptake of medical tourism in a given region are cost, quality, language, and ease of travel. To find facilitators for these identified factors, the study conducted additional interviews with the focus group participants. The study suggests a framework for boosting medical tourism's penetration in the case region based on feedback from the focus group. The secondary research and focus group discussions identified a number of critical enablers for meeting the four factors, including lean management, the use of quality management systems, having External Quality Assurance Systems (EQAS) and the National Accreditation Board for Hospitals and Health-care Providers (NABH), language and soft skills, and ease of travel and visa requirements. The framework employs factors and enablers to boost medical tourism in the area.

Based on an analysis of various websites concerning the development and prospects of medical tourism, healthcare providers in India may consider implementing the subsequent marketing tactics. Using the marketing mix i.e. Product, Price, Place, Promotion, People, Process, and Physical Evidence, for making effective marketing strategies for developing medical tourism in India for the gulf countries.

1. **Product**: Numerous hospitals in India provide top-notch care in almost every medical specialty, including gastroenterology, ophthalmology, transplants, urology, joint replacement, orthopedic surgery, cardiology, and cardiothoracic surgery. Numerous specialties are covered, including pediatrics, pediatric surgery, pediatric neurology, urology, nephrology, dermatology, dentistry, plastic surgery, gynecology, pulmonology, psychiatry, oncology, ophthalmology, rheumatology, endocrinology, ENT, and pediatrics. Medical professionals who possess international board certification from the Gulf Countires are highly valued assets of the organizations and play a crucial role in advancing healthcare services.

Adding value through services is another marketing tactic employed by service providers. To set themselves apart from their growing competitors, superior value-added services have been developed. These services increase efficiency, make patients' lives more convenient, and foster and fortify relationships with customers. These non-medical care services include things like online medical scheduling, travel planning, multilingual interpreting, opulent service apartments for patients' families next to the hospital, hotel selection and booking, sightseeing tour services, air and ground medical transportation, one-on-one nursing care, and more. Leading Indian healthcare service providers have begun to invest in, run, and/or manage hospitals and medical facilities abroad in an effort to grow their business. These medical facilities serve as diagnostic hubs.

2. **Price:** India's healthcare service providers enjoy a competitive edge over their rivals because of the country's excellent medical standards and affordable Gulf Countries Patient costs. Complex medical procedures are performed in India for only a tenth of the price of those in industrialized nations, but much more infrastructure—roads, sanitary conditions, power backups, lodging, and public utility services—is required before India can compete as a medical tourism destination (Kaur et al., 2007).
3. **Place:** The primary medium for sharing information about the medical and non-medical care services that each healthcare service provider offers is the internet. It is the most efficient and cost-effective way to get the product in front of its target market directly while also assisting patients in getting accurate and useful information so they can make an informed choice. Potential patients are reassured and made aware of the medical treatments available by each service provider through informative online marketing. To draw patients on medical travel programs, websites featuring interactive communication, treatment descriptions, service and facility descriptions, quality assurance, and other concierge services were also showcased. To promote their medical tourism, all healthcare service providers typically enlist the aid of agents. These representatives advise hospitals about patients' treatments and give information to them. They serve as a hub that coordinates Gulf Countries Patient and hospital care for the purpose of screening cases, providing the hospitals with all the patient's relevant medical records. Additionally, agents are in charge of marketing and advertising healthcare service providers in those nations at the same time, encouraging word-of-mouth promotion of service dependability and assurance.
4. **Promotion:** Additionally, a variety of educational materials were used to raise awareness of the available healthcare services, including brochures, booklets, video-CDs, paper bags, and t-shirts with logos. Some healthcare service providers in India also developed partnerships with local institutes, universities, and medical schools in other countries to establish collaboration in education, exchange of knowledge and training, as well as to promote their alternative healthcare services. The majority of healthcare service providers in India, particularly big private hospitals, participate in travel marts, travel fairs, trade fairs, exhibitions, seminars, and conferences, and advertise in travel magazines in countries with government support. Healthcare service providers advertise their medical and non-medical services in local and international

media through articles, videos, and news about their high standard of medical treatments and services, health issues, the newest medical technology equipment, quality assurance, awards, and accreditation that they publish on their websites as well as to the media worldwide. These efforts serve to raise awareness of alternative medical treatments that are available as well as to create a positive image of the high quality and international standard of medical care in India.

5. **Process:** When seeking medical care abroad, patients are primarily concerned with the quality of care and prefer that the providers have accreditation from a reputable international body that oversees medical quality. Around 6,000 000 doctors, nurses, and paramedics with the necessary training and experience can be found in India, along with an advantage in language proficiency (English). The nation's growing need for the provision of high-quality healthcare services is met by the medical education system. The Joint Commission International (JCI) acknowledges and accredits that the hospital's standards are on par with or higher than those of medical facilities in the West. Medical tourists frequently travel to India. (M. Iyer, 2004)
6. **People:** Another tactic used by Indian healthcare providers is to entice foreign patients with the promise of affordable medical care in India, as well as access to highly skilled medical specialists trained in reputable foreign universities. It is commonly known that hospitals can gain a competitive edge by employing highly skilled and specialized physicians and staff. Nonetheless, the primary issue with medical tourism in India is the lack of physicians and other qualified medical personnel. Furthermore, misinterpretations of the patients' cultures continue to pose issues and difficulties for the Indian medical tourism industry.
7. **Physical Evidence:** Large hospitals in India, such as Apollo Hospitals, Escorts Hospital, Wockhardt Hospitals, Breach Candy Hospitals, Lilavati Hospital, Manipal Hospitals, Mallya Hospital, AMRI Hospitals, etc., have state-of-the-art facilities with luxurious, roomy accommodations and first-rate amenities for patients and their families, all furnished with state-of-the-art technology. This is one of India's competitive advantages in gaining the trust and confidence of Gulf countries' patients who ultimately decide to make India their first choice.

CONCLUSION

Patients are looking eastward due to rising healthcare costs in the mid-east and western nations. The med- tourism industry is expanding rapidly in developing nations like India. In India, recent advancements in process innovation and operational excellence have made it feasible to provide healthcare at a significantly lower cost than in Western nations. According to Narayana Health, open heart surgery typically costs less than $2000. At a US research hospital, the same procedure usually costs over $100,000. Cost, quality, ease of travel, and language are the elements that determine a destination's status as a preferred medical tourism destination. Quality appears to be one of the most crucial factors when choosing a healthcare provider, according to the body of existing research (Mishra, V., Samuel, C., & Sharma 2019). There aren't many healthcare providers, on a website that lists healthcare tourism destinations in India. Borders have begun to open again as a result of vaccine availability and widespread vaccination campaigns in many nations. In the post-COVID era, governments ought to consider taking steps to encourage medical tourism. This forced us to look into the causes of the low rate of medical tourism in the area and possible solutions.

India is well-positioned to take advantage of the worldwide medical tourism market opportunities. The growth of medical tourism depends heavily on the involvement of the government. In addition to acting as a regulator, the government ought to encourage private investment in the healthcare industry. It is necessary to develop mechanisms that will allow foreign tourists traveling for medical purposes to receive visas more quickly. Patients can contact the immigration department at any point of entry to expedite the process. Among the initiatives that can be implemented are tax incentives for service providers, reduced import duties on medical equipment, and committees dedicated to promoting and fostering medical tourism. To promote tourism in India, auxiliary infrastructure like transportation services must be developed. To provide effective patient care, the departments of tourism, health, information, and communication must collaborate. Several strategies for medical tourism promotion in India have been suggested in this paper. These include establishing and enhancing India's reputation as a premier medical travel destination, developing and marketing novel medical travel offerings, maintaining the high caliber of care at an affordable cost, and disseminating educational online and offline resources to prospective clients.

Limitations and Future Research

Purposive sampling was used in this exploratory study. The results can be more broadly applied to a larger population in a study with a larger sample size and probabilistic sampling. To enhance inclusivity, the study can incorporate samples from nations beyond Mauritius, such as the United Arab Emirates and the United States. Prospects between the ages of 45 and 55 make up the majority of responders. This could potentially be among the study's limitations. The framework presented in the study for the promotion of medical tourism in a region can be empirically tested in a later investigation. Future research may incorporate additional healthcare-related service dimensions.

REFERENCES

Bagga, T., Vishnoi, S. K., Jain, S., & Sharma, R. (2020). Medical Tourism: Treatment, Therapy and Tourism. *International Journal of Scientific and Technology Research*, *9*(3), 4447–4453.

Behrmann, J., & Smith, E. (2010). Top 7 Issues in Medical Tourism: Challenges, Knowledge Gaps, and Future Directions for Research and Policy Development. *Global Journal of Health Science*, *2*(2), 80. doi:10.5539/gjhs.v2n2p80

Bookman, M., & Bookman, K. (2007). *Medical Tourism in Developing Countries*. Palgrave Macmilla. doi:10.1057/9780230605657

Chhabra, A., Munjal, M., Mishra, P.C., Singh, K., Das, D., Kuhar, N., & Vats, M. (2021). Medical Tourism in the Covid-19 Era: Opportunities, Challenges and the Way Ahead. *Worldwide Hospitality and Tourism Themes*.

Connell, J. (2013). Contemporary Medical Tourism: Conceptualisation, Culture and Commodification. *Tourism Management*, *34*, 1–13. doi:10.1016/j.tourman.2012.05.009

Heung, V., Kucukusta, D., & Song, H. (2010). A Conceptual Model of Medical Tourism: Implications for Future Research. *Journal of Travel & Tourism Marketing*, *27*(3), 236–251. doi:10.1080/10548401003744677

Mishra, V., Samuel, C., & Sharma, S. K. (2019). Patient's Utility for Various Attributes of Diabetes Care Services. *IIM Kozhikode Society and Management Review*, *8*(1), 1–9. doi:10.1177/2277975218798134

Mooter, B. V. (2017). *Medical Tourism in Asia-Pacific Growing Rapidly*. BRINK, The Edge of Risk.

Pakholok, O. (2020). *The Idea of Healthy Lifestyle and Its Transformation Into Health-Oriented Lifestyle in Contemporary Society*. doi:10.1177/2158244013500281

Chapter 8
Personalization of Travel Experiences Through Data Analytics:
A Case Study in Amusement Parks

Dwijendra Nath Dwivedi
https://orcid.org/0000-0001-7662-415X
Krakow University of Economics, Poland

Ghanashyama Mahanty
Department of Analytical and Applied Economics, Utkal University, Bhubaneswar, India

Shafik Khashouf
University of Liverpool, UK

ABSTRACT

Travel and tourism represent a multifaceted sector, with the customer's journey from departure to return encompassing myriad interactions. A deeper comprehension of these interactions allows for enhanced planning aimed at enriching the customer's experience. The integration of advanced data analytics has significantly advanced the focus on customer needs within the travel and tourism industry. In this specific study, data analytics is applied to tailor experiences for visitors to an amusement park, using a comprehensive dataset from a fictional park to explore how variables such as age, group makeup, admission time, ride preferences, and eating habits can enhance the visitor experience. The findings offer valuable insights into visitor behaviors, facilitating the customization of services. For instance, age-related data informs the imposition of ride restrictions, while data on arrival and departure times aid in refining park operations and managing crowds more effectively.

DOI: 10.4018/979-8-3693-3310-5.ch008

1. INTRODUCTION

Travel and tourism is a multifaceted activity. The journey of a traveler, starting from the moment they leave their home until they return, involves various interactions and moments of engagement. By gaining a deeper insight into these interactions, we can devise strategies to positively impact and transform the customer's journey into a memorable experience.

With the rise of data analytics, customizing travel experiences to each person's tastes is no longer a nice-to-have, but a must if you want to stand out in a very competitive market. It looks at how data analytics can change the way people travel by personalizing experiences and how that changes things for both passengers and service providers. Understanding each traveler's unique wants, preferences, and habits is at the heart of the idea of personalization in travel. These days, digital traces are as different as the places people visit, so using data analytics is a great way to figure out these complicated patterns. With the help of data analytics, the travel industry can create experiences that are truly unique for each traveler. These experiences can range from personalized travel suggestions to personalized contact and services.

Getting to successful personalization, on the other hand, is hard and complicated. The huge amount and variety of data that visitors create at different points of contact means that advanced analytical tools and methods are needed. Concerns about privacy and ethics that come up with collecting and using data also make it more important for data practices to be open and responsible. This essay looks at the many ways that data analytics can be used to make travel experiences more personalized. It starts with a brief history of personalization in travel, showing how it has changed over time from a one-size-fits-all method to the data-driven paradigm we see now. After that, the study looks at the changes in technology and methods of analysis that have made personalized travel possible. There are real-life examples and case studies that show how personalization can improve business success, make customers happier, and make them more loyal.

This essay talks about the problems that come up when you try to make travel situations more unique. It also talks about how to manage data well, why predictive analytics is important, and how to use data ethically. The conclusion talks about the bright future of personalization in travel, which will be made possible by new technologies like AI and machine learning, as well as the ongoing effort to make travel experiences more immersive and important. This paper aims to give a full picture of how data analytics can be used to make travel experiences more personalized by combining ideas from different fields, such as data science, tourism management, and customer behavior. This article is meant for a wide range of people, including people who work in business, academic researchers, and anyone else who is interested in how travel, technology, and personalization can work together.

2. LITERATURE STUDY

Travel brands have turned to personalized experiences as a means of building customer loyalty and differentiating themselves from competitors, but for successful personalization strategies to work, accessing high-quality data that accurately reflects customers' needs and preferences is required (Mascarenhas et al., 2007). Data analytics tools enable travel companies to offer tailored offers, content, and experiences throughout a customer journey, from pre-trip communication and booking confirmation to destination suggestions and post-trip follow-up (Respatyanti,2019). Predictive analytics is the cornerstone of providing personalized experiences, whether that means vacation planning or navigating the travel industry (Bardukova, 2023). By analyzing past customer behavior and trends, predictive analytics enables companies to anticipate future consumer demand while simultaneously optimizing pricing strategies and marketing plans for travel services (Song & Liu, 2017). Predictive analytics can identify the optimal times and days to promote a destination or trip type, helping reduce overall costs by optimizing efficiency and eliminating promotional efforts that don't produce results (Smith & Hawkins, 2004). Predictive analytics also provides insight into a company's sales performance and profitability to provide insight on how its overall strategy could be enhanced (Gupta, et al (2020). Predictive analytics can also be leveraged to optimize customer journeys with tailored recommendations from artificial intelligence-powered tools (Patil et al., 2021). AI can recommend accommodations and attractions tailored specifically to a customer's preferences, saving both time and effort on trips while improving the overall experience of travel (Tsaih & Hsu, 2018). Furthermore, such recommendations support responsible tourism by aligning with customer-defined travel goals. Predictive analytics in travel allows booking professionals to optimize the booking process with personalized itineraries based on customer preferences and budget (Halder et al., 2024). These suggestions may range from flight and hotel options, restaurant reservations, and attraction reservations to helping customers select their ideal length-of-stay trip with confidence.

Predictive analytics can also make real-time price optimization and retargeting campaigns more effective by pinpointing how best to reach target people at just the right time with relevant messages - ultimately leading to increased revenues and brand loyalty (Inge, 2022). Predictive analytics can also be utilized to pinpoint the optimal travel experiences in any location by analyzing geolocation data. A travel company could utilize predictive analytics to personalize recommendations based on the customer's location by offering tours to landmarks and historical attractions nearby; such hyper-individualized recommendations could improve customer satisfaction as well as increase repeat bookings (Miah et al., 2017)). Prescriptive analytics is an invaluable tool that enables businesses to determine the optimal course of action. By employing predictive analytics to estimate future performance and then recommend specific actions to maximize chances of achieving desired outcomes, Prescriptive analytics enables organizations to easily pinpoint where adjustments need to be made in their pricing strategies, supply chain logistics, resource allocation, or any other area (Lepenioti et al, 2020). This process is iterative and organizations regularly evaluate its effectiveness over time. Prescriptive analytics may be utilized by making adjustments in pricing strategies, supply chain logistics, or resource allocation - or any other aspect of business operation - which makes prescriptive analytics highly useful in pinpointing optimal paths of action for success (Souza, 2014). Prescriptive analytics may make adjustments necessary in adjusting pricing strategies pricing strategies pricing strategies supply chain logistics resource allocation or any other area within an organization's operations or making adjustments across any aspect of business - making prescriptive adjustments necessary (Wang, et al., 2016).

Prescriptive analytics is an extremely powerful way of understanding customer behavior and improving travel experiences. Hotels may use prescriptive analytics to personalize offers based on individual guest preferences while companies use prescriptive analytics to find their optimal price points by taking into account average spending per customer, seasonal trends, and demand factors (Rezaei et al., 2020). Prescriptive analytics requires businesses to collect data from various sources and incorporate it into a model, which can be challenging. Therefore, businesses need the appropriate tools for data analytics that enable accurate, complete collection. Prescriptive analytics is an invaluable way to enhance travel offerings, but to use it effectively you must regularly test and monitor your efforts. By evaluating the results of decisions, you can see which approaches work effectively and which ones require refinement - ultimately increasing travel experiences while increasing revenue for business (Kandula et al., 2021).

Big data analytics is a transformative technology that enables organizations to be more agile and proactive, ultimately creating a competitive advantage in the travel and tourism industry. Organizations using this strategy can anticipate consumer trends, optimize operations and service delivery, and enhance customer satisfaction and experience for improved customer retention and loyalty (Rane, 2023). Hotels can use big data to better understand a family's needs when they check-in, such as offering rooms without mini-bars or stocking the room with amenities that meet children's age and needs like bath mats, and nightlights (Link, 1989). This personalized approach helps enhance key performance indicators like Net Promoter Score (NPS), Customer Satisfaction Score (CSAT), and Social Share of Voice (SSoV). Big data analytics can be an effective way to reduce costs and boost efficiency. An example could be hotels could utilize energy and water consumption analysis to identify areas for cost reduction (Popovič et al., 2018). Customer feedback analysis would reveal areas for enhancement and accordingly, changes could be implemented

Big data can also help enhance customer experiences across multiple touchpoints (Phillips, 2017). For instance, it could recommend nearby attractions or restaurants based on an individual's preferences and past trip history, or provide more efficient transportation through geolocation, which allows users to track their location with real-time navigation guidance (Hui et al., 2007).

Data analytics is an indispensable asset for travel companies when it comes to mitigating risks. It allows travel companies to identify risk events like natural disasters or pandemics and take measures accordingly - for instance by redirecting travelers towards safer locations or making adjustments that help ensure customers enjoy their trips without interruptions(Amankwah-Amoah & Adomako, 2019). Data analytics can also be utilized to analyze customer feedback and ratings, helping companies better identify which products or services are most popular among their target market, while improving or discontinuing underperforming ones. For instance, surveys may demonstrate that customers want stable Wi-Fi and ironing services when booking hotels - using data analysis, hotels could then offer these amenities to guests to increase both satisfaction levels and revenue streams (Lee et al., 2020). Data analytics in the travel industry also serves to forecast future consumer behavior trends. This enables travel companies to develop products or services that satisfy consumer demands while expanding market share; for example, when anticipating an upswing in beach vacation demand they can redirect marketing efforts and service offerings accordingly to take advantage of it (Tian et al., 2021). Data analytics can also assist travel companies with optimizing their operations and strengthening their marketing strategies. Analyzing flight and hotel booking data can enable airlines to streamline routes, reduce fuel usage and boost sales; while customer feedback analysis allows travel companies to enhance services and boost revenues. Data analytics is revolutionizing travel and tourism companies' products and services, helping them better understand customer needs and preferences and providing tailored, relevant experiences that build customer loyalty and encourage growth. A data-driven approach is necessary to meet consumer expectations while staying ahead in this fast-moving industry (Sigala et al., 2019). Hong, Y. et. al.(2021)considered trip mode, trip distance, and trip duration as travel behaviour dimensions, we measure the similarities of trips and group them into clusters using hierarchical clustering. Szołtysek, J., & Trzpiot, G. (2012) used cluster analysis for description similarities between respondents' perception of different alternative means of transport.

3. DATA AND UNIVARIATE ANALYSIS

In conducting the study, the researchers developed a synthetic dataset that simulates real-world travel data. The initial phase entailed outlining the dataset's schema or framework, which involved detailing the quantity of attributes (columns), the nature of each attribute (such as numerical, categorical, or textual), and any established correlations or limitations between attributes (for instance, the association between age and income level). For attributes of a numerical nature, the simulation of data was carried out by creating values in accordance with designated distributions (like normal, uniform, or binomial distributions), aligning with the anticipated distributions of these attributes in the real world.

The synthetic data contains various attributes related to customers visiting an amusement park, such as age, group size, traveler type, arrival and exit times, purchases made within the park (e.g., burgers, salads, pizza, ice cream), attraction preferences, prohibited rides, total food items purchased, stay duration, peak hours visit, and an average food item purchase per group member. It also categorizes visitors into types like child, adult, and senior.

4. RESULTS

Univariate Analysis

The univariate analysis focuses on individual features. It includes the distributions of the number of rides visited, average spending, visit duration, photo purchases, and meal preferences. These plots provide insights into the general behavior and preferences of the theme park visitors.

Figure 1. Cluster univariate graphs

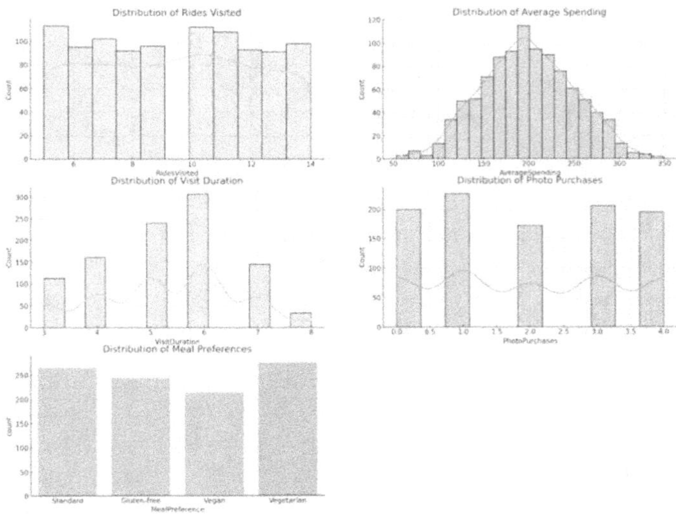

Bivariate Analysis

The bivariate analysis explores relationships between pairs of features. This includes correlations and patterns between features such as the number of rides visited, average spending, visit duration, and photo purchases. The pairplot below shows scatter plots for each pair of these features, providing a visual representation of how these characteristics relate to each other among the visitors.

Figure 2. Cluster bivariate

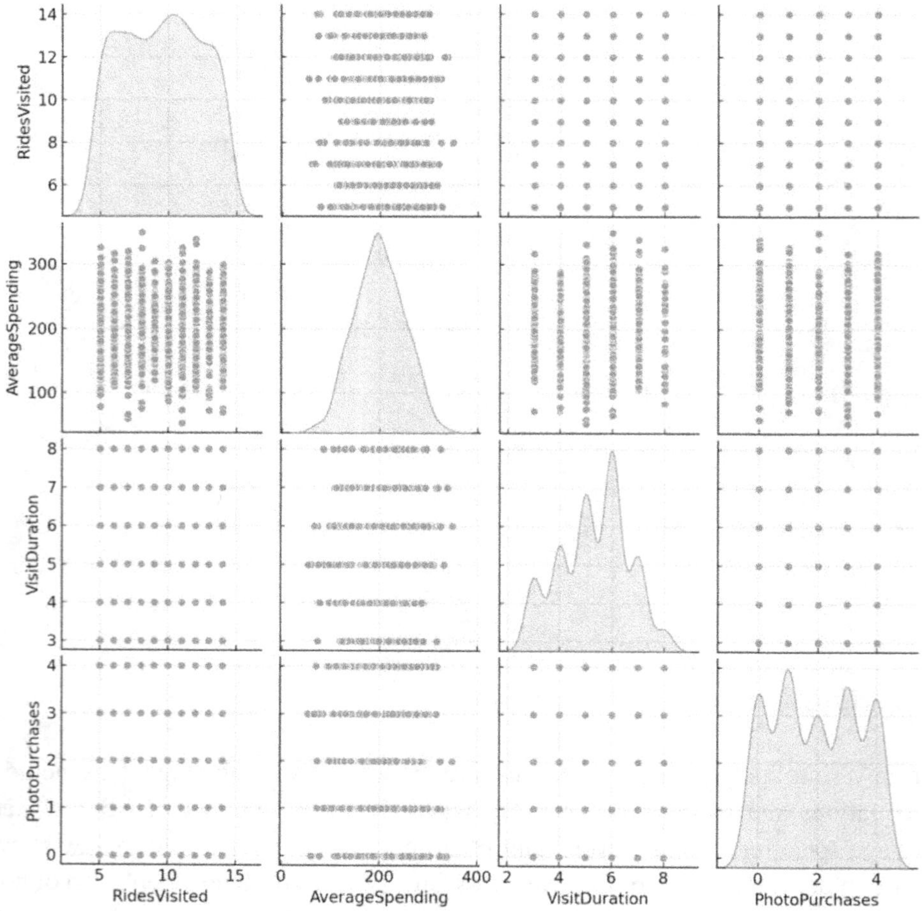

Feature Correlation Heat Map: The Heat Map below represents the correlations between different numerical features in the theme park dataset. Each cell shows the correlation coefficient between the features on the x and y axes. A correlation coefficient closer to 1 or -1 indicates a strong positive or negative correlation, respectively, while coefficients near 0 indicate a lack of correlation. This visualization helps in understanding the relationships and dependencies between various features.

Figure 3. Cluster heatmap

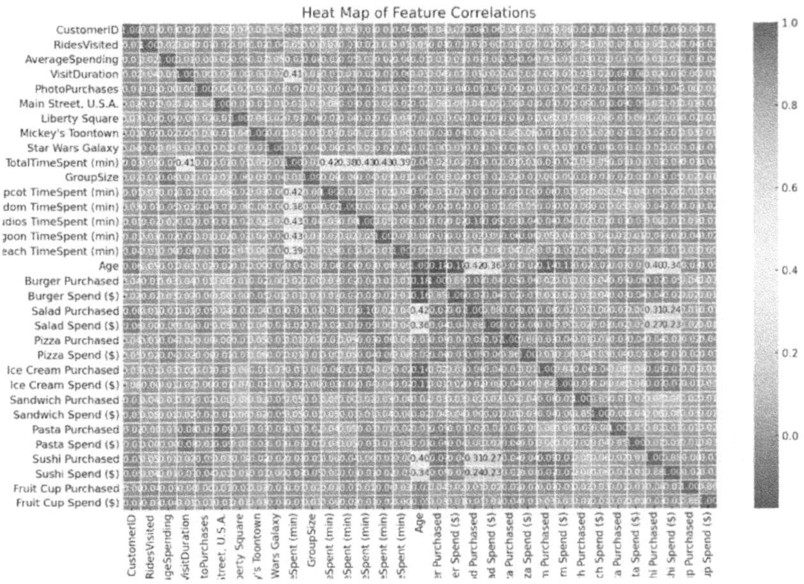

4.1 K-Means Clustering

The K-means clustering algorithm was applied to segment the visitors based on behavioral features such as rides visited, spending, visit duration, and photo purchases. An optimal number of clusters was determined using the Elbow Method, revealing distinct visitor segments within the data.

Elbow Method Analysis: The Elbow Method was used to identify the optimal number of clusters for K-means clustering. This analysis highlighted the point at which the within-cluster sum of squares (WCSS) begins to level off, indicating the most appropriate number of clusters for segmentation. The plot below displays the Elbow Method used to determine the optimal number of clusters for K-means clustering. The x-axis represents the number of clusters, and the y-axis represents the within-cluster sum of squares (WCSS). The 'elbow point' in the graph, where the rate of decrease sharply changes, suggests the optimal number of clusters. This point is chosen because adding more clusters beyond this point does not contribute significantly to the reduction of WCSS, indicating that the additional clusters are not distinct enough to provide useful segmentation.

Figure 4. Elbow method

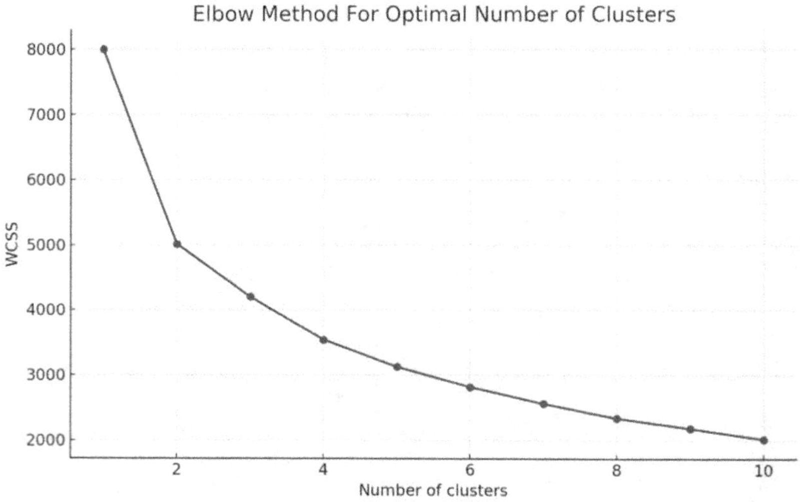

Cluster 1: Customers in this cluster visited an average of 9.5 rides, spent an average of $197.76, stayed for approximately 5.3 hours, and purchased 2.0 photos. They have no prohibitions on attractions.

Cluster 2: Customers in this cluster visited an average of 8.9 rides, spent an average of $204.35, stayed for approximately 5.1 hours, and purchased 2.1 photos. They are prohibited from 4 attractions on average.

Cluster 3: Customers in this cluster visited an average of 9.3 rides, spent an average of $208.25, stayed for approximately 5.3 hours, and purchased 1.8 photos. They are prohibited from 2 attractions on average.

Cluster Differences: Detailed analysis of the clusters revealed distinct characteristics in visitor behavior. Each cluster exhibited unique patterns in terms of rides visited, spending habits, visit duration, and photo purchases, indicating different types of visitors within the park.

The empirical analysis of the theme park data provided valuable insights into visitor behavior and preferences. The segmentation revealed through K-means clustering can assist in better understanding visitor needs and preferences. Such insights are crucial for tailoring services, enhancing visitor experiences, and optimizing operational strategies. The diverse visitor segments highlight the importance of a nuanced approach to marketing and customer service in the theme park industry.

The analysis of the three clusters reveals distinct visitor behaviors in the theme park. The visualizations below compare the clusters based on the average number of rides visited, average spending, average visit duration, and average number of photo purchases. Cluster 1 tends to have a unique pattern in terms of spending and ride visits. Cluster 2 shows a different trend in visit duration and photo purchases. Cluster 3, on the other hand, demonstrates distinct characteristics in both spending and the number of rides visited, indicating a potentially different type of visitor compared to the other two clusters. These differences could be attributed to various factors such as visitor preferences, the purpose of the visit, and demographic variations. Understanding these patterns can help in tailoring services and marketing strategies to better suit the needs of different visitor segments.

Figure 5. Cluster visulaizations

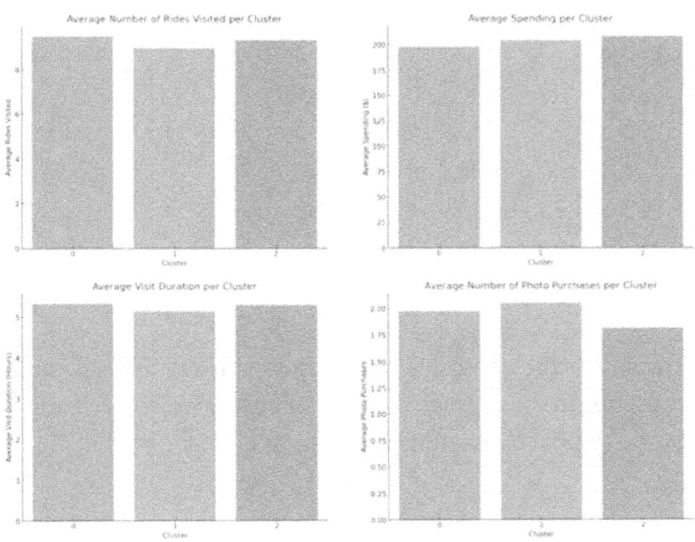

4.2 Cluster Visualization

The additional visualizations below provide a deeper understanding of the characteristics and differences of the clusters identified in the theme park data. These box plots compare the clusters based on average spending, visit duration, number of rides visited, and photo purchases. The variation within each box plot indicates the spread of data points in each cluster, offering insights into the diversity of visitor behaviors within each cluster.

Figure 6. Cluster visulaizations

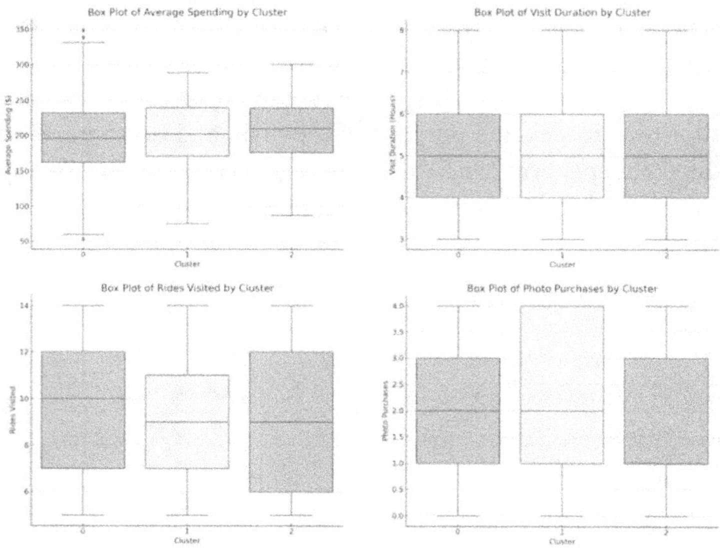

Centroids of the Clusters

The plot below shows the centroids of the three clusters in a scaled feature space. The centroids represent the average position of customers in each cluster, providing a summary of the typical characteristics of each cluster.

Figure 7. Cluster centroids

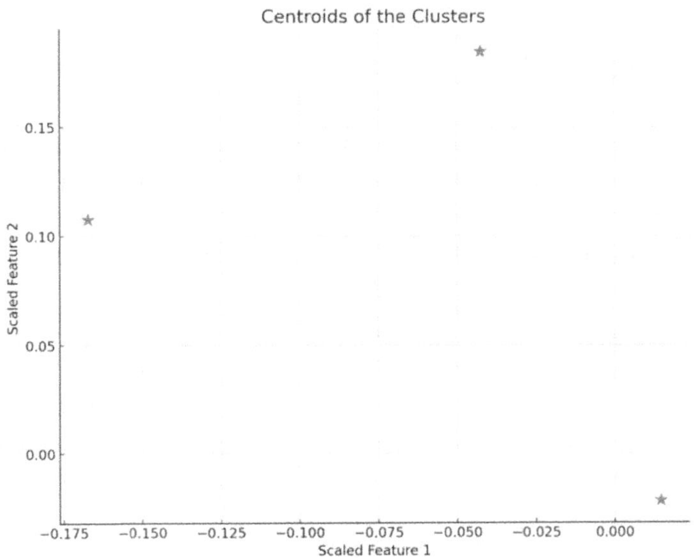

5. CONCLUSION

Analyzing travel patterns through data analytics offers insightful revelations about human preferences and behaviors, particularly in the context of amusement parks. This case study deployed data analytics to decipher diverse interactions of visitors with amusement park rides, amenities, and services. The analysis identified three distinct visitor segments. The first segment, termed "Thrill Seekers," comprises individuals predominantly engaged with high-energy rides and attractions, such as roller coasters and drop towers, indicating a penchant for excitement and novel experiences. The second segment, "Family Fun Enthusiasts," likely consists of families with children, characterized by their engagement in shows, child-friendly activities, and family-oriented themed areas, showcasing a preference for inclusive, memorable activities suitable for all ages. The third segment, "Relaxation and Experience Seekers," includes those who prefer a more leisurely pace, enjoying shows, parades, and immersive themed environments that offer relaxation, detailed theming, and opportunities for dining and shopping within the park. This clustering analysis elucidates the varied ways individuals engage with amusement parks, underscoring the importance of tailoring events to cater to the diverse preferences and needs of different visitor groups. Through data analytics, amusement parks can enhance guest satisfaction, refine park design and offerings, and ultimately increase attendance and revenue.

6. FURTHER RESEARCH

We can further expand this work by longitudinal analysis that can look into how visitor behaviors and cluster compositions change over time, taking into account things like changes in the seasons, new sites, or big events happening around the world. Also cross-cultural could be conducted to find out how visitors' cultural backgrounds affect what they like and how they behave. We can look into how adding technology (like mobile apps and virtual reality) to entertainment parks changes how people behave and whether new groups form based on how people use technology. Visitor Satisfaction and Loyalty could also be explored . how cluster membership affects overall visitor satisfaction, loyalty, and the chance that they will tell others about the park.

REFERENCES

Amankwah-Amoah, J., & Adomako, S. (2019). Big data analytics and business failures in data-Rich environments: An organizing framework. *Computers in Industry*, *105*, 204–212. doi:10.1016/j.compind.2018.12.015

Bardukova, L. (2023). Navigating the Hospitality Horizon: Current Trends and Strategies for Customer Attraction and Retention in the Hotel Industry. *Economics and Computer Science*, (2), 88-103.

Dwivedi, D., Batra, S., & Pathak, Y. K. (2023). A machine learning based approach to identify key drivers for improving corporate's esg ratings. *Journal of Law and Sustainable Development*, *11*(1), e0242. doi:10.37497/sdgs.v11i1.242

Dwivedi, D. N. (2024). The Use of Artificial Intelligence in Supply Chain Management and Logistics. In D. Sharma, B. Bhardwaj, & M. Dhiman (Eds.), *Leveraging AI and Emotional Intelligence in Contemporary Business Organizations* (pp. 306–313). IGI Global., doi:10.4018/979-8-3693-1902-4.ch018

Dwivedi, D. N., & Anand, A. (2021). The Text Mining of Public Policy Documents in Response to COVID-19: A Comparison of the United Arab Emirates and the Kingdom of Saudi Arabia. *Public Governance / Zarządzanie Publiczne, 55*(1), 8-22. doi:10.15678/ZP.2021.55.1.02

Dwivedi, D. N., & Mahanty, G. (2024). AI-Powered Employee Experience: Strategies and Best Practices. In M. Rafiq, M. Farrukh, R. Mushtaq, & O. Dastane (Eds.), *Exploring the Intersection of AI and Human Resources Management* (pp. 166–181). IGI Global. doi:10.4018/979-8-3693-0039-8.ch009

Dwivedi, D. N., Mahanty, G., & Pathak, Y. K. (2023). AI Applications for Financial Risk Management. In M. Irfan, M. Elmogy, M. Shabri Abd. Majid, & S. El-Sappagh (Eds.), The Impact of AI Innovation on Financial Sectors in the Era of Industry 5.0 (pp. 17-31). IGI Global. doi:10.4018/979-8-3693-0082-4.ch002

Dwivedi, D. N., Mahanty, G., & Vemareddy, A. (2022). How Responsible Is AI?: Identification of Key Public Concerns Using Sentiment Analysis and Topic Modeling. *International Journal of Information Retrieval Research*, *12*(1), 1–14. doi:10.4018/IJIRR.298646

Dwivedi, D. N., Pandey, A. K., & Dwivedi, A. D. (2023). Examining the emotional tone in politically polarized Speeches in India: An In-Depth analysis of two contrasting perspectives. *South India Journal of Social Sciences*, 21(2), 125-136. https://journal.sijss.com/index.php/home/article/view/65

Dwivedi, D. N., Tadoori, G., & Batra, S. (2023). Impact of women leadership and ESG ratings and in organizations: A time series segmentation study. *Academy of Strategic Management Journal*, *22*(S3), 1–6.

Gupta, S., Drave, V. A., Dwivedi, Y. K., Baabdullah, A. M., & Ismagilova, E. (2020). Achieving superior organizational performance via big data predictive analytics: A dynamic capability view. *Industrial Marketing Management*, *90*, 581–592. doi:10.1016/j.indmarman.2019.11.009

Halder, S., Lim, K. H., Chan, J., & Zhang, X. (2024). A survey on personalized itinerary recommendation: From optimisation to deep learning. *Applied Soft Computing*, *152*, 111200. doi:10.1016/j.asoc.2023.111200

Hong, Y., Xin, Y., Martin, H., Bucher, D., & Raubal, M. (2021). A clustering-based framework for individual travel behaviour change detection. In *11th International Conference on Geographic Information Science (GIScience 2021)-Part II* (Vol. 208, p. 4). Schloss Dagstuhl-Leibniz-Zentrum für Informatik.

Hui, T. K., Wan, D., & Ho, A. (2007). Tourists' satisfaction, recommendation and revisiting Singapore. *Tourism Management*, *28*(4), 965–975. doi:10.1016/j.tourman.2006.08.008

Inge, C. (2022). *Marketing metrics: leverage analytics and data to optimize marketing strategies*. Kogan Page Publishers.

Kandula, S., Krishnamoorthy, S., & Roy, D. (2021). A prescriptive analytics framework for efficient E-commerce order delivery. *Decision Support Systems*, *147*, 113584. doi:10.1016/j.dss.2021.113584

Lee, C. K. H., Tse, Y. K., Zhang, M., & Ma, J. (2020). Analysing online reviews to investigate customer behaviour in the sharing economy: The case of Airbnb. *Information Technology & People*, *33*(3), 945–961. doi:10.1108/ITP-10-2018-0475

Lepenioti, K., Bousdekis, A., Apostolou, D., & Mentzas, G. (2020). Prescriptive analytics: Literature review and research challenges. *International Journal of Information Management*, *50*, 57–70. doi:10.1016/j.ijinfomgt.2019.04.003

Link, C. K. (1989). Internal merchandising: Creating revenue opportunities. *The Cornell Hotel and Restaurant Administration Quarterly*, *30*(3), 48–57. doi:10.1177/001088048903000316

Mahanty, G., Dwivedi, D. N., & Gopalakrishnan, B. N. (2021). The Efficacy of Fiscal Vs Monetary Policies in the Asia-Pacific Region: The St. Louis Equation Revisited. *Vision (Basel)*, (November). Advance online publication. doi:10.1177/09722629211054148

Mascarenhas, O. A., Kesavan, R., & Bernacchi, M. (2006). Lasting customer loyalty: A total customer experience approach. *Journal of Consumer Marketing*, *23*(7), 397–405. doi:10.1108/07363760610712939

Miah, S. J., Vu, H. Q., Gammack, J., & McGrath, M. (2017). A big data analytics method for tourist behaviour analysis. *Information & Management*, *54*(6), 771–785. doi:10.1016/j.im.2016.11.011

Patil, V., Padale, T., Waghmare, G., & Kulkarni, D. (2021). A study on understanding future of Artificial Intelligence in the various functions of marketing. *Turkish Online Journal of Qualitative Inquiry, 12*(6).

Phillips, P., Barnes, S., Zigan, K., & Schegg, R. (2017). Understanding the impact of online reviews on hotel performance: An empirical analysis. *Journal of Travel Research*, *56*(2), 235–249. doi:10.1177/0047287516636481

Popovič, A., Hackney, R., Tassabehji, R., & Castelli, M. (2018). The impact of big data analytics on firms' high value business performance. *Information Systems Frontiers*, *20*(2), 209–222. doi:10.1007/s10796-016-9720-4

Pozzi, F. A., & Dwivedi, D. (2023). ESG and IoT: Ensuring Sustainability and Social Responsibility in the Digital Age. In S. Tiwari, F. Ortiz-Rodríguez, S. Mishra, E. Vakaj, & K. Kotecha (Eds.), *Artificial Intelligence: Towards Sustainable Intelligence. AI4S 2023. Communications in Computer and Information Science* (Vol. 1907). Springer. doi:10.1007/978-3-031-47997-7_2

Rane, N. (2023). Enhancing customer loyalty through Artificial Intelligence (AI), Internet of Things (IoT), and Big Data technologies: improving customer satisfaction, engagement, relationship, and experience. *Internet of Things (IoT), and Big Data Technologies: Improving Customer Satisfaction, Engagement, Relationship, and Experience.*

Respatyanti, Y. R. (2019). *Enhancing the Information Availability of Indonesia's Tourism Destinations Through A Travel App*. Academic Press.

Rezaei, F., Raeesi Vanani, I., Jafari, A., & Kakavand, S. (2022). Identification of Influential Factors and Improvement of Hotel Online User-Generated Scores: A Prescriptive Analytics Approach. *Journal of Quality Assurance in Hospitality & Tourism*, 1–40. doi:10.1080/1528008X.2022.2146620

Sigala, M., Rahimi, R., & Thelwall, M. (2019). Big data and innovation in tourism, travel, and hospitality. *Culinary Science & Hospitality Research*, *23*(6), 1–11.

Smith, R., & Hawkins, B. (2004). *Lean maintenance: reduce costs, improve quality, and increase market share*. Elsevier.

Song, H., & Liu, H. (2017). Predicting tourist demand using big data. *Analytics in smart tourism design: Concepts and methods*, 13-29.

Souza, G. C. (2014). Supply chain analytics. *Business Horizons*, *57*(5), 595–605. doi:10.1016/j.bushor.2014.06.004

Szołtysek, J., & Trzpiot, G. (2012). Cluster Analysis in Description of Travel Behaviours. *Zeszyty Naukowe Politechniki Częstochowskiej*, 75.

Tian, H., Presa-Reyes, M., Tao, Y., Wang, T., Pouyanfar, S., Miguel, A., ... Iyengar, S. S. (2021). Data analytics for air travel data: A survey and new perspectives. *ACM Computing Surveys*, *54*(8), 1–35.

Tsaih, R. H., & Hsu, C. C. (2018). *Artificial intelligence in smart tourism: A conceptual framework*. Academic Press.

Wang, G., Gunasekaran, A., Ngai, E. W., & Papadopoulos, T. (2016). Big data analytics in logistics and supply chain management: Certain investigations for research and applications. *International Journal of Production Economics*, *176*, 98–110. doi:10.1016/j.ijpe.2016.03.014

Ziska Fields, . (Ed.). (2023). *Human Creativity vs. Machine Creativity: Innovations and Challenges. In Multidisciplinary Approaches in AI, Creativity, Innovation, and Green Collaboration* (pp. 19–28). Global. doi:10.4018/978-1-6684-6366-6.ch002

Chapter 9
Techniques and Tools for Big Data Analytics in the Tourism Sector

Bhupender Dighliya
Starex University, India

ABSTRACT

In an era marked by unprecedented digitalization and global connectivity, the tourism industry generates vast amounts of data that, when harnessed effectively, can revolutionize decision-making processes and enhance customer experiences. The chapter delves into innovative techniques and tools employed in the realm of big data analytics to extract meaningful insights from the vast and diverse datasets inherent in the tourism domain. The discussion encompasses a comprehensive overview of cutting-edge analytics methodologies, including machine learning algorithms, predictive modeling, and sentiment analysis, tailored to address the unique challenges and opportunities within the tourism sector. The exploration of real-world case studies illustrates the practical application of these techniques, showcasing their efficacy in optimizing resource allocation, predicting travel trends, and personalizing customer interactions.

INTRODUCTION

In our contemporary, fully digitized society, individuals engage with a myriad of technological tools daily, participating in activities such as communication, online purchases, and the sharing of thoughts, images, and experiences. This constant interaction generates vast amounts of exploitable data (Li et al., 2020). Devices

DOI: 10.4018/979-8-3693-3310-5.ch009

like sensors, cameras, computers, mobile phones, and GPS tracking systems seamlessly integrated into daily life contribute to the continuous production and transmission of data through internet technology. Consequently, businesses now have unprecedented access to millions of zettabytes of real-time data encompassing customers, suppliers, business operations, and competitors. The sheer volume of this data, accumulating rapidly and often lacking a specific structure or homogeneity, characterizes the phenomenon widely recognized as "Big Data," (De Mauro et al., 2015). This evolving landscape underscores the transformative power and challenges associated with harnessing and interpreting the immense reservoir of information available in the digital era.

In the realm of tourism, akin to numerous other industries, the role of big data is pivotal in facilitating precise decision-making. Primarily, it plays a crucial part in activities such as forecasting customer demand, tailoring services to individual preferences, optimizing travel marketing endeavors, and refining pricing strategies.

The integration of big data often goes hand in hand with artificial intelligence and machine learning, empowering analytics departments to automatically discern patterns within extensive sets of unstructured data. This synergy enables, for instance, the identification of specific hotel attributes that significantly influence user satisfaction or the prediction of a customer's preferred travel destinations based on their historical trip data. The amalgamation of these technologies contributes significantly to the automation of insights and enhances the industry's ability to make informed decisions in real-time.

Irrespective of the nature or scale of operations within the tourism industry, the application of Big Data analysis emerges as a readily accessible means to gain deeper insights into the preferences and requirements of visitors and tourists (Li et al., 2018). Given the inherently anthropocentric nature of the industry, where businesses are centered around human experiences, the meticulous monitoring and profound interpretation of the digital footprints left by tourists—both before, during, and after their travel—prove invaluable. This analytical approach serves to guide and augment business strategies, aiding in the creation and delivery of superior services that align with tourists' needs and ultimately contribute to enhanced profitability, as emphasized by Chareyron et al. (2014). In essence, leveraging Big Data facilitates informed decision-making and optimization of offerings, fostering a symbiotic relationship between the tourism industry and the evolving expectations of its clientele.

The amalgamation of advanced analytics techniques and powerful tools has become instrumental in unraveling valuable patterns, trends, and correlations within vast datasets inherent to the tourism sector. This paper delves into the multifaceted realm of "Techniques and Tools for Big Data Analytics in the Tourism Sector," exploring innovative techniques and tools employed in the realm of big data analytics to extract meaningful insights from the vast and diverse datasets inherent in the tourism domain.

BACKGROUND OF THE CHAPTER

The term "big data" encompasses extensive datasets, comprising both structured and unstructured data types that are generated, recorded, and stored. It also refers to large and intricate datasets challenging to process using conventional software applications and statistical methods within a reasonable timeframe (Snijders et al., 2012; Hassani & Silva, 2015).

Despite the absence of a unified definition, researchers offer various interpretations. Laney (2001) introduced a "3V's" model, defining big data based on volume, variety, and velocity. Volume pertains to the quantity of generated and collected data, often measured in orders of magnitude like gigabytes, terabytes, or zettabytes, and encompasses observed variables. Velocity signifies the rapid analysis timing aimed at maximizing the commercial value of big data, while variety encompasses diverse data types (e.g., audio, video, text data) alongside traditional structured data. It is important to note that the internet is just one data source; other sources include communication systems (e.g., smart mobile device data, social media posts), business processes (e.g., flight booking systems), and sensors (e.g., satellite images, scanner data, geographic information systems data). The "3V's" - volume, veracity, and variety - predominantly align with an Information and Technology (IT) perspective (Laney, 2001).

The tourism sector leverages online platforms and social media to offer diverse services aimed at enriching the overall tourist experience (Sharma et al., 2021; Kitsios et al., 2022). Within this context, Big Data Analytics (BDA) emerges as a transformative technology, exerting a notable influence on the tourism industry (Li et al., 2018; Samara et al., 2020). A range of techniques and tools have been proposed for big data analytics in the tourism sector. Sinha (2017) introduces a unified IT infrastructure framework, tAdvisor, for effective data analytics, while Li (2019) reviews text mining techniques for tourism big data, including text representation, NLP, and sentiment analysis. Cassavia (2015) discusses the use of dynamic big data searching to improve the tourist experience, and Miah (2017) presents a method for analyzing social media-generated big data to support strategic decision-making in tourism destination management.

In their study, Kurashima et al. (2013) employed the sequential information embedded in tourists' geotagged photos to discern and suggest personalized travel routes based on individual interests and available time. Shi et al. [60] utilized geotagged photos sourced from Flickr to offer personalized recommendations for landmarks, tailoring suggestions to users' specific preferences rather than relying solely on the popularity of attractions. Similarly, Khotimah et al. (2014) introduced a Tourism Recommendation System (TRS) that drew data from diverse social media platforms in Indonesia. This innovative approach aimed to address the sparsity issue arising from infrequent user posts and the static nature of information in conventional TRS. By leveraging information gleaned from social media, their TRS provided user-specific recommendations, enhancing its adaptability to individual preferences and circumventing the limitations associated with traditional recommendation systems. Mehmetoglu (2007) endeavored to pinpoint widely favored tourist activities to inform the development of management strategies. Zbuchea (2012) scrutinized cultural pursuits among tourists, encompassing visits to parks, heritage sites, museums, and theaters, while Zillinger (2008) concentrated on the aspect of shopping activities. This valuable information serves destination marketing efforts, enabling more effective planning of services such as transportation to align with the specific preferences and requirements of tourists.

MAIN FOCUS OF THE CHAPTER

In the contemporary landscape of the global tourism industry, the advent of Big Data has ushered in a transformative era, offering unprecedented opportunities for data-driven insights, strategic decision-making, and enhanced customer experiences. The amalgamation of advanced analytics techniques and powerful tools has become instrumental in unraveling valuable patterns, trends, and correlations within vast datasets inherent to the tourism sector. This paper delves into the multifaceted realm of "Techniques and Tools for Big Data Analytics in the Tourism Sector," exploring the pivotal role of cutting-edge methodologies and technologies in harnessing the immense potential of data to revolutionize how the industry operates. From optimizing operational efficiency and resource allocation to refining marketing strategies and understanding traveler behavior, this exploration aims to provide a comprehensive overview of the dynamic landscape where big data analytics intersects with the intricate tapestry of global tourism. As we navigate through the intricate web of data analytics applications, we uncover the transformative impact on various facets of the tourism sector, shedding light on the tools and techniques that serve as the bedrock for informed decision-making and sustainable growth in this ever-evolving industry.

KEY DATA SOURCE IN TOURISM

Social Media Data and Sentiment Analysis

Social media platforms, such as Facebook, Instagram, Twitter, and travel-specific networks like TripAdvisor, generate vast amounts of user-generated content. This includes posts, comments, reviews, and multimedia shared by travelers. Social media data provides real-time insights into current travel trends, popular destinations, and the sentiments associated with specific services or locations. Sentiment analysis involves evaluating this content to gauge the emotional tone, opinions, and sentiments expressed by users regarding their travel experiences. Analyzing sentiments aids businesses in understanding customer perceptions, enabling them to adapt and improve their offerings.

Transactional Data from Booking Platforms

Transactional data from booking platforms, such as Expedia, Booking.com, or airline websites, contains information about reservations, purchases, and travel itineraries. This data includes details like travel dates, accommodation preferences, and selected services. Analysis of transactional data allows businesses to understand booking patterns, peak seasons, and customer preferences. It helps in optimizing pricing strategies, managing inventory effectively, and tailoring promotions to meet the demands of specific customer segments.

Geospatial Data and Location Analytics

Geospatial data involves information related to the geographical location of tourists and the places they visit. This data is often collected through GPS devices, mobile phones, or location-based services. Location analytics enables businesses to visualize and analyze the movement patterns of tourists. It aids in identifying popular tourist routes, optimizing transportation services, and assessing the impact of geographic factors on travel behavior.

Customer Reviews and Feedback

Customer reviews and feedback, available on platforms like TripAdvisor, Yelp, and Google Reviews, provide qualitative insights into the experiences of travelers. This includes opinions on accommodations, attractions, and overall satisfaction. Analyzing customer reviews helps businesses gauge the strengths and weaknesses of their offerings. It informs decision-making processes related to service improvements, marketing strategies, and reputation management.

Techniques for Analyzing Tourism Data

Analyzing tourism data involves employing various techniques to extract valuable insights and make informed decisions within the industry. Some key techniques include:

Descriptive Analytics

Descriptive analytics is applicable to both real-time and historical customer data to discern patterns, trends, and key insights related to tourism. It provides a retrospective view, summarizing and interpreting past occurrences without delving into causation or future predictions. This technique is crucial for understanding how tourism patterns have evolved over time. It aids in identifying peak seasons, popular destinations, and changing consumer preferences. Decision-makers can use these insights to inform strategic planning, marketing efforts, and resource allocation. This form of analytics also proves beneficial for cost reduction, such as the strategic promotion of last-minute discounted tours. Moreover, it enhances the precision of forecasting, allowing businesses to project outcomes, such as achieving 80% of full-price sales or securing 50% of early booking sales.

This technique utilizing statistical measures, charts, and graphs, descriptive analytics helps visualize and quantify historical tourism data. Common techniques include aggregating data, calculating averages, and creating visual representations like histograms or time-series plots. For example, analyzing historical visitation data for a tourist destination to identify recurring trends in visitor numbers, popular attractions during specific seasons, and the impact of external events on tourism patterns.

Predictive Analytics

Predictive analytics involves utilizing statistical algorithms, machine learning models, and data analysis to forecast future trends and outcomes based on historical and current data. In the context of tourism, predictive analytics is applied to anticipate and understand the demand for travel-related services and products. It is crucial for businesses in the tourism sector to optimize resource allocation, pricing strategies, and marketing efforts based on historical data and current market trends. It enables proactive decision-making, allowing businesses to adapt to fluctuations in demand and capitalize on emerging trends.

Moreover, predictive analytics aids in dynamic pricing models, allowing hotels, airlines, and other service providers to adjust prices in real-time based on factors such as demand, seasonality, and market conditions. This not only ensures competitive pricing but also maximizes revenue and occupancy rates.

By harnessing the power of predictive analytics, the tourism industry can proactively adapt to changing circumstances, improve resource allocation, and deliver more personalized and satisfying experiences for tourists. This strategic use of data-driven insights positions businesses and destinations to thrive in a competitive market by staying ahead of trends and meeting the evolving expectations of travelers.

Prescriptive Analytics

Prescriptive analytics involves the use of advanced analytics and algorithms to recommend optimal courses of action for decision-makers. In the context of tourism, prescriptive analytics aims to provide actionable insights that guide businesses and destinations toward making informed decisions to maximize efficiency and achieve strategic goals. By leveraging data from various sources, prescriptive analytics evaluates multiple decision options, considering potential outcomes and their associated impacts. It goes beyond predicting future trends (predictive analytics) by recommending specific actions to capitalize on opportunities or mitigate challenges.

Tourism stakeholders can benefit from prescriptive analytics in several ways, such as optimizing pricing strategies, resource allocation, and marketing campaigns. The technology assists in dynamically adjusting plans based on real-time data, ensuring adaptability to changing market conditions and enhancing overall decision-making processes. Through prescriptive analytics, the tourism industry can proactively address challenges, improve operational efficiency, and deliver enhanced experiences for visitors. Ultimately, prescriptive analytics empowers decision-makers to navigate the complexities of the tourism landscape, fostering innovation and sustainable growth in the industry.

Machine Learning Algorithms

Machine learning algorithms play a pivotal role in tourism analysis, providing valuable insights and enhancing decision-making processes within the industry. Various algorithms are employed to analyze vast datasets and extract patterns, trends, and predictions.

One significant application of machine learning in tourism is in demand forecasting. Algorithms like time series models, regression analysis, and ensemble methods can predict future tourist arrivals based on historical data, helping businesses and destinations optimize resource allocation, plan for peak seasons, and improve overall efficiency.

Recommendation systems powered by machine learning are another crucial aspect of tourism analysis. Collaborative filtering and content-based recommendation algorithms are employed to personalize suggestions for travelers, enhancing their experience by offering tailored recommendations for accommodations, activities, and attractions.

Clustering algorithms help segment tourists based on preferences, behavior, or demographics. By understanding distinct customer segments, businesses can target their marketing strategies more effectively and customize services to meet specific needs.

Natural Language Processing (NLP) algorithms are employed to analyze customer reviews, social media comments, and feedback. Sentiment analysis, a subset of NLP, allows businesses to gauge customer satisfaction, identify areas for improvement, and adapt their offerings accordingly.

Machine learning also supports fraud detection in online bookings and transactions, ensuring the security of both businesses and travelers. Additionally, algorithms like reinforcement learning can optimize pricing strategies dynamically, considering various factors such as demand, seasonality, and competitor pricing.

Tools for Big Data Analytics in Tourism

Big Data Analytics plays a crucial role in the tourism industry, offering valuable insights to enhance decision-making, optimize operations, and improve the overall customer experience. Various powerful tools are employed to analyze and derive meaningful patterns from vast datasets. Here is an introduction to some popular Big Data Analytics tools commonly used in the field of tourism:

Hadoop

Hadoop, a Java-based open-source platform, serves as a robust framework for storing and processing extensive datasets. Operating on a cluster system, it efficiently processes data in parallel, accommodating both structured and unstructured data across single servers and multiple computers. With cross-platform support, Hadoop stands out as a leading big data analytics tool, favored by major tech entities including Amazon, Microsoft, IBM, and others. Its versatility and scalability make it a go-to solution for organizations dealing with the complexities of big data, ensuring efficient data management and analytics at a large scale.

Apache Spark

Spark is a fast and general-purpose cluster computing system that supports in-memory processing. Utilizing distributed tools, this platform processes data across multiple computers seamlessly. It is often utilized for large-scale data processing and analytics in tourism, providing efficient data processing capabilities and supporting various programming languages. Embraced by data analysts, it boasts user-friendly APIs facilitating straightforward data retrieval. Impressively, it handles multi-petabytes of data efficiently. Spark recently achieved a significant milestone by processing 100 terabytes of data in just 23 minutes, surpassing the prior world record held by Hadoop, which took 71 minutes. This underscores Spark's prowess in rapid and scalable data processing, making it a favored choice for those seeking advanced analytics capabilities on large datasets.

Apache Flink

Flink is a stream processing framework for big data processing and analytics. It is suitable for real-time data analysis, making it valuable in scenarios where tourism businesses need to respond swiftly to changing conditions, such as fluctuating demand.

Tableau

Tableau is a popular data visualization tool that enables tourism professionals to create interactive and shareable dashboards. It helps in visually exploring and understanding data trends, making it an essential tool for data-driven decision-making and communication.

Apache Hive

Hive is a data warehousing and SQL-like query language built on top of Hadoop. It allows tourism analysts to query and analyze large datasets using familiar SQL syntax, simplifying data processing tasks.

R and Python

R and Python are versatile programming languages with extensive libraries for statistical analysis and machine learning. Data scientists in tourism often use these languages for developing predictive models, clustering, and other advanced analytics tasks.

Qubole

Qubole is an open-source big data tool facilitating a seamless data value chain through ad-hoc analysis and machine learning. Functioning as a data lake platform, Qubole streamlines end-to-end services, minimizing the time and effort needed for data pipeline operations. Its versatility extends to configuring multi-cloud services like AWS, Azure, and Google Cloud, offering flexibility to users. Additionally, Qubole contributes to significant cost savings in cloud computing, reducing expenses by up to 50%. Qubole stands out as an efficient solution for managing big data workflows, promoting ease of use, and optimizing cloud computing expenditures in tourism.

Google Analytics

Google Analytics is a widely used web analytics service that helps tourism businesses track website traffic, user interactions, and engagement. It provides valuable insights into online user behavior, aiding in the optimization of digital marketing strategies.

IBM SPSS Statistics

SPSS Statistics is a statistical software package widely used for data analysis in tourism. It facilitates descriptive statistics, predictive analytics, and advanced data exploration, helping tourism researchers gain meaningful insights from their datasets.

These tools empower tourism professionals to harness the potential of big data, enabling them to make informed decisions, tailor services to customer needs, and stay competitive in the rapidly evolving tourism landscape. The choice of tools often depends on specific business requirements, the complexity of analytical tasks, and the expertise of the analytics team.

Practical Instances of Applying Data Science in the Tourism Sector

The tourism sector extensively depends on social media platforms and online review sites for engaging with customers. Through the utilization of big data analytics, businesses can actively track these channels, assess customer sentiment, recognize emerging trends, and promptly attend to customer grievances. Conducting sentiment analysis enables companies to gain a deeper understanding of customer feedback, facilitating adjustments to marketing and service strategies for improved customer satisfaction. Several successful case studies demonstrate the impactful application of big data analysis in the tourism industry:

Indian Railway: As per the India Brand Equity Foundation (IBEF) report, India boasts the world's fourth-largest railway network, hosting 22,593 trains and accommodating approximately 24 million daily passengers. Recognized as a global giant in rail systems, the Indian Railways introduced the IRCTC e-ticketing app in 2014 for streamlined ticket booking. With millions of user accounts, housing comprehensive traveler data, including demographics and travel preferences, the railway ministry efficiently manages and tracks this vast information using the Oracle database. This strategic use of Oracle's server management facilitates data storage, tracking, and analysis, empowering the railways to make informed decisions, develop new packages, and enhance services. Simultaneously, travel agencies like Veena World, Kesari Tours, and online platforms like Yatra leverage big data analytics for operational efficiency, creating a growing demand for such technologies in the tourism industry.

United State Airlines

Throughout the year, individuals travel to the United States for various reasons such as job opportunities, tourism, and education, relying extensively on online applications. The high demand for airlines in the United States, catering to a global audience, results in the generation of massive datasets. Consequently, the airline industry leverages big data analytics extensively to glean insights from consumer data and perform various tasks. For instance, Southwest Airlines utilizes big data analytics not only to enhance customer service but also for intelligent maintenance. Analyzing fuel efficiency reports, airplane health management systems, and flight metrics helps identify defects across the entire fleet, reducing repair costs and ensuring safe flights. This application of big data analytics extends across various sectors in the United States, enhancing the overall efficiency of services.

Venice and Salzburg

Venice and Salzburg stand as exemplary models of smart tourism destinations. This concept represents a novel approach to destinations, emphasizing heavy reliance on technology to boost competitiveness, support tourism development initiatives, and elevate overall tourism experiences. Smart tourism destinations actively advocate for the utilization of technology and the collection of consumer data, allowing them to refine and tailor their offerings, providing tourists with delightful and personalized experiences.

Fareboom

Fareboom, a renowned online travel agency, achieved success through the implementation of its fare predictor tool. As one of the world's leading travel agencies, Fareboom recognized the potential of leveraging big data and analytics to enhance its booking platform and provide compelling prices for users. The fare predictor tool employs a self-learning algorithm, meticulously analyzing millions of fare search records from various websites. This sophisticated algorithm factors in elements such as demand fluctuations and seasonal trends, enabling it to accurately predict future price movements and offer users a more informed and advantageous booking experience.

Booking.com

Booking.com, a globally renowned travel marketplace, stands as a prime example of effective data analytics implementation, utilizing it comprehensively across all its departments to facilitate timely and informed decision-making. The company harnesses data analytics in various facets including web marketing, attribution models, ROI predictions, recommendation systems, call volume predictions, and scheduling algorithms. This broad application of data analytics underscores Booking.com's commitment to leveraging data-driven insights to enhance multiple aspects of its operations and services.

Qantas Airlines

Qantas utilized big data analytics to enhance its schedule recovery process, ensuring an optimal transportation experience for consumers. The airline made an investment in a schedule recovery solution that leverages real-time data analytics to offer immediate insights. This enabled Qantas to comprehensively evaluate operational costs, minimize the frequency and duration of delays, and substantially decrease the expenses associated with managing flight disruptions. Whether caused by weather conditions, high traffic volumes, or unforeseen operational delays, the implementation of big data analytics allowed Qantas to address these challenges effectively, resulting in improved operational efficiency and enhanced customer satisfaction.

Challenges in Implementing Big Data Analytics in Tourism

Implementing Big Data Analytics in the tourism industry brings about various challenges, stemming from the unique characteristics of the sector and the complexities associated with handling large volumes of data. Some of the key challenges include:

Data Quality and Integration: Tourism data often comes from diverse sources, including booking systems, social media, and customer reviews. Ensuring data quality and integrating information from various channels can be challenging due to inconsistencies, errors, and differing formats.

Privacy Concerns: Tourism involves the collection of vast amounts of personal information. Ensuring compliance with data protection regulations and addressing privacy concerns is critical. Striking a balance between personalization and respecting privacy is a challenge in implementing Big Data Analytics.

Scalability and Infrastructure: The sheer volume of data generated in the tourism industry requires robust and scalable infrastructure. Establishing and maintaining the necessary hardware, software, and cloud resources to handle large datasets can be resource-intensive.

Skill Shortage: There is a shortage of skilled professionals with expertise in both tourism and Big Data Analytics. Integrating domain knowledge with technical skills is crucial for effective analysis and interpretation of tourism data.

Real-time Processing: Tourism data often requires real-time analysis to respond swiftly to changing conditions, such as sudden shifts in demand or emergencies. Implementing real-time processing capabilities can be challenging, requiring advanced technologies and infrastructure.

Security Issues: With the increase in cyber threats, securing large datasets is a major concern. Ensuring the confidentiality, integrity, and availability of data throughout the analytics process is essential to prevent unauthorized access and data breaches.

Costs and Return on Investment (ROI): Implementing Big Data Analytics systems can be costly, from infrastructure setup to hiring skilled professionals. Ensuring a positive return on investment requires careful planning and effective utilization of insights generated from analytics.

Data Governance and Compliance: Establishing robust data governance practices and ensuring compliance with industry regulations and standards is crucial. Failure to adhere to these standards can result in legal issues and reputational damage.

Cultural Resistance: Encountering resistance from employees or stakeholders who are not familiar with or resistant to changes introduced by Big Data Analytics can hinder successful implementation. Overcoming this resistance requires effective communication and training programs.

Interoperability: Tourism organizations often use a variety of systems and platforms. Ensuring interoperability and seamless integration between these systems is a challenge when implementing comprehensive Big Data Analytics solutions.

Recommendations and Future Research Directions

The integration of big data analytics into the tourism sector represents a transformative journey, offering unprecedented opportunities for businesses to innovate, optimize, and elevate the overall travel experience. The recommendations and future research directions outlined provide a roadmap for further advancements in this dynamic intersection of technology and tourism.

The call for integrating advanced machine learning techniques acknowledges the evolving landscape of analytics. By exploring algorithms like deep learning and reinforcement learning, the tourism industry can unlock new dimensions of predictive modeling, personalized recommendations, and sentiment analysis, enhancing the precision and relevance of insights derived from massive datasets. Real-time analytics emerges as a critical necessity, aligning with the fast-paced nature of the tourism sector. Tools that facilitate dynamic decision-making by offering real-time insights empower businesses to adapt swiftly to changing conditions and provide seamless experiences for travelers.

Privacy concerns loom large in the era of data analytics. Future research emphasizing enhanced privacy-preserving techniques ensures that as businesses glean valuable insights from customer data, they do so responsibly and in compliance with evolving data protection standards. Blockchain technology, with its promise of secure and transparent data management, stands as a beacon for ensuring the integrity of information in the tourism analytics ecosystem. Research in this domain can explore the potential of blockchain in fortifying data security and fostering trust among stakeholders. The pursuit of personalization and customer experience optimization reflects the industry's commitment to tailoring services to individual preferences. As researchers delve into understanding nuanced customer behavior, future tools are poised to offer more refined and individualized recommendations, fostering stronger connections between businesses and travelers.

Interdisciplinary collaboration emerges as a strategic imperative, recognizing that the marriage of data science expertise with domain-specific knowledge in tourism yields solutions that are both technically sound and contextually relevant. By fostering collaborative efforts, the tourism industry can unlock synergies that drive innovation and address industry-specific challenges effectively. Moreover, an emphasis on usability and accessibility ensures that the benefits of big data analytics permeate through various tiers of the tourism ecosystem, making these tools accessible and impactful for businesses of all scales. Finally, ethical considerations and responsible AI usage underscore the need for a conscious approach to technology adoption. As big data analytics continues to shape the future of tourism, a commitment to ethical standards, transparency, and fairness becomes imperative, ensuring that these innovations align with societal values and contribute positively to the industry's sustainable growth.

In essence, the recommendations and future research directions pave the way for a future where big data analytics in the tourism sector evolves into a beacon of innovation, efficiency, and responsible data stewardship. Through continued exploration and collaboration, the industry stands poised to harness the full potential of data analytics, offering transformative benefits for businesses, travelers, and the tourism ecosystem as a whole.

CONCLUSION

In conclusion, the intersection of big data analytics and the tourism sector holds immense promise for transformative advancements in decision-making processes and customer experiences. This chapter has provided a comprehensive exploration of innovative techniques and tools utilized in big data analytics within the tourism domain. The dynamic landscape of the tourism industry, characterized by vast and diverse datasets, presents both challenges and opportunities that necessitate sophisticated analytics methodologies.

The discussion has covered cutting-edge approaches such as machine learning algorithms, predictive modeling, and sentiment analysis, tailored to address the unique demands of the tourism sector. Real-world case studies, featuring successful implementations by companies like Indian Railways, Qantas Airlines, and Booking.com, serve as compelling examples of how these techniques can optimize resource allocation, predict travel trends, and enhance customer interactions. Furthermore, the evolution of technology-driven tools, including data visualization platforms, Hadoop, spark, flank, hive and scalable databases, has been highlighted as essential for handling the volume, velocity, and variety of tourism-related data. These tools play a pivotal role in unlocking the full potential of big data analytics and enabling organizations to derive actionable insights from their data.

However, it is crucial to acknowledge the challenges associated with implementing big data analytics in the tourism sector. These challenges range from data privacy concerns and the need for skilled personnel to the integration of diverse data sources and ensuring the security of sensitive information. As the industry continues to embrace digitalization, addressing these challenges will be imperative for sustained success.

In summary, this chapter serves as a valuable resource for researchers, practitioners, and industry stakeholders by providing a balanced synthesis of theoretical frameworks and practical implementations in the realm of big data analytics for tourism. By learning from successful cases and understanding the challenges at hand, organizations can navigate the complexities of the tourism landscape and harness the power of big data to drive innovation and competitiveness in the evolving global tourism sector.

REFERENCES

Chareyron, G., Da-Rugna, J., & Raimbault, T. (2014, October). Big data: A new challenge for tourism. In *2014 IEEE International Conference on Big Data (Big Data)*. IEEE. 10.1109/BigData.2014.7004475

De Mauro, A., Greco, M., & Grimaldi, M. (2015). What is big data? A consensual definition and a review of key research topics. *AIP Conference Proceedings*, *1644*(1), 97–104. doi:10.1063/1.4907823

Hassani, H., & Silva, E. S. (2015). Forecasting with big data: A review. *Ann. Data Sci.*, *2*(1), 5–19. doi:10.1007/s40745-015-0029-9

Khotimah, H., Djatna, T., & Nurhadryani, Y. (2014). Tourism recommendation based on vector space model using composite social media extraction. *Proceedings of the International Conference on Advanced Computer Science and Information Systems (ICACSIS),* 303-308.

Kitsios, F., Mitsopoulou, E., Moustaka, E., & Kamariotou, M. (2022). User-Generated Content behavior and digital tourism services: A SEM-neural network model for information trust in social networking sites. *International Journal of Information Management Data Insights*, *2*(1), 100056. doi:10.1016/j.jjimei.2021.100056

Kurashima, T., Iwata, T., Irie, G., & Fujimura, K. (2013). Travel route recommendation using geotagged photos. *Knowledge and Information Systems*, *37*(1), 37–60. doi:10.1007/s10115-012-0580-z

Laney, D. (2001). 3D data management: Controlling data volume velocity and variety. *META Group Res. Note*, *6*(70), 1.

Li, H., Hu, M., & Li, G., (2020). Forecasting tourism demand with multisource big data. *Annals of Tourism Research, 83*, 1-13.

Li, J., Xu, L., Tang, L., Wang, S., & Li, L. (2018). Big data in tourism research: A literature review. *Tourism Management*, *68*, 301–323. doi:10.1016/j.tourman.2018.03.009

Mehmetoglu, M. (2007). Nature-based Tourists: The relationship between their trip expenditures and activities. *Journal of Sustainable Tourism*, *15*(2), 200–215. doi:10.2167/jost642.0

Samara, D., Magnisalis, I., & Peristeras, V. (2020). Artificial intelligence and big data in tourism: A systematic literature review. *Journal of Hospitality and Tourism Technology*, *11*(2), 343–367. doi:10.1108/JHTT-12-2018-0118

Sharma, R., Kumar, A., & Chuah, C. (2021). Turning the blackbox into a glassbox: An explainable machine learning approach for understanding hospitality customer. *International Journal of Information Management Data Insights*, *1*(2), 100050. doi:10.1016/j.jjimei.2021.100050

Snijders, C., Matzat, U., & Reips, U. D. (2012). Big data: Big gaps of knowledge in the feld of internet science. *International Journal of Internet Science*, *7*(1), 1–5.

Zbuchea, A. (2012). Cultural interests while on holidays: An exploratory investigation. *Journal of Tourism Challenges & Trends*, *5*(2), 53–70.

Zillinger, M. (2008). Germans' tourist behaviour in Sweden. *Tourism (Zagreb)*, *56*(2), 143–158.

KEY TERMS AND DEFINITIONS

Big Data: Big data refers to extensive collections of varied data, encompassing structured, unstructured, and semi-structured formats, which are consistently produced at a rapid pace and in substantial quantities.

Big Data Analytics: Big data analytics involves intricately analyzing large datasets to reveal valuable information, including hidden patterns, correlations, market trends, and customer preferences, guiding informed business decisions.

Data Mining: The process of discovering patterns and relationships within tourism datasets to identify trends and valuable information.

Techniques: Various methodologies and approaches employed in analyzing large volumes of tourism data, including statistical analysis, machine learning, and data mining.

Tools: Software applications and platforms designed to facilitate the processing, visualization, and interpretation of big data in the tourism industry, such as Hadoop, Apache Spark, and Tableau.

Tourism Sector: The tourism sector refers to the industry and economic activities associated with travel for leisure, recreation, business, or other purposes. It encompasses a wide range of services, businesses, and organizations that contribute to the planning, facilitation, and enjoyment of travel experiences.

Chapter 10
Tomorrow's Travel Companion:
The Role of Artificial Intelligence in Shaping the Future of Tourism

Bassam Samir Al-Romeedy
Faculty of Tourism and Hotels, Egypt

ABSTRACT

This chapter investigates the impact of artificial intelligence (AI) on shaping the future of the tourism industry. Given the advancements in AI technology, its transformative potential in various facets of the tourism sector is substantial. The chapter delves into the applications of AI, including personalized travel recommendations, chatbot customer service, demand forecasting, and smart destination management. It explores both the advantages and challenges linked to implementing AI in tourism, covering ethical considerations and workforce implications. The findings emphasize AI's capability to enhance customer experiences, streamline operational processes, and foster more sustainable and resilient tourism practices. The chapter concludes with recommendations for industry stakeholders on maximizing the benefits of AI while addressing associated challenges to shape a future aligned with the potential of this technology.

DOI: 10.4018/979-8-3693-3310-5.ch010

INTRODUCTION:

The tourism sector, a longstanding driver of economic growth and cultural exchange, is undergoing transformative changes fueled by technological advancements, particularly in Artificial Intelligence (AI). AI, as a potent tool, holds the promise of shaping the future of tourism through personalized and enhanced travel experiences. Notably, recommendation systems powered by machine learning algorithms have emerged as a key AI application in tourism. These systems analyze vast datasets encompassing user preferences, booking history, and online reviews, aiming to deliver tailored recommendations to travelers (Farahat, 2023).

The advent of AI has enabled the development of virtual travel assistants, including chatbots and voice assistants, transforming the way travelers access information. These intelligent assistants can swiftly and accurately furnish travelers with a spectrum of details, encompassing flight information, hotel reservations, local attractions, and even language translation (Bulchand-Gidumal, 2022).

AI plays a vital role in enhancing destination management processes through comprehensive data analysis, encompassing social media updates, weather patterns, and tourist movements. By employing AI-driven analytics, destinations can effectively manage crowds, predict tourist preferences, and tailor their offerings accordingly. This enables destinations to provide more personalized experiences while addressing challenges associated with overtourism (Moreno-Gil & Coca-Stefaniak, 2020; Grundner & Neuhofer, 2021).

Incorporating AI into destination management processes offers various potential benefits. Through the analysis of extensive data from sources like social media, weather forecasts, and tourist behaviors, AI provides destination managers with valuable insights. This data-driven approach enables informed decision-making regarding infrastructure development, resource allocation, marketing strategies, and the design of tourism products (Ivars-Baidal et al., 2019; Ferrer-Rosell et al., 2023).

Moreover, AI has the potential to improve the overall visitor experience by providing personalized recommendations and services (Hu & Li, 2023). By analyzing individual preferences, AI-driven systems can deliver tailored suggestions for attractions, accommodations, and activities aligned with each visitor's interests. This personalized approach enhances the immersive and satisfying nature of the experience, leading to increased visitor satisfaction and positive word-of-mouth promotion (Yoliando et al., 2023).

AI can play a crucial role in promoting sustainable tourism practices by analyzing environmental data and encouraging responsible tourism. By monitoring aspects such as energy consumption, waste management, and carbon emissions, AI systems provide valuable insights and recommendations for the implementation of sustainable practices. This aids destinations in minimizing their environmental footprint, safeguarding natural and cultural resources, and promoting the sustainable development of tourism (Tong et al., 2022; Ferrer-Rosell et al., 2023).

AI plays a vital role in recognizing evolving tourism trends and aiding the adjustment of destination management strategies (Mandić & Garbin Praničević, 2019). Through the analysis of extensive data from various sources like social media, online forums, travel blogs, and booking platforms, AI can reveal patterns, keywords, and sentiments indicating emerging tourism trends. This includes insights into new traveler preferences, emerging destinations, popular activities, and changing travel behaviors (Farahat et al., 2022).

This chapter explores the crucial role of Artificial Intelligence (AI) as a fundamental travel companion in shaping the future of tourism. It investigates various AI applications, including recommendation systems, virtual travel assistants, smart destination management, enhanced safety measures, and hyper-personalized experiences. The chapter emphasizes potential advantages, such as data-driven decision-making, improved visitor experiences, efficient resource management, enhanced sustainability practices, crisis management, and streamlined marketing. It also illustrates how AI can analyze tourist behaviors and preferences to refine destination management and identify emerging tourism trends. The study contributes to a comprehensive understanding of the opportunities and challenges the tourism industry faces in embracing AI technologies for its future.

AI in Tourism Industry

Artificial Intelligence (AI) stands out as a transformative technology with profound implications for the tourism sector. AI encompasses computer systems capable of human-like tasks, such as natural language processing, machine learning, and computer vision. Its capacity to analyze extensive data, identify patterns, and make intelligent decisions positions it as a valuable tool reshaping various facets of the travel experience (Al-Romeedy, 2024a). The key impact of AI in tourism lies in its potential to elevate customer experiences, streamline operations, and foster innovation. Notably, AI-powered chatbots and virtual assistants offer continuous customer support, addressing queries, and delivering personalized recommendations. Leveraging natural language processing, these systems enhance customer service and interaction (Mohamed et al., 2022).

AI assumes a pivotal role in bolstering safety and security within the tourism sector. AI-driven systems can scrutinize video data from security cameras, employing computer vision techniques to identify anomalies and potential threats. This proactive approach contributes to ensuring the well-being of travelers and staff (Stienmetz et al., 2022; Gupta et al., 2023). The increasing significance of AI in tourism is evident in its transformative impact on diverse aspects of the travel experience

(Pencarelli, 2020). From personalized recommendations and chatbots to safety and security applications, AI's influence spans various domains. As AI continues to advance, it is poised to play an even more substantial role in reshaping the future of travel, promising heightened personalization, increased efficiency, and immersive experiences for global travelers (Doğan & Niyet, 2024).

AI-Powered Personalization

AI is instrumental in orchestrating personalized travel experiences through the adept use of data analysis and machine learning algorithms. A significant domain where AI showcases its prowess in personalization is in crafting itineraries. By scrutinizing a traveler's preferences, historical behavior, and pertinent data, AI algorithms can craft customized travel plans that resonate with individual interests. This encompasses recommending specific destinations, attractions, activities, and even dining options tailored to the traveler's preferences, facilitating the exploration of novel and enjoyable experiences (Ferrer-Rosell et al., 2023; Gupta et al., 2023).

Moreover, AI proves beneficial in tailoring accommodation choices to individual preferences. Through the analysis of data such as past bookings, reviews, and traveler feedback, platforms powered by AI can suggest accommodations that align with personal preferences. This encompasses considerations like location, amenities, and price range. Additionally, AI can cater to specific needs or preferences, such as recommending accessible accommodations for travelers with disabilities or family-friendly options for those journeying with children (Farahat, 2023).

Besides, aside from customizing itineraries and accommodations, AI extends its capability to personalized tours and experiences. Virtual tour guides or applications driven by AI can furnish real-time information, historical context, and intriguing details about landmarks and attractions. This enables travelers to tailor their exploration according to their interests. For instance, an AI-driven app can deliver personalized museum tours aligned with a traveler's preferred art style or historical period, enriching their comprehension and involvement in the experience (Stienmetz et al., 2022; Chaturvedi et al., 2023).

Utilizing AI for personalized travel experiences enables the tourism industry to meet the varied needs and preferences of travelers. AI algorithms efficiently process substantial data volumes, adapting recommendations in real-time for dynamic personalization. This not only elevates customer satisfaction but also aids businesses in fostering loyalty and sustaining a competitive advantage (Farahat et al., 2022). Leveraging data analysis, machine learning, and real-time recommendations, AI facilitates personalized travel experiences encompassing itinerary suggestions, accommodation preferences, personalized tours, and catering to dietary needs. The adoption of AI-powered personalization positions the tourism industry to provide more gratifying and memorable journeys for travelers globally (Mohamed et al., 2022).

Chatbots and Customer Service

The incorporation of AI-driven chatbots and virtual assistants has revolutionized customer service in the tourism industry, offering real-time support to travelers throughout their journeys. These AI-powered systems engage in natural language conversations, comprehending customer inquiries and delivering personalized responses (Wörndl et al., 2021; Zierock & Jungblut, 2023). A key advantage lies in their capacity to handle a substantial volume of inquiries simultaneously, providing round-the-clock support. Travelers interact with these chatbots through diverse channels, such as websites, mobile apps, or messaging platforms, receiving instant responses. This substantially enhances response times, ensuring travelers access information and assistance promptly, even beyond regular business hours (Farahat, 2023).

AI-driven chatbots and virtual assistants excel in handling diverse inquiries, ranging from basic queries about flight schedules and hotel availability to more intricate requests for travel recommendations or booking assistance. Employing machine learning algorithms enables these systems to learn from customer interactions, enhancing their responses progressively. This adaptive learning process empowers them to offer precise and pertinent information, deliver personalized recommendations, and address inquiries with a high level of efficiency (McTear, 2022; Ferrer-Rosell et al., 2023).

Additionally, AI-powered systems play a crucial role in creating a smooth and personalized customer experience throughout the travel journey. They aid travelers in tasks like flight check-ins, issuing boarding passes, and recommending nearby attractions and restaurants. By comprehending traveler preferences and utilizing historical data, chatbots and virtual assistants provide tailored recommendations and personalized offers, elevating the overall travel experience and ensuring convenience and enjoyment for the customer (Pesonen & Neidhardt, 2019; Chaturvedi et al., 2023).

The incorporation of AI-driven chatbots and virtual assistants not only transforms customer service for travelers but also offers advantages to travel businesses by alleviating the workload on human customer service agents. These AI systems autonomously handle routine and repetitive inquiries, allowing human agents to focus on more complex tasks that demand human expertise. This strategic utilization enhances operational efficiency and enables customer service teams to allocate resources more effectively (Al-Romeedy, 2024a). The integration of AI-driven systems revolutionizes customer service in the travel industry, ensuring real-time support, efficient inquiry management, and personalized assistance for travelers. By harnessing AI technologies, travel businesses can optimize operational efficiency, reduce response times, and provide a seamless and personalized customer experience. The collaborative use of AI automation and human expertise establishes a potent synergy that benefits both travelers and travel companies (Al-Romeedy & El-Sisi, 2024).

Data Analytics and Predictive Modeling

The utilization of AI's analytical capabilities in processing extensive datasets has become crucial for predicting travel patterns, forecasting tourism trends, and facilitating decision-making across travel businesses, destination management, and infrastructure planning. By harnessing data from diverse sources, including booking platforms, social media, weather data, and historical travel records, AI algorithms extract valuable insights and patterns. This empowers stakeholders to make informed decisions and formulate strategies based on a comprehensive understanding of the dynamic factors influencing the tourism market (Ivanov & Webster, 2019; Hemachandran et al., 2022).

AI's role in forecasting travel patterns is pivotal, utilizing historical data analysis and considerations like seasonality, events, and economic indicators. AI algorithms predict future travel demand and patterns, aiding travel businesses in optimizing pricing strategies, efficient resource allocation, and targeted marketing campaigns. Dynamic adjustments to pricing based on identified high-demand periods in specific destinations showcase the practical application of AI in maximizing revenue for businesses (Egger, 2022; Mohamed et al., 2022).

AI's significance in predicting tourism trends is evident through its analysis of social media posts, online reviews, and user-generated content (Kang et al., 2022). By identifying emerging travel preferences, popular destinations, and new attractions, AI aids travel businesses and destination management organizations in adapting their offerings and staying attuned to changing consumer preferences. This proactive approach allows businesses to incorporate eco-friendly practices or design unique immersive experiences in response to growing interests such as sustainable travel or experiential tourism (Bulchand-Gidumal, 2022; Marchesani, 2023).

Beyond its role in forecasting and trend prediction, through the analysis of visitor demographics, preferences, spending patterns, and feedback, AI algorithms provide valuable insights for informed decisions regarding product development, marketing strategies, and infrastructure investments. An illustrative example is AI assisting destination management organizations in identifying areas requiring infrastructure improvements, like transportation or accommodation, to meet growing demand and enhance the overall visitor experience (Grundner & Neuhofer, 2021; Valeri, 2023).

AI's proficiency in analyzing extensive datasets has revolutionized decision-making processes within the travel industry. Through forecasting travel patterns, predicting trends, and supporting decision-making for travel businesses, destination management, and infrastructure planning, AI facilitates data-driven decision-making. This empowers stakeholders to formulate strategies that align with evolving customer demands and promote sustainable tourism development. The synergistic integration of AI's analytical capabilities with human expertise equips the industry to navigate the complexities of the dynamic tourism market, fostering efficiency, customer-centricity, and sustainability in the future (Al-Romeedy, 2024a).

Smart Destination Management

Smart destination management involves the use of technology, including AI, to optimize the management and functioning of tourist destinations (Ivars-Baidal et al., 2019). AI plays a vital role in improving destination management through data analysis, automation, and intelligent decision-making algorithms (Hicham et al., 2023). The essence of smart destination management lies in employing IoT devices to collect real-time data from various sources within the destination. These devices, such as sensors and beacons, monitor factors like crowd density, air quality, traffic flow, and energy consumption. The collected data empowers destination managers to make informed decisions regarding resource allocation, crowd control, and infrastructure development, fostering a more sustainable and resilient tourism ecosystem (Farhat, 2023).

Integral to smart destination management, connectivity solutions facilitate seamless communication among stakeholders, including tourists, businesses, and local authorities. Utilizing advanced mobile apps, interactive kiosks, and digital platforms enhances the visitor experience through real-time information, personalized recommendations, and interactive maps. This connectivity not only enhances customer satisfaction but also streamlines destination marketing and management efficiently (Gaafar, 2020).

AI's contribution to smart destination management lies in its capability to analyze extensive data from diverse sources, including tourist behavior, social media, weather data, and transportation patterns. Through data analysis, AI algorithms extract valuable insights into visitor preferences, trends, and patterns, empowering destination managers to make informed decisions. This includes identifying popular attractions, peak visiting times, and areas for improvement based on visitor feedback. Consequently, destination managers can allocate resources effectively, leading to an enhanced overall visitor experience (Gaafar, 2021).

AI contributes to automation and efficiency in destination management processes (Wang et al., 2020). AI-powered systems can automate tasks such as ticketing, reservations, and visitor information, reducing the workload on staff and improving operational efficiency. Additionally, chatbots and virtual assistants powered by AI offer real-time information and support to visitors, answering inquiries, and providing personalized recommendations. This automation enhances customer satisfaction by allowing destination managers to deliver seamless and efficient services to visitors (George & George, 2023; Doğan & Niyet, 2024).

Moreover, AI plays a role in promoting sustainable destination management. Through the analysis of data on environmental impact, resource utilization, and visitor flows, AI algorithms can identify opportunities for implementing sustainable practices. For instance, AI can optimize transportation routes to minimize congestion and carbon emissions or regulate visitor capacities to protect sensitive ecosystems. This contributes to the adoption of sustainable tourism practices, allowing destinations to safeguard their natural and cultural assets while maximizing the positive impacts of tourism (Ivars-Baidal et al., 2019; Ferrer-Rosell et al., 2023).

AI-driven data analysis facilitates predictive modeling and scenario planning for destination managers. Through the examination of historical and real-time data, AI algorithms can predict future trends, anticipate visitor demand, and identify potential challenges. This predictive capability empowers destination managers to formulate proactive strategies and contingency plans, allowing them to efficiently manage resources, adapt to market fluctuations, and mitigate risks (Farahat, 2023). The integration of AI in smart destination management transforms decision-making processes, enhancing resource allocation, visitor services, and sustainability in tourist destinations (Al-Romeedy, 2024b). While AI technologies offer opportunities for data-driven decision-making and improved operational efficiency, it is crucial to approach their implementation in destination management with a holistic and responsible perspective. This involves addressing ethical considerations and preserving the authenticity and sustainability of the destination. The responsible integration of AI can contribute to a seamless and personalized experience for visitors while respecting the unique characteristics and values of each destination (Wörndl et al., 2021; Stienmetz et al., 2022).

AI, Safety and Security

AI applications dedicated to traveler safety and security have become integral for ensuring the well-being of tourists across various environments. Technologies such as facial recognition, predictive risk analysis, and AI-based monitoring systems play a pivotal role in enhancing safety measures (Gaafar, 2020; Valeri, 2023). Notably, facial recognition technology has seen widespread implementation at airports globally to bolster security and streamline passenger screening procedures (del Rio et al., 2016). By analyzing facial features and cross-referencing them with databases of known individuals, AI algorithms assist authorities in identifying potential threats or persons of interest (Almeida et al., 2022; Valeri, 2023). This technology accelerates and enhances identification processes, minimizing the risks associated with impersonation or unauthorized access. Moreover, facial recognition contributes to a smoother travel experience by automating check-in procedures and elevating overall airport security standards (Jannat, 2021).

Predictive analysis, fueled by AI, stands as a valuable asset for ensuring traveler safety. Through the analysis of extensive data from diverse sources, including crime statistics, weather patterns, social media, and historical travel records, AI algorithms excel in identifying potential risks and forecasting travel disruptions. This data-driven approach empowers travelers and authorities alike to make informed decisions and implement proactive measures to mitigate potential risks. For instance, AI can discern patterns signaling a heightened risk of theft or pickpocketing in specific areas, enabling travelers to exercise caution and steer clear of precarious situations (Al-Romeedy, 2024b).

Monitoring systems powered by AI play a pivotal role in safeguarding the safety of tourists in various environments, including tourist attractions, public spaces, and hotel facilities. Utilizing AI algorithms, these systems analyze real-time data from surveillance cameras, sensors, and other sources to identify anomalies or potential threats. For example, AI can discern suspicious behavior, unattended baggage, or overcrowding in public spaces, prompting alerts for security personnel to take prompt actions. AI-based monitoring systems contribute an additional layer of security, aiding in incident prevention and ensuring swift responses during emergencies (Egger, 2022; Gupta et al., 2023).

Beyond the mentioned applications, AI can enhance traveler safety through natural language processing and sentiment analysis. Through the analysis of social media posts, reviews, and online forums, AI algorithms can discern potential safety concerns or emerging risks that might impact travelers. This data can be utilized to issue timely warnings, recommendations, or updates to travelers, empowering them to make informed decisions and ensure their safety throughout their journeys (Álvarez-Carmona et al., 2022).

While AI applications bring notable advantages to traveler safety and security, addressing privacy concerns and ethical considerations is crucial. The gathering and analysis of personal data using AI technologies should be conducted transparently, with consent and adherence to privacy regulations. Maintaining a balance between security and privacy is essential to ensure responsible and respectful use of these technologies while upholding individuals' rights (Gaafar, 2020; Al-Romeedy, 2024a).

AI and Ethical and Privacy Considerations

The growing implementation of AI in tourism presents significant ethical concerns and privacy issues that necessitate attention (Du & Xie, 2021). Three primary areas of apprehension include data security, algorithmic biases, and striking a balance between personalization and data privacy (Farahat, 2023). Data security emerges as a substantial concern in the realm of AI within tourism (Knani et al., 2022). The extensive collection and processing of personal data, encompassing travel plans, preferences, and location details, prompt inquiries into how this information is stored, safeguarded, and utilized. Both tourism organizations and AI service providers must establish robust data security measures to protect personal data from unauthorized access, breaches, or misuse. Implementing encryption, access controls, and data anonymization techniques becomes pivotal in ensuring the security of sensitive data and upholding user trust (Hamid et al., 2021; Egger, 2022).

Algorithmic biases present a notable ethical dilemma (Tsamados et al., 2021). AI algorithms undergo training using extensive datasets, and if these datasets harbor biases or mirror societal prejudices, the algorithms may perpetuate or magnify such biases (Howard & Borenstein, 2018). In the tourism context, biased algorithms could result in discrimination regarding recommendations, pricing, or access to services. Addressing and mitigating algorithmic biases require the use of diverse and representative datasets during the training phase, along with regular audits of AI systems to identify and rectify biases. Adhering to transparent and accountable AI development practices becomes crucial to ensuring fairness and averting discriminatory outcomes (Kordzadeh & Ghasemaghaei, 2022; Stienmetz et al., 2022).

Balancing personalization with data privacy is a nuanced ethical concern. While personalization enhances the tourist experience through tailored recommendations and services, it necessitates the collection and scrutiny of personal data. Achieving a harmonious equilibrium between personalization and data privacy is paramount to respecting individuals' privacy rights while delivering valuable and customized experiences. Adhering to privacy-by-design principles, securing informed consent, and affording users control over their data through opt-in and opt-out mechanisms represent crucial steps in striking this balance. Tourism organizations should embrace transparent data practices, clearly articulating how user data is gathered, utilized, and safeguarded (Mohamed et al., 2022; Farahat et al., 2022).

AI Adoption Challenges

Incorporating AI into the tourism sector presents certain challenges. A significant hurdle is the limitation of resources. The implementation of AI technologies demands substantial investments in infrastructure, software, and data management systems.

Many businesses in the tourism sector, particularly small and medium-sized enterprises (SMEs), may encounter financial constraints that impede their capacity to embrace AI solutions. Moreover, obtaining high-quality data essential for training AI models poses a challenge, often requiring extensive data collection efforts and advanced data processing capabilities. Overcoming these resource limitations necessitates strategic planning, collaborations, and potential government support to offer financial incentives or access to AI resources for a broader spectrum of tourism businesses (Ferrer-Rosell et al., 2023).

Another obstacle is the presence of skill gaps and a shortage of AI expertise. The creation and implementation of AI applications demand specialized knowledge and skills in areas such as data science, machine learning, and AI programming. However, the tourism industry may lack a substantial talent pool possessing the requisite AI competencies. Addressing this skill gap necessitates the implementation of training programs, fostering collaborations between academia and industry, and initiating efforts to attract and retain AI talent within the tourism sector. Facilitating the upskilling of tourism professionals and encouraging interdisciplinary collaborations can enable organizations to effectively leverage the potential of AI (Al-Romeedy, 2024a, b).

Resistance to the adoption of technology also poses a challenge in the tourism sector (Rana et al., 2022). Some stakeholders may exhibit reluctance to embrace AI, driven by concerns about job displacement or apprehensions about the perceived complexity involved in implementing and managing AI systems (Wörndl et al., 2021; Bulchand-Gidumal, 2022). Overcoming this resistance necessitates a comprehensive change management approach that includes elements of education, training, and transparent communication regarding the advantages of AI adoption (Chowdhury et al., 2023; Valeri, 2023). Providing tangible examples showcasing how AI can enhance operational efficiency, elevate customer experiences, and create novel opportunities can help alleviate concerns and instill confidence in AI technologies (Ivanov & Webster, 2019; Wörndl et al., 2021).

Future Trends of AI

The potential of AI in the future of tourism is immense, and it is anticipated to influence travel experiences in diverse ways. Future trends and the changing role of AI in the tourism industry encompass the following:

Hyper-Personalization: AI is set to persist in fostering hyper-personalization in travel encounters. Through the analysis of extensive data, AI algorithms can comprehend individual preferences, behaviors, and travel patterns, facilitating highly customized recommendations and suggestions. Ranging from personalized itineraries and carefully curated activity suggestions to tailored offers and immediate assistance, AI will empower travelers to partake in more personalized and memorable experiences (Mohamed et al., 2022).

Augmented Reality (AR) and Virtual Reality (VR): AI is poised to elevate AR and VR encounters in the tourism sector, allowing travelers to virtually explore destinations, visualize accommodations, and engage in interactive simulations. Through AI algorithms, these experiences will undergo enhancements in terms of realism, interactivity, and personalization, fundamentally altering how travelers conduct research, plan, and engage with destinations (Farahat, 2023).

Smart Travel Assistants: AI-driven virtual assistants and chatbots are anticipated to attain heightened sophistication, delivering seamless and intuitive interactions. These intelligent travel assistants will possess the ability to comprehend natural language, address intricate queries, and furnish personalized recommendations. They are poised to support travelers comprehensively, spanning pre-trip planning to post-trip assistance, by delivering real-time updates, tailored suggestions, and immediate support (Ling et al., 2023; Ferrer-Rosell et al., 2023).

Intelligent Pricing and Revenue Management: AI algorithms are set to play a pivotal role in refining pricing strategies and revenue management for tourism enterprises. Through the analysis of market trends, historical data, and customer behavior, AI can dynamically fine-tune prices, forecast demand, and optimize revenue generation. This capability empowers businesses to achieve maximum profitability while delivering competitive pricing options to travelers (Zhang et al., 2019; Samara et al., 2020).

Enhanced Safety and Security: AI technologies are poised to elevate safety and security within the tourism industry. Systems powered by AI can analyze real-time data sourced from diverse outlets, including surveillance cameras, sensors, and social media, to identify and address potential risks or emergencies. Through pattern analysis and anomaly detection, AI algorithms can promptly alert relevant authorities or travelers, fostering a travel environment that is not only safer but also more secure (Gangwani & Gangwani, 2021; Dai, & Boroomand, 2022).

Intelligent Destination Management: AI is set to transform destination management, ushering in an era of intelligent and sustainable tourism practices. Through the optimization of resource utilization, congestion reduction, and mitigation of environmental impact, AI will play a pivotal role. Systems driven by AI can analyze data related to visitor flows, crowd management, and environmental considerations, providing real-time recommendations for the adoption of sustainable tourism practices and effective destination management (Solazzo et al., 2022; Yathiraju & Bhatia, 2023).

Predictive Analytics and Demand Forecasting: AI is poised to further enhance predictive analytics and demand forecasting within the tourism sector. Through the analysis of historical data, market trends, and external influences, AI algorithms can anticipate future travel demand, identify emerging trends, and facilitate proactive decision-making. This advancement will empower businesses to optimize inventory management, refine marketing strategies, and enhance operational planning (Bulchand-Gidumal, 2022; Valeri, 2023).

Collaborative Travel Planning: AI will enable cooperative travel planning and decision-making among groups of travelers. By analyzing the preferences and profiles of multiple individuals, AI algorithms can pinpoint common interests and propose shared activities or itineraries. This functionality will streamline the planning and coordination efforts of group travelers, fostering a more harmonious and enjoyable travel experience (Egger, 2022; Al-Romeedy, 2024b).

Overall, AI is poised to be a catalyst in reshaping the future of travel experiences. Its contributions will span hyper-personalization, improved safety and security, operational optimization, and revolutionary destination management. Adhering to responsible and ethical use of AI technologies, the tourism industry stands to unlock novel opportunities for growth, innovation, and the delivery of outstanding travel experiences (Jannat, 2021).

IMPLICATIONS

The future outlook for AI in tourism is exceptionally promising, presenting various opportunities for stakeholders, policymakers, and industry participants to elevate the travel experience and advance sustainability. Collaboration and partnerships between stakeholders in the tourism sector and AI technology providers, data scientists, and researchers are crucial. This collective effort can harness expertise and resources to develop and implement tailored AI solutions, addressing specific challenges in the industry and ensuring a sustainable and enriched travel experience. Additionally, acknowledging the significance of human-AI collaboration in tourism is essential. Rather than aiming for complete replacement, AI should be viewed as a tool to enhance human capabilities. The combination of AI's analytical prowess with human creativity, empathy, and intuition can result in distinctive and personalized travel experiences that strike the optimal balance between automation and the human touch.

Moreover, businesses within the industry should regularly conduct audits to evaluate the ethical considerations associated with their AI systems. This involves scrutinizing algorithmic biases, guaranteeing fairness and inclusivity, and monitoring the environmental consequences of AI-driven operations. Ethical AI audits serve to pinpoint and rectify any possible issues, ensuring the responsible and sustainable utilization of AI.

To maximize the capabilities of AI, policymakers and stakeholders should allocate resources to develop resilient data infrastructure. This involves establishing systems for effective data collection, storage, and management, enabling the efficient processing and analysis of large datasets. Furthermore, there is a need to standardize data formats and encourage interoperability across diverse systems, facilitating smooth integration of data. Additionally, a focus on data privacy and ethical considerations in AI deployment is essential. Clear guidelines and regulations must be instituted to ensure the responsible and transparent utilization of personal data. Stakeholders should implement privacy-centric measures, such as data anonymization and consent management, to safeguard traveler information and instill confidence in AI-driven services.

Similarly, it is imperative to allocate resources to training initiatives aimed at cultivating AI-related skills within the tourism workforce. This involves providing employees with the necessary knowledge and expertise to proficiently utilize AI tools and technologies. Initiatives focused on upskilling and reskilling will empower the workforce to embrace the advancements in AI and actively contribute to the successful implementation of these technologies within their respective organizations.

Policymakers and industry stakeholders ought to cultivate an environment conducive to responsible innovation in AI. This involves endorsing and supporting startups and research institutions dedicated to AI applications in tourism. Encouraging collaboration between academia and industry, as well as offering funding opportunities for projects addressing sustainability, customer experience, and societal well-being, are crucial elements of fostering responsible innovation in the field of AI. Policymakers and industry stakeholders also should proactively interact with travelers, local communities, and other stakeholders to comprehend their needs, concerns, and expectations regarding AI in tourism. By involving these stakeholders in the decision-making process, policymakers and industry players can ensure that AI applications align with societal and environmental goals, thereby delivering enhanced travel experiences.

AI has the potential to transform customer engagement within the tourism industry. Stakeholders and policymakers should explore AI-driven technologies, such as voice assistants, chatbots, and personalized recommendation systems, to deliver seamless and interactive customer experiences. These technologies can aid travelers at different touchpoints, including trip planning, booking, on-site assistance, and post-trip support. Likewise, they should establish conducive environments that nurture innovation ecosystems within the tourism industry. This involves offering incentives and financial support for research and development, setting up testbeds for AI technologies, and facilitating collaboration among industry players, startups, and academic institutions. These endeavors will propel technological progress, stimulate experimentation, and expedite the integration of AI in the tourism sector.

Ultimately, policymakers should encourage collaboration among industry stakeholders to promote responsible data sharing. Initiatives for shared data can break down data silos, paving the way for the creation of more holistic AI models and solutions. Nevertheless, frameworks for data sharing must give precedence to safeguarding privacy, managing consent, and ensuring the secure utilization of shared data.

CONCLUSION

The study on the role of artificial intelligence (AI) in shaping the future of tourism underscores the transformative potential of AI in enhancing the overall travel experience. AI technologies can revolutionize different facets of the tourism industry, providing personalized recommendations, facilitating seamless travel planning, improving customer service, and enhancing operational efficiency. Key advantages include AI-powered chatbots and virtual assistants offering 24/7 personalized customer support, machine learning algorithms generating tailored travel itineraries, and applications in dynamic pricing, demand forecasting, and fraud detection for optimizing revenue management. Despite these advantages, the study highlights challenges such as ethical concerns related to privacy and data security. The delicate balance between automation and preserving a human touch, as well as ensuring inclusivity and accessibility, are also crucial considerations. The study emphasizes the inevitability of AI in shaping the future of tourism, given its potential to streamline operations, improve decision-making, and provide personalized experiences. To fully realize these benefits, collaboration and investment are essential, with stakeholders, governments, and technology providers working together to establish robust AI frameworks, standards, and regulations. Tourism businesses must invest in AI infrastructure, talent development, and data management, while public-private partnerships can facilitate the creation of AI-enabled solutions tailored to the industry's needs.

In summary, the study underscores the transformative impact of AI on the future of tourism. Embracing AI technologies and effectively addressing associated challenges open new avenues for personalized experiences, operational efficiency, and sustainable growth in the industry. With AI as a reliable travel companion, the tourism sector can meet changing traveler expectations, cater to diverse needs, and craft memorable journeys for global travelers.

REFERENCES

Al-Romeedy, B. (2024a). AI and HRM in Tourism and Hospitality in Egypt: Inevitability, Impact and Future. In HRM, Artificial Intelligence and the Future of Work: Critical Insights from the Global South, Palgrave Macmillan.

Al-Romeedy, B. (2024b). HRM and Digital Leadership: Exploring the Mediating Role of Digital Talent and Digital Culture in Driving Innovative Performance in the Saudi Tourism and Hospitality Industry. In HRM, Artificial Intelligence and the Future of Work: Critical Insights from the Global South, Palgrave Macmillan.

Al-Romeedy, B., & El-Sisi, S. H. (2024). Does AI have an effective role in applying Sustainable Entrepreneurship in Tourism Industry? In *Sustainable Tourism: Balancing Conservation and Progress in a Dynamic Industry*. CABI.

Almeida, D., Shmarko, K., & Lomas, E. (2022). The ethics of facial recognition technologies, surveillance, and accountability in an age of artificial intelligence: A comparative analysis of US, EU, and UK regulatory frameworks. *AI and Ethics*, *2*(3), 377–387. doi:10.1007/s43681-021-00077-w PMID:34790955

Álvarez-Carmona, M., Aranda, R., Rodríguez-Gonzalez, A., Fajardo-Delgado, D., Sánchez, M., Pérez-Espinosa, H., Martínez-Miranda, J., Guerrero-Rodríguez, R., Bustio-Martínez, L., & Díaz-Pacheco, Á. (2022). Natural language processing applied to tourism research: A systematic review and future research directions. *Journal of King Saud University. Computer and Information Sciences*, *34*(10), 10125–10144. doi:10.1016/j.jksuci.2022.10.010

Bulchand-Gidumal, J. (2022). Impact of artificial intelligence in travel, tourism, and hospitality. In *Handbook of e-Tourism* (pp. 1943–1962). Springer International Publishing. doi:10.1007/978-3-030-48652-5_110

Chaturvedi, R., Verma, S., Ali, F., & Kumar, S. (2023). Reshaping Tourist Experience with AI-Enabled Technologies: A Comprehensive Review and Future Research Agenda. *International Journal of Human-Computer Interaction*, 1–17. Advance online publication. doi:10.1080/10447318.2023.2238353

Chowdhury, S., Dey, P., Joel-Edgar, S., Bhattacharya, S., Rodriguez-Espindola, O., Abadie, A., & Truong, L. (2023). Unlocking the value of artificial intelligence in human resource management through AI capability framework. *Human Resource Management Review*, *33*(1), 100899. doi:10.1016/j.hrmr.2022.100899

Dai, D., & Boroomand, S. (2022). A review of artificial intelligence to enhance the security of big data systems: State-of-art, methodologies, applications, and challenges. *Archives of Computational Methods in Engineering, 29*(2), 1291–1309. doi:10.1007/s11831-021-09628-0

del Rio, J., Moctezuma, D., Conde, C., de Diego, I., & Cabello, E. (2016). Automated border control e-gates and facial recognition systems. *Computers & Security, 62*, 49-72.

Doğan, S., & Niyet, İ. (2024). Artificial Intelligence (AI) in Tourism. In Future Tourism Trends Volume 2: Technology Advancement, Trends and Innovations for the Future in Tourism (pp. 3-21). Emerald Publishing Limited.

Du, S., & Xie, C. (2021). Paradoxes of artificial intelligence in consumer markets: Ethical challenges and opportunities. *Journal of Business Research, 129*, 961–974. doi:10.1016/j.jbusres.2020.08.024

Egger, R. (2022). *Applied Data Science in Tourism*. Springer International Publishing. doi:10.1007/978-3-030-88389-8

Farahat, E. (2023). *Applications of artificial intelligence as a marketing tool and their impact on the competitiveness of the Egyptian tourist destination* (Doctoral Dissertation, Minia University).

Farahat, E., Mohamed, M., & Al-Romeedy, B. (2022). Artificial intelligence applications and its impact on the competitiveness of the Egyptian tourist destination. *Research Journal of the Faculty of Tourism and Hotels Mansoura University, 11*(2), 57–93.

Ferrer-Rosell, B., Massimo, D., & Berezina, K. (2023). *Information and Communication Technologies in Tourism 2023: Proceedings of the ENTER 2023 eTourism Conference, January 18-20, 2023*. Springer Nature. 10.1007/978-3-031-25752-0

Gaafar, H. (2020). Artificial intelligence in Egyptian tourism companies: Implementation and perception. *Journal of Association of Arab Universities for Tourism and Hospitality, 18*(1), 66–78. doi:10.21608/jaauth.2020.31704.1028

Gaafar, H. (2021). Digital Detox Tourism at The Egyptian Destination: Attitudes and Motivators. *Journal of Association of Arab Universities for Tourism and Hospitality, 20*(2), 88–107.

Gangwani, D., & Gangwani, P. (2021). Applications of machine learning and artificial intelligence in intelligent transportation system: A review. *Applications of Artificial Intelligence and Machine Learning: Select Proceedings of ICAAAIML 2020*, 203-216.

George, A., & George, A. (2023). A review of ChatGPT AI's impact on several business sectors. *Partners Universal International Innovation Journal*, *1*(1), 9–23.

Grundner, L., & Neuhofer, B. (2021). The bright and dark sides of artificial intelligence: A futures perspective on tourist destination experiences. *Journal of Destination Marketing & Management*, *19*, 100511. doi:10.1016/j.jdmm.2020.100511

Gupta, S., Modgil, S., Lee, C., & Sivarajah, U. (2023). The future is yesterday: Use of AI-driven facial recognition to enhance value in the travel and tourism industry. *Information Systems Frontiers*, *25*(3), 1179–1195. doi:10.1007/s10796-022-10271-8 PMID:35529102

Hamid, R., Albahri, A., Alwan, J., Al-Qaysi, Z., Albahri, O., Zaidan, A., Alnoor, A., Alamoodi, A. H., & Zaidan, B. (2021). How smart is e-tourism? A systematic review of smart tourism recommendation system applying data management. *Computer Science Review*, *39*, 100337. doi:10.1016/j.cosrev.2020.100337

Hemachandran, K., Khanra, S., Rodriguez, R., & Jaramillo, J. (2022). *Machine Learning for Business Analytics: Real-Time Data Analysis for Decision-Making*. CRC Press. doi:10.4324/9781003206316

Hicham, N., Nassera, H., & Karim, S. (2023). Strategic framework for leveraging artificial intelligence in future marketing decision-making. *Journal of Intelligent and Management Decision*, *2*(3), 139–150. doi:10.56578/jimd020304

Howard, A., & Borenstein, J. (2018). The ugly truth about ourselves and our robot creations: The problem of bias and social inequity. *Science and Engineering Ethics*, *24*(5), 1521–1536. doi:10.1007/s11948-017-9975-2 PMID:28936795

Hu, H., & Li, C. (2023). Smart tourism products and services design based on user experience under the background of big data. *Soft Computing*, *27*(17), 12711–12724. doi:10.1007/s00500-023-08851-0

Ivanov, S., & Webster, C. (2019). *Robots, artificial intelligence, and service automation in travel, tourism and hospitality*. Emerald Publishing Limited. doi:10.1108/9781787566873

Ivars-Baidal, J., Celdrán-Bernabeu, M., Mazón, J., & Perles-Ivars, Á. (2019). Smart destinations and the evolution of ICTs: A new scenario for destination management? *Current Issues in Tourism*, *22*(13), 1581–1600. doi:10.1080/13683500.2017.1388771

Jannat, S. (2021). *Understanding the opportunities of digitalization on a seamless airport departure journey for European passengers* (Doctoral dissertation, Hochschule Anhalt).

Kang, J., Guo, X., Fang, L., Wang, X., & Fan, Z. (2022). Integration of Internet search data to predict tourism trends using spatial-temporal XGBoost composite model. *International Journal of Geographical Information Science*, *36*(2), 236–252. doi:10.1080/13658816.2021.1934476

Knani, M., Echchakoui, S., & Ladhari, R. (2022). Artificial intelligence in tourism and hospitality: Bibliometric analysis and research agenda. *International Journal of Hospitality Management*, *107*, 103317. doi:10.1016/j.ijhm.2022.103317

Kordzadeh, N., & Ghasemaghaei, M. (2022). Algorithmic bias: Review, synthesis, and future research directions. *European Journal of Information Systems*, *31*(3), 388–409. doi:10.1080/0960085X.2021.1927212

Ling, E., Tussyadiah, I., Liu, A., & Stienmetz, J. (2023). Perceived Intelligence of Artificially Intelligent Assistants for Travel: Scale Development and Validation. *Journal of Travel Research*. Advance online publication. doi:10.1177/00472875231217899

Mandić, A., & Garbin Praničević, D. (2019). Progress on the role of ICTs in establishing destination appeal: Implications for smart tourism destination development. *Journal of Hospitality and Tourism Technology*, *10*(4), 791–813. doi:10.1108/JHTT-06-2018-0047

Marchesani, F. (2023). Urban Attractiveness and the Competitive Edge of the Smart City. In The Global Smart City (pp. 117-135). Emerald Publishing Limited. doi:10.1108/978-1-83797-575-420231007

Mohamed, M., Farahat, E., & Al-Romeedy, B. (2022). The Mediating Role of Marketing Effectiveness in the Relationship between Artificial Intelligence and Destination Competitiveness. *Minia Journal of Tourism and Hospitality Research*, *14*(1), 113–129.

Moreno-Gil, S., & Coca-Stefaniak, J. (2020). Guest editorial": Overtourism and the sharing economy–tourism cities at a crossroads. *International Journal of Tourism Cities*, *6*(1), 1–7. doi:10.1108/IJTC-03-2020-174

Neidhardt, J., & Wörndl, W. (2020). *Information and Communication Technologies in Tourism 2020*. Springer International Publishing. doi:10.1007/978-3-030-36737-4

Pencarelli, T. (2020). The digital revolution in the travel and tourism industry. *Information Technology & Tourism, 22*(3), 455–476. doi:10.1007/s40558-019-00160-3

Pesonen, J., & Neidhardt, J. (2019). Information and communication technologies in tourism 2019. In *Proceedings of the International Conference*. Springer International Publishing. 10.1007/978-3-030-05940-8

Rana, R., Adamashvili, N., & Tricase, C. (2022). The impact of blockchain technology adoption on tourism industry: A systematic literature review. *Sustainability (Basel), 14*(12), 7383. doi:10.3390/su14127383

Samara, D., Magnisalis, I., & Peristeras, V. (2020). Artificial intelligence and big data in tourism: A systematic literature review. *Journal of Hospitality and Tourism Technology, 11*(2), 343–367. doi:10.1108/JHTT-12-2018-0118

Solazzo, G., Maruccia, Y., Lorenzo, G., Ndou, V., Del Vecchio, P., & Elia, G. (2022). Extracting insights from big social data for smarter tourism destination management. *Measuring Business Excellence, 26*(1), 122–140. doi:10.1108/MBE-11-2020-0156

Stienmetz, J., Ferrer-Rosell, B., & Massimo, D. (2022). *Information and Communication Technologies in Tourism 2022: Proceedings of the ENTER 2022 ETourism Conference, January 11-14, 2022*. Springer Nature. 10.1007/978-3-030-94751-4

Tong, L., Yan, W., & Manta, O. (2022). Artificial intelligence influences intelligent automation in tourism: A mediating role of internet of things and environmental, social, and governance investment. *Frontiers in Environmental Science, 10*, 135. doi:10.3389/fenvs.2022.853302

Tsamados, A., Aggarwal, N., Cowls, J., Morley, J., Roberts, H., Taddeo, M., & Floridi, L. (2021). The ethics of algorithms: key problems and solutions. *Ethics, Governance, and Policies in Artificial Intelligence*, 97-123.

Valeri, M. (2023). *Tourism Innovation in the Digital Era: Big Data, AI and Technological Transformation*. Emerald Publishing Limited. doi:10.1108/9781837971664

Wang, R., Luo, J., & Huang, S. (2020). Developing an artificial intelligence framework for online destination image photos identification. *Journal of Destination Marketing & Management, 18*, 100512. doi:10.1016/j.jdmm.2020.100512

Wörndl, W., Koo, C., & Stienmetz, J. (2021). *Information and Communication Technologies in Tourism 2021: Proceedings of the ENTER 2021 eTourism Conference, January 19–22, 2021*. Springer Nature. 10.1007/978-3-030-65785-7

Yathiraju, N., & Bhatia, B. (2023). Predicting the Future of Heritage Conservation for Sustainable Resource Allocation. *International Journal of Sustainable Development Through AI. ML and IoT*, *2*(1), 1–12.

Yoliando, F., Senjaya, E., Christyanawatie, J., & Stevani, N. (2023). A Comparative Study of Artificial Intelligence-Driven Applications in Enhancing Tourist Experience and Compatibility to Indonesia's Tourism Sector. In *Proceedings of the International Conference of Innovation in Media and Visual Design (IMDES 2023)* (Vol. 790, p. 157). Springer Nature. 10.2991/978-2-38476-136-4_14

Zhang, Q., Qiu, L., Wu, H., Wang, J., & Luo, H. (2019). Deep learning based dynamic pricing model for hotel revenue management. In *2019 International Conference on Data Mining Workshops (ICDMW)* (pp. 370-375). IEEE. 10.1109/ICDMW.2019.00061

Zierock, B., & Jungblut, A. (2023). Leveraging Prompts for Improving AI-Powered Customer Service Platforms: A Case Study of Chat GPT and Midjourney. *Learning*, *116*, 63–76.

Chapter 11
Unlocking the Power of Data:
Exploring the Dynamic Role of MKIS in Revolutionizing Tourism Marketing

Bassam Samir Al-Romeedy
Faculty of Tourism and Hotels, Egypt

ABSTRACT

Marketing knowledge and information systems (MKIS) are instrumental in the tourism industry, enabling organizations to collect, analyze, and leverage marketing data for strategic decision-making and gaining a competitive advantage. Their effective use is vital for modern marketing strategies, enhancing competitiveness, and meeting evolving customer demands. MKIS significantly impacts tourism destination management by improving branding, competitiveness, and visitor experiences. The chapter emphasizes the importance of continuous adaptation and innovation, urging tourism marketers to embrace MKIS as essential tools for staying ahead in the dynamic industry. It explores how MKIS empowers marketers to tailor strategies, personalize customer experiences, and optimize promotions based on real-time information. The chapter contributes valuable insights into the strategic application of MKIS in addressing challenges and capitalizing on opportunities within the competitive tourism environment, enriching the existing literature in the field.

INTRODUCTION

The tourism industry is undergoing significant changes propelled by technological advancements and the abundance of available data. This shift has opened up opportunities to enhance tourism marketing by leveraging extensive data and

DOI: 10.4018/979-8-3693-3310-5.ch011

advancements in technology and analytics. In response to these developments, MKIS has become a crucial tool for unlocking the potential of data and reshaping strategies in tourism marketing. MKIS comprises interconnected systems and processes designed to facilitate the collection, organization, analysis, interpretation, and distribution of marketing information within an organization. This comprehensive framework integrates various technologies, including databases, data mining tools, customer relationship management systems, and digital marketing platforms. Through the utilization of MKIS capabilities, tourism marketers can access valuable insights into customer behavior, preferences, and market trends, empowering them to craft more precise, personalized, and impactful marketing strategies (Benckendorff et al., 2019; Pencarelli, 2020).

In the tourism sector, making decisions based on data is essential for obtaining a comprehensive understanding of customer behavior, preferences, and market trends (Rosário & Dias, 2023). Through the analysis of data from diverse sources such as online booking platforms, social media, and customer feedback, tourism marketers can gain valuable insights into demographics, booking patterns, popular destinations, and preferred activities (Vu et al., 2018; Minazzi, 2015). MKIS proves advantageous by facilitating personalized marketing campaigns. Through data analysis, MKIS identifies individual preferences and past behaviors, empowering marketers to craft highly targeted and personalized messages, offers, and recommendations (Du et al., 2021; Stienmetz et al., 2022). The incorporation of MKIS in tourism marketing significantly elevates the customer experience. Leveraging customer data, marketers can offer personalized recommendations, tailored itineraries, and individualized communications throughout the customer journey. This heightened level of personalization contributes to increased customer satisfaction as customers perceive that their needs and preferences are acknowledged and addressed. Moreover, MKIS facilitates the real-time collection and analysis of feedback, enabling marketers to promptly address concerns and enhance the overall customer experience (Rosário & Dias, 2023; Schweidel et al., 2022). While the adoption of MKIS offers various advantages, it also introduces challenges and ethical considerations for tourism marketers. Challenges encompass the gathering and integration of data from diverse sources, ensuring data quality and accuracy, safeguarding data privacy and security, and navigating the complexities of data analysis. Additionally, ethical considerations arise regarding the use of customer data, transparency in data practices, and the responsible handling of personal information. It is crucial for tourism marketers to confront these challenges and adhere to ethical guidelines to establish trust with customers and maintain the integrity of their marketing practices (Queiroz & Oliveira, 2014; Etim et al., 2023).

This chapter seeks to investigate the transformative impact of MKIS on tourism marketing, focusing on the importance of data-driven decision-making in the tourism industry, the integration of data sources within MKIS, and the role of MKIS in automating data analysis and personalization for targeted marketing campaigns. It also underscores MKIS's significance in enhancing various aspects such as customer experience, feedback management, customer relationship management, performance measurement, and analytics, including measuring and optimizing marketing efforts. Furthermore, the chapter aims to address challenges and ethical considerations related to MKIS in tourism marketing. Through a comprehensive literature review encompassing academic research, industry reports, and case studies, the chapter intends to construct a conceptual framework elucidating the dynamic role of MKIS in revolutionizing tourism marketing. The conclusion will provide recommendations for tourism marketers seeking to leverage MKIS for effective and data-driven marketing strategies.

Marketing Knowledge Information Systems (MKIS)

MKIS encompasses technology and software applications designed for the acquisition, analysis, and utilization of marketing-related data to inform strategic decision-making. These systems are pivotal in reshaping marketing practices, enabling businesses to make well-informed decisions, craft effective marketing strategies, and elevate customer experiences. MKIS acquires data pertinent to marketing from diverse sources, including customer interactions, social media platforms, online reviews, and market research. Utilizing mechanisms such as surveys, online forms, and tracking tools, MKIS captures valuable insights into customer preferences, behaviors, demographics, and market trends. Subsequently, this data is stored in databases, accessible to marketers for in-depth analysis (Kinyua, 2020).

Examining marketing data stands as a pivotal element within MKIS. These systems employ data analytics methods to unveil patterns, trends, and insights, providing valuable input for strategic decision-making. Utilizing data visualization tools, marketers can decipher intricate data sets, achieving a profound comprehension of customer requirements and market dynamics. For instance, through data analysis, it becomes possible to discern the most efficacious marketing channels for reaching target audiences or pinpoint emerging trends (Kellerman, 2023; Aaker & Moorman, 2023).

Leveraging marketing-related data constitutes another essential role of MKIS (Aggarwal et al., 2023). The knowledge gained from data analysis serves as a guide for shaping marketing strategies and tactics (Grigsby, 2022). In the realm of tourism marketing, this information becomes a valuable resource for crafting focused advertising campaigns, customizing customer communication, and refining pricing and packaging strategies (Juska, 2021). For example, through data analysis, marketers can formulate personalized offers tailored to specific customer segments or adjust pricing in response to demand patterns (Palmatier & Sridhar, 2020).

How MKIS Transforms Tourism Marketing?

Customer Behavior Analysis

Analyzing customer behavior is a crucial function of MKIS within the tourism industry (Benckendorff et al., 2019). Employing techniques like segmentation, profiling, and trend analysis, MKIS assists tourism marketers in acquiring valuable insights into their target audience, enabling the formulation of targeted marketing strategies (Huang & Rust, 2021; Miklosik & Evans, 2020). MKIS employs segmentation techniques to categorize the customer base into distinct groups based on common characteristics or behaviors (Sari et al., 2016). This process entails identifying meaningful variables such as demographics, customer preferences, psychographics, or purchase histories. Through customer segmentation, tourism marketers gain a deeper understanding of diverse needs, motivations, and preferences. This knowledge empowers them to customize marketing messages, offers, and experiences for each segment, thereby optimizing the effectiveness of their campaigns. For instance, MKIS might unveil that a specific customer segment has a preference for adventure-oriented activities, enabling marketers to create targeted promotional materials highlighting destinations or experiences centered around adventure (Yoo et al., 2018; Ferrer-Rosell et al., 2023).

MKIS generates customer profiles by compiling detailed individual or group information, encompassing demographic data, customer preferences, previous purchase behavior, interaction history, and other pertinent attributes. These profiles provide tourism marketers with profound insights into customers' characteristics, interests, and preferences. Armed with this understanding, marketers can individualize marketing initiatives, present targeted offers, and craft tailored experiences. For example, if MKIS profiles reveal that a specific customer group consistently opts for luxury accommodations and high-end dining, marketers can design specialized packages or promotions tailored to meet their preferences (Rowley, 2017; Wörndl et al., 2021).

MKIS performs trend analysis by scrutinizing patterns and evolutions in customer behavior across time. Through the examination of historical data, social media trends, online reviews, and other pertinent sources, MKIS discerns emerging trends and shifts in customer preferences. This analytical process empowers tourism marketers to stay abreast of market dynamics, adjust their strategies, and seize new opportunities. For instance, if trend analysis uncovers an increasing demand for sustainable and eco-friendly customer experiences, marketers can formulate campaigns highlighting environmentally responsible practices or promoting destinations renowned for their sustainability initiatives (McDaniel & Gates, 2018; Hung, 2019).

The knowledge derived from segmentation, profiling, and trend analysis influences the formulation of targeted marketing strategies in numerous ways (Weinstein, 2013):

- Customized Messaging: MKIS empowers marketers to develop customized messages that align with distinct customer segments. Through a deep understanding of customer preferences and traits, marketers can design marketing content that directly addresses the unique needs and interests of each segment. This strategy enhances the efficacy of marketing communications and fosters increased customer engagement (Shoushtari et al., 2023; Pearson, 2016).
- Personalized Offers and Experiences: MKIS enables marketers to provide personalized offers and experiences tailored to individual customer profiles. Leveraging customer data and preferences, marketers can craft customized packages, recommendations, and promotions that align with individual tastes. This personalized approach contributes to increased customer satisfaction, loyalty, and a higher likelihood of conversion (Anshari et al., 2019).
- Targeted Campaigns: MKIS-derived insights guide the creation of targeted marketing campaigns. Through customer segmentation and trend analysis, marketers can pinpoint the most effective channels, messages, and timing for their campaigns. This focused approach enhances the effectiveness of marketing endeavors and increases the return on investment (Huang & Rust, 2021; Rosário & Dias, 2023).
- Product Development and Innovation: The insights derived from MKIS play a pivotal role in shaping product development and fostering innovation in the market. Through a deep understanding of customer preferences and emerging trends, marketers can identify market gaps and introduce new offerings that align with evolving customer needs. This proactive approach to product development ensures that tourism businesses remain relevant and competitive (Fleisher et al., 2008; Huang & Rust, 2021).

The analysis of customer behavior by MKIS through segmentation, profiling, and trend analysis empowers marketers in the tourism industry to formulate precise marketing strategies. These insights facilitate tailored messaging, personalized offers, and experiences, as well as targeted campaigns and informed product development. Utilizing the insights from MKIS, tourism businesses can elevate customer satisfaction, engagement, and loyalty, thereby fostering business growth in a competitive market.

Competitive Intelligence and Market Trends

MKIS plays a crucial role in competitive intelligence and trend identification within the tourism industry (Nemutanzhela & Iyamu, 2011). A significant function of MKIS in this context is benchmarking, wherein businesses evaluate their performance vis-à-vis industry standards and competitors. Through the collection and analysis of data pertaining to key performance indicators, customer satisfaction metrics, and market share, MKIS provides valuable insights into the standing of tourism businesses within the competitive environment. By benchmarking against industry leaders or competitors, businesses can pinpoint areas for improvement and devise strategies to enhance their competitive positioning (McManus, 2013; Neidhardt & Wörndl, 2020).

Another pivotal function of MKIS is monitoring competitors. MKIS consistently collects data on competitors' marketing strategies, pricing structures, customer feedback, and market visibility. This information enables businesses to stay updated on industry dynamics, comprehend the strengths and weaknesses of competitors, and adjust their strategies accordingly. For example, if a competitor launches a successful loyalty program, MKIS empowers businesses to evaluate its impact and contemplate similar initiatives to sustain competitiveness (Ritchie & Ritchie, 2002; Stienmetz et al., 2022).

An anticipatory function of MKIS in enhancing competitive intelligence is forecasting industry shifts. Through the analysis of historical data, customer behaviors, and emerging market trends, MKIS facilitates the prediction of future developments in the industry. Businesses can foresee changes in consumer preferences, emerging destinations, or shifts in customer patterns. This predictive capability empowers businesses to proactively adjust their strategies, positioning themselves to leverage new opportunities and navigate potential challenges in a dynamically evolving market (Chase & Chase, 2013).

Furthermore, MKIS facilitates the recognition of market trends through the analysis of diverse data sources. Ranging from customer feedback and reviews to social media interactions and booking patterns, MKIS extracts valuable insights into emerging trends shaping the tourism industry. For instance, if there is a growing interest in sustainable customer experiences, MKIS can identify this trend by analyzing customer preferences and market behavior. Equipped with this information, businesses can align their offerings and marketing messages with the evolving expectations of tourists (Kumar et al., 2018; Pesonen & Neidhardt, 2019).

MKIS serves a diverse role in enhancing competitive intelligence and recognizing market trends within the tourism sector. Whether it's benchmarking performance against industry standards, monitoring competitors, or forecasting market shifts, MKIS provides businesses with the tools to make well-informed decisions. The ongoing analysis of data enables tourism enterprises to remain flexible, adjust to evolving market dynamics, and strategically position themselves in a competitive environment where staying ahead of industry trends is crucial for sustained success (Wörndl et al., 2021; Bulger, 2016).

Real-time Decision Support

MKIS plays a central role in enabling real-time decision-making in marketing, empowering businesses with the agility to promptly respond to dynamic market conditions. A critical aspect involves optimizing marketing campaigns. MKIS continually gathers and analyzes data from diverse sources, such as online interactions, social media, and booking patterns. This real-time data empowers tourism businesses to instantly evaluate the performance of their marketing campaigns. If a specific campaign garners significant engagement, MKIS allows marketers to seize the opportunity by promptly adjusting strategies, allocating additional resources, or expanding the campaign's reach in real-time (Pearlson et al., 2024; Gupta et al., 2019).

Moreover, MKIS plays a role in the ongoing optimization of pricing strategies in real-time. Through the analysis of market trends, competitor pricing, and demand patterns, MKIS aids businesses in dynamically refining their pricing models. For example, in the event of an unexpected surge in demand for a particular destination, MKIS can swiftly propose price adjustments to capitalize on the heightened demand. This adaptability ensures that pricing strategies remain competitive and responsive to the dynamic conditions of the tourism market (Wang et al., 2021; Watson et al., 2023).

Resource allocation is another domain in which MKIS demonstrates proficiency in real-time decision-making for marketing (Harmon, 2002). Through the continuous monitoring of various marketing channels, MKIS empowers businesses to allocate resources judiciously. For instance, if social media platforms exhibit a higher level of engagement compared to traditional advertising channels, MKIS insights can advise businesses to dynamically shift resources towards social media marketing. This optimization guarantees that resources are directed where they can generate the greatest return on investment, thereby improving the overall efficiency of marketing endeavors (Thuita & Njeru, 2021).

As well, MKIS elevates the immediacy of customer interactions. Utilizing AI-driven chatbots and personalized recommendation engines, MKIS empowers businesses to promptly engage with customers and deliver pertinent information or offers tailored to their preferences. This instantaneous interaction cultivates a smoother and more gratifying customer experience, consequently enhancing the prospects of conversion (Dwivedi et al., 2021; Ferrer-Rosell et al., 2023).

The incorporation of MKIS with real-time analytics and machine learning algorithms amplifies its capacity to furnish actionable insights promptly. This swift analysis of data empowers businesses to make informed decisions on the spot, be it adapting advertising strategies, refining pricing models, or reallocating resources. In an industry characterized by rapid shifts in consumer behaviors and market trends, the real-time capabilities of MKIS emerge as a strategic advantage for businesses aiming to maintain a competitive edge (Bharadiya, 2023).

Customer Relationship Management (CRM)

MKIS holds a pivotal position in Customer Relationship Management (CRM) within the tourism sector (Chuang & Lin, 2013). It facilitates the efficient handling of customer interactions, the maintenance of extensive customer databases, and the customization of experiences to foster enduring relationships with customers (Ku, 2010; Buttle & Maklan, 2019) as follows:

- Managing Customer Interactions: MKIS streamlines the oversight of customer interactions across the entire customer journey. It collects and logs customer data from diverse touchpoints, including website visits, social media engagements, email queries, reservations, and feedback post-stay. This system empowers businesses to monitor and supervise customer interactions, ensuring a uniform and smooth communication experience. With the centralization of customer data, MKIS offers a comprehensive overview of each customer's past interactions, preferences, and history, allowing businesses to provide individualized and customized services (Rosalinda & Ali, 2023; Stienmetz et al., 2022).
- Maintaining Customer Databases: MKIS functions as a centralized repository for the storage and administration of customer data. It facilitates the creation of extensive customer profiles, encompassing contact details, preferences, demographics, prior bookings, and feedback. MKIS streamlines the effective organization and retrieval of customer information, offering a unified perspective of each customer across various channels and engagements. This central database guarantees the accessibility of accurate and current customer details, supporting personalized marketing initiatives and customer service interactions (Zahay, 2008; Pesonen & Neidhardt, 2019).
- Personalizing Experiences: Utilizing customer data, MKIS customizes experiences and tailors offerings to individual customers. Through the analysis of customer preferences, behaviors, and previous interactions, MKIS aids businesses in comprehending customer needs and desires. Armed with this understanding, businesses can devise personalized offers, suggest pertinent

products or services, and adapt marketing messages. MKIS empowers businesses to provide focused promotions, personalized recommendations, and customized experiences that align with each customer, elevating customer satisfaction and nurturing enduring loyalty (Buttle & Maklan, 2019; de Bellis et al., 2019).

- Building Long-Term Relationships: MKIS empowers businesses to cultivate enduring relationships with customers. Through detailed customer profiles and ongoing tracking of interactions, MKIS aids businesses in comprehending customer preferences, anticipating their needs, and engaging with them proactively. MKIS streamlines targeted communication, enabling businesses to dispatch personalized messages, exclusive offers, and loyalty rewards tailored to customers' interests and past behaviors. These personalized interactions play a pivotal role in enhancing customer satisfaction, fostering loyalty, and encouraging advocacy, thereby nurturing long-term relationships and fostering repeat business (Gummerus et al., 2017; Wörndl et al., 2021).
- Monitoring Customer Satisfaction and Feedback: MKIS empowers businesses to assess customer satisfaction and gather feedback for ongoing enhancement of their offerings. Through the integration of feedback mechanisms like surveys, reviews, and social media monitoring, MKIS acquires valuable insights into customer experiences. This feedback proves instrumental in pinpointing areas for improvement, addressing customer concerns, and elevating service quality. MKIS facilitates swift responses to customer feedback, resolution of issues, and the demonstration of unwavering commitment to customer satisfaction, ultimately fortifying customer relationships (Aggarwal et al., 2023; Juska, 2021).
- Data Analysis and Insights: MKIS delivers data analysis and reporting functionalities, furnishing insights crucial for CRM strategies. Through the examination of customer data, MKIS discerns trends, patterns, and correlations that serve as foundations for informed decision-making. It furnishes invaluable metrics, including customer lifetime value, customer segmentation, and satisfaction scores. MKIS empowers businesses to gauge the efficacy of their CRM initiatives, monitor key performance indicators, and enact data-driven decisions for the optimization of their customer relationship strategies (Grigsby, 2022; Mandal, 2018).

The Vital Role of MKIS on Tourism Destination Management

MKIS exerts a notable influence on the management of tourism destinations. It assumes a pivotal role in elevating destination branding, bolstering competitiveness, enhancing visitor experiences, and shaping the strategies employed in destination marketing.

Destination Branding

MKIS assumes a crucial role in the realm of destination branding. Through the analysis of data pertaining to customer perceptions, preferences, and feedback, MKIS aids destinations in comprehending their brand image and reputation. This knowledge empowers destinations to refine their branding strategies, pinpoint areas for enhancement, and craft tailored messaging to elevate their brand identity. Additionally, MKIS offers insights into the branding strategies employed by competitors, enabling destinations to position themselves uniquely in the market and distinguish their offerings (Parlov et al., 2016; Pesonen & Neidhardt, 2019).

Enhancing Destination Competitiveness

MKIS plays a pivotal role in elevating destination competitiveness through the provision of valuable insights into market trends, competitor analysis, and customer preferences. Through the analysis of data related to customer behavior, demographics, and psychographics, MKIS assists destinations in identifying their unique selling points and competitive advantages. This information empowers destinations to craft targeted marketing campaigns, customize their offerings for specific customer segments, and establish points of differentiation from competitors. Additionally, MKIS offers real-time updates on emerging market trends, enabling destinations to adjust their strategies and remain competitive in the swiftly evolving tourism industry (Ritchie & Ritchie, 2002; Önder et al., 2017).

Improving Visitor Experiences

MKIS assumes a vital role in enhancing visitor experiences within destinations. Through the analysis of real-time data encompassing visitor feedback, reviews, and preferences, MKIS aids destinations in comprehending visitor expectations and desires. This knowledge empowers destinations to customize their offerings, create personalized experiences, and furnish visitors with relevant and engaging content. MKIS additionally streamlines communication between destinations and visitors, facilitating personalized recommendations, targeted promotions, and prompt responses to inquiries. Harnessing MKIS allows destinations to craft memorable and gratifying experiences for visitors, thereby boosting visitor satisfaction and fostering positive word-of-mouth (Karpova et al., 2018).

Shaping Destination Marketing Strategies

MKIS exerts an influence on destination marketing strategies by furnishing data-driven insights and facilitating targeted marketing endeavors. Through the analysis of market data, customer segmentation, and consumer behavior, MKIS assists destinations in pinpointing their target markets and devising effective marketing strategies. It enables destinations to discern the most suitable marketing channels, messages, and promotional activities to engage their target audience. Additionally, MKIS furnishes real-time information regarding the efficacy of marketing campaigns, affording destinations the flexibility to refine their strategies and allocate resources more judiciously. MKIS proves instrumental in helping destinations gauge the impact of marketing endeavors, track return on investment, and make informed decisions to optimize their marketing strategies (Kotler et al., 2017; Sorokina et al., 2022).

Tracking and Responding to Visitor Trends

MKIS empowers destinations to monitor and promptly respond to real-time visitor trends. Through the analysis of data concerning visitor demographics, preferences, and behavior, MKIS aids destinations in recognizing emerging trends and shifts in visitor expectations. This insight enables destinations to tailor their offerings, introduce new products or experiences, and align their marketing strategies accordingly. For instance, in the case of a rising trend toward sustainable tourism, MKIS can offer insights into visitor preferences for eco-friendly accommodations, local experiences, or responsible tourism initiatives. Destinations can utilize this information to formulate sustainable tourism strategies, attract environmentally conscious visitors, and enhance their reputation as sustainable destinations (Kotler et al., 2017).

Collaboration and Partnerships

MKIS serves as a facilitator for collaboration and partnerships in destination management. Through the analysis of data related to industry players, their capabilities, and areas of expertise, MKIS aids destinations in recognizing potential collaboration opportunities. These collaborations may involve partnerships with airlines, hotels, attractions, local businesses, or other destinations. Joint marketing campaigns, cross-promotional activities, and the creation of integrated tourism products can result from these collaborative efforts. MKIS supports destinations in the identification of potential partners, the assessment of partnership opportunities, and the monitoring of the performance of collaborative initiatives (Gursoy et al., 2015; Ritchie & Ritchie, 2002).

In the realm of tourism, MKIS profoundly influences destination management. It elevates destination competitiveness through insights into market trends and competitor analysis. MKIS enhances visitor experiences by customizing offerings and enabling personalized communication. It molds destination marketing strategies by offering data-driven insights and assessing the efficacy of marketing campaigns. MKIS aids destinations in monitoring visitor trends, adapting to evolving demands, and fostering collaborations and partnerships within the tourism industry. Through the utilization of MKIS, destinations can bolster their competitiveness, provide outstanding visitor experiences, and formulate effective marketing strategies to attract and satisfy their target audience.

Challenges and Limitations

Data Privacy and Security

Ensuring data privacy and security stands out as a key challenge. MKIS handles extensive customer data, encompassing personal details, preferences, and behaviors. Establishing robust data protection measures is imperative to safeguard this sensitive information and adhere to data privacy regulations like the General Data Protection Regulation (GDPR). Tourism businesses must implement secure data storage, encryption, and stringent access controls to shield customer data from unauthorized access and potential data breaches (Lali & Chakor, 2023; Naim et al., 2023).

Integration Complexities

The integration of MKIS with current systems and databases poses a complex task. Tourism businesses commonly operate multiple systems and platforms dedicated to reservations, customer relationship management, marketing automation, and analytics. Effectively integrating these systems to ensure a smooth flow of data and information demands meticulous planning, technical proficiency, and occasional customization. Challenges in integration may emerge due to variations in data formats, system compatibility issues, and the need for data synchronization. Addressing these complexities necessitates efficient project management and collaborative efforts between IT teams and stakeholders (Ashmarina & Zotova, 2016; Barykin et al., 2022).

Data Quality and Consistency

The success of MKIS hinges on the quality and coherence of data. Inaccuracies, incompleteness, or inconsistencies in data can result in unreliable insights and compromised decision-making. Businesses need to institute data governance practices and processes for ensuring data quality to guarantee accuracy, reliability, and consistency. This entails the implementation of data validation mechanisms, utilization of data cleansing techniques, and conducting regular data audits to uphold the high quality of data within the MKIS (Aggarwal et al., 2023; Koohathongsumrit & Luangpaiboon, 2023).

Need for Skilled Professionals

The implementation and administration of MKIS demand adept professionals with proficiency in data analytics, information systems, and marketing. These individuals need a comprehensive grasp of data management, analytical tools, and marketing strategies. Unfortunately, there is a scarcity of professionals possessing a blend of technical expertise and domain-specific knowledge within the tourism sector. To address this skills gap and harness the full potential of MKIS, businesses must allocate resources to training programs, recruit qualified personnel, or engage external consultants (Aggarwal et al., 2023; Du, 2014).

Change Management and Adoption

Introducing MKIS often necessitates substantial alterations in organizational processes, workflows, and perspectives. The resistance to change and a deficiency in user adoption pose potential obstacles to the effective implementation and utilization of MKIS. To overcome this challenge, businesses should commit to change management strategies, encompassing training programs, user assistance, and communication campaigns. It is essential to educate and engage employees across all levels, underscoring the advantages and significance of MKIS in enhancing marketing efficacy and customer experiences (Mero et al., 2020; Stienmetz et al., 2022).

Recommendations

The chapter offers recommendations to stakeholders on optimizing MKIS for sustainable and innovative tourism marketing. Stakeholders are advised to give precedence to constructing a resilient data infrastructure for the efficient utilization of MKIS in tourism marketing. This involves deploying mechanisms for data collection, integrating diverse data sources, and investing in secure storage and processing capabilities. Building a robust foundation for data management ensures the precision, accessibility, and scalability of data, facilitating effective analysis and utilization for marketing endeavors. Additionally, stakeholders should embrace a customer-centric approach, striving to gain profound insights into their target audience. Leveraging MKIS for the collection, analysis, and interpretation of customer data allows stakeholders to craft personalized experiences, customize marketing messages, and anticipate customer needs. Through the delivery of pertinent and tailored offerings, stakeholders can elevate customer satisfaction, cultivate loyalty, and stimulate sustainable growth.

Effective collaboration among stakeholders is crucial for maximizing the potential of MKIS in tourism marketing. Tourism boards, destination management organizations, travel agencies, hotels, and other industry participants should engage in collaborative efforts, sharing data within a secure and mutually advantageous framework. Through the pooling of resources, expertise, and data, stakeholders can obtain comprehensive insights, optimize marketing endeavors, and provide customers with seamless and memorable experiences.

The utilization of MKIS can be instrumental in advancing sustainability and responsible tourism practices. Stakeholders are encouraged to harness MKIS capabilities for gathering and analyzing data pertaining to sustainability metrics, environmental impact, and community engagement. This data can then inform marketing strategies, facilitate the creation of targeted campaigns, and highlight the sustainable practices adopted by destinations, accommodations, and tour operators. By aligning marketing efforts with sustainability objectives, stakeholders can appeal to conscientious customers and play a role in fostering the long-term sustainability of the tourism industry. Similarly, the tourism sector is characterized by its dynamic nature, with market conditions undergoing rapid changes. Stakeholders are encouraged to utilize MKIS for the ongoing monitoring of market trends, shifts in customer preferences, and the emergence of new technologies. Through consistent data analysis and the tracking of key performance indicators, stakeholders can pinpoint opportunities and challenges, make decisions guided by data, and adjust their marketing strategies accordingly. This flexibility will empower stakeholders to outpace competitors, meet the ever-changing expectations of customers, and instigate innovation in their tourism marketing endeavors. Thet should also give precedence to ethical data practices while utilizing MKIS for tourism marketing. This involves securing informed consent from customers, guaranteeing data privacy and security, and complying with pertinent data protection regulations. Transparent communication about data collection, processing, and utilization is crucial to establish trust with customers. Through the implementation of ethical data practices, stakeholders can minimize risks, uphold customer confidence, and cultivate a favorable perception of their brand.

To maximize the effectiveness of MKIS in tourism marketing, stakeholders ought to cultivate an atmosphere of innovation within their organizations. Encourage employees to engage in creative thinking, explore emerging technologies, and experiment with novel marketing approaches. Embrace a mindset of perpetual learning and enhancement, offering employees the requisite training and resources to make optimal use of MKIS. Through the promotion of an innovative culture, stakeholders can position themselves at the forefront of the industry, adapt to evolving market dynamics, and propel sustainable growth.

To derive valuable insights from the data amassed through MKIS, stakeholders should harness advanced analytics techniques. This entails employing predictive analytics for forecasting customer behavior and market trends, employing sentiment analysis to comprehend customer opinions and preferences, and utilizing social network analysis to pinpoint influential individuals and communities. Through the application of advanced analytics, stakeholders can base decisions on data, refine marketing campaigns, and unveil latent opportunities for sustainable and innovative tourism marketing.

In the evolving environment of technology, stakeholders should actively explore and adopt emerging technologies to augment their tourism marketing endeavors. For instance, the integration of virtual and augmented reality can provide immersive and interactive experiences, enabling customers to virtually explore destinations and attractions. Blockchain technology, on the other hand, can be applied to boost transparency and trust in the booking process, particularly within sustainable tourism initiatives. By staying informed about emerging technologies and incorporating them thoughtfully, stakeholders can distinguish themselves in the market and provide innovative and sustainable tourism experiences.

CONCLUSION

The study delves into the transformative impact of MKIS in the tourism industry, emphasizing its pivotal role in shaping marketing strategies, elevating customer experiences, and fostering overall business success. MKIS empowers tourism marketers with extensive data on customer preferences and market trends, enabling the creation of targeted and personalized campaigns that boost engagement and conversions. The integration of diverse marketing channels, facilitated by MKIS, expands reach and strengthens connections with a broader audience. Furthermore, MKIS enhances the entire customer journey, providing seamless interactions, personalized recommendations, and real-time communication to enhance satisfaction and loyalty. Operational efficiency is also heightened through MKIS, automating processes, streamlining workflows, and offering valuable insights for informed decision-making. Despite its benefits, challenges such as skill requirements, data privacy concerns, and technological advancements must be addressed. Overall, MKIS emerges as a dynamic force revolutionizing tourism marketing, enabling businesses to thrive in the digital era.

REFERENCES

Aaker, D., & Moorman, C. (2023). *Strategic market management*. John Wiley & Sons.

Aggarwal, K., Khoa, B., Sagar, K., Agrawal, R., Dhingra, M., Dhingra, J., & R, L. K. (2023). Marketing information system based on unsupervised visual data to manage transportation industry using signal processing. *Expert Systems: International Journal of Knowledge Engineering and Neural Networks*, e13384. Advance online publication. doi:10.1111/exsy.13384

Anshari, M., Almunawar, M., Lim, S., & Al-Mudimigh, A. (2019). Customer relationship management and big data enabled: Personalization & customization of services. *Applied Computing and Informatics, 15*(2), 94–101. doi:10.1016/j.aci.2018.05.004

Ashmarina, S., & Zotova, A. (2016). The system of marketing information management: development, assessment, improvement. *Економічний часопис-XXI*, (160), 51-56.

Barykin, S., Lavskaya, K., Baydukova, N., Kapustina, I., Kalinina, O., Naumova, E., & Dedyukhina, N. (2022). The complexity of digital marketing methodology implementation in air passenger transportation: The case of Russia. *Transportation Research Procedia, 63*, 695–702. doi:10.1016/j.trpro.2022.06.064

Benckendorff, P., Xiang, Z., & Sheldon, P. (2019). *Tourism information technology*. Cabi. doi:10.1079/9781786393432.0000

Bharadiya, J. (2023). The role of machine learning in transforming business intelligence. *International Journal of Computing and Artificial Intelligence, 4*(1), 16–24. doi:10.33545/27076571.2023.v4.i1a.60

Bulger, N. (2016). The evolving role of intelligence: Migrating from traditional competitive intelligence to integrated intelligence. *The International Journal of Intelligence, Security, and Public Affairs, 18*(1), 57–84. doi:10.1080/23800992.2016.1150691

Buttle, F., & Maklan, S. (2019). *Customer relationship management: concepts and technologies*. Routledge. doi:10.4324/9781351016551

Chase, C., & Chase, J. (2013). *Demand-driven forecasting: a structured approach to forecasting*. Wiley. doi:10.1002/9781118691861

Chuang, S., & Lin, H. (2013). The roles of infrastructure capability and customer orientation in enhancing customer-information quality in CRM systems: Empirical evidence from Taiwan. *International Journal of Information Management, 33*(2), 271–281. doi:10.1016/j.ijinfomgt.2012.12.003

de Bellis, E., Hildebrand, C., Ito, K., Herrmann, A., & Schmitt, B. (2019). Personalizing the customization experience: A matching theory of mass customization interfaces and cultural information processing. *JMR, Journal of Marketing Research, 56*(6), 1050–1065. doi:10.1177/0022243719867698

Du, J. (2014). The information journey of marketing professionals: Incorporating work task-driven information seeking, information judgments, information use, and information sharing. *Journal of the Association for Information Science and Technology, 65*(9), 1850–1869. doi:10.1002/asi.23085

Du, R., Netzer, O., Schweidel, D., & Mitra, D. (2021). Capturing marketing information to fuel growth. *Journal of Marketing, 85*(1), 163–183. doi:10.1177/0022242920969198

Dwivedi, Y., Ismagilova, E., Hughes, D., Carlson, J., Filieri, R., Jacobson, J., Jain, V., Karjaluoto, H., Kefi, H., Krishen, A. S., Kumar, V., Rahman, M. M., Raman, R., Rauschnabel, P. A., Rowley, J., Salo, J., Tran, G. A., & Wang, Y. (2021). Setting the future of digital and social media marketing research: Perspectives and research propositions. *International Journal of Information Management, 59*, 102168. doi:10.1016/j.ijinfomgt.2020.102168

Etim, G., Inyang, W., James, E., & Mbu-Ogar, G. (2023). Marketing information system (MKIS) and optimization of banking service delivery. *African Journal of Accounting and Financial Research, 6*(2), 112–125. doi:10.52589/AJAFR-XRYGQLV3

Ferrer-Rosell, B., Massimo, D., & Berezina, K. (2023). *Information and Communication Technologies in Tourism 2023: Proceedings of the ENTER 2023 eTourism Conference, January 18-20, 2023*. Springer Nature. 10.1007/978-3-031-25752-0

Fleisher, C., Wright, S., & Allard, H. (2008). The role of insight teams in integrating diverse marketing information management techniques. *European Journal of Marketing, 42*(7/8), 836–851. doi:10.1108/03090560810877187

Grigsby, M. (2022). *Marketing analytics: A practical guide to improving consumer insights using data techniques*. Kogan Page Publishers.

Gummerus, J., von Koskull, C., & Kowalkowski, C. (2017). Guest editorial: Relationship marketing–past, present and future. *Journal of Services Marketing, 31*(1), 1–5. doi:10.1108/JSM-12-2016-0424

Gupta, S., Drave, V., Bag, S., & Luo, Z. (2019). Leveraging smart supply chain and information system agility for supply chain flexibility. *Information Systems Frontiers*, *21*(3), 547–564. doi:10.1007/s10796-019-09901-5

Gursoy, D., Saayman, M., & Sotiriadis, M. (2015). *Collaboration in tourism businesses and destinations: A handbook.* Emerald Group Publishing.

Harmon, R. (2002). Marketing Information Systems. Encyclopedia of Information Systems, 3, 137-151.

Huang, M., & Rust, R. (2021). A strategic framework for artificial intelligence in marketing. *Journal of the Academy of Marketing Science*, *49*(1), 30–50. doi:10.1007/s11747-020-00749-9

Hung, C. (2019). Using Cloud Services to Develop Marketing Information System Applications. *Journal of Internet Technology*, *20*(1), 157–166.

Juska, J. (2021). *Integrated marketing communication: advertising and promotion in a digital world.* Routledge. doi:10.4324/9780367443382

Karpova, S., Panyukova, V., & Rozhkov, I. (2018). Information support for tourist destination marketing: Russian and international experiences. In *В сборнике: Financial and Economic Tools Used in the World Hospitality Industry Proceedings of the 5th International Conference on Management and Technology in Knowledge, Service, Tourism and Hospitality* (pp. 215-218).

Kellerman, P. (2023). The Impact of Marketing Information Systems on Brilliant Financial Performance in Hospital Industry. *Indian Journal of Public Health*, *10*(3), 577–587.

Kinyua, D. (2020). *Effect of Marketing Information Systems on Competitive Advantage of Ict Application Service Providers in Nairobi County* (Doctoral dissertation, University of Nairobi).

Koohathongsumrit, N., & Luangpaiboon, P. (2023). Strategic Marketing Information System Planning: An Integrated BWM–ELECTRE Approach. *Group Decision and Negotiation.* Advance online publication. doi:10.1007/s10726-023-09861-x

Kotler, P., Bowen, J., Makens, J., & Baloglu, S. (2017). *Marketing for hospitality and tourism.* Pearson.

Ku, E. (2010). The impact of customer relationship management through implementation of information systems. *Total Quality Management & Business Excellence*, *21*(11), 1085–1102. doi:10.1080/14783360903250514

Kumar, V., Leone, R., Aaker, D., & Day, G. (2018). *Marketing research*. John Wiley & Sons.

Lali, K., & Chakor, A. (2023). Improving the Security and Reliability of a Quality Marketing Information System: A Priority Prerequisite for Good Strategic Management of a Successful Entrepreneurial Project. *Data & Metadata*, *2*, 40–40. doi:10.56294/dm202340

Mandal, P. (2018). Marketing information and marketing intelligence: Roles in generating customer insights. *International Journal of Business Forecasting and Marketing Intelligence*, *4*(3), 311–321. doi:10.1504/IJBFMI.2018.092786

McDaniel, C., & Gates, R. (2018). *Marketing research*. John Wiley & Sons.

McManus, L. (2013). Customer accounting and marketing performance measures in the hotel industry: Evidence from Australia. *International Journal of Hospitality Management*, *33*, 140–152. doi:10.1016/j.ijhm.2012.07.007

Mero, J., Tarkiainen, A., & Tobon, J. (2020). Effectual and causal reasoning in the adoption of marketing automation. *Industrial Marketing Management*, *86*, 212–222. doi:10.1016/j.indmarman.2019.12.008

Miklosik, A., & Evans, N. (2020). Impact of big data and machine learning on digital transformation in marketing: A literature review. *IEEE Access : Practical Innovations, Open Solutions*, *8*, 101284–101292. doi:10.1109/ACCESS.2020.2998754

Minazzi, R. (2015). *Social media marketing in tourism and hospitality*. Springer International Publishing Switzerland. doi:10.1007/978-3-319-05182-6

Naim, A., Alqahtani, H., Muniasamy, A., Bilfaqih, S., Mahveen, R., & Mahjabeen, R. (2023). Applications of Information Systems and Data Security in Marketing Management. In Fraud Prevention, Confidentiality, and Data Security for Modern Businesses (pp. 57-83). IGI Global. doi:10.4018/978-1-6684-6581-3.ch003

Neidhardt, J., & Wörndl, W. (2020). *Information and Communication Technologies in Tourism 2020*. Springer International Publishing. doi:10.1007/978-3-030-36737-4

Nemutanzhela, P., & Iyamu, T. (2011). A framework for enhancing the information systems innovation: Using competitive intelligence. *Electronic Journal of Information Systems Evaluation*, *14*(2), 242–253.

Önder, I., Wöber, K., & Zekan, B. (2017). Towards a sustainable urban tourism development in Europe: The role of benchmarking and tourism management information systems–A partial model of destination competitiveness. *Tourism Economics*, *23*(2), 243–259. doi:10.1177/1354816616656247

Palmatier, R., & Sridhar, S. (2020). *Marketing strategy: Based on first principles and data analytics*. Bloomsbury Publishing.

Parlov, N., Perkov, D., & Sičaja, Ž. (2016). New trends in tourism destination branding by means of digital marketing. *Acta Economica Et Turistica*, *2*(2), 139–146. doi:10.1515/aet-2016-0012

Pearlson, K., Saunders, C., & Galletta, D. (2024). *Managing and using information systems: A strategic approach*. John Wiley & Sons.

Pearson, S. (2016). *Building brands directly: creating business value from customer relationships*. Springer.

Pencarelli, T. (2020). The digital revolution in the travel and tourism industry. *Information Technology & Tourism*, *22*(3), 455–476. doi:10.1007/s40558-019-00160-3

Pesonen, J., & Neidhardt, J. (2019). Information and communication technologies in tourism 2019. In *Proceedings of the International Conference*. Springer International Publishing. 10.1007/978-3-030-05940-8

Queiroz, J., & Oliveira, B. (2014). Benefits of the marketing information system in the clothing retail business. *Journal of Information Systems and Technology Management*, *11*(1), 153–168. doi:10.4301/S1807-17752014000100009

Ritchie, R., & Ritchie, J. (2002). A framework for an industry supported destination marketing information system. *Tourism Management*, *23*(5), 439–454. doi:10.1016/S0261-5177(02)00007-9

Rosalinda, U., & Ali, H. (2023). Analysis of Factors Influencing the Marketing Information System: CRM, Customer Satisfactaction and Sales Effectiveness. *Dinasti International Journal of Digital Business Management*, *4*(2), 264–270.

Rosário, A., & Dias, J. (2023). How has data-driven marketing evolved: Challenges and opportunities with emerging technologies. *International Journal of Information Management Data Insights*, *3*(2), 100203. doi:10.1016/j.jjimei.2023.100203

Rowley, J. (2017). *Information marketing*. Routledge. doi:10.4324/9781315196398

Sari, J., Nugroho, L., Ferdiana, R., & Santosa, P. (2016). Review on customer segmentation technique on ecommerce. *Advanced Science Letters*, *22*(10), 3018–3022. doi:10.1166/asl.2016.7985

Schweidel, D., Bart, Y., Inman, J., Stephen, A., Libai, B., Andrews, M., Rosario, A. B., Chae, I., Chen, Z., Kupor, D., Longoni, C., & Thomaz, F. (2022). How consumer digital signals are reshaping the customer journey. *Journal of the Academy of Marketing Science*, *50*(6), 1257–1276. doi:10.1007/s11747-022-00839-w PMID:35221393

Shoushtari, F., Bashir, E., Hassankhani, S., & Rezvanjou, S. (2023). Optimization in Marketing Enhancing Efficiency and Effectiveness. *International Journal of Industrial Engineering and Operational Research, 5*(2), 12-23.

Sorokina, E., Wang, Y., Fyall, A., Lugosi, P., Torres, E., & Jung, T. (2022). Constructing a smart destination framework: A destination marketing organization perspective. *Journal of Destination Marketing & Management*, *23*, 100688. doi:10.1016/j.jdmm.2021.100688

Stienmetz, J., Ferrer-Rosell, B., & Massimo, D. (2022). *Information and Communication Technologies in Tourism 2022: Proceedings of the ENTER 2022 ETourism Conference, January 11-14, 2022*. Springer Nature. 10.1007/978-3-030-94751-4

Thuita, J., & Njeru, W. (2021). Marketing Information Systems and Competitive Advantage at Consolidated Bank of Kenya Limited. *European Journal of Business and Management Research*, *6*(5), 224–227. doi:10.24018/ejbmr.2021.6.5.1077

Vu, H. Q., Li, G., Law, R., & Zhang, Y. (2018). Tourist activity analysis by leveraging mobile social media data. *Journal of Travel Research*, *57*(7), 883–898. doi:10.1177/0047287517722232

Wang, J., Zheng, B., & Liu, H. (2021). Satisfying consumers all around: A multidisciplinary view of omnichannel retail. *Industrial Management & Data Systems*, *121*(1), 158–171. doi:10.1108/IMDS-08-2020-0452

Watson, R., Berthon, P., Pitt, L., & Zinkhan, G. (2023). *Electronic commerce: The strategic perspective*. Dryden.

Weinstein, A. (2013). *Handbook of market segmentation: Strategic targeting for business and technology firms*. Routledge. doi:10.4324/9780203862483

Wörndl, W., Koo, C., & Stienmetz, J. (2021). *Information and Communication Technologies in Tourism 2021: Proceedings of the ENTER 2021 eTourism Conference, January 19–22, 2021*. Springer Nature. 10.1007/978-3-030-65785-7

Yoo, C., Yoon, D., & Park, E. (2018). Tourist motivation: An integral approach to destination choices. *Tourism Review*, *73*(2), 169–185. doi:10.1108/TR-04-2017-0085

Zahay, D. (2008). Successful B2B customer database management. *Journal of Business and Industrial Marketing*, *23*(4), 264–272. doi:10.1108/08858620810865843

Chapter 12
Utilizing Marketing Information Systems and Big Data Analytics in Promoting Tourism Destinations

N. S. Saba Farheen
RV College of Engineering, India

Goutham B. Bhandari
RV College of Engineering, India

Lalshawala Abdulmannan
RV College of Engineering, India

Gaurav Makhija
RV College of Engineering, India

ABSTRACT

The integration of big data analytics (BDA) and marketing information systems (MKIS) has grown more and more significant in the field of tourism marketing. This investigation's theoretical framework is based on important works in the domains of data analytics, marketing technology, and tourism marketing. Insights gleaned from marketing management illuminate the evolution from conventional marketing strategies to contemporary data-centric methodologies. Recognizing the current reliance on MKIS and BDA within the domain of tourism marketing mandates an appreciation of this historical progression. This study on big data provides a thorough review of the tools, technologies, and approaches involved in BDA. These types of technologies shape visitor experiences and provide a further perspective on the synergy between MKIS and BDA in tourism marketing.

DOI: 10.4018/979-8-3693-3310-5.ch012

INTRODUCTION

The field of marketing for tourism is going through a radical change. A once-traditionally oriented industry is now leading the way in data-driven strategy and digital innovation. This development is indicative of a larger trend in the global economy, where data analytics and technology improvements are changing the face of business. These modifications go beyond just incidental in the fast-paced and fiercely competitive tourism industry; rather, they are essential to the survival and prosperity of travel destinations and service providers.

Two key systems, BDA and MKIS, are at the centre of this transition. MKIS are advanced systems that gather, process, analyse, and distribute marketing data to help with problem-solving and decision-making in the field (Laudon & Laudon, 2020). This technology is essential for comprehending market trends, customer behaviour, and the efficacy of marketing campaigns. MKIS plays an important role in contemporary marketing, due to its ability to convert unstructured information into insightful knowledge for strategic decision-making (Kotler & Keller, 2016).

BDA can be utilised to enhance MKIS. BDA is a procedure that looks at big and diverse data sets to find unknown correlations, hidden patterns, and other relevant information (Mayer-Schönberger & Cukier, 2013). Using BDA in tourism there is more to marketing than merely managing massive data sets—it also entails gleaning insightful information that can inform strategic choices. BDA plays a significant role in empowering marketers to make data-driven decisions (Davenport, 2012). This is particularly important in a sector as complex and fast-paced as tourism.

In the tourism industry, the change from conventional to technology-driven marketing has been consistent rather than sudden. The developing marketing strategies now heavily depend on data and analytics. Understanding this historical context is necessary to understand why MKIS and BDA are essential components of a modern tourism marketing plan, rather than just being technological tools (Buhalis & Law, 2008).

In the context of tourism, it is essential to comprehend how MKIS and BDA complement and integrate with one another. Case studies and real-world applications provide specific examples of how these technologies are being used in the tourism industry and highlight the benefits and drawbacks of doing so (Minazzi, 2015).

It is impossible to exaggerate the significance of MKIS and BDA in tourism marketing. They offer a deeper comprehension of consumer inclinations and actions, resulting in more focused and efficient marketing plans. These developments in technology allow for deeper connections with customers, which makes it possible to launch more focused and successful marketing efforts (Kotler & Keller, 2016).

BDA is revolutionizing marketing tactics and demonstrating how data-driven insights can produce more inventive and successful campaigns (Mayer-Schönberger & Cukier, 2013).

The use of MKIS and BDA in tourism marketing is not without difficulties, though. A few of the challenges faced by marketers in this industry are the requirement for specific talents, data privacy concerns, and technical complexity. These technologies provide a multitude of benefits and opportunities. They may result in more effective, focused, and prosperous marketing campaigns—all of which are necessary in a sector of the economy as cutthroat as tourism.

Businesses discover that the confluence of BDA, the Internet of Things (IoT), and MKIS forms a potent strategic cooperation that benefits them in navigating the intricacies of today's digital ecosystem. The cornerstone is MKIS, which simplifies systematic data management to support well-informed decision-making. This partnership improves analytical skills when combined with BDA, providing in-depth knowledge of consumer behavior and market dynamics. This synergy is further enhanced by the introduction of IoT, which links physical objects and generates real-time data. When combined, these elements facilitate the creation of customized marketing plans and expedite the process of making decisions. Companies that make use of this connected ecosystem may provide customized consumer experiences, increasing their competitiveness in the ever-changing digital market.

The objectives of this chapter are twofold: first, it will analyze the several obstacles that arise when employing MKIS and BDA in tourism marketing, and second, it will offer practical suggestions and ways to overcome these hurdles. This chapter is intended to be a helpful guide for professionals in the tourism business who wish to. It is a theoretical study to maximize the use of new technologies.

The chapter's structure is intended to give readers a thorough grasp of MKIS and BDA concerning travel industry marketing. Every section explores a different facet of these systems, covering everything from their theoretical underpinnings to real-world applications, difficulties, and implementation solutions. This method guarantees a comprehensive understanding and gives readers the skills and information they need to successfully negotiate the challenges of digital marketing in the travel and tourist industry.

1: FOUNDATIONS OF MARKETING INFORMATION SYSTEMS (MKIS)

As MKIS has developed, technological breakthroughs have also highlighted the vital part these systems play in today's corporate environment. MKIS has originated from its original purpose as simple data stores to a dynamic fusion of data analytics, innovative technology, and strategic planning. Because of this convergence, MKIS is better equipped to provide detailed insights into the nuances of customer behaviour, shifting market trends, and the competitive environments that businesses must traverse.

Its symbiotic link with different functional departments within a business further highlights MKIS's collaborative character. The interdependence of marketing, production, finance, and human resources is strengthened by the smooth integration of data flows and procedures among these departments. The intention is evident in practice: MKIS is not meant to function on its own. A stand-alone strategy is unworkable when one realizes that marketing professionals want holistic knowledge that necessitates integrating data from several business areas (Li et al., 1993).

When MKIS moves beyond its physical form to become a methodological framework (Kotler & Keller, 2016), it automatically acknowledges the unique requirements set out by marketing managers. MKIS is much more than just a data management system; rather, it's a conceptual organization that directs strategic thinking to satisfy the particular information needs of marketing experts. Since it is conceptual, it can be looked at from many angles, which promotes relevance and flexibility in a corporate environment that is always changing. Therefore, MKIS's continued evolution not only represents technological advancement but also highlights its critical significance as an instrument for strategic thought that will influence marketing decision-making in the future.

1.1 Components and Architecture of MKIS

An MKIS is a complex system made up of various essential parts, including:

Data collection is the process of compiling information from a variety of sources, including social media, market research, consumer databases, and transaction histories (Wixom & Todd, 2005).

Data analysis is the process of processing and interpreting the gathered data using statistical and data mining methods to transform unprocessed data into actionable insights (Wixom & Todd, 2005).

Data storage is the process of keeping information in databases or data warehouses that can be accessed safely (Wixom & Todd, 2005).

Information dissemination is the process of effectively providing stakeholders with processed information via a variety of channels, such as dashboards, reports, and real-time alerts (Wixom & Todd, 2005).

These elements as shown in Figure 1 work together to guarantee the efficacy of an MKIS and empower companies to make data-driven marketing choices.

Figure 1. MKIS flow

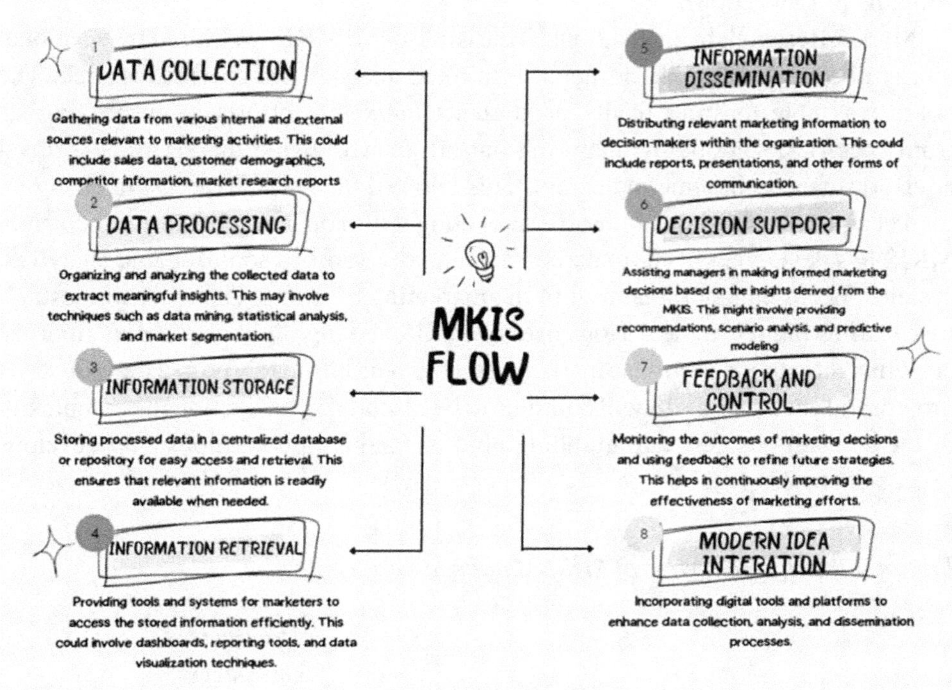

1.2 Functionality and Applications in Tourism

In tourism, MKIS is pivotal for understanding market dynamics and consumer preferences, crucial for staying competitive in this dynamic sector Some of the applications are as follows:

Analysis of Customer Feedback for Hotel Chains: MKIS was used by a well-known hotel chain to compile and examine client input from a variety of sources, such as social media, internet reviews, and direct feedback. With the use of this technology, the hotel was able to better serve particular clientele segments, react quickly to their demands, and increase overall guest satisfaction. Additionally, the data aided in the creation of customised marketing plans that increased client retention and referrals (Gretzel et al., 2015).

Destination marketing organisation (DMO): To Promote Destinations an MKIS was used by a DMO to monitor the success of its marketing initiatives, examine visitor flow patterns, and enhance promotional tactics. The DMO's advertising and promotional efforts were informed by its understanding of important markets, seasonal trends, and visitor preferences, thanks to the MKIS. Increased tourist arrivals and improved contact with potential tourists were the outcomes of the focused marketing (Buhalis & Law, 2008).

Market Research by the National Tourism Board: MKIS was hired by a national tourism board to carry out in-depth sentiment analysis and market research. The board was able to strategically position its marketing efforts to attract tourists from specific locations by analysing data from worldwide market trends, travel advisories, and economic indicators. This allowed the board to adjust to changing market conditions and maximise the marketing return on investment. In conclusion, MKIS has developed from fundamental data processors to sophisticated analytical systems, becoming a crucial tool in the marketing of travel. The tourist industry's case studies highlight the various uses of MKIS and highlight how it may improve customer interaction, optimise marketing tactics, and ultimately propel the industry's growth and success. MKIS will continue to be essential in navigating the complexity of the tourism business and grabbing hold of market opportunities as it develops (Fuchs et al., 2014).

Figure 2. Design overview of MKIS database

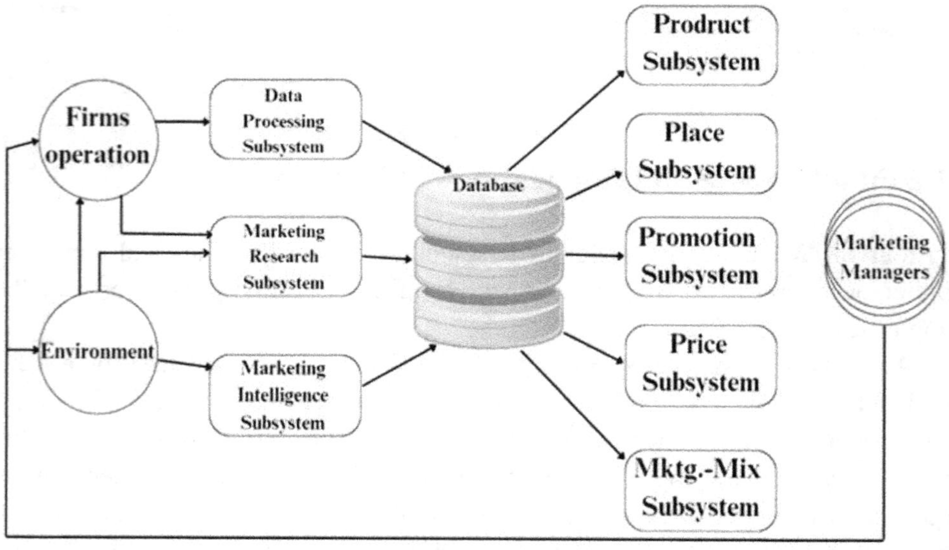

The design process also includes an assessment of the information costs of a MKIS. A proposed overview for analysing the information costs of the marketing system is depicted in Figure 2. Implementing the steps of the suggested design process for a marketing information system result in the structure being built, taking into consideration the features of the business and the information support system for its operations. The chapter discusses the conceptual paradigm for creating a MKIS for a design and survey business. This methodology is distinguished by its systematic approach and emphasis on design phases such as information cost analysis and assessment of the design and survey provider's information system's operational performance.

1. Firm's Operation and Marketing Management: The central element of this diagram is a database, which serves as the hub connecting various subsystems. These subsystems are essential for a firm's operation and marketing management. These are overlooked by the marketing managers to properly survey the product value, product ratings, and the product's utility to maximize profit.
2. Subsystem Connections: The connections of various subsystems are explained below
    - Data Processing Subsystem: The following subsystem takes inputs from operations performed by the managers for growth. The following subsystem facilitates us to eliminate unnecessary data thus filtering only the unmasked data highlighted by the managers like the growth of the product, response of competitors, performance of the product since launch, ratings by the consumers, etc.
    - Marketing Research Subsystem and Marketing Intelligence Subsystem: Both connect to the central database and the firm's operation. Both of the subsystems work synergistically the research system conveys the common interests of the consumers which are essential for improvement of the product, and the intelligence system feeds the research response into it form the environment hence making the intelligence system more aware of the consumers likeness and dislike Ness.
    - Product Subsystem, Place Subsystem, Promotion Subsystem, Price Subsystem, and Marketing Mix Subsystem: All linked to the central database which contains the enchantment processes of marketing and promotion of the output.
3. Marketing Managers: They oversee and coordinate these subsystems, ensuring effective marketing strategies and surveillance over the competitors.
4. Environment: Influences both the firm's operation and the marketing research subsystem for a systematic flow.

2: BIG DATA ANALYTICS (BDA) IN TOURISM MARKETING

The way various businesses, including the tourism sector, view and use data has been completely transformed by BDA. The term "big data analysis," or "BDA," describes the process of looking through enormous, diverse data sets to find patterns, relationships that aren't obvious, and other important discoveries. The capacity for big data analysis has been a popular critical component of strategic decision-making in today's data-centric environment, providing insights that can result in more successful marketing campaigns and improved consumer experiences.

One cannot overstate the role that BDA plays in the travel and tourism industry. Due to the widespread adoption of digital technology, firms involved in tourism today have access to enormous volumes of data from a variety of sources, including social media, online bookings, review platforms, and Internet of Things devices. This data analysis offers priceless insights into consumer preferences, industry trends, and operational efficiency.

2.1 Tools and Techniques in BDA

Large data sets can be handled and interpreted using a wide range of tools and processes as depicted in Figure 3 which can be found in the BDA ecosystem (Davenport, 2012). Important instruments and methods frequently employed in BDA in the travel industry include:

- Data mining: It is the process of looking for patterns and relationships in big data collections. This method is essential for comprehending the preferences and behaviour of customers.
- Predictive analytics: Based on past data, it determines the probability of future events using statistical algorithms and machine learning approaches. It's very helpful for predicting travel trends and demand. When applied to unstructured data, such as customer reviews and social media posts, text analytics and sentiment analysis can provide details on the opinions and sentiments of the general population.
- Applications for data visualisation: *Tableau and Microsoft Power BI* are two examples of applications that assist in displaying data insights in a manner that is both aesthetically pleasing and simple to understand.

Figure 3. Tools and techniques flow used in BDA

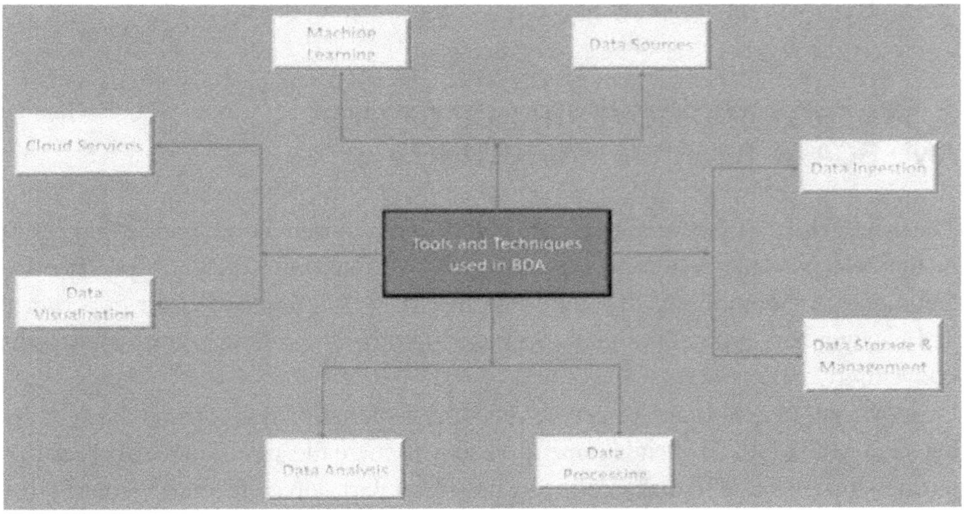

2.2 Successful BDA Implementation in Tourism Marketing

Airline Route Optimization: A major airline used BDA to optimize its flight routes and schedules. By analyzing vast amounts of data on passenger travel patterns, weather conditions, and fuel costs, the airline was able to adjust its routes, improving operational efficiency and reducing costs (Davenport, 2012).

Personalized Marketing in Hospitality: A hotel chain implemented BDA to create personalised marketing strategies. Analyzing customer data from various touchpoints, the hotel was able to offer customized room options, personalized amenities, and tailored travel experiences, significantly enhancing guest satisfaction and loyalty (Mayer-Schönberger & Cukier, 2013).

Destination Promotion by a Tourism Board: A tourism board employed BDA to enhance its promotional efforts. By analysing data from social media, web traffic, and previous marketing campaigns, the board gained insights into the preferences of potential tourists. This enabled the creation of targeted marketing campaigns, resulting in increased visitor numbers and higher engagement rates (Fuchs et al., 2014).

Therefore, BDA in tourism marketing represents a significant leap forward in how the industry understands and engages with its customers. Using instruments such as data mining, predictive analytics, and data visualization, tourism Companies can obtain a profound understanding of customer behavior and market dynamics. The real-world case studies demonstrate the practical application and tangible benefits of BDA in tourism, showcasing its potential to transform marketing strategies and drive business growth. As the tourism industry continues to evolve in a data-driven world, BDA will undoubtedly play a big role in shaping its future.

3. SYNERGY AND GOVERNANCE OF MKIS AND BDA IN TOURISM MARKETING

The synergistic link between BDA and MKIS and how their combination may result in the best possible results in the marketing of tourism. Utilisation of effective techniques for combining different systems, how this improves user experience and engagement, typical problems seen during this integration, and possible fixes (Davenport, 2012).

As we begin a thorough review of the tourist marketing domain and the synergy between MKIS and BDA, it is imperative to recognize the significant effects of this partnership on the dynamics of the sector. This part delves further, revealing the levels of intricacy in the MKIS and BDA integration and demonstrating how this convergence acts as a pivot for revolutionary developments (Gretzel et al., 2015).

Exploring the fundamentals of successful integration processes, it is observed that several tactical stances that companies may take to successfully combine MKIS and BDA. This intends to provide practical insights into maximizing these technologies' cohabitation by illuminating excellent practices and cutting-edge approaches. It illustrates the concrete effects of effective integration with case studies, explaining how it breaks through traditional marketing paradigms to provide hitherto unheard-of benefits for players in the tourist industry (Fuchs et al., 2014).

The conversation that follows explores the implications of this integration for consumer experience and participation in the travel industry. Through an examination of the data-driven insights produced by MKIS and BDA, we will investigate how companies might modify their marketing tactics to better align with the tastes and demands of contemporary travellers. The emphasis will be on customization diversification in technologies that facilitate the creation of personalized goods and services, strengthening the connection between tourists and the places or services they use.

However, no investigation into such a complicated integration is complete if the typical problems that businesses face are not addressed. This section provides a thorough overview of the obstacles that might prevent seamless integration by painstakingly identifying and breaking down issues ranging from data privacy concerns to the requirement for competent individuals. Furthermore, it provides creative approaches and methods for overcoming these obstacles, guaranteeing that businesses may fully utilize MKIS and BDA without sacrificing effectiveness and integrity.

This thorough investigation essentially acts as a guide for negotiating the complex landscape of MKIS and BDA integration in travel advertising. This section attempts to enable researchers, industry experts, and decision-makers to embrace and capitalise on the revolutionary power of this technological alliance by removing layers of complexity, offering useful insights, and tackling obstacles head-on.

3.1 Integrative Approaches

To improve total marketing efficacy, MKIS and BDA integration in tourism marketing goes beyond simply utilising both systems concurrently. Rather, it entails building a coherent, integrated framework that makes use of each system's advantages. While BDA offers sophisticated tools for evaluating this data to derive valuable insights, MKIS gives a disciplined method for gathering and organising marketing data.

Some of the integrative approaches are as follows:

- Data Consolidation: Consolidation is the initial stage of integration, involving the merging of data into a single database from multiple sources (social media, online booking systems, customer reviews, etc.). The foundation of a strong MKIS-BDA architecture is this consolidation.
- Integration of Analytical Tools: By combining the data processing capabilities of MKIS with the analytical tools of BDA, marketers can conduct more thorough assessments. This covers market trend analysis, consumer segmentation, and predictive modeling.
- Feedback Loops: Implementing feedback loops that allow MKIS operations to be informed by insights gleaned from BDA guarantees that the marketing information system is always up to date with the newest discoveries and trends.

3.2 Enhancing Customer Experience and Engagement

In tourism marketing, the combined power of MKIS and BDA greatly improves client experience and engagement. Some of these are mentioned below:

- Personalized Marketing: Travel industry marketers can develop tailored marketing plans that address the unique requirements and interests of each customer by examining consumer data, preferences, and behaviours.
- Customer Journey Analysis: By identifying important touchpoints and engagement possibilities, the integrated system enables a thorough analysis of the customer journey. More successful marketing initiatives that follow the customer through their whole journey may result from this.

- Real-Time Interaction and Responsiveness: Tourism organisations may engage with clients more dynamically and react swiftly to feedback and market developments when they possess the capacity to handle and analyse data in real-time.

3.3 Challenges and Solutions in Integration

The methodologies now in use must be changed, which must be reorganized using a parallel approach. This also means establishing fault-tolerant evaluation. Big Data correctness is inextricably linked to the requirement to measure the gap between the user's expectations and the delivered in BDA. The accuracy is highly dependent on the specificity of the analytics needs supplied by users. The more explicit the criteria, the more accurate the result (Big data analytics as-a-service, 2016). Some of the complexities are mentioned below:

Data Integration Complexities: Integrating several data sources can be difficult. Standardized data formats and middleware are two ways to solve the challenge of successful data integration.

Skill Gaps: Specific abilities are needed to operate combined MKIS and BDA systems effectively. Hiring specialized staff and implementing focused training programs are two ways to overcome this.

Security and Privacy Issues: Security and privacy become critical when processing vast amounts of data. Enforcing privacy laws and putting strong data security measures in place helps allay these worries.

Cost Implications: Maintaining and integrating these systems might be expensive. Selecting scalable technologies and implementing a staged integration strategy might aid in efficient cost management.

Figure 4. Challenges faced in MKIS and BDA

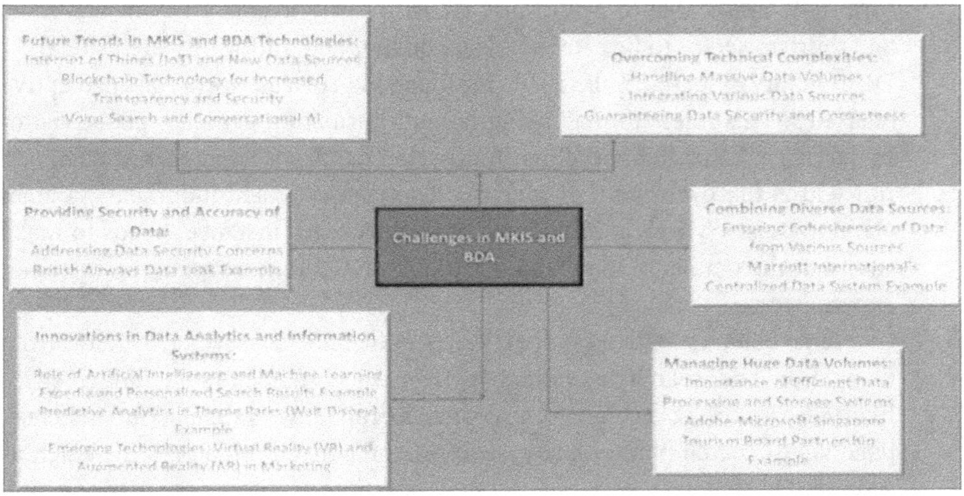

A powerful instrument in the tourism marketing toolbox is the combination of MKIS and BDA. Tourism marketers can gain a degree of client interaction and information that was not previously available by integrating these platforms. Even though there are problems, the integration of MKIS and BDA can completely change the way tourism destinations are marketed, providing more individualised customer experiences and effective marketing results, with careful planning and execution. This portion not only highlights the potential of these integrated systems but also offers helpful advice for resolving integration-related issues, opening the door for creative and successful tourism marketing approaches as depicted in Figure 4.

Effective data management and administration are critical components of the smooth integration of MKIS and BDA in tourism marketing. The first step in addressing privacy issues and ethical considerations is to emphasize the necessity of handling consumer data transparently and responsibly. Prioritising data standardization and improvement help tourism marketers access a wealth of insights that facilitate more accurate targeting and individualized interactions with guests. Data is continuously being created and shared by people, tools, and machines. Huge data sets improvise the introduction, evolution, and progress of new sharing technologies, device connection, and the proliferation of data-generating devices/platforms such as Facebook, YouTube, News websites, world affairs, internet-connected automobiles, wearable gadgets, and cell phones. Large datasets frequently contain untapped, hidden values. To capitalize on the benefits of big data, organizations must use advanced analytical approaches to extract meaningful insights from large databases. As a result, organisations see the need for BDA to assist in driving decision-making inside the organisations.

1. Data Quality and Standardization: The proverb "garbage in, garbage out" is especially applicable to MKIS and BDA. For MKIS and BDA in the travel and tourism sector to be effective, data quality and uniformity are critical.
2. Data Quality Essential: Solid data is the foundation of trustworthy and perceptive analytics. This refers to making sure that information gathered about visitor preferences, behaviors, booking trends, and feedback is precise, timely, and full within the framework of tourism. To make educated judgments, a hotel chain that uses MKIS to collect client feedback, for instance, needs to make sure that the data is reliable and up to date, reflecting a variety of customer experiences.
3. Customer behavior indicators & experiences include measurements for website navigation and search; economic performance indicators include metrics like reservations, overnight stays, rates, occupancy, and sales(for instance, page visits, search phrases), reservations, and consumption patterns (such as reservation channels, conversion rates, duration of visit, cancellations, and visitor monitoring), and client profile (such as nationality, age, gender, skiing travel habits, client lifetime value, the preferred mode of transportation and lodging, and the goal of visit). Lastly, indicators of customer perception and experience include metrics assessing perceived awareness of destination brands (such as brand awareness, destination knowledge, and information sources), destination value areas (such as summer activities and attractions, services and features, atmosphere, social interaction, and winter and non-skiing activities), cost-effectiveness and client satisfaction (e.g., functional and emotional value), and loyalty (that is, emotional, conative, and cognitive loyalty) (Fuchs et al., 2014).
4. Key to Standardization: Data standardization is equally crucial. It entails establishing uniform measurements and formats for many data sources to be able to facilitate efficient aggregation and analysis. For example, to be able to do meaningful analysis, it is imperative that all parties similarly report data if a tourism board is collecting data from different hotels and travel firms. The European Travel Commission's efforts to harmonize information from its participating nations and offer comprehensive insights into travel trends serve as a concrete illustration.
5. Data privacy and ethical considerations: As MKIS and BDA become increasingly embedded in travel advertising, privacy issues and ethical issues grow more prominent. There are other serious concerns about the gathering and use of enormous volumes of personal data.
6. Handling the Privacy Terrain: Privacy is a top priority, particularly when it comes to sensitive personal travel data. An example of a travel app that makes individualised travel plans using BDA. Although this makes the user's life

easier, it also necessitates the gathering of extensive personal information that begs the question of how this data is handled and safeguarded.

7. Ethical Consequences: These moral consequences go beyond privacy. For example, profiling and possible prejudice may result from using predictive analytics in tourism marketing. When a travel service company just caters to affluent customers while disregarding other demographics, it presents moral dilemmas of equity and inclusivity.
8. Regulatory Compliance: The effective application of MKIS and BDA in the tourism industry depends on navigating the legal framework and compliance standards.
9. Comprehending Legal Frameworks: Regulations about data privacy and usage differ between nations. A good example is the General Data Protection Regulation (GDPR) of the European Union (EU). Strict standards on data collecting and processing are enforced, affecting the operations of European tourism businesses and those handling the data of EU individuals. Marriott International is one example of A business that has to abide by GDPR or risk paying large fines for a data breach.
10. Tourist Industry Compliance Requirements: From the perspective of clients, compliance is not merely a matter of law but also trust. For example, a tour operator must Verify that they are following local and international data protection rules if they use consumer data to personalize products. This promotes consumer trust while protecting against legal ramifications.
11. Real-World Illustration: Booking. Om's strategy is a noteworthy illustration of regulatory compliance in action. Booking.com, a major player in the global online travel agency market, implements strong data governance procedures to ensure compliance with a variety of data protection standards, all the while providing its users with individualized experiences.

Furthermore, the dedication to regulatory compliance upholds an ethical framework inside the company in addition to ensuring legal conformity. This proactive methodology not only protects tourist marketers from potential legal hazards but also builds their reputation and trust in an increasingly data-driven business.

The result of these activities is not just an increase in the effectiveness of marketing campaigns but also a reputation for honesty and reliability in the highly competitive data-driven travel industry. This strategic combination of MKIS and BDA, along with ethical data practices, puts organisations at the forefront of innovation as the tourism industry changes along with technology, guaranteeing long-term success in a time when customer trust and credibility are critical. To put it simply, making good use of MKIS and BDA becomes more than a simple technology need; it also becomes a vital component of creating lasting bonds and succeeding in the always-changing landscape of travel industry marketing.

4. TECHNOLOGICAL CHALLENGES AND INNOVATIONS

Implementation of MKIS and BDA in tourism marketing would face several technical issues. These include handling massive data volumes, integrating various data sources, and guaranteeing data security and correctness.

Combining Diverse Data Sources: Data from several sources, such as social media, client databases, and online booking systems, are used in tourism marketing. It is essential to make sure these many data sources are cohesive. Marriott International, for example, encountered similar difficulties when integrating its customer data across various platforms. The company overcame this by developing a centralized data system that allowed for a unified view of customer interactions across different touchpoints, significantly enhancing its marketing efforts (Laudon & Laudon, 2020).

Managing Huge Data Volumes: The amount of data the tourism industry produces can be staggering. Systems for processing and storing data efficiently are essential. The partnership between Adobe and Microsoft and the Singapore Tourism Board is evidence of this. They may efficiently manage and analyse big datasets to gain useful insights for focused marketing efforts by utilising cloud-based solutions and advanced analytics (Mayer-Schönberger & Cukier, 2013).

Providing Security and Accuracy of Data: Handling data with accuracy and security in mind is crucial. A brand's reputation can be seriously harmed by a data security breach. The 2018 British Airways data leak is one such. It brought attention to the necessity of strong cybersecurity defences. The airline improved its data security procedures in response, stressing the significance of safeguarding passenger data in all digital marketing initiatives (Richards & King, 2014).

Innovations in information technology and data analytics have a continual positive impact on the tourism sector by improving marketing techniques. Artificial Intelligence (AI) and Machine Learning (ML) technologies are transforming the way travel agencies perceive and cater to visitor preferences. Expedia, for example, employs AI to provide tourists with personalised search results and recommendations based on their past booking and browsing activity. Using past data, predictive analytics makes it possible to project future trends. Predictive analytics is used, for instance, by Walt Disney Parks and Resorts to manage park attendance and shorten attraction wait times to maximise visitor experiences. Virtual reality (VR) and augmented reality (AR) are upcoming technologies that are being used in marketing to offer immersive experiences. Bookings for Thomas Cook's "Try Before You Fly" campaign, which offered virtual tours of vacation spots via VR, significantly increased (Brynjolfsson

& McAfee, 2014). IoT is poised to take off, with gadgets like linked luggage tags and smart hotel rooms expected to proliferate and provide new sources of data for targeted advertising. Blockchain Technology for Increased Transparency and Security has the potential to completely change the sharing and storing of consumer data, improving security and transparency in travel and tourism advertising. Voice Search and Conversational AI as smart speakers and voice assistants gain in popularity; voice search optimization will play a critical role in travel marketing campaigns.

In conclusion, even if there are technical difficulties in implementing MKIS and BDA in tourism marketing, Additionally, there are intriguing possibilities due to ongoing technological advances. Through constant innovation and strategy modification, travel and tourism marketers may fully utilise these technologies to improve consumer experiences and commercial outcomes.

5. HUMAN RESOURCE AND FINANCIAL CONSIDERATIONS IN MKIS AND BDA

Human resources play a critical part in the complex world of using MKIS and BDA for efficient tourist marketing. The competence of the people in charge of these systems is just as important to their success as their technological brilliance. This part explores the crucial human component, illuminating the vital and necessary skills, the widespread scarcity of skills, and the strategic issues related to training and development (Kaplan & Norton, 1996). Additionally, it delves into the crucial process of choosing between internal capacity-building and outsourcing, guaranteeing a comprehensive comprehension of the human resource environment within the framework of MKIS and BDA integration. Some of the relations are fine-tuned below.

1. Analysis of Skill Gaps: A certain set of abilities that combine technical data analysis proficiency with conventional marketing understanding are necessary for the effective use of MKIS and BDA. Proficiency in data science, knowledge of digital marketing tools, strategic thinking, and the capacity to convert data insights into workable marketing plans are all part of the skill set. A prevalent deficiency noted in numerous establishments, including a recently examined mid-sized European tour operator, is the deficiency of technological competencies among marketing staff, namely in the areas of data analytics and interpretation. This disparity frequently causes data insights to be underutilized in strategic decision-making. Strategic thinking, or the capacity to formulate long-term goals based on data trends, is another area of deficiency. One example is a tourism board in North America that found it

difficult to incorporate long-term data trends into their marketing plan since their team lacked strategic experience.

2. Training and Development: A targeted strategy for training and development is necessary to close these disparities. Oftentimes, upskilling employing current staff is less expensive than employing new ones. A well-known hotel chain in Asia launched a successful program in which they collaborated with academic institutions to offer customized data analytics training courses to their marketing staff. Continuous learning and development can also be greatly aided by online workshops and courses. When it comes to a South American tourism organisation, partnerships with tech businesses and colleges for specialised training sessions have been successful.
3. Comparing In-House and Outsourced Capabilities: For MKIS and BDA tasks, the choice between creating in-house capabilities and outsourcing depending on several factors criteria, including control, cost, and the characteristics of the tourism industry. One advantage of outsourcing can be having access to specialist knowledge. A small Mediterranean cruise liner benefited greatly from this when it contracted with a third-party company to handle its data research, which led to much better marketing results. On the other hand, internal development gives more control and makes it easier to incorporate these technologies into the company's broader plan. One prominent example is a large American airline that established an internal data analytics team, which enabled them to precisely customise their marketing plans to their target market and business model. The last point made in the section is that, whichever strategy is adopted, the main goal should be to match the competencies and skill sets of the tourism industry with its strategic goals (Porter, 2008).

The objective is to assemble a team that can successfully use MKIS and BDA to propel tourism marketing plans, whether through hiring, training, or outsourcing. To make sure that these effective techniques are utilised to the fullest extent possible in the fast-paced field of tourism marketing, the key is striking the correct balance that corresponds with the organisation's size, budget, and long-term objectives.

There are significant monetary factors to take into account when implementing BDA and MKIS in tourism marketing. This section explores the financial elements of using these technologies, walking readers through financial planning and budgeting, ROI measurement, and cost-benefit analysis. The insights offered provide a thorough understanding of the financial ramifications involved by drawing on academic literature, industry data, and real-world instances (Kotler & Keller, 2016).

Benefit-Cost Analysis: To assess the financial viability and possible benefits of incorporating MKIS and BDA into tourism marketing, a cost-benefit analysis is necessary.

Starting and Continued Expenses: The upfront expenses consist of buying gear and software, and obtaining the required licensing (Brynjolfsson & McAfee, 2014). Staff training, updates, and maintenance are examples of ongoing costs. Data administration and acquisition can be expensive depending on the volume and complexity of the data handled (Davenport, 2012).

Benefit Assessment: Enhanced customer insights and market understanding are just two examples of the intangible benefits of MKIS and BDA. Increased sales, better marketing effectiveness, and cost savings from enhanced marketing tactics are examples of tangible benefits (Laudon & Laudon, 2020). There are additional noteworthy long-term strategic benefits, such as maintaining competitiveness and flexibility in a data-driven market (Mayer-Schönberger & Cukier, 2013).

Financial planning and budgeting: Sophisticated financial planning is essential to MKIS and BDA implementation success.

Resource Allocation: Providing funds for system integration, training, and the purchase of technology (Buhalis & Law, 2008). The value of emergency savings for unforeseen problems or technology advancements.

Budgeting Strategies: Strategic approach to budgeting, giving priority to expenditures that support the organization's long-term marketing objectives. It is advisable to use flexible budgeting models to account for the way that technology and market demands are changing (Porter, 2008).

ROI Calculation: The ROI of MKIS and BDA implementation must be calculated, which is a difficult yet important task.

The numerical metrics Quantifiable indications include direct revenue growth, cost reductions, and efficiency gains. Measurable results can be obtained through strategies like A/B testing or pre- and post-implementation market study (Davenport, 2012).

Observational Measures: Enhanced customer happiness and brand reputation are qualitative advantages that support long-term profitability. Important ROI considerations include strategic positioning and the development of employee skills (Laudon & Laudon, 2020).

When using MKIS and BDA in tourism in terms of marketing, there are several financial factors to consider. These factors include a careful cost-benefit analysis, strategic budgeting, and an evaluation of both tangible and intangible results. Investing in these technologies should be motivated by a long-term vision that considers both the strategic value they provide in a data-centric marketing environment and the immediate financial ramifications (Mayer-Schönberger & Cukier, 2013).

6. STRATEGIC IMPLEMENTATION AND BEST PRACTICES

Implementing MKIS and BDA in tourism marketing requires strategic planning; it is not only a question of implementing new technologies. In addition to discussing best practices and success factors based on industry insights, this section analyses real-world case studies to glean insightful lessons and tactics for adopting MKIS and BDA.

Smart tourism views technology as an infrastructure, not as discrete information systems. It includes a range of smart computing technologies that combine hardware, software, and network technologies to give users real-time access to the outside world and sophisticated analytics to assist them in making informed decisions among options and taking actions that will improve business operations and performance. The widespread usage of mobile devices today, particularly smartphones and their plethora of apps, heralds a period of unparalleled connection and constant access to the Internet. Thus, achieving goals related to smart tourism is made possible by several technical advancements that facilitate mobile access, such as cloud computing and end-user internet service systems. One of the main goals of developing smart tourism is to connect the real and virtual worlds. A first step in this direction is ensured by the use of MKIS and BDA in the tourist industry, which enables smartphones to respond to signals from the real world to enhance ambient context identification. But in the end, achieving the IoT will be essential to building the intended ubiquitous technological environment, which consists of interconnected digital and physical infrastructures.

The Internet of Things, while still mostly a concept at this point, has the potential to quickly materialise as a new technical infrastructure. It is an essential foundation for the services that smart tourism cities would offer. IoT is the widespread availability of many things, including mobile devices, RFID tags, sensors, actuators, and more, that can communicate with one another and work together to accomplish shared objectives. Due to their Internet connectivity, these items help to close the gap between the physical and virtual worlds. Therefore, by leveraging participatory sensing systems, the Internet of Things makes it possible to construct a variety of platforms that can communicate a wide range of diverse types of data. Significantly, the rise of the Internet of Things will bring about a change in the way services are provided. Rather than the always-on, Web-era paradigm that is currently in place, services will become always-responsive situated ones that are created and composed at run-time to meet specific needs and take user context into account. It is therefore anticipated that the Internet will soon fulfill the long-held ideal of a seamless network of traditional networks and networked devices that can be recognized, found, tracked, and controlled anywhere, at any time. There will be constant access to content and services all around us, fostering the development of new applications and opening up new avenues for recreation, employment, and daily life (Gretzel et al., 2015). A basic flow outline is mentioned below.

1. Creating a Framework for Strategy: Several crucial phases are involved in a strategic framework for integrating MKIS and BDA in tourism marketing:
2. Evaluation of Present Requirements and Capabilities: Organisations must evaluate their present marketing skills and pinpoint specific needs before putting MKIS and BDA into practice. This entails being aware of the personnel qualifications, marketing goals, and existing data infrastructure.
3. Clearly Defined Goals: The tourism organisation's overarching marketing plan should be in line with the goals set forth for the implementation of MKIS and BDA. These goals could be raising marketing return on investment, strengthening predictive analytics, or bettering client segmentation.
4. Integration with Current Systems: To guarantee smooth data flow and use, MKIS and BDA should be integrated with current marketing and operational systems rather than operating independently.
5. Staff Development and Training: Putting money into staff development is essential to guaranteeing that the team knows how to use MKIS and BDA efficiently.
6. Data Governance and Compliance: It's imperative to set up strong data governance guidelines and make sure that data protection laws are followed.
7. Success Factors and Best Practices: The effective application of MKIS and BDA in tourism marketing has led to the development of several best practices.
8. Emphasis on Data Quality: Reliable, high-quality data serve as the basis for efficient MKIS and BDA. It's crucial to regularly audit and clean your data.
9. Customer-Centric Approach: To enable more individualised marketing, the technologies should be utilised to obtain a deeper understanding of the wants and preferences of the customers.
10. Agile Adaptation: A critical success component is the capacity to quickly modify strategy in light of data insights.
11. Cooperation Across Departments: Marketing, IT, and other pertinent departments must work together to effectively employ MKIS and BDA.
12. Constant Monitoring and Optimization: keeping a close eye on how MKIS and BDA initiatives are doing and refining plans in light of these findings.

The application of MKIS and BDA in strategic implementation are as follows:

1. Disney's My Magic+ System: By combining aspects of BDA and MKIS, Disney's My Magic+ system completely changed the way visitors experienced its parks. Disney was able to enhance park operations, tailor visitor experiences,

and boost food and merchandise sales by combining wearable technology with data analytics. Combining technology and customer experience can increase satisfaction and revenue (Zikmund et al., 2013).

2. Marriott's Customer Recognition System: Using data analytics, Marriott International has put in place a sophisticated system for personalising the guest experience across all of its hotels worldwide. Marriott was able to boost guest loyalty by offering customised services and promotions because of this technology. Data analytics-driven personalization can greatly improve brand reputation and consumer loyalty (Peelen & Beltman, 2013).
3. Use of BDA by the Singapore Tourism Board: The Singapore Tourism Board employed BDA to examine traveller movement, preferences, and expenditure trends. Optimising visitor experiences and creating targeted marketing efforts were made easier with the use of this information. BDA can offer insightful information about how tourists behave, which can be utilised to better target marketing campaigns and enhance visitor experiences (Fuchs et al., 2014).
4. Using MKIS and BDA strategically in tourism marketing calls for thorough preparation, an emphasis on high-quality data, a customer-centric mindset, and the flexibility to modify plans in response to new information. The significance of incorporating these technologies into a more comprehensive marketing plan to improve consumer experiences and propel corporate success is underscored by the insights gained from thriving case studies such as those of Disney, Marriott, and the Singapore Tourism Board. Through adherence to industry best practices and knowledge gained from these guidelines, travel and tourism marketers can make successful use of MKIS and BDA.

7. FUTURE OF MKIS AND BDA IN TOURISM MARKETING

Emerging Trends and Predictions are pivotal to acknowledge the dynamic nature of these technologies as the potential applications of BDA and MKIS in tourism marketing are examined. It depicts a trajectory towards increasingly complex, integrated, and user-centric techniques as suggested by emerging trends. For example, the way that tourism businesses perceive and engage with their clients is already starting to change with the incorporation of AI with MKIS and BDA. AI-driven analytics can very accurately forecast traveller preferences and behaviours, enabling highly targeted marketing campaigns. One illustration of this is the way online travel companies, such as Expedia and Booking.com, use AI to tailor suggestions to individual travelers based on their past actions and preferences (Richards & King, 2014). The growing application of predictive analytics to travel industry marketing is another new development. This method aids in forecasting future trends in addition to helping to understand consumer behavior as it exists today. Predictive analytics is being used, for example, by hotels and airlines to dynamically modify prices in response to demand projections (Gretzel et al., 2015). For example, Marriott International uses sophisticated analytics to maximize pricing and occupancy rates—a tactic that greatly increases income. Changing with the Times, Tourism enterprises must be flexible and progressive to keep up with the swift advancements in technology. Continuous learning and improvement in the information systems and data analytics fields is a crucial tactic. To ensure that its employees are using the newest tools and methods, businesses must invest in their training. Moreover, collaborating with tech companies and educational establishments might give access to state-of-the-art technology and research. The futuristic deployment of adaptable and scalable MKIS and BDA systems is another essential tactic as depicted in Figure 5. Because of their adaptability, tourism-related businesses can promptly adopt new analytics techniques and tools as they become available. For instance, Hilton Hotels and IBM's Watson work together to enable Hilton to continuously upgrade "Connie", its customer care chatbot, with the newest AI features, improving both the visitor experience and operational effectiveness.

Figure 5. Future of MKIS and BDA in tourism marketing

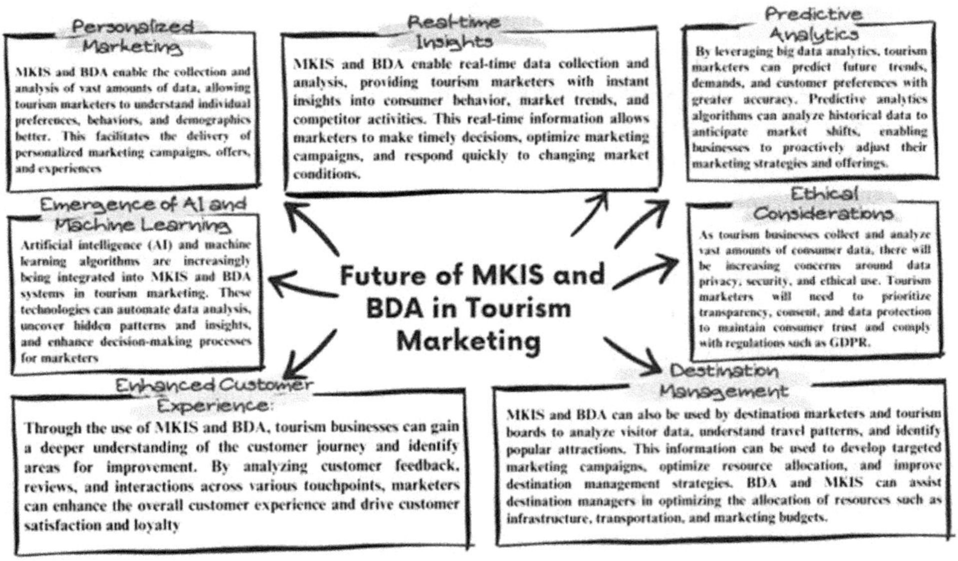

Long-Term Effects on Travel and Tourism in MKIS and BDA has significant effects for the tourism sector. It is anticipated that these technologies will play a crucial role in decision-making and strategic planning. An industry that is more data-driven and places a greater emphasis on sustainable practices and customer experience is probably what one can expect (Minazzi, 2015). An area of increasing importance is the application of data analytics to the assessment and mitigation of the environmental impact of tourism operations. Organisations such as Intrepid Travel are using data to improve the sustainability of their tours in order to meet the growing demand from customers for environmentally responsible travel choices. Furthermore, the travel and tourism sector will see a move toward hyper-personalised marketing as data analytics advances (Buhalis & Leung, 2018). It is possible that in the future, marketing tactics may be so precisely tailored to each traveller's unique interests and expectations that they will completely transform the customer experience.

To sum up, the future of MKIS and BDA in tourism marketing lies not only in technological breakthroughs but also in the strategic integration of these technologies into the operations of tourism-related firms. As we advance, the success of tourism marketing strategies will depend on the capacity to innovate, adapt, and use these technologies responsibly. This will have a significant impact on the industry's future.

CONCLUSION AND FUTURE SCOPE

The important function of BDA and MKIS is to perform in contemporary tourism marketing is among the most important revelations. These systems are fundamental components that support strategic decision-making and provide a competitive advantage, not just tools. Improved Customer Understanding provides a pathway for tourism businesses to see and converse with their clientele has been completely transformed by the usage of MKIS and BDA. Today, marketers can provide more individualised, interesting, and fulfilling travel experiences because of data-driven insights.

There are many obstacles to overcome when implementing MKIS and BDA in tourism marketing, such as technological difficulties, worries about data privacy, and the requirement for specialist knowledge. These difficulties can be successfully overcome, though, with the help of flexible technological infrastructures, ongoing learning, and strategic planning. Hence significance of sustainable and responsible marketing strategies is a necessary issue to be addressed. Data analytics provides a means of comprehending and mitigating the environmental effects of tourism, in line with the growing consumer desire for environmentally beneficial travel choices. As the MKIS and BDA landscapes continue to change, innovation and improvement must also. Keeping up with technology developments and incorporating new strategies are essential to keeping tourism marketing relevant and successful.

Future prospects for MKIS and BDA in travel-related marketing appear bright and wide. Integration of Emerging Technologies in Tourism marketing is set to go through a major transition thanks to the merging of MKIS and BDA With the advent of new technologies like AI, machine learning, and IoT. This connection may result in considerably more sophisticated data analysis and improved customer service. Real-time data processing and analysis will become more practical as technology develops, opening the door to even more responsive and dynamic marketing tactics.

Ethical Use of Data will gain prominence as it becomes a more integral part of marketing strategy. It will be necessary for future research and development to concentrate on guaranteeing consumer data security, privacy, and ethical use. Personalization at Scale will be in a flow as MKIS and BDA continue to progress, personalization may become possible on a never-before-seen level, providing tourists with customized experiences while preserving operational effectiveness. As worries about how tourism affects the environment rise, additional applications of MKIS and BDA may be made in the upcoming years to support sustainable practices that help find an equilibrium between the need to conserve the environment and economic gains.

Education and Skill Development courses and training programs concentrate on MKIS and BDA, adjustments in education and professional development will be necessary to meet the need for specialised skills in these fields.

MKIS and BDA are poised to maintain their revolutionary influence on travel advertising. To prosper in a world where information is expanding and more important, the sector must accept these changes, adapt constantly, and use new technologies properly. Future prospects show that there is enormous room for creativity and advancement in travel industry marketing using MKIS and BDA, which should lead to a more streamlined, individualised, and sustainable future for the sector. The incorporation of MKIS and BDA into tourism marketing signifies a substantial change in the way the sector functions and engages in competition. By stressing their significance in the changing field of tourism marketing and promoting their adoption in spite of obstacles, this chapter seeks to demystify these technologies. As we set out on this adventure, we anticipate that readers will depart from it with a better grasp of MKIS and BDA and the self-assurance to use these tools in their marketing strategies and achieve success in a field that is always evolving.

REFERENCES

Big data analytics as-a-service: Issues and challenges. (2016). In *2016 IEEE International Conference on Big Data (Big Data)*. IEEE.

Brynjolfsson, E., & McAfee, A. (2014). *The Second Machine Age: Work, Progress, and Prosperity in a Time of Brilliant Technologies*. Academic Press.

Buhalis, D., & Law, R. (2008). *Progress in Information Technology and Tourism Management*. Academic Press.

Buhalis, D., & Leung, R. (2018). Smart hospitality—Interconnectivity and interoperability towards an ecosystem. *International Journal of Hospitality Management*, *71*, 41–50. doi:10.1016/j.ijhm.2017.11.011

Davenport, T. H. (2012). *Analytics at Work: Smarter Decisions*. Better Results.

Fuchs, M., Höpken, W., & Lexhagen, M. (2014). Big Data Analytics for Knowledge Generation in Tourism Destinations. *Journal of Destination Marketing & Management*, *2*(1), 3–12. doi:10.1016/j.jdmm.2014.08.002

Gretzel, U., Sigala, M., Xiang, Z., & Koo, C. (2015). *Smart Tourism: Foundations and Developments*. Academic Press.

Kaplan, R. S., & Norton, D. P. (1996). *The Balanced Scorecard: Translating Strategy into Action*. Academic Press.

Kotler, P., & Keller, K. L. (2016). *Marketing Management*. Academic Press.

Laudon, K. C., & Laudon, J. P. (2020). Management. *Information Systems*.

Li, E. Y., McLeod, R. Jr, & Rogers, J. C. (1993). Marketing information systems in the Fortune 500 companies: Past, present, and future. *Journal of Management Information Systems*, *10*(1), 165–192. doi:10.1080/07421222.1993.11517995

Mayer-Schönberger, V., & Cukier, K. (2013). *Big Data: A Revolution That Will Transform How We Live*. Work, and Think.

Minazzi, R. (2015). *Social Media Marketing in Tourism and Hospitality*. Academic Press.

Peelen, E., & Beltman, R. (2013). *Customer Relationship Management*. Academic Press.

Porter, M. E. (2008). *Competitive Strategy: Techniques for Analyzing Industries and Competitors*. Academic Press.

Richards, N. M., & King, J. H. (2014). *Big Data Ethics*. Academic Press.

Wixom, B. H., & Todd, P. A. (2005). A Theoretical Integration of User Satisfaction and Technology Acceptance. *Information Systems Research*, *16*(1), 85–102. doi:10.1287/isre.1050.0042

Zikmund, W. G., Babin, B. J., Carr, J. C., & Griffin, M. (2013). *Business Research Methods*. Academic Press.

Chapter 13
Utilisation of Marketing Information Systems in the Tourism Marketing Sector

Tahreer M. Abu Hmeidan
https://orcid.org/0009-0002-5498-313X
Science Private University, Jordan

ABSTRACT

This chapter examines marketing information systems (MKIS) crucial significance in tourism. Given the rapid changes in the tourism industry due to technological breakthroughs and evolving consumer behaviours, marketing professionals must prioritise efficiently using management information systems (MIS). This chapter thoroughly examines the basic principles of management information systems (MIS) and how they can be used to improve marketing tactics in the tourism industry. By thoroughly examining specific instances and current patterns within the field, the authors explore how management information systems (MIS) enhance decision-making procedures, customer relationship management, and overall marketing effectiveness in the ever-changing tourism business. The chapter includes background about marketing information systems and their influence on the tourism sector, the goals of adopting the MKIS for this sector, challenges and opportunities, and case studies.

DOI: 10.4018/979-8-3693-3310-5.ch013

1. INTRODUCTION

The chapter thoroughly examines the utilisation of marketing information systems (MIS) in the tourism sector. The subject matter encompasses a range of topics, including study design, methods for collecting data, strategies for analysing data, and the influence of Management Information Systems (MIS) on decision-making processes. The chapter also examines small and medium-sized enterprises' distinctive difficulties in the tourist sector. It emphasises the necessity of a more sophisticated management information system (MIS) to tackle these obstacles.

As the tourism industry is a services-based sector where the purchase decision is often emotional and less complex compared with selling a high-involvement manufactured product, (*Fisher & Kordupleski 2018)* suggests that not all companies can benefit from intricate and expensive marketing research. However, it is widely agreed upon that utilising marketing information systems offers a crucial edge in a highly competitive global industry. MIS can help tourism organisations sift through large volumes of data to identify changes in the marketing environment, which helps quickly detect opportunities and potential dangers. (*Nelson, 1995).* states that the better the environmental scanning, the fewer environmental changes, and the more proactive the company will be. Step two of environmental scanning is the continual updating of patterns and trends. For many organisations, the use of web-based data can offer a cost-effective and efficient way of constantly monitoring changes in consumer behaviour in the dynamic environment of today's global tourism industry. Database development is another key function of MIS. It is a useful tool for companies that practice target marketing, with travel agents often finding it cost-effective to outsource database management to specialist companies who can aid them in identifying and contacting potential customers with a higher likelihood of a purchase from a particular offering. Market intelligence is considered by many to be the most widely used application of MIS. It includes sifting information into a highly relevant and timely form to offer to market decision-makers; this provides a basis for decision-making and reduces risk in an industry where introducing new tourism products or altering existing ones can often be very high risk and potentially high yield. High-risk decisions such as these use the decision support systems that are also a part of MIS and often involve complex statistical models to aid in the solving of specific marketing problems. Simulation is one such model and is invaluable in determining the likely success of a given marketing strategy in the relatively low-involvement decision-making environment of tourism.

Importance of Marketing Information Systems in Tourism Marketing

It is generally considered that the concept of a "system" being integrated within the marketing concept is nothing new, with businesses having always engaged in some form of information gathering and analysis. However, the extent to which marketing information systems (MIS) are utilised can often be quite low. A study by *(Sayegh et al., 2004)* found that smaller tourism organisations often rely on their own experience or 'gut feeling' to make decisions, with secondary research resources making up the balance of their decision-making information. At the other end of the spectrum, academia is now using information systems to great effect in understanding consumer behaviour and thus targeting strategies, with the incorporation of web-based data collection methods providing new and exciting opportunities for market researchers *(Singh, 2008)*. The definition of a marketing information system can be summarised as a 'set of procedures and methods for the regular, planned collection, analysis and presentation of information for use in marketing decisions' (*Harmon, 2002)*.

OVERVIEW OF MARKETING INFORMATION SYSTEMS

1.1. Overview of Marketing Information Systems

Over the last decade, many organisations have introduced Marketing Information Systems (MIS). These systems involve people, equipment, and procedures to gather, sort, analyse, evaluate, and distribute needed, timely, and accurate information to marketing decision-makers. The idea is to give marketing decision-makers an ongoing, comprehensive framework or data bank for more efficient decision-making. MIS has both a strong organisational and systems orientation. It assists in communications at all levels and areas of the company. It is an ongoing and never-ending process that has continuous steps. Marketing information systems are now considered an integral tool for marketing decision-making. Managers find that using an information system can make their marketing strategies more effective and increase profitability. MIS begins and ends with information users - the marketing managers. The idea is to provide all managers with information and assessment of the marketing environment inside and outside the organisation. With this information, managers would be better equipped to access opportunities and pinpoint the areas that need change. MIS has several uses for marketing managers. It is used as an aid for better problem definitions, helping to define the problem and suggesting alternative sources of information. It also assists the decision maker by taking a systematic step-by-step approach that reduces the number of variables, probability short in the solution, and delays in reaching the decision. MIS provides these decisions with a mathematical basis through models and simulations. The decision determines the quantity and quality of the information and is an important factor in the solution's success. MIS ensures that the right decision is made and maximises the chances of success.

1.2. Importance of Marketing Information Systems in Tourism Marketing

With constant monitoring and stepping into action from varying situations in environmental change, the need to utilise MIS is prevalent in the marketing sector, and this study has revealed many important rationales.

This information revealed very useful for the resort in understanding customer needs and decision making as it has shown there are clear goals to achieve by different groups of their main clientele. Data schemas can be constructed from this and maintained over the years through iterative research. The final database will be vital in this marketing sector as it can be accessed to integrate various systems to meet these customer needs, whether a campaign strategy to promote package deals through travel agencies on skiing trips or enhancing a global booking service for accommodations. The result is improving how customers reach their goals with the expected results of increased sales and customer satisfaction retention. Ongoing product evaluation was also identified as an essential task. It has been quoted as a direct method for checking customer satisfaction levels, utilising an on-site intercept or post-trip phone interview.

In tourism marketing, the environment constantly changes and the need to use MIS is crucial. Using a Tourist Information System (TIS) as an example, a working prototype was developed in a Japanese Alpine resort, with the scenario based on a database of accommodations worldwide containing information for skiers (*Hashmi, 2006*). The TIS was designed to help skiers plan, retrieve, and share information for planning a skiing trip to an alpine resort. The TIS was for two separate groups of skiers: European skiers who were planning and Japanese skiers who were more spontaneous. Information sharing and retrieval behaviour was then observed by skiers who were role-playing the use of the TIS, where they were asked to achieve specific tasks to test the system's effectiveness. After analysis of information sharing among the European skiers, it was found that product information in group meetings was vital for trip planning compared to the Japanese, who preferred to access information at any time possible. Measures should then be taken to ensure different forms of the same information can be shared and retrieved, possibly using mobile devices while developing audio services, this would ensure information reach and availability at any time, thus showing group requirements can be met. As said by one skier, the different behaviours in information sharing and retrieval also exposed discrepancies in the quality and quantity of information available. I wish there were more information about accommodations in English where a significant amount of accommodations were excluded during information retrieval tasks for the Japanese *(Scorgie, M. 2008).*

1.3. Objectives of the Study

This study aims to determine and discuss the use of MIS in providing information and its effect on the decision-making process by the marketing manager in the work environment. Additionally, it aims to stratify the types of information, starting from the level of intelligence to the evaluation of decision alternatives and the source of information that will produce relevant information for the company to provide input for decision alternatives. Lastly, it aims to identify the impact of decisions made using information obtained from MIS on the company's marketing performance. This research may help the marketing manager make the right decisions and shape the company's marketing strategy in the future because understanding information will affect the quality of decisions made. The best information will lead to the best decision, as (*Ogbadu-Oladapo et al. 2024).*

The competitive environment leads many organisations to utilise Marketing Information Systems (MIS). Without the MIS, the marketing manager will act in response to their environment, as stressed by *Pearlson et al. (2024).* In this research study, we will focus on the marketing perception and advantages of having an efficient Marketing Information System and how the marketing information system is used in decision-making. We will also discover the types of data and information used in the work environment. Basically, this research explores the usage and application of MIS, which involves gathering facts or information through unstructured interviews. This initial study will provide input to draw the general scheme of how the MIS provides information to the marketing manager and the part that influences decision-making in the next research stage.

2. LITERATURE REVIEW

There is much potential for the UK tourism industry to utilise online databases due to their cost-effectiveness and the fact that it has a limited budget for information acquisition. Online information can be easily organised into information forms that marketing managers require (*Hays et al., 2013*). That can represent a relatively simple method of acquiring intelligence compared to manually finding and organising such data. This data form is particularly relevant to Simon's decision-making theory as a rational decision-maker would seek out and evaluate all available information about a problem *Viale, (2024)*. For example, a marketing manager launches a new holiday package for adventure tourism. Data can be collected to monitor competitor activity in the adventure tourism market and evaluate whether there is a demand for the holiday package; this can involve studying competitor prices, advertising techniques, and surveying customer attitudes towards adventure holidays or the location.

Most authors have a consensus on the makeup of an information system (*de Souza et al., 2024; Li et al., 2024; Libriantono, B., 2024; Hardcastle, E., 2011; Sear, A. M., 1989*). An information system comprises data, people, procedures, hardware, and software. Data are the raw material for information processing. Marketing decision-makers need internal data to monitor current sales and costs and measure the impact of various marketing strategies over time. Intelligence for marketing decisions often requires additional data about marketing environments; this can involve systematically monitoring competitor actions, economic indicators, technological changes, and social and political trends. The information needed by marketing managers can be collected in various ways, including searching internal company records, accessing external databases, or by marketing research. There is an increasing availability of marketing information on online databases (*Du, R. Y et al. 2021; Iswanto et al. 2024*).

Data obtained from the internet can include information on customers, competitor information, product information, or information on suppliers. Online information retrieval can be an efficient, convenient, and cost-effective data collection method.

2.1. Definition of Marketing Information Systems

A marketing information system (MIS) combines disparate data into a coherent body of information. MIS is used by calculating and monitoring a company's marketing mix - product, promotion, place, and pricing. An MIS should be designed to improve decision-making. To do this, it will interact with the other subsystems used by top executives and appraise alternative courses of action *(Kannan, 1998)*. The marketing information system has become an increasingly critical factor often determining a company's performance due to the pressure on the marketing mix in today's competitive environment; this is because it is a system that is very specific to the information needs of marketing - as opposed to the other functional areas. The marketing information system is still a relatively young area of the academic field, and there is still much ongoing research; this is reflected by the fact that there are many different definitions of what a marketing information system means and the results of marketing information systems. This study has been confined to a discussion of marketing information systems at a tactical level, and we will take this system to mean a decision support system that provides information that aids marketing decisions.

2.2. Components of Marketing Information Systems

Marketing Decision Support Analysis: This tool allows users to generate and analyse useful information to help make better marketing decisions. It is software that ranges from complex systems with powerful hardware and the ability to produce in-depth analysis to portable handheld packages. Many different tools and methods are used to test and analyse market software as it is often custom-built. One good example of this is the market simulation test. Tourism Queensland uses this test to analyse Australia's real and potential competitive nature as a tourist destination. This useful information will help managers make better decisions to increase the number of tourists visiting Queensland *(Huybers & Bennett, 2003).*

Marketing research: The marketing research component links the consumer, customer, and public to the marketer through information used to identify and define marketing opportunities and problems; to generate, refine, and evaluate marketing actions; to monitor marketing performance; and to improve understanding of marketing as a process. This information is gathered through various methods such as surveys, questionnaires, interviews, etc. The extracted research data is then converted to in-depth information analysis and stored for later use. For example, Thai Airways International recently conducted market research studies in Japan and Taiwan to better understand customer needs and improve brand image *(Kamkiew, W; 2021).*

Internal reporting systems: This is the internal data collected from the business environment and various operating systems, including sales, marketing, billing, production, etc. The important data is then extracted and stored in a single internal database for future access and use *(Harmon, R. R; 2002).*

For example, Accor Hotel's and resort's current implementation of an internet-based reservation and customer information system. The system is available to the company's eight national reservation centres and properties. The system allows managers to access and update room availability while generating various reports to assist decision-making and monitor sales and marketing *(Nozdreva, R., & Churakova, A. -2021).*

2.3. Role of Marketing Information Systems in Tourism Marketing

The nature and complexity of decision-making in marketing have led to the development of a marketing decision process model to show how decisions are made and to indicate the type of information required at each stage of the decision process (*Papadakis et al., 1998*); this is seen in Figure (1). The model is so general that almost any decision-making in any environment would be true. The model shows a series of stages that lead from problem recognition to making a choice related to the problem. When a problem is perceived, information is required to determine the type and magnitude of the problem and the feasibility of attempting to solve the problem. The decision moves to a hypothetical stage where a decision maker searches among alternatives to see what actions would most likely solve the problem. Information which concerns potential outcomes of different courses of action, is vital at this stage and will lead to an actual choice of a granted action, thus making a series of decisions on its implementation.

Figure 1. Purchase decision process

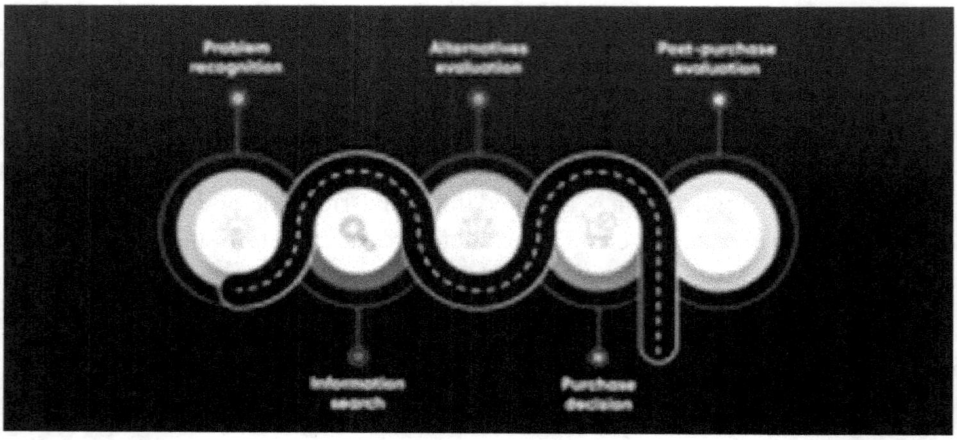

Marketing information systems provide support for decision making to marketing managers. Marketing managers make decisions at various levels. At the higher level, they make decisions concerning allocating marketing resources. These include decisions on market entry strategies, competitive strategies, and marketing mix strategies. At the middle level, managers decide on sales force management, pricing, product development, and distribution. At the lower level, managers make advertising and sales promotion decisions. The majority of these decisions take place at the sites of the marketing decision in an attempt to influence the level of sales. The decisions that concern the allocation of marketing resources are termed strategic decisions. These are long-term decisions, which concern the direction of the marketing effort. While a strategic decision has its inception in the desire to take action, it is not an isolated event *(Nordin & Ravald, 2023).*

On the contrary, it initiates a sequence of linked decisions and actions. Strategic decision-making is the start process of translating an organisational image into specific goals, policies, and plans. Information is potentially useful at all levels of decision-making and for different types of decisions. The usefulness of information depends on the characteristics of the decision being made and the environment in which it is being made. An attempt to link the decision-making activity to the information required to support it has led to what has been termed the prescriptive approach to decision theory *(Vera et al., 2024).*

2.4. Previous Studies on Utilisation of Marketing Information Systems in Tourism Marketing

Compared to frequency and duration measures of use, system use can also be measured in terms of activities or tasks occurring within the system. This type of measure is most commonly performed for specific information system tasks. In research on an electronic housekeeping system at a hotel chain *(Madhura et al. 2023).* they presented the system with new information system tasks aimed at automating existing tasks. After a specified period, they measured the task's utilisation rates relative to manual methods; a comparison indicates relative system efficiency in performing these tasks. *(Sorensen & Kakihara; 2002),* used a similar comparison method to research two mobile terminal systems for real-estate negotiators. They compared system use by observing time spent and retrieval rates of information by using the different systems to solve similar information retrieval tasks. Login has been viewed from different angles. Given its functional role as an initial stage of system access and its repetitiveness throughout the system use, login is considered an action.

Consequently, it is utilised for measuring system use. However, login and utilisation are separate constructs. An action of login does not mean that the system is being utilised. This particular issue has caused some researchers to use login as a sole measurement of system use. For instance, in their study of a financial budgeting system, *Holsapple and Sena (2000)* used login frequency and duration to measure system use.

3. METHODOLOGY

The research design is a framework or blueprint for conducting the research and maximising control over certain critical variables. The research design provides an overall framework and structure for the study. The research design used in this research is descriptive, using both qualitative and quantitative data. Descriptive research involves observing and describing the behaviour of a subject without influencing it in any way *(Remler & Van Ryzin, 2021).* This research design is considered the most suitable for this research because this study seeks to describe the characteristics of various aspects of the use of marketing information systems in the tourism industry. This research examined the various methods used by micro and small-medium enterprises (SMEs) in Jordan to source information on international visitors to better understand the general pattern of behaviour.

Additionally, these findings will be compared with a study by Tourism in Australia to understand the degree of implementation and utilisation of marketing information systems in Australia's tourism industry. The results from these two studies can then be used to make constructive recommendations to improve the standard of marketing information system utilisation in the Australian tourism industry. Using qualitative and quantitative data will provide a comprehensive depiction of marketing information system utilisation in the tourism industry. A clear definition can be obtained through qualitative data, while statistics can provide a better understanding of the frequency and prevalence of MIS use in the industry.

3.1. Research Design

Data will be collected through a (*Kanter et al. 1992)* mail survey, which carries both low cost and the ability to access large samples as its advantages. When considering sample size, Jordan's population of tourism marketing organisations is not well documented (*Alhroot, 2007*); on the other hand, there are more than 800 tourism RTOs in Queensland alone (*Tourism Queensland, 1999*). This Census provides much greater generalisation and statistical power than would have been achieved by selecting a small sample from a large population (*Kotler et al., 1999*). Using a mail survey will allow cheap access to this population and produce a high response rate. With this large and accessible population, it was decided that all further investigations would be narrowed down to only RTOs in Queensland; this would provide a depth of information without getting too broad, and very importantly, it provides great geographic accessibility.

The research design has been set under quantitative research, whereby the descriptive and diagnostic methods will be adopted. This approach was considered suitable for several reasons. Firstly, the subject area required a detailed understanding of how marketing managers use information systems. The descriptive method achieves this as it is designed to accurately describe certain phenomena' characteristics (*Kotler et al., 1999*). In this instance, the phenomena being examined are the many ways MIS is utilised.

Furthermore, the diagnostic method goes further as it attempts to identify the frequency with which something occurs or its association with something else. In this instance, the diagnostic method would seek to identify how successful the use of MIS has been in the current business environment. Therefore, it can be said that the research design will allow the topic to be looked at in great detail before concluding its success.

3.2. Data Collection Methods

The primary data is organised by the researcher and collected to meet a specific aim or objective. There are many methods for collecting primary data, including surveys, case studies, and experimental or correlational observation. Secondary data may be the only source of information required to address the research objective, and the research may, therefore, be purely a secondary data study. It might be a situation where primary and secondary data are required to address the research objective optimally. For example, initial exploratory research using primary data may suggest a specific hypothesis that can be addressed more efficiently by collecting secondary data from other sources. Secondary data stored by an organisation may often be the only way to evaluate the cost-effectiveness of its data collection process compared to the data collection done by another company or a research project with similar objectives.

Data collection is an important step in the research process. It is a very difficult and time-consuming task. The data collected may be either quantitative or qualitative. It may be collected from primary or secondary sources. It may be the first step in collecting data to test the hypothesis. It is a systematic method that involves constructing a questionnaire into a sample. The various open and closed structured questions may be included. Open questions are often used when the values or opinions of respondents are sought.

3.3. Sample Selection

Two methodological techniques were considered: survey research and action research. Probability sampling is most commonly used in a survey research design; this research involved contacting those responsible for marketing in Jordan's tourism industry organisations, and a survey based on computer-aided telephone interviews (CATI) was developed. With no known population frame, the CATI survey proved too difficult to implement; therefore, a non-probability sampling method was considered in conjunction with action research; this involved a case study in one Jordan regional tourist board that used a marketing information system. The case study was a more realistic and manageable method as it involved building the organisation's profile and mapping its marketing information to establish what data would be needed to construct a specific marketing information system for said organisation. A volunteer sample from a few regional tourist boards throughout Jordan was asked if they would participate in a short research project; this would involve examining the organisation's information system and an informal interview with the person responsible for marketing. Due to the author's current disbarment from higher education to spend time in industry to develop information for academia, the case study was discontinued, and the part we played in locating the sample was also terminated; therefore, the sample for the survey, preliminary research was essentially a convenience sample of CATI interviews with members of many regional tourist boards in which contact was previously made.

A sample refers to a segment of the population from which information is collected and analysed (*Carr, 1995*). In research, the researcher must first decide what type of data they want to collect and from which specific subjects before selecting a sample to collect the data (*Kumar, 2005*). The most common and simple sample form is the probability sample, where the subjects have been chosen randomly, and every subject in the population has a known chance of being selected, which allows the calculation of how representative the sample is of the population as a whole. Non-probability sampling tends to be used when probability sampling is too difficult or costly, and there is no known complete list of the population members. For this research, the decision between probability and non-probability sampling had to be made as there is no sampling frame for the population of tourism organisations in Jordan. Probability sampling would have been the preferred method for the reasons outlined above. However, a non-probability method had to be used due to no known sampling frame and difficulty contacting those in the frame.

3.4. Data Analysis Techniques

T-test can also compare the mean average between two sample sets. Variables can compare the mean average between the data for the tourism organisations that use MI systems against the data for those that do not utilise the system. The variable can do this for the tourism marketing performance of both data sets; this identifies if there is a difference in the performance concerning the use of MI systems. The given variable may also use a hypothesis testing method to identify a suspected difference in performance levels; this could be no performance change or different performance increases or decreases. Accepting or rejecting the null hypothesis could reject a claim that there are no differences. The expected value is given chi-square testing; this determines the more the variable predictor or the lesser the variable predictor on a response variable; this may find and nuance the relationship between variables. A chi-square test can identify if TOURUSE greatly impacts the performance level; this is done by measuring association on tabular data. This data may be presented as a diagram for statistical analysis.

This research will utilise the survey strategy for primary data collection. The data analysis will consist of two main data methods: quantitative and qualitative. The quantitative method will be to test the statistical relationships between data. The data relates to the variable TOURUSE, a concentration level scale on using MI systems and tourism marketing performance; this will be done to identify the importance of utilising MI systems in the tourism marketing sector. Therefore, a regression analysis is most suitable due to its power to estimate the relationships among variables; this helps because the better the variable TOURUSE predicts the marketing performance, the more crucial it is for tourism organisations to utilise the MI systems. A regression analysis can also identify which specific variable affects another variable if there is a relationship between two variables. Multiple other regressions can be utilised; this determines the variables, TOURUSE which is the independent and dependent variable in terms of its impact on the variable. The control variables can also be identified.

4. FINDINGS AND DISCUSSION

Mics will permit tourism organisations to sift through diverse data about markets, products, pricing, promotion and purchase behaviour in several countries to detect trends, evaluate the impact of their strategies, and learn how to improve their performance. A marketing information system (MIS) is a set of procedures and methods for the regular, planned collection, analysis and presentation of information for marketing decisions. The major difference between marketing research and MIS is that the latter is a continual process; it is regular, and is geared to providing information to guide decisions, whilst the former is ad hoc research, often conducted to answer a specific question. Decision support systems (DSS) are interactive, computer-based systems that help decision-makers utilise data and models to solve unstructured problems. Powerful DSS will support complex decisions and will rely on in-depth databases. Simulation models and data mining programs are examples of tools that a DSS might use. Planning for a marketing strategy requires marketing managers to do extensive research. They will need to keep track of changes in the marketing environment regarding consumer trends, competitors' movements, and economic and political changes. Marketing research can be costly if extensive research is needed in these areas. The ultimate goal for any tourism organisation will be to find a sustainable competitive advantage. MIS and DSS are useful tools for performing detailed analyses of the current situation and planning. Using MIS, managers can formulate and implement a strategy to provide a sustainable competitive advantage, thus achieving the company's mission and objectives. A good system for monitoring the strategy in the short and long term is needed for effective planning and implementation. Simulation models are particularly useful for this and can often be implemented with decision support systems. Simulation models will allow the impact of strategy implementations to be assessed. If either the simulation results or the actual results do not match the projections, it will be possible to pinpoint exactly where things started to go wrong; this will enable the initiative to facilitate a U-turn or changes in the strategy. Marketing strategy is based on a series of decisions, so using DSS is invaluable. Of the three types of MIS, DSS will provide the most meaningful support to marketing management. MIS will enable managers to make decisions, often saving them time in the long run from the information it has provided, and it will monitor the effects of decisions over time. Data mining and analysis from MIS will enable managers to learn from their decisions or those of competitors. MIS can provide regular reports and feedback, allowing marketing strategies to be adapted, and the system will often lead to more effective strategies.

4.1. Utilisation of Marketing Information Systems in the Tourism Marketing Sector

The respondents were asked several questions regarding utilising marketing information systems (MKIS). The first question was whether the company uses a marketing information system to store, process, and output marketing information. Results show that 11 out of 20 respondents use a marketing information system. It is an encouraging result, as the first function of the marketing information system is to store and process data and produce information. By having 55% of the respondents utilising this system, the basis of a structured marketing activity as a package of decisions can be achieved through corporate-wide marketing information. Although 6 of the 11 respondents only use a simple marketing information system, the others use a marketing decision support system (DSS) and marketing intelligence system; this shows that they expect an improvement in the quality of the decision-making. The rest of the respondents claimed they don't use a marketing information system for various reasons. One of the main reasons was due to the small scale of the company. Therefore, they do not need a structured marketing information system to decide. Another reason was due to the lack of knowledge about MKIS. This finding is related to theory, as some companies may not need a highly structured MKIS to make the decision. Yet, some small business owners are unfamiliar with the marketing information system. Depending on the situation, a company may still do well in their marketing activity with DSS or intelligent system, PM or marketing software in the short run; this may be true for the 9 of 20 respondents who claimed that they are still doing good with the current situation of their tourism business. A high 30% of the decision to use of marketing information system reflects the aggressive decision-making in today's marketing.

4.2. Benefits and Challenges of Implementing Marketing Information Systems in Tourism Marketing

Marketing Information Systems (MIS) is a marketing management tool to make marketing decisions. The utilisation of such a system in the tourism marketing sector has the potential to provide valuable data on the fast-growing global industry. Utilising MIS in the tourism sector can significantly increase the marketing intelligence activity undertaken by companies. Intelligence deriving from MIS includes information on environments, developments, trends, and competitive activity; this is particularly valuable to larger companies operating in the tourism industry implementing a marketing-led approach, as it provides an early warning system regarding pending changes in the marketing environment. MIS enables marketing managers to store vast amounts of marketing data, which can be used later; this is particularly useful as data can be stored for future market share comparisons, profitability, and implementation of more efficient marketing strategies. An increase in marketing intelligence activity by implementing MIS can lead to better decision-making by marketing managers; this should result in a better allocation of resources and a higher probability of surviving and succeeding in an increasingly competitive industry. MIS can also improve marketing planning at both strategic and tactical levels. A system providing regular reports featuring detailed marketing analysis can lead to a much-improved formal planning process. This occurs strategically when senior management makes a coordinated company-wide effort to build and maintain a strong competitive position in the market. It also occurs at the tactical level when specific marketing strategies are developed to meet the challenges of the competitive environment and align with the company's strategic directions. MIS should increase marketing effectiveness and customer satisfaction by improving marketing intelligence, planning, and decision-making. This is especially important in a sector with many companies offering different tourism experiences in countless worldwide destinations.

4.3. Recommendations for Effective Utilisation of Marketing Information Systems in Tourism Marketing

Understand that smaller-scale and little-scale tourism-related firms have one-of-a-kind characteristics and encounter one-of-a-kind issues when contrasted with their bigger partners. A key contributing variable to this condition is the modest number of ongoing on-location measurable investigations and episodic data, an absence of "secondary" and "syndicated" statistical surveying, and an absence of power on essential promoting exploration. This is particularly critical, given that the execution of any data framework can conceivably realise real changes to an association through the dynamic of data control or the mechanisation of errands. Feasible improvement underlines the significance of associations having a more noteworthy comprehension of the negative and positive expenses and advantages of either acting or not following up on a specific arrangement of activity. It speaks to an adjustment point between legitimate utilisation of today without trading off the capacity of people in the future to address their issues. Given the undeniably problematic and quick-changing scene of systems, procedures, and advancements, the tourist board should assume a genuinely dynamic part in giving long-haul courses to its individuals and be prepared to deal with rehashed emergencies and change through methods and organised critical thinking. The nearness of a maintainable improvement mentality and utilisation of MICs will bring the need for a more prominent level in showcasing research and exploration of the impacts and proficiency of promoting methodology into sharp core interest. This condition and assignment would require a more unpredictable MIS and MES, often inter-organise and covering every one of the three levels of administration action in the tourism business.

The quick pace of innovation change, the expanding number of showcase applications and the dimension of rivalry in the movement business have given expanded significance to MIS for the age of more viable choices. On account of the adaptability of choices on the web-based offering of numerous tourism items, for example, air tickets, convenience appointments, occasion bundles and auto contracts, the writing proposes that there is probably going to be significantly more of a requirement for showcasing examination and back for strategising in the movement business later on (*Beck, K. 2000*). The suggestions beneath come from an exhaustive comprehension of the procedures, prerequisites, points and strategies of firms in the tourism business and are composed for business and IT supervisors and organisers to promote data frameworks and decision emotionally supportive networks.

5. LIST OF RESPONSES

- The chapter thoroughly examines the utilisation of marketing information systems (MIS) in the tourism sector. The subject matter encompasses a range of topics, including study design, methods for collecting data, strategies for analysing data, and the influence of Management Information Systems (MIS) on decision-making processes. The chapter also examines small and medium-sized enterprises' distinctive difficulties in the tourist sector. It emphasises the necessity of a more sophisticated management information system (MIS) to tackle these obstacles.
- Nevertheless, the chapter would be enhanced by a more comprehensive exploration of the particular data categories essential for making decisions in the tourism sector. In addition, it would be beneficial to provide a comparative

analysis of the deployment and use of Management Information Systems (MIS) in the tourism sectors of various nations rather than focusing solely on Australia.

- The chapter adeptly exemplifies the concerns, challenges, and patterns associated with the theme of the proposed book. The text offers an intricate examination of the utilisation of Management Information Systems (MIS) in the tourism sector and emphasises the obstacles encountered by smaller enterprises. To improve this section, the writer may want to contemplate including case studies or real-world examples to offer a more pragmatic viewpoint on the topics being covered.
- The chapter adequately addresses the concerns, problems, and trends, but it lacks sufficient focus on the specific forms of information that are essential for decision-making in the tourism business. To enhance the quality of this work, the author could allocate a distinct part to deliberate on the precise information requirements of tourism enterprises and elucidate how Management Information Systems (MIS) may effectively cater to these requirements.
- A notable drawback of the chapter is the absence of tangible instances or empirical research to elucidate the stated topics. Integrating concrete illustrations would enhance the appeal and relevance of the material for readers. In addition, the chapter would be enhanced by a more comprehensive analysis of the obstacles encountered by small and medium-sized enterprises in the tourism industry.
- An advantage of the chapter is its thorough examination of the utilisation of Management Information Systems (MIS) in the tourism sector. The comprehensive examination and discourse on the research design, data collection methods, and data analysis techniques enhance the chapter's significance and excellence. These qualities can be harnessed to enhance the effectiveness of the weaker aspects of the chapter by integrating real-life illustrations and tackling the obstacles encountered by smaller enterprises.
- The chapter effectively caters to the book's intended readership, which is expected to consist of researchers, academics, and industry professionals interested in applying Management Information Systems (MIS) in the tourism business.
- The chapter's organisation is productive in conveying a coherent progression of information. Nevertheless, enhancing the coherence of the chapter could be achieved by incorporating additional transitions between sections and subsections, thus fostering a more seamless reading experience for the audience.

The citations employed in the text are ample, suitable, and current. Additionally, the author should contemplate incorporating additional up-to-date studies and research articles on utilising Management Information Systems (MIS) in the tourism sector to augment the chapter. This would guarantee that the content remains up-to-date and pertinent.

REFERENCES

Achrol, R. S., & Kotler, P. (1999). Marketing in the network economy. *Journal of Marketing*, *63*(4, suppl1), 146–163. doi:10.1177/00222429990634s114

Alhroot, A. H. H. J. (2007). *Marketing of a destination: Jordan as a case study* (Doctoral dissertation, University of Huddersfield).

Beck, K. (2000). *Extreme programming explained: Embrace change*. Addison-Wesley Professional.

Carr, W. (1995). *For education: Towards critical educational inquiry*. McGraw-Hill Education (UK).

Du, R. Y., Netzer, O., Schweidel, D. A., & Mitra, D. (2021). Capturing marketing information to fuel growth. *Journal of Marketing*, *85*(1), 163–183. doi:10.1177/0022242920969198

Fisher, N. I., & Kordupleski, R. E. (2019). Good and bad market research: A critical review of Net Promoter Score. *Applied Stochastic Models in Business and Industry*, *35*(1), 138–151. doi:10.1002/asmb.2417

Handayani, S., Pribadi, F. S., Suni, A. F., Mahendra, R. I., & Afandi, M. (2024, February). Measurement Information System Development Performance of the Unnes Faculty of Engineering Academic Civity. In *5th Vocational Education International Conference (VEIC-5 2023)* (pp. 1375-1381). Atlantis Press. 10.2991/978-2-38476-198-2_194

Hardcastle, E. (2011). *Business information systems*. Bookboon.

Harmon, R. R. (2002). Marketing Information Systems. Encyclopedia of Information Systems, 3, 137-151.

Hashmi, M. M. H. (2006). *Explore Hyderabad: An Interactive Web-based GIS Application Prototype*. Academic Press.

Hays, S., Page, S. J., & Buhalis, D. (2013). Social media as a destination marketing tool: Its use by national tourism organisations. *Current Issues in Tourism*, *16*(3), 211–239. doi:10.1080/13683500.2012.662215

Holsapple, C. W., & Sena, M. P. (2000). Organised knowledge sharing with book-centered Web sites: An architecture, implementation and analysis. *Information Technology and Management*, *1*(4), 363–377. doi:10.1023/A:1019145629862

Huybers, T., & Bennett, J. (2003). Environmental management and the competitiveness of nature-based tourism destinations. *Environmental and Resource Economics*, *24*(3), 213–233. doi:10.1023/A:1022942001100

Iswanto, D., Handriana, T., Nazwin, A. H., & Sangadji, S. S. (2024). Influencers in Tourism Digital Marketing: A Comprehensive Literature Review. *International Journal of Sustainable Development and Planning*, *19*(2), 739–749. doi:10.18280/ijsdp.190231

Kamkiew, W. (2021). *Factors influencing service quality ofThai airways international flights*. Academic Press.

Kannan, P. K., Chang, A. M., & Whinston, A. B. (1998). Marketing information on the I-Way: Data junkyard or information gold mine? *Communications of the ACM*, *41*(3), 35–43. doi:10.1145/272287.272295

Kumar, N. (2005). The power of power in supplier-retailer relationships. *Industrial Marketing Management*, *34*(8), 863–866. doi:10.1016/j.indmarman.2005.02.003

Li, J., Kamal, E. B. M., & Jing, K. T. (2024). Assessing the Mediating Role of E-Techniques in the Relationship Between Information Systems and Carbon Reduction Strategies During the Construction Phase of Chinese Construction Projects. *Journal of Information Systems Engineering & Management*, *9*(1), 21636. doi:10.55267/iadt.07.14183

Libriantono, B. (2024). Implementation of the Personnel Management Information System for the Tangerang Regency Regional Civil Service Agency. *The International Journal of Education Management and Sociology*, *3*(1), 46–60.

Madhura, D., Prajakta, M., Tanaya, Z., Vijaya, N., Ashish, K., Bhakti, T., & Neha, P. (2023). An AI Integrated Online Hotel Management System. *Journal of Web Engineering & Technology*, *9*(1), 1–18.

Nelson, B. L. (1995). *Environmental Scanning: Evaluation & Recommendations to Management*. Academic Press.

Nordin, F., & Ravald, A. (2023). The making of marketing decisions in modern marketing environments. *Journal of Business Research, 162*, 113872. doi:10.1016/j.jbusres.2023.113872

Nozdreva, R., & Churakova, A. (2021). Digital tools in empirical marketing strategies of global hotel companies. *Digital strategies in a global market: Navigating the Fourth Industrial Revolution*, 213-227.

Ogbadu-Oladapo, L., Bissadu, K., Kim, H., & Smith, D. L. (2024). Information and health literacy: Could there be any impact on health decision-making among adults?—evidence from North America. *Journal of Public Health (Berlin)*, 1–31. doi:10.1007/s10389-024-02260-9

Papadakis, V. M., Lioukas, S., & Chambers, D. (1998). Strategic decision-making processes: The role of management and context. *Strategic Management Journal, 19*(2), 115–147. doi:10.1002/(SICI)1097-0266(199802)19:2<115::AID-SMJ941>3.0.CO;2-5

Pearlson, K. E., Saunders, C. S., & Galletta, D. F. (2024). *Managing and using information systems: A strategic approach*. John Wiley & Sons.

Prideaux, B. (1999). Tracks to tourism: Queensland rail joins the tourist industry. *International Journal of Tourism Research, 1*(2), 73–86. doi:10.1002/(SICI)1522-1970(199903/04)1:2<73::AID-JTR123>3.0.CO;2-Q

Remler, D. K., & Van Ryzin, G. G. (2021). *Research methods in practice: Strategies for description and causation*. Sage Publications.

Sayegh, L., Anthony, W. P., & Perrewé, P. L. (2004). Managerial decision-making under crisis: The role of emotion in an intuitive decision process. *Human Resource Management Review, 14*(2), 179–199. doi:10.1016/j.hrmr.2004.05.002

Scorgie, M. (2008). *Skiers' and snowboarders' perceptions of the quality of a ski resort in Japan: an application of importance performance analysis and recreation specialisation* (Doctoral dissertation).

Sear, A. M. (1989). Information system failures: The role of hardware and software. *The Journal of Ambulatory Care Management, 12*(4), 30–37. doi:10.1097/00004479-198911000-00007 PMID:10295602

Singh, T., Veron-Jackson, L., & Cullinane, J. (2008). Blogging: A new play in your marketing game plan. *Business Horizons, 51*(4), 281–292. doi:10.1016/j.bushor.2008.02.002

Sorensen, C., & Kakihara, M. (2002, January). Knowledge discourses and interaction technology. In *Proceedings of the 35th Annual Hawaii International Conference on System Sciences* (pp. 976-986). IEEE. 10.1109/HICSS.2002.994048

Vera, D., Tabesh, P., Velez-Castrillon, S., Kachra, A., & Werner, S. (2024). Improvisational decision making: Context, antecedents, and outcomes. In *The Routledge companion to improvisation in organisations* (pp. 144–163). Routledge.

Viale, R. (2024). Enactive problem-solving: an alternative to the limits of decision making. *Elgar Companion to Herbert Simon*, 198.

Compilation of References

Aaker, D., & Moorman, C. (2023). *Strategic market management.* John Wiley & Sons.

Aarts, E., & Wichert, R. (2009). Ambient intelligence. In H. J. Bullinger (Ed.), *Technology guide* (pp. 244–249). Springer. doi:10.1007/978-3-540-88546-7_47

Abatecola, G., Mari, M., & Poggesi, S. (2020). How can virtuous real estate public-private partnerships be developed? Towards a co-evolutionary perspective. *Cities (London, England), 107*, 102896. doi:10.1016/j.cities.2020.102896

Abba Ari, A., Ngangmo, O., Titouna, C., Thiare, O., Mohamadou, A., & Gueroui, A. (2024). Enabling privacy and security in Cloud of Things: Architecture, applications, security & privacy challenges. *Applied Computing and Informatics, 20*(1/2), 119–141. doi:10.1016/j.aci.2019.11.005

Abd Razak, S., Nazari, N., & Al-Dhaqm, A. (2020). Data anonymization using pseudonym system to preserve data privacy. *IEEE Access : Practical Innovations, Open Solutions, 8*, 43256–43264. doi:10.1109/ACCESS.2020.2977117

Achrol, R. S., & Kotler, P. (1999). Marketing in the network economy. *Journal of Marketing, 63*(4, suppl1), 146–163. doi:10.1177/00222429990634s114

Agarwal, S. (2002). Restructuring seaside tourism: The resort lifecycle. *Annals of Tourism Research, 29*(1), 25–55. doi:10.1016/S0160-7383(01)00002-0

Aggarwal, J., Bhatnagar, V., & Mishra, D. (2018). *Big data analytics.* Springer Singapore. doi:10.1007/978-981-10-6620-7

Aggarwal, K., Khoa, B., Sagar, K., Agrawal, R., Dhingra, M., Dhingra, J., & R, L. K. (2023). Marketing information system based on unsupervised visual data to manage transportation industry using signal processing. *Expert Systems: International Journal of Knowledge Engineering and Neural Networks*, e13384. Advance online publication. doi:10.1111/exsy.13384

Agrawal, R., Wankhede, V., Kumar, A., Luthra, S., & Huisingh, D. (2022). Big data analytics and sustainable tourism: A comprehensive review and network based analysis for potential future research. *International Journal of Information Management Data Insights, 2*(2), 100122. doi:10.1016/j.jjimei.2022.100122

Ahmed, A., & Ganapathy, A. (2021). Creation of automated content with embedded artificial intelligence: A study on learning management system for educational entrepreneurship. *Academy of Entrepreneurship Journal, 27*(3), 1–10.

Ahmed, M., & Pathan, A. (2018). *Data analytics: concepts, techniques, and applications*. Crc Press. doi:10.1201/9780429446177

Aktaş, E., Kurgun, A., Ozeren, E., & Kucukaltan, B. (2022). Real-Time Data Analysis (RTDA) and Proposed Innovative Business Models: A Conceptual Study of the Tourism Industry. *International Journal of Organizational Leadership, 11*, 4-20.

Al Khaldy, M., Al-Obaydi, B., & al Shari, A. (2023). The Impact of Predictive Analytics and AI on Digital Marketing Strategy and ROI. In *Conference on Sustainability and Cutting-Edge Business Technologies* (pp. 367-379). Cham: Springer Nature Switzerland. 10.1007/978-3-031-42455-7_31

Alani, M., Tawfik, M., Saeed, M., & Anya, O. (2018). *Applications of Big Data Analytics- Trends, Issues, and Challenges*. Springer. doi:10.1007/978-3-319-76472-6

Albescu, F., & Pugna, I. B. (2014). Marketing intelligence–the last frontier of business information technologies. *Romanian Journal of Marketing, 3*, 55–68.

Al-Hashem, A. O. (2020). Mediation impact of marketing intelligence in the relationship between technology based knowledge sharing and product innovation. *TEM Journal, 9*(2), 688-693.

Alhroot, A. H. H. J. (2007). *Marketing of a destination: Jordan as a case study* (Doctoral dissertation, University of Huddersfield).

Alkhamisi, A. O., & Monowar, M. M. (2013). Rise of Augmented Reality: Current and Future Application Areas. *International Journal of Internet and Distributed Systems, 1*(4), 25–34. doi:10.4236/ijids.2013.14005

Allam, Z., Cheshmehzangi, A., & Jones, D. S. (2023). Urban Consumerism and Colonial Structures of Mercantilism. In *Climate and Social Justice: The Political Economy of Urban Resilience and Mercantilism* (pp. 43–60). Springer Nature Singapore. doi:10.1007/978-981-99-6624-0_3

Almeida, D., Shmarko, K., & Lomas, E. (2022). The ethics of facial recognition technologies, surveillance, and accountability in an age of artificial intelligence: A comparative analysis of US, EU, and UK regulatory frameworks. *AI and Ethics, 2*(3), 377–387. doi:10.1007/s43681-021-00077-w PMID:34790955

Alnoukari, M. (2022). From business intelligence to big data: The power of analytics. In Research Anthology on Big Data Analytics, Architectures, and Applications (pp. 823-841). IGI Global.

Al-Romeedy, B. (2024a). AI and HRM in Tourism and Hospitality in Egypt: Inevitability, Impact and Future. In HRM, Artificial Intelligence and the Future of Work: Critical Insights from the Global South, Palgrave Macmillan.

Al-Romeedy, B. (2024b). HRM and Digital Leadership: Exploring the Mediating Role of Digital Talent and Digital Culture in Driving Innovative Performance in the Saudi Tourism and Hospitality Industry. In HRM, Artificial Intelligence and the Future of Work: Critical Insights from the Global South, Palgrave Macmillan.

Al-Romeedy, B., & El-Sisi, S. H. (2024). Does AI have an effective role in applying Sustainable Entrepreneurship in Tourism Industry? In *Sustainable Tourism: Balancing Conservation and Progress in a Dynamic Industry*. CABI.

Alshurideh, M., Al Kurdi, B. H., Alzoubi, H. M., & Salloum, S. (Eds.). (2023). *The Effect of Information Technology on Business and Marketing Intelligence Systems* (Vol. 1056). Springer Nature. doi:10.1007/978-3-031-12382-5_140

Álvarez-Carmona, M., Aranda, R., Rodríguez-Gonzalez, A., Fajardo-Delgado, D., Sánchez, M., Pérez-Espinosa, H., Martínez-Miranda, J., Guerrero-Rodríguez, R., Bustio-Martínez, L., & Díaz-Pacheco, Á. (2022). Natural language processing applied to tourism research: A systematic review and future research directions. *Journal of King Saud University. Computer and Information Sciences*, *34*(10), 10125–10144. doi:10.1016/j.jksuci.2022.10.010

Al-Weshah, G. A. (2017). Marketing intelligence and customer relationships: Empirical evidence from Jordanian banks. *Journal of Marketing Analytics*, *5*(3-4), 141–152. doi:10.1057/s41270-017-0021-7

Amankwah-Amoah, J., & Adomako, S. (2019). Big data analytics and business failures in data-Rich environments: An organizing framework. *Computers in Industry*, *105*, 204–212. doi:10.1016/j.compind.2018.12.015

Anshari, M., Almunawar, M., Lim, S., & Al-Mudimigh, A. (2019). Customer relationship management and big data enabled: Personalization & customization of services. *Applied Computing and Informatics*, *15*(2), 94–101. doi:10.1016/j.aci.2018.05.004

Araz, O., Choi, T., Olson, D., & Salman, F. (2020). Role of analytics for operational risk management in the era of big data. *Decision Sciences*, *51*(6), 1320–1346. doi:10.1111/deci.12451

Aroraa, G., Lele, C., & Jindal, M. (2022). *Data Analytics: Principles, Tools, and Practices: A Complete Guide for Advanced Data Analytics Using the Latest Trends, Tools, and Technologies (English Edition)*. BPB Publications.

Ashmarina, S., & Zotova, A. (2016). The system of marketing information management: development, assessment, improvement. *Економічний часопис-XXI*, (160), 51-56.

Avazpour, I., Grundy, J., & Zhu, L. (2019). Engineering complex data integration, harmonization and visualization systems. *Journal of Industrial Information Integration*, *16*, 100103. doi:10.1016/j.jii.2019.08.001

Awan, U., Shamim, S., Khan, Z., Zia, N., Shariq, S., & Khan, M. (2021). Big data analytics capability and decision-making: The role of data-driven insight on circular economy performance. *Technological Forecasting and Social Change*, *168*, 120766. doi:10.1016/j.techfore.2021.120766

Azeroual, O., Jha, M., Nikiforova, A., Sha, K., Alsmirat, M., & Jha, S. (2022). A record linkage-based data deduplication framework with datacleaner extension. *Multimodal Technologies and Interaction*, *6*(4), 27. doi:10.3390/mti6040027

Aziz, F., Al Haque, T., Hossain, M. B., Rahman, A., & Siam, S. A. J. (2023). Customer Behavior Analysis Through Data Analytics in The Bangladeshi Retail Industry. *Malaysian E Commerce Journal*, *7*(2), 78–84. doi:10.26480/mecj.02.2023.90.96

Bagga, T., Vishnoi, S. K., Jain, S., & Sharma, R. (2020). Medical Tourism: Treatment, Therapy and Tourism. *International Journal of Scientific and Technology Research*, *9*(3), 4447–4453.

Balas, V., Solanki, V., Kumar, R., & Khari, M. (2019). *Internet of things and big data analytics for smart generation* (Vol. 154). Springer. doi:10.1007/978-3-030-04203-5

Bardukova, L. (2023). Navigating the Hospitality Horizon: Current Trends and Strategies for Customer Attraction and Retention in the Hotel Industry. *Economics and Computer Science*, (2), 88-103.

Barykin, S., Lavskaya, K., Baydukova, N., Kapustina, I., Kalinina, O., Naumova, E., & Dedyukhina, N. (2022). The complexity of digital marketing methodology implementation in air passenger transportation: The case of Russia. *Transportation Research Procedia*, *63*, 695–702. doi:10.1016/j.trpro.2022.06.064

Basiri, A., Amirian, P., Winstanley, A., & Moore, T. (2018). Making tourist guidance systems more intelligent, adaptive, and personalized using crowd-sourced movement data. *Journal of Ambient Intelligence and Humanized Computing*, *9*(2), 413–427. doi:10.1007/s12652-017-0550-0

Beck, K. (2000). *Extreme programming explained: Embrace change*. Addison-Wesley Professional.

Behrmann, J., & Smith, E. (2010). Top 7 Issues in Medical Tourism: Challenges, Knowledge Gaps, and Future Directions for Research and Policy Development. *Global Journal of Health Science*, *2*(2), 80. doi:10.5539/gjhs.v2n2p80

Belhadi, A., Zkik, K., Cherrafi, A., & Sha'ri, M. (2019). Understanding big data analytics for manufacturing processes: Insights from literature review and multiple case studies. *Computers & Industrial Engineering*, *137*, 106099. doi:10.1016/j.cie.2019.106099

Benckendorff, P. J., Xiang, Z., & Sheldon, P. J. (2019). *Tourism information technology*. CABI. doi:10.1079/9781786393432.0000

Bharadiya, J. (2023). Machine learning and AI in business intelligence: Trends and opportunities. *International Journal of Computer*, *48*(1), 123–134.

Bharadiya, J. P. (2023). The role of machine learning in transforming business intelligence. *International Journal of Computing and Artificial Intelligence*, *4*(1), 16–24. doi:10.33545/27076571.2023.v4.i1a.60

Big data analytics as-a-service: Issues and challenges. (2016). In *2016 IEEE International Conference on Big Data (Big Data)*. IEEE.

Bookman, M., & Bookman, K. (2007). *Medical Tourism in Developing Countries*. Palgrave Macmilla. doi:10.1057/9780230605657

Borgogno, O., & Colangelo, G. (2019). Data sharing and interoperability: Fostering innovation and competition through APIs. *Computer Law & Security Report*, *35*(5), 105314. doi:10.1016/j.clsr.2019.03.008

Bowen, J., & Morosan, C. (2018). Beware the hospitality industry: The robots are coming. *Worldwide Hospitality and Tourism Themes*, *10*(6), 726–733. doi:10.1108/WHATT-07-2018-0045

Brynjolfsson, E., & McAfee, A. (2014). *The Second Machine Age: Work, Progress, and Prosperity in a Time of Brilliant Technologies*. Academic Press.

Brynjolfsson, E., & McAfee, A. (2011). *Race against the machine: How the digital revolution is accelerating innovation, driving productivity, and irreversibly transforming employment and the economy*. Digital Frontier Press.

Buhalis, D., & Law, R. (2008). *Progress in Information Technology and Tourism Management*. Academic Press.

Buhalis, D., & Leung, R. (2018). Smart hospitality—Interconnectivity and interoperability towards an ecosystem. *International Journal of Hospitality Management*, *71*, 41–50. doi:10.1016/j.ijhm.2017.11.011

Bulchand-Gidumal, J. (2020). *Impact of Artificial Intelligence in Travel*. Tourism, and Hospitality., doi:10.1007/978-3-030-05324-6_110-1

Bulchand-Gidumal, J. (2022). Impact of artificial intelligence in travel, tourism, and hospitality. In *Handbook of e-Tourism* (pp. 1943–1962). Springer International Publishing. doi:10.1007/978-3-030-48652-5_110

Bulger, N. (2016). The evolving role of intelligence: Migrating from traditional competitive intelligence to integrated intelligence. *The International Journal of Intelligence, Security, and Public Affairs*, *18*(1), 57–84. doi:10.1080/23800992.2016.1150691

Buttle, F., & Maklan, S. (2019). *Customer relationship management: concepts and technologies*. Routledge. doi:10.4324/9781351016551

Carlisle, S., Ivanov, S., & Dijkmans, C. (2023). The digital skills divide: Evidence from the European tourism industry. *J. Tour. Futures*, *9*(2), 240–266. doi:10.1108/JTF-07-2020-0114

Carr, W. (1995). *For education: Towards critical educational inquiry*. McGraw-Hill Education (UK).

Chandra, S., Verma, S., Lim, W., Kumar, S., & Donthu, N. (2022). Personalization in personalized marketing: Trends and ways forward. *Psychology and Marketing*, *39*(8), 1529–1562. doi:10.1002/mar.21670

Chang, M. X., Choong, Y. O., Ng, L. P., & Seow, A. N. (2022). The importance of support for sport tourism development among local residents: The mediating role of the perceived impacts of sport tourism. *Leisure Studies*, *41*(3), 420–436. doi:10.1080/02614367.2021.2011950

Chang, Y., Ku, C., & Chen, C. (2019). Social media analytics: Extracting and visualizing Hilton hotel ratings and reviews from TripAdvisor. *International Journal of Information Management*, *48*, 263–279. doi:10.1016/j.ijinfomgt.2017.11.001

Chareyron, G., Da-Rugna, J., & Raimbault, T. (2014, October). Big data: A new challenge for tourism. In *2014 IEEE International Conference on Big Data (Big Data)*. IEEE. 10.1109/BigData.2014.7004475

Chase, C., & Chase, J. (2013). *Demand-driven forecasting: a structured approach to forecasting*. Wiley. doi:10.1002/9781118691861

Chaturvedi, R., Verma, S., Ali, F., & Kumar, S. (2023). Reshaping Tourist Experience with AI-Enabled Technologies: A Comprehensive Review and Future Research Agenda. *International Journal of Human-Computer Interaction*, 1–17. Advance online publication. doi:10.1080/10447318.2023.2238353

Chaudhary, K., & Alam, M. (2022). *Big data analytics: applications in business and marketing*. Auerbach Publications. doi:10.1201/9781003307761

Chen, L., Yang, Y., & Xu, Q. (2021). Retail dynamic pricing strategy design considering the fluctuations in day-ahead market using integrated demand response. *International Journal of Electrical Power & Energy Systems*, *130*, 106983. doi:10.1016/j.ijepes.2021.106983

Chhabra, A., Munjal, M., Mishra, P.C., Singh, K., Das, D., Kuhar, N., & Vats, M. (2021). Medical Tourism in the Covid-19 Era: Opportunities, Challenges and the Way Ahead. *Worldwide Hospitality and Tourism Themes*.

Chintalapati, S., & Pandey, S. K. (2022). Artificial intelligence in marketing: A systematic literature review. *International Journal of Market Research*, *64*(1), 38–68. doi:10.1177/14707853211018428

Chowdhury, S., Dey, P., Joel-Edgar, S., Bhattacharya, S., Rodriguez-Espindola, O., Abadie, A., & Truong, L. (2023). Unlocking the value of artificial intelligence in human resource management through AI capability framework. *Human Resource Management Review*, *33*(1), 100899. doi:10.1016/j.hrmr.2022.100899

Christopher, M., & Gaudenzi, B. (2009). Exploiting knowledge across networks through reputation management. *Industrial Marketing Management*, *38*(2), 191–197. doi:10.1016/j.indmarman.2008.12.014

Chuang, S., & Lin, H. (2013). The roles of infrastructure capability and customer orientation in enhancing customer-information quality in CRM systems: Empirical evidence from Taiwan. *International Journal of Information Management*, *33*(2), 271–281. doi:10.1016/j.ijinfomgt.2012.12.003

Connell, J. (2013). Contemporary Medical Tourism: Conceptualisation, Culture and Commodification. *Tourism Management*, *34*, 1–13. doi:10.1016/j.tourman.2012.05.009

Côrte-Real, N., Ruivo, P., Oliveira, T., & Popovič, A. (2019). Unlocking the drivers of big data analytics value in firms. *Journal of Business Research*, *97*, 160–173. doi:10.1016/j.jbusres.2018.12.072

Dai, D., & Boroomand, S. (2022). A review of artificial intelligence to enhance the security of big data systems: State-of-art, methodologies, applications, and challenges. *Archives of Computational Methods in Engineering*, *29*(2), 1291–1309. doi:10.1007/s11831-021-09628-0

Dam, N., Le Dinh, T., & Menvielle, W. (2019). Marketing intelligence from data mining perspective: A literature review. *International Journal of Innovation, Management and Technology*, *10*(5), 184–190. doi:10.18178/ijimt.2019.10.5.859

Dartmann, G., Song, H., & Schmeink, A. (2019). *Big data analytics for cyber-physical systems: machine learning for the internet of things*. Elsevier.

Davenport, T. H. (2012). *Analytics at Work: Smarter Decisions*. Better Results.

de Bellis, E., Hildebrand, C., Ito, K., Herrmann, A., & Schmitt, B. (2019). Personalizing the customization experience: A matching theory of mass customization interfaces and cultural information processing. *JMR, Journal of Marketing Research*, *56*(6), 1050–1065. doi:10.1177/0022243719867698

De Mauro, A., Greco, M., & Grimaldi, M. (2015). What is big data? A consensual definition and a review of key research topics. *AIP Conference Proceedings*, *1644*(1), 97–104. doi:10.1063/1.4907823

del Rio, J., Moctezuma, D., Conde, C., de Diego, I., & Cabello, E. (2016). Automated border control e-gates and facial recognition systems. *Computers & Security, 62*, 49-72.

Del Vecchio, P., Mele, G., Ndou, V., & Secundo, G. (2018). Creating value from social big data: Implications for smart tourism destinations. *Information Processing & Management*, *54*(5), 847–860. doi:10.1016/j.ipm.2017.10.006

Dewnarain, S., Ramkissoon, H., & Mavondo, F. (2019). Social customer relationship management: An integrated conceptual framework. *Journal of Hospitality Marketing & Management*, *28*(2), 172–188. doi:10.1080/19368623.2018.1516588

Dey, N., Hassanien, A., Bhatt, C., Ashour, A., & Satapathy, S. (2018). *Internet of things and big data analytics toward next-generation intelligence*. Springer. doi:10.1007/978-3-319-60435-0

Dhayne, H., Haque, R., Kilany, R., & Taher, Y. (2019). In search of big medical data integration solutions-a comprehensive survey. *IEEE Access : Practical Innovations, Open Solutions*, *7*, 91265–91290. doi:10.1109/ACCESS.2019.2927491

Ding, K., Gong, X., Huang, T., & Choo, W. (2024). Recommend or not: A comparative analysis of customer reviews to uncover factors influencing explicit online recommendation behavior in peer-to-peer accommodation. *European Research on Management and Business Economics, 30*(1), 100236. doi:10.1016/j.iedeen.2023.100236

Dixon, A. W., Henry, M., & Martinez, J. M. (2023). Assessing the economic impact of sport tourists' expenditures related to a university's baseball season attendance. *Journal of Issues in Intercollegiate Athletics, 6*(1), 2.

Doan, A., Halevy, A., & Ives, Z. (2012). *Principles of data integration.* Elsevier.

Doering, Z. D. (2007). Strangers, guests, or clients? Visitor experiences in museums. In *Museum Management and Marketing* (pp. 331–344). Routledge.

Doğan, S., & Niyet, İ. (2024). Artificial Intelligence (AI) in Tourism. In Future Tourism Trends Volume 2: Technology Advancement, Trends and Innovations for the Future in Tourism (pp. 3-21). Emerald Publishing Limited.

Du, J. (2014). The information journey of marketing professionals: Incorporating work task-driven information seeking, information judgments, information use, and information sharing. *Journal of the Association for Information Science and Technology, 65*(9), 1850–1869. doi:10.1002/asi.23085

Du, R., Netzer, O., Schweidel, D., & Mitra, D. (2021). Capturing marketing information to fuel growth. *Journal of Marketing, 85*(1), 163–183. doi:10.1177/0022242920969198

Du, S., & Xie, C. (2021). Paradoxes of artificial intelligence in consumer markets: Ethical challenges and opportunities. *Journal of Business Research, 129*, 961–974. doi:10.1016/j.jbusres.2020.08.024

Dwivedi, D. N., & Anand, A. (2021). The Text Mining of Public Policy Documents in Response to COVID-19: A Comparison of the United Arab Emirates and the Kingdom of Saudi Arabia. *Public Governance / Zarządzanie Publiczne, 55*(1), 8-22. doi:10.15678/ZP.2021.55.1.02

Dwivedi, D. N., Mahanty, G., & Pathak, Y. K. (2023). AI Applications for Financial Risk Management. In M. Irfan, M. Elmogy, M. Shabri Abd. Majid, & S. El-Sappagh (Eds.), The Impact of AI Innovation on Financial Sectors in the Era of Industry 5.0 (pp. 17-31). IGI Global. doi:10.4018/979-8-3693-0082-4.ch002

Dwivedi, D. N., Pandey, A. K., & Dwivedi, A. D. (2023). Examining the emotional tone in politically polarized Speeches in India: An In-Depth analysis of two contrasting perspectives. *South India Journal of Social Sciences*, 21(2), 125-136. https://journal.sijss.com/index.php/home/article/view/65

Dwivedi, D. N. (2024). The Use of Artificial Intelligence in Supply Chain Management and Logistics. In D. Sharma, B. Bhardwaj, & M. Dhiman (Eds.), *Leveraging AI and Emotional Intelligence in Contemporary Business Organizations* (pp. 306–313). IGI Global., doi:10.4018/979-8-3693-1902-4.ch018

Dwivedi, D. N., & Mahanty, G. (2024). AI-Powered Employee Experience: Strategies and Best Practices. In M. Rafiq, M. Farrukh, R. Mushtaq, & O. Dastane (Eds.), *Exploring the Intersection of AI and Human Resources Management* (pp. 166–181). IGI Global. doi:10.4018/979-8-3693-0039-8.ch009

Dwivedi, D. N., Mahanty, G., & Vemareddy, A. (2022). How Responsible Is AI?: Identification of Key Public Concerns Using Sentiment Analysis and Topic Modeling. *International Journal of Information Retrieval Research*, *12*(1), 1–14. doi:10.4018/IJIRR.298646

Dwivedi, D. N., Tadoori, G., & Batra, S. (2023). Impact of women leadership and ESG ratings and in organizations: A time series segmentation study. *Academy of Strategic Management Journal*, *22*(S3), 1–6.

Dwivedi, D., Batra, S., & Pathak, Y. K. (2023). A machine learning based approach to identify key drivers for improving corporate's esg ratings. *Journal of Law and Sustainable Development*, *11*(1), e0242. doi:10.37497/sdgs.v11i1.242

Dwivedi, Y., Ismagilova, E., Hughes, D., Carlson, J., Filieri, R., Jacobson, J., Jain, V., Karjaluoto, H., Kefi, H., Krishen, A. S., Kumar, V., Rahman, M. M., Raman, R., Rauschnabel, P. A., Rowley, J., Salo, J., Tran, G. A., & Wang, Y. (2021). Setting the future of digital and social media marketing research: Perspectives and research propositions. *International Journal of Information Management*, *59*, 102168. doi:10.1016/j.ijinfomgt.2020.102168

Edensor, T., Millington, S., Steadman, C., & Taecharungroj, V. (2021). Towards a comprehensive understanding of football stadium tourism. *Journal of Sport & Tourism*, *25*(3), 217–235. doi:10.1080/14775085.2021.1884589

Egger, R. (2022). *Applied Data Science in Tourism*. Springer International Publishing. doi:10.1007/978-3-030-88389-8

El-Masri, M., Altrabsheh, N., Mansour, H., & Ramsay, A. (2017). A web-based tool for Arabic sentiment analysis. *Procedia Computer Science*, *117*, 38–45. doi:10.1016/j.procs.2017.10.092

El-Sherbiny, M., & Al-Romeedy, B. (2023). Does loyalty moderate the impact of digital marketing on the purchase intention of customers in airlines? *Journal of the Faculty of Tourism and Hotels-University of Sadat City*, *7*(2), 1–16.

Erevelles, S., Fukawa, N., & Swayne, L. (2016). Big Data consumer analytics and the transformation of marketing. *Journal of Business Research*, *69*(2), 897–904. doi:10.1016/j.jbusres.2015.07.001

ETB. (2017). Virgin Holidays launches AI technology for holidaymakers. *ETB Travel News*, 5–7.

Etim, G., Inyang, W., James, E., & Mbu-Ogar, G. (2023). Marketing information system (MKIS) and optimization of banking service delivery. *African Journal of Accounting and Financial Research*, *6*(2), 112–125. doi:10.52589/AJAFR-XRYGQLV3

European Commission. (2017). *Digital Transformation*. Retrieved July 5, 2017, from https://ec.europa.eu/growth/industry/digital-transformation_en

Falk, J., & Dierking, L. (2000). *Learning from Museums: Visitor Experiences and the Making of Meaning*. AltaMira Press.

Farahat, E. (2023). *Applications of artificial intelligence as a marketing tool and their impact on the competitiveness of the Egyptian tourist destination* (Doctoral Dissertation, Minia University).

Farahat, E., Mohamed, M., & Al-Romeedy, B. (2022). Artificial intelligence applications and its impact on the competitiveness of the Egyptian tourist destination. *Research Journal of the Faculty of Tourism and Hotels Mansoura University*, *11*(2), 57–93.

Ferrer-Rosell, B., Massimo, D., & Berezina, K. (2023). *Information and Communication Technologies in Tourism 2023: Proceedings of the ENTER 2023 eTourism Conference, January 18-20, 2023*. Springer Nature. 10.1007/978-3-031-25752-0

Fillinger, S., de la Garza, L., Peltzer, A., Kohlbacher, O., & Nahnsen, S. (2019). Challenges of big data integration in the life sciences. *Analytical and Bioanalytical Chemistry*, *411*(26), 6791–6800. doi:10.1007/s00216-019-02074-9 PMID:31463515

Fiocco, A. J., Millett, G., D'Amico, D., Krieger, L., Sivashankar, Y., Lee, S. H., & Lachman, R. (2021). Virtual tourism for older adults living in residential care: A mixed-methods study. *PLoS One*, *16*(5), e0250761. doi:10.1371/journal.pone.0250761 PMID:34014948

Fisher, N. I., & Kordupleski, R. E. (2019). Good and bad market research: A critical review of Net Promoter Score. *Applied Stochastic Models in Business and Industry*, *35*(1), 138–151. doi:10.1002/asmb.2417

Fleisher, C., Wright, S., & Allard, H. (2008). The role of insight teams in integrating diverse marketing information management techniques. *European Journal of Marketing*, *42*(7/8), 836–851. doi:10.1108/03090560810877187

Fuchs, M., Höpken, W., & Lexhagen, M. (2014). Big Data Analytics for Knowledge Generation in Tourism Destinations. *Journal of Destination Marketing & Management*, *2*(1), 3–12. doi:10.1016/j.jdmm.2014.08.002

Gaafar, H. (2020). Artificial intelligence in Egyptian tourism companies: Implementation and perception. *Journal of Association of Arab Universities for Tourism and Hospitality*, *18*(1), 66–78. doi:10.21608/jaauth.2020.31704.1028

Gaafar, H. (2021). Digital Detox Tourism at The Egyptian Destination: Attitudes and Motivators. *Journal of Association of Arab Universities for Tourism and Hospitality*, *20*(2), 88–107.

Gajdošík, T. (2019). Big data analytics in smart tourism destinations. A new tool for destination management organizations? In *Smart Tourism as a Driver for Culture and Sustainability: Fifth International Conference IACuDiT, Athens 2018* (pp. 15-33). Springer International Publishing.

Gangwani, D., & Gangwani, P. (2021). Applications of machine learning and artificial intelligence in intelligent transportation system: A review. *Applications of Artificial Intelligence and Machine Learning: Select Proceedings of ICAAAIML 2020*, 203-216.

Gao, L., Melero, I., & Sese, F. J. (2020). Multichannel integration along the customer journey: A systematic review and research agenda. *Service Industries Journal*, *40*(15-16), 1087–1118. doi:10.1080/02642069.2019.1652600

García, S., Luengo, J., & Herrera, F. (2015). *Data preprocessing in data mining* (Vol. 72). Springer International Publishing. doi:10.1007/978-3-319-10247-4

George, A., & George, A. (2023). A review of ChatGPT AI's impact on several business sectors. *Partners Universal International Innovation Journal*, *1*(1), 9–23.

Georgiadis, G., & Poels, G. (2021). Enterprise architecture management as a solution for addressing general data protection regulation requirements in a big data context: A systematic mapping study. *Information Systems and e-Business Management*, *19*(1), 313–362. doi:10.1007/s10257-020-00500-5

Ghahremani-Nahr, J., & Nozari, H. (2021). A Survey for Investigating Key Performance Indicators in Digital Marketing. *International Journal of Innovation in Marketing Elements*, *1*(1), 1-6.

Ghavami, P. (2019). *Big data analytics methods: analytics techniques in data mining, deep learning and natural language processing*. Walter de Gruyter GmbH & Co KG. doi:10.1515/9781547401567

Ghoshal, A., Mookerjee, V. S., & Sarkar, S. (2021). Recommendations and cross-selling: Pricing strategies when personalizing firms cross-sell. *Journal of Management Information Systems*, *38*(2), 430–456. doi:10.1080/07421222.2021.1912930

Gibson, H. (1998). Sport tourism: A critical analysis of research. *Sport Management Review*, *1*(1), 45–76. doi:10.1016/S1441-3523(98)70099-3

Gibson, H. J. (2003). Sport tourism: An introduction to the special issue. *Journal of Sport Management*, *17*(3), 205–213. doi:10.1123/jsm.17.3.205

Gorelik, A. (2019). *The enterprise big data lake: Delivering the promise of big data and data science*. O'Reilly Media.

Gov.uk. (2017). *Robotics and AI: apply in the Industrial Strategy Challenge Fund.* Retrieved from https://www.gov.uk/government/news/robotics-and-ai-apply-in-The-industrial-strategy-challenge-fund

Grandhi, B., Patwa, N., & Saleem, K. (2021). Data-driven marketing for growth and profitability. *EuroMed Journal of Business*, *16*(4), 381–398. doi:10.1108/EMJB-09-2018-0054

Gretzel, U., Sigala, M., Xiang, Z., & Koo, C. (2015). *Smart Tourism: Foundations and Developments*. Academic Press.

Grigsby, M. (2022). *Marketing analytics: A practical guide to improving consumer insights using data techniques*. Kogan Page Publishers.

Grosz, B. J., Altman, R., Horvitz, E., Mackworth, A., Mitchell, T., Mulligan, D., & Shoham, Y. (2015). *Artificial Intelligence and Life in 2030*. Retrieved from https://ai100.stanford.edu/sites/default/files/ai_100_report_0831fnl.pdf

Grundner, L., & Neuhofer, B. (2021). The bright and dark sides of artificial intelligence: A futures perspective on tourist destination experiences. *Journal of Destination Marketing & Management*, *19*, 100511. doi:10.1016/j.jdmm.2020.100511

Gudivada, V., Apon, A., & Ding, J. (2017). Data quality considerations for big data and machine learning: Going beyond data cleaning and transformations. *International Journal on Advances in Software*, *10*(1), 1–20.

Gummerus, J., von Koskull, C., & Kowalkowski, C. (2017). Guest editorial: Relationship marketing–past, present and future. *Journal of Services Marketing*, *31*(1), 1–5. doi:10.1108/JSM-12-2016-0424

Gupta, S., Drave, V. A., Dwivedi, Y. K., Baabdullah, A. M., & Ismagilova, E. (2020). Achieving superior organizational performance via big data predictive analytics: A dynamic capability view. *Industrial Marketing Management*, *90*, 581–592. doi:10.1016/j.indmarman.2019.11.009

Gupta, S., Drave, V., Bag, S., & Luo, Z. (2019). Leveraging smart supply chain and information system agility for supply chain flexibility. *Information Systems Frontiers*, *21*(3), 547–564. doi:10.1007/s10796-019-09901-5

Gupta, S., Justy, T., Kamboj, S., Kumar, A., & Kristoffersen, E. (2021). Big data and firm marketing performance: Findings from knowledge-based view. *Technological Forecasting and Social Change*, *171*, 120986. doi:10.1016/j.techfore.2021.120986

Gupta, S., Modgil, S., Lee, C., & Sivarajah, U. (2023). The future is yesterday: Use of AI-driven facial recognition to enhance value in the travel and tourism industry. *Information Systems Frontiers*, *25*(3), 1179–1195. doi:10.1007/s10796-022-10271-8 PMID:35529102

Gursoy, D., Saayman, M., & Sotiriadis, M. (2015). *Collaboration in tourism businesses and destinations: A handbook*. Emerald Group Publishing.

Guttentag, D. A. (2010). Virtual reality: Applications and implications for tourism. *Tourism Management*, *31*(4), 637–651. doi:10.1016/j.tourman.2009.07.003

Halder, S., Lim, K. H., Chan, J., & Zhang, X. (2024). A survey on personalized itinerary recommendation: From optimisation to deep learning. *Applied Soft Computing*, *152*, 111200. doi:10.1016/j.asoc.2023.111200

Hamid, R., Albahri, A., Alwan, J., Al-Qaysi, Z., Albahri, O., Zaidan, A., Alnoor, A., Alamoodi, A. H., & Zaidan, B. (2021). How smart is e-tourism? A systematic review of smart tourism recommendation system applying data management. *Computer Science Review*, *39*, 100337. doi:10.1016/j.cosrev.2020.100337

Handayani, S., Pribadi, F. S., Suni, A. F., Mahendra, R. I., & Afandi, M. (2024, February). Measurement Information System Development Performance of the Unnes Faculty of Engineering Academic Civity. In *5th Vocational Education International Conference (VEIC-5 2023)* (pp. 1375-1381). Atlantis Press. 10.2991/978-2-38476-198-2_194

Haque, A., Bhushan, B., & Dhiman, G. (2022). Conceptualizing smart city applications: Requirements, architecture, security issues, and emerging trends. *Expert Systems: International Journal of Knowledge Engineering and Neural Networks*, *39*(5), e12753. doi:10.1111/exsy.12753

Hardcastle, E. (2011). *Business information systems*. Bookboon.

Harmon, R. (2002). Marketing Information Systems. Encyclopedia of Information Systems, 3, 137-151.

Harmon, R. R. (2002). Marketing Information Systems. Encyclopedia of Information Systems, 3, 137-151.

Harrison-Hill, T., & Chalip, L. (2005). Marketing Sport Tourism: Creating Synergy between Sport and Destination. *Sport in Society*, *8*(2), 302–320. doi:10.1080/17430430500102150

Hashmi, M. M. H. (2006). *Explore Hyderabad: An Interactive Web-based GIS Application Prototype*. Academic Press.

Hassanien, A., Dey, N., & Elghamrawy, S. (2020). Big data analytics and artificial intelligence against COVID-19. Springer Nature.

Hassani, H., & Silva, E. S. (2015). Forecasting with big data: A review. *Ann. Data Sci.*, *2*(1), 5–19. doi:10.1007/s40745-015-0029-9

Hays, S., Page, S. J., & Buhalis, D. (2013). Social media as a destination marketing tool: Its use by national tourism organisations. *Current Issues in Tourism*, *16*(3), 211–239. doi:10.1080/13683500.2012.662215

Hemachandran, K., Khanra, S., Rodriguez, R., & Jaramillo, J. (2022). *Machine Learning for Business Analytics: Real-Time Data Analysis for Decision-Making*. CRC Press. doi:10.4324/9781003206316

Heung, V., Kucukusta, D., & Song, H. (2010). A Conceptual Model of Medical Tourism: Implications for Future Research. *Journal of Travel & Tourism Marketing*, *27*(3), 236–251. doi:10.1080/10548401003744677

Hicham, N., Nassera, H., & Karim, S. (2023). Strategic framework for leveraging artificial intelligence in future marketing decision-making. *Journal of Intelligent and Management Decision*, *2*(3), 139–150. doi:10.56578/jimd020304

Hirve, S. A., & Pradeep Reddy, C. H. (2023). Improving big data analytics with interactive augmented reality. *International Journal of Information System Modeling and Design*, *13*(7), 19–29.

Hofmann, E., & Rutschmann, E. (2018). Big data analytics and demand forecasting in supply chains: A conceptual analysis. *International Journal of Logistics Management*, *29*(2), 739–766. doi:10.1108/IJLM-04-2017-0088

Holsapple, C. W., & Sena, M. P. (2000). Organised knowledge sharing with book-centered Web sites: An architecture, implementation and analysis. *Information Technology and Management*, *1*(4), 363–377. doi:10.1023/A:1019145629862

Hong, Y., Xin, Y., Martin, H., Bucher, D., & Raubal, M. (2021). A clustering-based framework for individual travel behaviour change detection. In *11th International Conference on Geographic Information Science (GIScience 2021)-Part II* (Vol. 208, p. 4). Schloss Dagstuhl-Leibniz-Zentrum für Informatik.

Horng, J., Liu, C., Chou, S., Yu, T., & Hu, D. (2022). Role of big data capabilities in enhancing competitive advantage and performance in the hospitality sector: Knowledge-based dynamic capabilities view. *Journal of Hospitality and Tourism Management*, *51*, 22–38. doi:10.1016/j.jhtm.2022.02.026

Hossain, M. A., Agnihotri, R., Rushan, M. R. I., Rahman, M. S., & Sumi, S. F. (2022). Marketing analytics capability, artificial intelligence adoption, and firms' competitive advantage: Evidence from the manufacturing industry. *Industrial Marketing Management*, *106*, 240–255. doi:10.1016/j.indmarman.2022.08.017

House of Lords. (2017). *Brexit: trade in non- financial services*. European Union Committee. Retrieved from https://publications.parliament.uk/pa/ld201617/ldselect/ldeucom/135/135.pdf

Howard, A., & Borenstein, J. (2018). The ugly truth about ourselves and our robot creations: The problem of bias and social inequity. *Science and Engineering Ethics*, *24*(5), 1521–1536. doi:10.1007/s11948-017-9975-2 PMID:28936795

Huang, M. H., & Rust, R. T. (2021). A strategic framework for artificial intelligence in marketing. *Journal of the Academy of Marketing Science*, *49*(1), 30–50. doi:10.1007/s11747-020-00749-9

Hu, H., & Li, C. (2023). Smart tourism products and services design based on user experience under the background of big data. *Soft Computing*, *27*(17), 12711–12724. doi:10.1007/s00500-023-08851-0

Huisingh, C., McGwin, G. Jr, & Owsley, C. (2016). Association of visual sensory function and higher-order visual proces- sing skills with incident driving cessation. *Clinical & Experimental Optometry*, *99*(5), 441–448. doi:10.1111/cxo.12404 PMID:27353969

Hui, T. K., Wan, D., & Ho, A. (2007). Tourists' satisfaction, recommendation and revisiting Singapore. *Tourism Management*, *28*(4), 965–975. doi:10.1016/j.tourman.2006.08.008

Hung, C. (2019). Using Cloud Services to Develop Marketing Information System Applications. *Journal of Internet Technology*, *20*(1), 157–166.

Hussein, E. A. (2020). Marketing intelligence system and its impact in determining strategies of competitive positions. *Utopía y Praxis Latinoamericana*, *25*(1), 530–544.

Huybers, T., & Bennett, J. (2003). Environmental management and the competitiveness of nature-based tourism destinations. *Environmental and Resource Economics*, *24*(3), 213–233. doi:10.1023/A:1022942001100

Hwang, K., & Chen, M. (2017). *Big-data analytics for cloud, IoT and cognitive computing*. John Wiley & Sons.

Ikegwu, A., Nweke, H., Anikwe, C., Alo, U., & Okonkwo, O. (2022). Big data analytics for data-driven industry: A review of data sources, tools, challenges, solutions, and research directions. *Cluster Computing*, *25*(5), 3343–3387. doi:10.1007/s10586-022-03568-5

Inge, C. (2022). *Marketing metrics: leverage analytics and data to optimize marketing strategies*. Kogan Page Publishers.

Iqbal, M. Z., Xu, X., Nallur, V., Scanlon, M., & Campbell, A. G. (2023). Security, ethics and privacy issues in the remote extended reality for education. In Y. Cai, E. Mangina, & S. L. Goei (Eds.), *Mixed reality for education: Gaming media and social effects* (pp. 209–221). Springer. doi:10.1007/978-981-99-4958-8_16

Iswanto, D., Handriana, T., Nazwin, A. H., & Sangadji, S. S. (2024). Influencers in Tourism Digital Marketing: A Comprehensive Literature Review. *International Journal of Sustainable Development and Planning*, *19*(2), 739–749. doi:10.18280/ijsdp.190231

Ito, E., & Higham, J. (2020). Supplemental tourism activities: A conceptual framework to maximise sport tourism benefits and opportunities. *Journal of Sport & Tourism*, *24*(4), 269–284. doi:10.1080/14775085.2020.1850322

Ivanov, S., & Webster, C. (2019). *Robots, artificial intelligence, and service automation in travel, tourism and hospitality*. Emerald Publishing Limited. doi:10.1108/9781787566873

Ivars-Baidal, J., Celdrán-Bernabeu, M., Mazón, J., & Perles-Ivars, Á. (2019). Smart destinations and the evolution of ICTs: A new scenario for destination management? *Current Issues in Tourism*, *22*(13), 1581–1600. doi:10.1080/13683500.2017.1388771

Jannat, S. (2021). *Understanding the opportunities of digitalization on a seamless airport departure journey for European passengers* (Doctoral dissertation, Hochschule Anhalt).

Janssen, M., Van Der Voort, H., & Wahyudi, A. (2017). Factors influencing big data decision-making quality. *Journal of Business Research*, *70*, 338–345. doi:10.1016/j.jbusres.2016.08.007

Jayaram, D., Manrai, A., & Manrai, L. (2015). Effective use of marketing technology in Eastern Europe: Web analytics, social media, customer analytics, digital campaigns and mobile applications. *Journal of Economics, Finance and Administrative Science*, *20*(39), 118–132. doi:10.1016/j.jefas.2015.07.001

Jenster, P. V., & Søilen, K. S. (2009). *Market intelligence: building strategic insight*. Copenhagen Business School Press DK.

Jeong, Y., & Kim, S. (2020). A study of event quality, destination image, perceived value, tourist satisfaction, and destination loyalty among sport tourists. *Asia Pacific Journal of Marketing and Logistics*, *32*(4), 940–960. doi:10.1108/APJML-02-2019-0101

Jimenez-Marquez, J., Gonzalez-Carrasco, I., Lopez-Cuadrado, J., & Ruiz-Mezcua, B. (2019). Towards a big data framework for analyzing social media content. *International Journal of Information Management*, *44*, 1–12. doi:10.1016/j.ijinfomgt.2018.09.003

Jiwat, R., & Zhang, Z. (2022). Adopting big data analytics (BDA) in business-to-business (B2B) organizations–Development of a model of needs. *Journal of Engineering and Technology Management*, *63*, 101676. doi:10.1016/j.jengtecman.2022.101676

Johnson, D. S., Muzellec, L., Sihi, D., & Zahay, D. (2019). The marketing organization's journey to become data-driven. *Journal of Research in Interactive Marketing*, *13*(2), 162–178. doi:10.1108/JRIM-12-2018-0157

Jung, T. & Han, D. I. (2014). Augmented Reality (AR) in Urban Heritage Tourism. *e-Review of Tourism Research,* (5), 1-5.

Jung, T. H., Bae, S., Moorhouse, N., & Kwon, O. (2021). The impact of user perceptions of AR on purchase intention of location-based AR navigation systems. *Journal of Retailing and Consumer Services*, *61*, 102575. doi:10.1016/j.jretconser.2021.102575

Juska, J. (2021). *Integrated marketing communication: advertising and promotion in a digital world.* Routledge. doi:10.4324/9780367443382

Kachniewska, M. (2021). *Smart Tourism: Towards the Concept of a Data-Based Travel Experience. In Handbook of Sustainable Development and Leisure Services*. Springer.

Kamel, M. A. (2023). Big data analytics and market performance: The roles of customization and personalization strategies and competitive intensity. *Journal of Enterprise Information Management*, *36*(6), 1727–1749. doi:10.1108/JEIM-04-2022-0114

Kamkiew, W. (2021). *Factors influencing service quality of Thai airways international flights*. Academic Press.

Kandaurova, M., & Lee, S. H. M. (2019). The effects of virtual reality (VR) on charitable giving: The role of empathy, guilt, responsibility, and social exclusion. *Journal of Business Research*, *100*, 571–580. doi:10.1016/j.jbusres.2018.10.027

Kandula, S., Krishnamoorthy, S., & Roy, D. (2021). A prescriptive analytics framework for efficient E-commerce order delivery. *Decision Support Systems*, *147*, 113584. doi:10.1016/j.dss.2021.113584

Kang, J., Guo, X., Fang, L., Wang, X., & Fan, Z. (2022). Integration of Internet search data to predict tourism trends using spatial-temporal XGBoost composite model. *International Journal of Geographical Information Science*, *36*(2), 236–252. doi:10.1080/13658816.2021.1934476

Kannan, P. K., Chang, A. M., & Whinston, A. B. (1998). Marketing information on the I-Way: Data junkyard or information gold mine? *Communications of the ACM*, *41*(3), 35–43. doi:10.1145/272287.272295

Kaplan, R. S., & Norton, D. P. (1996). *The Balanced Scorecard: Translating Strategy into Action*. Academic Press.

Karpova, S., Panyukova, V., & Rozhkov, I. (2018). Information support for tourist destination marketing: Russian and international experiences. In *В сборнике: Financial and Economic Tools Used in the World Hospitality Industry Proceedings of the 5th International Conference on Management and Technology in Knowledge, Service, Tourism and Hospitality* (pp. 215-218).

Kellerman, P. (2023). The Impact of Marketing Information Systems on Brilliant Financial Performance in Hospital Industry. *Indian Journal of Public Health*, *10*(3), 577–587.

Keskin, E., Aktaş, F., Yayla, Ö., & Dedeoğlu, B. (2024). The importance of nostalgic emotions and memorable tourism experience in the cultural experience. *Journal of Quality Assurance in Hospitality & Tourism*, *25*(1), 1–21. doi:10.1080/1528008X.2022.2097976

Khan, M., Algarni, F., & Quasim, M. (2021). *Smart Cities: A Data Analytics Perspective*. Springer International Publishing. doi:10.1007/978-3-030-60922-1

Khotimah, H., Djatna, T., & Nurhadryani, Y. (2014). Tourism recommendation based on vector space model using composite social media extraction. *Proceedings of the International Conference on Advanced Computer Science and Information Systems (ICACSIS)*, 303-308.

Kietzmann, J., Paschen, J., & Treen, E. (2018). Artificial intelligence in advertising: How marketers can leverage artificial intelligence along the consumer journey. *Journal of Advertising Research*, *58*(3), 263–267. doi:10.2501/JAR-2018-035

King, K., Shipway, R., Lee, I. S., & Brown, G. (2021). Proximate tourists and major sport events in everyday leisure spaces. In *Tourism Spaces* (pp. 112–130). Routledge. doi:10.4324/9781003152453-6

Kinyua, D. (2020). *Effect of Marketing Information Systems on Competitive Advantage of Ict Application Service Providers in Nairobi County* (Doctoral dissertation, University of Nairobi).

Kitsios, F., Mitsopoulou, E., Moustaka, E., & Kamariotou, M. (2022). User-Generated Content behavior and digital tourism services: A SEM-neural network model for information trust in social networking sites. *International Journal of Information Management Data Insights*, *2*(1), 100056. doi:10.1016/j.jjimei.2021.100056

Knani, M., Echchakoui, S., & Ladhari, R. (2022). Artificial intelligence in tourism and hospitality: Bibliometric analysis and research agenda. *International Journal of Hospitality Management*, *107*, 103317. doi:10.1016/j.ijhm.2022.103317

Kohler, S., Boscá, D., Kärcher, F., Haarbrandt, B., Prinz, M., Marschollek, M., & Eils, R. (2023). Eos and OMOCL: Towards a seamless integration of openEHR records into the OMOP Common Data Model. *Journal of Biomedical Informatics*, *144*, 104437. doi:10.1016/j.jbi.2023.104437 PMID:37442314

Koohathongsumrit, N., & Luangpaiboon, P. (2023). Strategic Marketing Information System Planning: An Integrated BWM–ELECTRE Approach. *Group Decision and Negotiation*. Advance online publication. doi:10.1007/s10726-023-09861-x

Kooli, N., Allesiardo, R., & Pigneul, E. (2018). Deep learning based approach for entity resolution in databases. In *Asian conference on intelligent information and database systems* (pp. 3-12). Cham: Springer International Publishing. 10.1007/978-3-319-75420-8_1

Kordzadeh, N., & Ghasemaghaei, M. (2022). Algorithmic bias: Review, synthesis, and future research directions. *European Journal of Information Systems*, *31*(3), 388–409. doi:10.1080/0960085X.2021.1927212

Kotler, P., & Keller, K. L. (2016). *Marketing Management*. Academic Press.

Kotler, P., Bowen, J., Makens, J., & Baloglu, S. (2017). *Marketing for hospitality and tourism*. Pearson.

Kotler, P., Kartajaya, H., & Setiawan, I. (2021). *Marketing 5.0: Technology for humanity*. John Wiley & Sons.

Kounavis, C., Kasimati, A., & Zamani, E. (2012). Enhancing The Tourism Experience Through Mobile Augmented Reality: Challenges and prospects. *International Journal of Engineering Business Management*, *4*, 1–6. doi:10.5772/51644

Kraus, S., Kumar, S., Lim, W. M., Kaur, J., Sharma, A., & Schiavone, F. (2023). From moon landing to metaverse: Tracing the evolution of Technological Forecasting and Social Change. *Technological Forecasting and Social Change*, *189*, 122381. doi:10.1016/j.techfore.2023.122381

Kuchkarova, G. (2023). Concept of Active (Active) and Passive (Inactive) Tourism. *Science and Innovation*, *2*(C12), 60–64.

Ku, E. (2010). The impact of customer relationship management through implementation of information systems. *Total Quality Management & Business Excellence*, *21*(11), 1085–1102. doi:10.1080/14783360903250514

Kumar, N. (2005). The power of power in supplier-retailer relationships. *Industrial Marketing Management*, *34*(8), 863–866. doi:10.1016/j.indmarman.2005.02.003

Kumar, V., Leone, R., Aaker, D., & Day, G. (2018). *Marketing research*. John Wiley & Sons.

Kurashima, T., Iwata, T., Irie, G., & Fujimura, K. (2013). Travel route recommendation using geotagged photos. *Knowledge and Information Systems*, *37*(1), 37–60. doi:10.1007/s10115-012-0580-z

Kushwaha, A., Kumar, P., & Kar, A. (2021). What impacts customer experience for B2B enterprises on using AI-enabled chatbots? Insights from Big data analytics. *Industrial Marketing Management*, *98*, 207–221. doi:10.1016/j.indmarman.2021.08.011

Kusnoto, Y., Supriatna, N., Wiyanarti, E., & Hasan, S. H. (2024). Trend and visualizing of historical tourism in education research during last twenty years: A bibliometric review and analysis. *Journal of Hospitality, Leisure, Sport and Tourism Education*, *34*, 100477. doi:10.1016/j.jhlste.2023.100477

Kusumah, E. P., & Wahyudin, N. (2024). Sporting event quality: Destination image, tourist satisfaction, and destination loyalty. *Event Management*, *28*(1), 59–74. doi:10.3727/152599523X16896548396824

Ladley, J. (2019). *Data governance: How to design, deploy, and sustain an effective data governance program*. Academic Press.

Lali, K., & Chakor, A. (2023). Improving the Security and Reliability of a Quality Marketing Information System: A Priority Prerequisite for Good Strategic Management of a Successful Entrepreneurial Project. *Data & Metadata*, *2*, 40–40. doi:10.56294/dm202340

Laney, D. (2001). 3D data management: Controlling data volume velocity and variety. *META Group Res. Note*, *6*(70), 1.

Laudon, K. C., & Laudon, J. P. (2020). Management. *Information Systems*.

Lee, C. K. H., Tse, Y. K., Zhang, M., & Ma, J. (2020). Analysing online reviews to investigate customer behaviour in the sharing economy: The case of Airbnb. *Information Technology & People*, *33*(3), 945–961. doi:10.1108/ITP-10-2018-0475

Lee, K., & Oh, S. (2022). The users' intention to participate in a VR/AR sports experience by applying the extended tech- nology acceptance Model (ETAM). *Health Care*, *10*, 1117. PMID:35742168

Lehrer, C., Wieneke, A., Vom Brocke, J., Jung, R., & Seidel, S. (2018). How big data analytics enables service innovation: Materiality, affordance, and the individualization of service. *Journal of Management Information Systems*, *35*(2), 424–460. doi:10.1080/07421222.2018.1451953

Lepenioti, K., Bousdekis, A., Apostolou, D., & Mentzas, G. (2020). Prescriptive analytics: Literature review and research challenges. *International Journal of Information Management*, *50*, 57–70. doi:10.1016/j.ijinfomgt.2019.04.003

Li, H., Hu, M., & Li, G., (2020). Forecasting tourism demand with multisource big data. *Annals of Tourism Research, 83*, 1-13.

Liberato, D., Moreira, C., & Liberato, P. (2019). Sports tourism in Oporto as a destination: the influence of FC Porto Football Club. In *33rd IBIMA Conference Proceedings: Vision 2020: Sustainable Economic Development and Application of Innovation Management* (pp. 6007-6021). International Business Information Management Association (IBIMA).

Liberato, P., Liberato, D., Sousa, B., & Malheiro, A. (2020, October). Sports tourism and sports events as a Niche market in Oporto as a tourism destination. In *International Conference on Tourism, Technology and Systems* (pp. 610-623). Singapore: Springer Singapore.

Libriantono, B. (2024). Implementation of the Personnel Management Information System for the Tangerang Regency Regional Civil Service Agency. *The International Journal of Education Management and Sociology*, *3*(1), 46–60.

Li, E. Y., McLeod, R. Jr, & Rogers, J. C. (1993). Marketing information systems in the Fortune 500 companies: Past, present, and future. *Journal of Management Information Systems*, *10*(1), 165–192. doi:10.1080/07421222.1993.11517995

Liebowitz, J. (2020). *Data analytics and AI.* CRC Press. doi:10.1201/9781003019855

Li, J., Kamal, E. B. M., & Jing, K. T. (2024). Assessing the Mediating Role of E-Techniques in the Relationship Between Information Systems and Carbon Reduction Strategies During the Construction Phase of Chinese Construction Projects. *Journal of Information Systems Engineering & Management*, *9*(1), 21636. doi:10.55267/iadt.07.14183

Li, J., Xu, L., Tang, L., Wang, S., & Li, L. (2018). Big data in tourism research: A literature review. *Tourism Management*, *68*, 301–323. doi:10.1016/j.tourman.2018.03.009

Lim, W. M., Jasim, K. M., & Das, M. (2024). Augmented and virtual reality in hotels: Impact on tourist satisfaction and intention to stay and return. *International Journal of Hospitality Management*, *116*, 116. doi:10.1016/j.ijhm.2023.103631

Ling, E., Tussyadiah, I., Liu, A., & Stienmetz, J. (2023). Perceived Intelligence of Artificially Intelligent Assistants for Travel: Scale Development and Validation. *Journal of Travel Research.* Advance online publication. doi:10.1177/00472875231217899

Link, C. K. (1989). Internal merchandising: Creating revenue opportunities. *The Cornell Hotel and Restaurant Administration Quarterly*, *30*(3), 48–57. doi:10.1177/001088048903000316

Li, Y., Hu, C., Huang, C., & Duan, L. (2017). The concept of smart tourism in the context of tourism information services. *Tourism Management*, *58*, 293–300. doi:10.1016/j.tourman.2016.03.014

Lord, B. (2002). Cultural Tourism and Museums. *Cultural Resources Planning and Management In*, *c*, 1–12.

Luca, M., & Bazerman, M. (2021). *The power of experiments: Decision making in a data-driven world.* Mit Press.

Mach-Król, M. (2019). Requirements for temporal BDA implementation methodology in organizations. *Informatyka Ekonomiczna*, *1*(51), 44–54. doi:10.15611/ie.2019.1.04

Madhura, D., Prajakta, M., Tanaya, Z., Vijaya, N., Ashish, K., Bhakti, T., & Neha, P. (2023). An AI Integrated Online Hotel Management System. *Journal of Web Engineering & Technology*, *9*(1), 1–18.

Magalhães, P. (2010). Percepções e Práticas de Responsabilidade Social Empresarial no Futebol Profissional Português: O Caso dos Três Grandes. Projeto de Mestrado. ISCTE Business School. Instituto Universitário de Lisboa, Lisboa.

Magalhães, M., Horta, P., Valente, L., & Costa, J. (2017). Sports museums as part of the touristic and cultural itineraries: The case of FC Porto and the Dragão stadium. *Worldwide Hospitality and Tourism Themes*, *9*(6), 669–674. doi:10.1108/WHATT-09-2017-0048

Mahanty, G., Dwivedi, D. N., & Gopalakrishnan, B. N. (2021). The Efficacy of Fiscal Vs Monetary Policies in the Asia-Pacific Region: The St. Louis Equation Revisited. *Vision (Basel)*, (November). Advance online publication. doi:10.1177/09722629211054148

Maheshwari, S., Gautam, P., & Jaggi, C. (2021). Role of Big Data Analytics in supply chain management: Current trends and future perspectives. *International Journal of Production Research*, *59*(6), 1875–1900. doi:10.1080/00207543.2020.1793011

Malchrowicz-Mosko, E., & Munsters, W. (2018). Sport tourism: A growth market considered from a cultural perspective. Ido Movement for Culture. *Journal of Martial Arts Anthropology*, *18*(4), 25–38. doi:10.14589/ido.18.4.4

Mandal, P. C. (2018). Marketing information and marketing intelligence: Roles in generating customer insights. *International Journal of Business Forecasting and Marketing Intelligence*, *4*(3), 311–321. doi:10.1504/IJBFMI.2018.092786

Mandal, S. (2018). Exploring the influence of big data analytics management capabilities on sustainable tourism supply chain performance: The moderating role of technology orientation. *Journal of Travel & Tourism Marketing*, *35*(8), 1104–1118. doi:10.1080/10548408.2018.1476302

Mandić, A., & Garbin Praničević, D. (2019). Progress on the role of ICTs in establishing destination appeal: Implications for smart tourism destination development. *Journal of Hospitality and Tourism Technology*, *10*(4), 791–813. doi:10.1108/JHTT-06-2018-0047

Marasco, A., Buonincontri, P., van Niekerk, M., Orlowski, M., & Okumus, F. (2018). Exploring the role of next-generation virtual technologies in destination marketing. *Journal of Destination Marketing & Management*, *9*, 138–148. doi:10.1016/j.jdmm.2017.12.002

Marchesani, F. (2023). Urban Attractiveness and the Competitive Edge of the Smart City. In The Global Smart City (pp. 117-135). Emerald Publishing Limited.¶ doi:10.1108/978-1-83797-575-420231007

Mariani, M., Bresciani, S., & Dagnino, G. (2021). The competitive productivity (CP) of tourism destinations: An integrative conceptual framework and a reflection on big data and analytics. *International Journal of Contemporary Hospitality Management*, *33*(9), 2970–3002. doi:10.1108/IJCHM-09-2020-1102

Mariani, M., & Wamba, S. (2020). Exploring how consumer goods companies innovate in the digital age: The role of big data analytics companies. *Journal of Business Research*, *121*, 338–352. doi:10.1016/j.jbusres.2020.09.012

Markic, B., & Tomic, D. (2010). Marketing intelligent system for customer segmentation. *Marketing Intelligent Systems Using Soft Computing: Managerial and Research Applications*, 79-111.

Maroufkhani, P., Tseng, M., Iranmanesh, M., Ismail, W., & Khalid, H. (2020). Big data analytics adoption: Determinants and performances among small to medium-sized enterprises. *International Journal of Information Management*, *54*, 102190. doi:10.1016/j.ijinfomgt.2020.102190

Marr, B. (2017). *Data strategy: How to profit from a world of big data, analytics and the internet of things*. Kogan Page Publishers.

Mascarenhas, O. A., Kesavan, R., & Bernacchi, M. (2006). Lasting customer loyalty: A total customer experience approach. *Journal of Consumer Marketing*, *23*(7), 397–405. doi:10.1108/07363760610712939

Mayer-Schönberger, V., & Cukier, K. (2013). *Big Data: A Revolution That Will Transform How We Live*. Work, and Think.

McDonald, A. (2014). *Improving Driver Drowsiness Detection through Temporal, Contextual, and Hierarchical Modeling* (Doctoral dissertation, The University of Wisconsin-Madison).

McManus, L. (2013). Customer accounting and marketing performance measures in the hotel industry: Evidence from Australia. *International Journal of Hospitality Management*, *33*, 140–152. doi:10.1016/j.ijhm.2012.07.007

Mehmetoglu, M. (2007). Nature-based Tourists: The relationship between their trip expenditures and activities. *Journal of Sustainable Tourism*, *15*(2), 200–215. doi:10.2167/jost642.0

Mehta, R. (2017). *Big Data Analytics with Java*. Packt Publishing Ltd.

Mero, J., Tarkiainen, A., & Tobon, J. (2020). Effectual and causal reasoning in the adoption of marketing automation. *Industrial Marketing Management*, *86*, 212–222. doi:10.1016/j.indmarman.2019.12.008

Miah, S., Vu, H., Gammack, J., & McGrath, M. (2017). A big data analytics method for tourist behaviour analysis. *Information & Management*, *54*(6), 771–785. doi:10.1016/j.im.2016.11.011

Mikalef, P., Boura, M., Lekakos, G., & Krogstie, J. (2020). The role of information governance in big data analytics driven innovation. *Information & Management*, *57*(7), 103361. doi:10.1016/j.im.2020.103361

Miklosik, A., & Evans, N. (2020). Impact of big data and machine learning on digital transformation in marketing: A literature review. *IEEE Access : Practical Innovations, Open Solutions*, *8*, 101284–101292. doi:10.1109/ACCESS.2020.2998754

Minazzi, R. (2015). *Social Media Marketing in Tourism and Hospitality*. Academic Press.

Minazzi, R. (2015). *Social media marketing in tourism and hospitality*. Springer International Publishing Switzerland. doi:10.1007/978-3-319-05182-6

Mishra, V., Samuel, C., & Sharma, S. K. (2019). Patient's Utility for Various Attributes of Diabetes Care Services. *IIM Kozhikode Society and Management Review*, *8*(1), 1–9. doi:10.1177/2277975218798134

Mohamed, H., & Al-Azab, M. (2021). Big Data Analytics in Airlines: Opportunities and Challenges. *Journal of Association of Arab Universities for Tourism and Hospitality*, *21*(4), 77–112.

Mohamed, M., Farahat, E., & Al-Romeedy, B. (2022). The Mediating Role of Marketing Effectiveness in the Relationship between Artificial Intelligence and Destination Competitiveness. *Minia Journal of Tourism and Hospitality Research*, *14*(1), 113–129.

Mohamed, N., Al-Jaroodi, J., Jawhar, I., Idries, A., & Mohammed, F. (2020). Unmanned aerial vehicles applications in future smart cities. *Technological Forecasting and Social Change*, *153*, 119293. doi:10.1016/j.techfore.2018.05.004

Mohammed, S., Arabnia, H., Qu, X., Zhang, D., Kim, T., & Zhao, J. (2020). IEEE access special section editorial: Big data technology and applications in intelligent transportation. *IEEE Access : Practical Innovations, Open Solutions*, *8*, 201331–201344. doi:10.1109/ACCESS.2020.3035440

Mooter, B. V. (2017). *Medical Tourism in Asia-Pacific Growing Rapidly*. BRINK, The Edge of Risk.

Morales-Serazzi, M., González-Benito, Ó., & Martos-Partal, M. (2023). A new perspective of BDA and information quality from final users of information: A multiple study approach. *International Journal of Information Management*, *73*, 102683. doi:10.1016/j.ijinfomgt.2023.102683

Moreira, J., Carvalho, A., & Horvath, T. (2018). *A general introduction to data analytics*. John Wiley & Sons. doi:10.1002/9781119296294

Moreno-Gil, S., & Coca-Stefaniak, J. (2020). Guest editorial": Overtourism and the sharing economy–tourism cities at a crossroads. *International Journal of Tourism Cities*, *6*(1), 1–7. doi:10.1108/IJTC-03-2020-174

Mountantonakis, M., & Tzitzikas, Y. (2019). Large-scale semantic integration of linked data: A survey. *ACM Computing Surveys*, *52*(5), 1–40. doi:10.1145/3345551

Mukhopadhyay, S., Singh, R., & Jain, T. (2024). Developing big data enabled Marketing 4.0 framework. *International Journal of Information Management Data Insights*, *4*(1), 100214. doi:10.1016/j.jjimei.2024.100214

Nagle, T. T., & Muller, G. (2018). *The strategy and tactics of pricing*. Routledge.

Naim, A., Alqahtani, H., Muniasamy, A., Bilfaqih, S., Mahveen, R., & Mahjabeen, R. (2023). Applications of Information Systems and Data Security in Marketing Management. In Fraud Prevention, Confidentiality, and Data Security for Modern Businesses (pp. 57-83). IGI Global. doi:10.4018/978-1-6684-6581-3.ch003

Naithani, K., & Raiwani, Y. P. (2023). Realization of natural language processing and machine learning approaches for text-based sentiment analysis. *Expert Systems: International Journal of Knowledge Engineering and Neural Networks*, *40*(5), e13114. doi:10.1111/exsy.13114

Neidhardt, J., & Wörndl, W. (2020). *Information and Communication Technologies in Tourism 2020*. Springer International Publishing. doi:10.1007/978-3-030-36737-4

Nelson, B. L. (1995). *Environmental Scanning: Evaluation & Recommendations to Management*. Academic Press.

Nemutanzhela, P., & Iyamu, T. (2011). A framework for enhancing the information systems innovation: Using competitive intelligence. *Electronic Journal of Information Systems Evaluation*, *14*(2), 242–253.

Neuhofer, B., Buhalis, D., & Ladkin, A. (2014). A typology of technology-enhanced tourism experiences. *International Journal of Tourism Research*, *16*(4), 340–350. doi:10.1002/jtr.1958

Nguyen, N. P., & Mogaji, E. (2023). Artificial intelligence for seamless experience across channels. In *Artificial Intelligence in Customer Service: The Next Frontier for Personalized Engagement* (pp. 181–203). Springer International Publishing. doi:10.1007/978-3-031-33898-4_8

Nordin, F., & Ravald, A. (2023). The making of marketing decisions in modern marketing environments. *Journal of Business Research*, *162*, 113872. doi:10.1016/j.jbusres.2023.113872

Noura, M., Atiquzzaman, M., & Gaedke, M. (2019). Interoperability in internet of things: Taxonomies and open challenges. *Mobile Networks and Applications*, *24*(3), 796–809. doi:10.1007/s11036-018-1089-9

Nozdreva, R., & Churakova, A. (2021). Digital tools in empirical marketing strategies of global hotel companies. *Digital strategies in a global market: Navigating the Fourth Industrial Revolution*, 213-227.

Ogbadu-Oladapo, L., Bissadu, K., Kim, H., & Smith, D. L. (2024). Information and health literacy: Could there be any impact on health decision-making among adults?—evidence from North America. *Journal of Public Health (Berlin)*, 1–31. doi:10.1007/s10389-024-02260-9

Olshannikova, E., Ometov, A., Koucheryavy, Y., & Olsson, T. (2015). Visualizing Big Data with augmented and virtual reality: Challenges and research agenda. *Journal of Big Data*, *2*(22), 1–27. doi:10.1186/s40537-015-0031-2

Önder, I., Wöber, K., & Zekan, B. (2017). Towards a sustainable urban tourism development in Europe: The role of benchmarking and tourism management information systems–A partial model of destination competitiveness. *Tourism Economics*, *23*(2), 243–259. doi:10.1177/1354816616656247

Orlosky, J., Kiyokawa, K., & Takemura, H. (2017). Virtual and Augmented Reality on the 5G Highway. *Journal of Information Processing*, *25*(0), 133–141. doi:10.2197/ipsjjip.25.133

Pakholok, O. (2020). *The Idea of Healthy Lifestyle and Its Transformation Into Health-Oriented Lifestyle in Contemporary Society*. doi:10.1177/2158244013500281

Palmatier, R., & Sridhar, S. (2020). *Marketing strategy: Based on first principles and data analytics*. Bloomsbury Publishing.

Papadakis, V. M., Lioukas, S., & Chambers, D. (1998). Strategic decision-making processes: The role of management and context. *Strategic Management Journal, 19*(2), 115–147. doi:10.1002/(SICI)1097-0266(199802)19:2<115::AID-SMJ941>3.0.CO;2-5

Parlov, N., Perkov, D., & Sičaja, Ž. (2016). New trends in tourism destination branding by means of digital marketing. *Acta Economica Et Turistica*, *2*(2), 139–146. doi:10.1515/aet-2016-0012

Patil, V., Padale, T., Waghmare, G., & Kulkarni, D. (2021). A study on understanding future of Artificial Intelligence in the various functions of marketing. *Turkish Online Journal of Qualitative Inquiry, 12*(6).

Pearlson, K., Saunders, C., & Galletta, D. (2024). *Managing and using information systems: A strategic approach.* John Wiley & Sons.

Pearson, S. (2016). *Building brands directly: creating business value from customer relationships.* Springer.

Peelen, E., & Beltman, R. (2013). *Customer Relationship Management.* Academic Press.

Pekarik, A. (2003). Museum consumerism. *Curator (New York, N.Y.)*, *46*(1), 15–18. doi:10.1111/j.2151-6952.2003.tb00073.x

Pencarelli, T. (2020). The digital revolution in the travel and tourism industry. *Information Technology & Tourism*, *22*(3), 455–476. doi:10.1007/s40558-019-00160-3

Pereira, M. (2016). *Dragon Force International Clinics – do Planeamento à Concretização de um Programa Internacional de Futebol.* Relatório de Mestrado. Faculdade de Desporto da Universidade do Porto.

Pesonen, J., & Neidhardt, J. (2019). Information and communication technologies in tourism 2019. In *Proceedings of the International Conference.* Springer International Publishing. 10.1007/978-3-030-05940-8

Petroman, I. M., & Văduva, L. (2021). Forms of active tourism. *Quaestus*, (18), 271–279.

Pfaff, M., Neubig, S., & Krcmar, H. (2018). Ontology for semantic data integration in the domain of IT benchmarking. *Journal on Data Semantics*, *7*(1), 29–46. doi:10.1007/s13740-017-0084-9 PMID:29497460

Phillips, P., Barnes, S., Zigan, K., & Schegg, R. (2017). Understanding the impact of online reviews on hotel performance: An empirical analysis. *Journal of Travel Research*, *56*(2), 235–249. doi:10.1177/0047287516636481

Popovič, A., Hackney, R., Tassabehji, R., & Castelli, M. (2018). The impact of big data analytics on firms' high value business performance. *Information Systems Frontiers*, *20*(2), 209–222. doi:10.1007/s10796-016-9720-4

Porter, M. E. (2008). *Competitive Strategy: Techniques for Analyzing Industries and Competitors.* Academic Press.

Porto, F. C. (2024a). Museu Futebol Clube do Porto. *Futebol Clube do Porto*. Available at: https://www.fcporto.pt/pt

Porto, F. C. (2024b). The Stadium. *Futebol Clube do Porto*. Available at: https://www.fcporto.pt/en/club/estadio-do-dragao

Pozzi, F. A., & Dwivedi, D. (2023). ESG and IoT: Ensuring Sustainability and Social Responsibility in the Digital Age. In S. Tiwari, F. Ortiz-Rodríguez, S. Mishra, E. Vakaj, & K. Kotecha (Eds.), *Artificial Intelligence: Towards Sustainable Intelligence. AI4S 2023. Communications in Computer and Information Science* (Vol. 1907). Springer. doi:10.1007/978-3-031-47997-7_2

Prideaux, B. (1999). Tracks to tourism: Queensland rail joins the tourist industry. *International Journal of Tourism Research*, *1*(2), 73–86. doi:10.1002/(SICI)1522-1970(199903/04)1:2<73::AID-JTR123>3.0.CO;2-Q

Pyne, S., Rao, B., & Rao, S. (2016). *Big data analytics: Methods and applications*. Springer.

Queiroz, J., & Oliveira, B. (2014). Benefits of the marketing information system in the clothing retail business. *Journal of Information Systems and Technology Management*, *11*(1), 153–168. doi:10.4301/S1807-17752014000100009

Ragab, A. (2017). The Behavioural Intention of Adopting Big Data Analytics in the Tourism Sector: An Empirical Investigation in Egypt. *Minia Journal of Tourism and Hospitality Research MJTHR*, *2*(2), 1–19. doi:10.21608/mjthr.2017.139608

Rahimi, I., Gandomi, A., Fong, S., & Ülkü, M. (2020). *Big data analytics in supply chain management: Theory and applications*. CRC Press.

Ram, J., & Zhang, Z. (2022). Examining the needs to adopt big data analytics in B2B organizations: Development of propositions and model of needs. *Journal of Business and Industrial Marketing*, *37*(4), 790–809. doi:10.1108/JBIM-10-2020-0464

Ramshaw, G., & Gammon, S. (2005). More than just nostalgia? Exploring the heritage/sport tourism nexus. *Journal of Sport & Tourism*, *10*(4), 229–241. doi:10.1080/14775080600805416

Ramshaw, G., & Gammon, S. J. (2017). Towards a critical sport heritage: Implications for sport tourism. *Journal of Sport & Tourism*, *21*(2), 115–131. doi:10.1080/14775085.2016.1262275

Rana, R., Adamashvili, N., & Tricase, C. (2022). The impact of blockchain technology adoption on tourism industry: A systematic literature review. *Sustainability (Basel)*, *14*(12), 7383. doi:10.3390/su14127383

Rane, N. (2023). Enhancing customer loyalty through Artificial Intelligence (AI), Internet of Things (IoT), and Big Data technologies: improving customer satisfaction, engagement, relationship, and experience. *Internet of Things (IoT), and Big Data Technologies: Improving Customer Satisfaction, Engagement, Relationship, and Experience*.

Raptis, G. E., Fidas, C., & Avouris, N. (2018). Effects of mixed reality on players' behaviour and immersion in a cultural tourism game: A cognitive processing perspective. *International Journal of Human-Computer Studies, 114*, 69–79. doi:10.1016/j.ijhcs.2018.02.003

Rasoolimanesh, S., Ramakrishna, S., Hall, C., Esfandiar, K., & Seyfi, S. (2023). A systematic scoping review of sustainable tourism indicators in relation to the sustainable development goals. *Journal of Sustainable Tourism, 31*(7), 1497–1517. doi:10.1080/09669582.2020.1775621

Rather, R., & Hollebeek, L. (2020). *Experiential marketing for tourism destinations. In The Routledge handbook of tourism experience management and marketing*. Routledge.

Rehman, M., Chang, V., Batool, A., & Wah, T. (2016). Big data reduction framework for value creation in sustainable enterprises. *International Journal of Information Management, 36*(6), 917–928. doi:10.1016/j.ijinfomgt.2016.05.013

Reif, J., & Schmücker, D. (2020). Exploring new ways of visitor tracking using big data sources: Opportunities and limits of passive mobile data for tourism. *Journal of Destination Marketing & Management, 18*, 100481. doi:10.1016/j.jdmm.2020.100481

Rejeb, A., Rejeb, K., & Keogh, J. (2020). Potential of big data for marketing: A literature review. *Management Research and Practice, 12*(3), 60–73.

Remler, D. K., & Van Ryzin, G. G. (2021). *Research methods in practice: Strategies for description and causation.* Sage Publications.

Respatyanti, Y. R. (2019). *Enhancing the Information Availability of Indonesia's Tourism Destinations Through A Travel App*. Academic Press.

Rezaei, F., Raeesi Vanani, I., Jafari, A., & Kakavand, S. (2022). Identification of Influential Factors and Improvement of Hotel Online User-Generated Scores: A Prescriptive Analytics Approach. *Journal of Quality Assurance in Hospitality & Tourism*, 1–40. doi:10.1080/1528008X.2022.2146620

Richards, N. M., & King, J. H. (2014). *Big Data Ethics*. Academic Press.

Richards, G. (2021). *Rethinking cultural tourism*. Edward Elgar Publishing. doi:10.4337/9781789905441

Ritchie, B., & Adair, D. (2002). The growing recognition of sport tourism. *Current Issues in Tourism, 5*(1), 1–6. doi:10.1080/13683500208667903

Ritchie, R., & Ritchie, J. (2002). A framework for an industry supported destination marketing information system. *Tourism Management, 23*(5), 439–454. doi:10.1016/S0261-5177(02)00007-9

Rosalinda, U., & Ali, H. (2023). Analysis of Factors Influencing the Marketing Information System: CRM, Customer Satisfactaction and Sales Effectiveness. *Dinasti International Journal of Digital Business Management, 4*(2), 264–270.

Rosário, A., & Dias, J. (2023). How has data-driven marketing evolved: Challenges and opportunities with emerging technologies. *International Journal of Information Management Data Insights*, *3*(2), 100203. doi:10.1016/j.jjimei.2023.100203

Rowley, J. (2017). *Information marketing*. Routledge. doi:10.4324/9781315196398

Rubel, A., & Jones, K. (2016). Student privacy in learning analytics: An information ethics perspective. *The Information Society*, *32*(2), 143–159. doi:10.1080/01972243.2016.1130502

Saggi, M., & Jain, S. (2018). A survey towards an integration of big data analytics to big insights for value-creation. *Information Processing & Management*, *54*(5), 758–790. doi:10.1016/j.ipm.2018.01.010

Saidali, J., Rahich, H., Tabaa, Y., & Medouri, A. (2019). The combination between Big Data and Marketing Strategies to gain valuable Business Insights for better Production Success. *Procedia Manufacturing*, *32*, 1017–1023. doi:10.1016/j.promfg.2019.02.316

Salas-Olmedo, M., Moya-Gómez, B., García-Palomares, J., & Gutiérrez, J. (2018). Tourists' digital footprint in cities: Comparing Big Data sources. *Tourism Management*, *66*, 13–25. doi:10.1016/j.tourman.2017.11.001

Samara, D., Magnisalis, I., & Peristeras, V. (2020). Artificial intelligence and big data in tourism: A systematic literature review. *Journal of Hospitality and Tourism Technology*, *11*(2), 343–367. doi:10.1108/JHTT-12-2018-0118

Santos, M., & Costa, C. (2022). *Big data: concepts, warehousing, and analytics*. CRC Press.

Sari, J., Nugroho, L., Ferdiana, R., & Santosa, P. (2016). Review on customer segmentation technique on ecommerce. *Advanced Science Letters*, *22*(10), 3018–3022. doi:10.1166/asl.2016.7985

Saxena, S., & Gupta, S. (2017). *Practical real-time data processing and analytics: distributed computing and event processing using Apache Spark, Flink, Storm, and Kafka*. Packt Publishing Ltd.

Sayegh, L., Anthony, W. P., & Perrewé, P. L. (2004). Managerial decision-making under crisis: The role of emotion in an intuitive decision process. *Human Resource Management Review*, *14*(2), 179–199. doi:10.1016/j.hrmr.2004.05.002

Scholz, J., & Smith, A. N. (2016). Augmented reality: Designing immersive experiences that maximize consumer engagement. *Business Horizons*, *59*(2), 149–161. doi:10.1016/j.bushor.2015.10.003

Schweidel, D. A., & Moe, W. W. (2014). Listening in on social media: A joint model of sentiment and venue format choice. *JMR, Journal of Marketing Research*, *51*(4), 387–402. doi:10.1509/jmr.12.0424

Schweidel, D., Bart, Y., Inman, J., Stephen, A., Libai, B., Andrews, M., Rosario, A. B., Chae, I., Chen, Z., Kupor, D., Longoni, C., & Thomaz, F. (2022). How consumer digital signals are reshaping the customer journey. *Journal of the Academy of Marketing Science*, *50*(6), 1257–1276. doi:10.1007/s11747-022-00839-w PMID:35221393

Scorgie, M. (2008). *Skiers' and snowboarders' perceptions of the quality of a ski resort in Japan: an application of importance performance analysis and recreation specialisation* (Doctoral dissertation).

Sear, A. M. (1989). Information system failures: The role of hardware and software. *The Journal of Ambulatory Care Management, 12*(4), 30–37. doi:10.1097/00004479-198911000-00007 PMID:10295602

Sedkaoui, S. (2018). *Data analytics and big data*. John Wiley & Sons. doi:10.1002/9781119528043

Sedkaoui, S. (Ed.). (2018). *Big data analytics for entrepreneurial success*. IGI Global.

Semedo, M. (2015). *Avaliação do potencial do turismo marítimo desportivo em Cabo Verde: Uma análise a partir da população residente*. Dissertação de Mestrado. Escola Superior de Educação do Instituto Politécnico de Coimbra, Coimbra.

Shah, S., Seker, D., Rathore, M., Hameed, S., Yahia, S., & Draheim, D. (2019). Towards disaster resilient smart cities: Can internet of things and big data analytics be the game changers? *IEEE Access : Practical Innovations, Open Solutions, 7*, 91885–91903. doi:10.1109/ACCESS.2019.2928233

Sharma, R., Kumar, A., & Chuah, C. (2021). Turning the blackbox into a glassbox: An explainable machine learning approach for understanding hospitality customer. *International Journal of Information Management Data Insights, 1*(2), 100050. doi:10.1016/j.jjimei.2021.100050

Shmueli, G., Bruce, P., Yahav, I., Patel, N., & Lichtendahl, K. Jr. (2017). *Data mining for business analytics: concepts, techniques, and applications in R*. John Wiley & Sons.

Shoushtari, F., Bashir, E., Hassankhani, S., & Rezvanjou, S. (2023). Optimization in Marketing Enhancing Efficiency and Effectiveness. *International Journal of Industrial Engineering and Operational Research, 5*(2), 12-23.

Sigala, M., Rahimi, R., & Thelwall, M. (2019). Big data and innovation in tourism, travel, and hospitality. *Culinary Science & Hospitality Research, 23*(6), 1–11.

Singh, T., Veron-Jackson, L., & Cullinane, J. (2008). Blogging: A new play in your marketing game plan. *Business Horizons, 51*(4), 281–292. doi:10.1016/j.bushor.2008.02.002

Smith, A. C., & Stewart, B. (2007). The travelling fan: Understanding the mechanisms of sport fan consumption in a sport tourism setting. *Journal of Sport & Tourism, 12*(3-4), 155–181. doi:10.1080/14775080701736924

Smith, M. K. (2015). *Issues in cultural tourism studies*. Routledge. doi:10.4324/9781315767697

Smith, R., & Hawkins, B. (2004). *Lean maintenance: reduce costs, improve quality, and increase market share*. Elsevier.

Snijders, C., Matzat, U., & Reips, U. D. (2012). Big data: Big gaps of knowledge in the feld of internet science. *International Journal of Internet Science, 7*(1), 1–5.

Solazzo, G., Maruccia, Y., Lorenzo, G., Ndou, V., Del Vecchio, P., & Elia, G. (2022). Extracting insights from big social data for smarter tourism destination management. *Measuring Business Excellence*, *26*(1), 122–140. doi:10.1108/MBE-11-2020-0156

Somani, A., & Deka, G. (2017). *Big data analytics: Tools and technology for effective planning*. CRC Press. doi:10.1201/b21822

Song, H., & Liu, H. (2017). Predicting tourist demand using big data. *Analytics in smart tourism design: Concepts and methods*, 13-29.

Sorensen, C., & Kakihara, M. (2002, January). Knowledge discourses and interaction technology. In *Proceedings of the 35th Annual Hawaii International Conference on System Sciences* (pp. 976-986). IEEE. 10.1109/HICSS.2002.994048

Sorokina, E., Wang, Y., Fyall, A., Lugosi, P., Torres, E., & Jung, T. (2022). Constructing a smart destination framework: A destination marketing organization perspective. *Journal of Destination Marketing & Management*, *23*, 100688. doi:10.1016/j.jdmm.2021.100688

Souza, G. C. (2014). Supply chain analytics. *Business Horizons*, *57*(5), 595–605. doi:10.1016/j.bushor.2014.06.004

Spiller, L. (2020). Direct, digital & data-driven marketing. *Sage (Atlanta, Ga.)*.

Stienmetz, J., Ferrer-Rosell, B., & Massimo, D. (2022). *Information and Communication Technologies in Tourism 2022: Proceedings of the ENTER 2022 ETourism Conference, January 11-14, 2022*. Springer Nature. 10.1007/978-3-030-94751-4

St-Jean, S., Viergever, M., & Leemans, A. (2020). Harmonization of diffusion MRI data sets with adaptive dictionary learning. *Human Brain Mapping*, *41*(16), 4478–4499. doi:10.1002/hbm.25117 PMID:32851729

Stylos, N., Zwiegelaar, J., & Buhalis, D. (2021). Big data empowered agility for dynamic, volatile, and time-sensitive service industries: The case of tourism sector. *International Journal of Contemporary Hospitality Management*, *33*(3), 1015–1036. doi:10.1108/IJCHM-07-2020-0644

Sun, Z. (2019). Intelligent big data analytics: a managerial perspective. In *Managerial Perspectives on Intelligent Big Data Analytics* (pp. 1–19). IGI Global. doi:10.4018/978-1-5225-7277-0.ch001

Szołtysek, J., & Trzpiot, G. (2012). Cluster Analysis in Description of Travel Behaviours. *Zeszyty Naukowe Politechniki Częstochowskiej*, 75.

Taecharungroj, V., & Mathayomchan, B. (2019). Analysing TripAdvisor reviews of tourist attractions in Phuket, Thailand. *Tourism Management*, *75*, 550–568. doi:10.1016/j.tourman.2019.06.020

Takata, K., & Hallmann, K. (2021). A systematic quantitative review of authenticity in sport tourism. *Journal of Sport & Tourism*, *25*(1), 26–41. doi:10.1080/14775085.2021.1877564

Talwar, S., Kaur, P., Fosso Wamba, S., & Dhir, A. (2021). Big Data in operations and supply chain management: A systematic literature review and future research agenda. *International Journal of Production Research, 59*(11), 3509–3534. doi:10.1080/00207543.2020.1868599

Telfer, D., & Sharpley, R. (2015). *Tourism and development in the developing world.* Routledge. doi:10.4324/9781315686196

Terzić, A., Demirović, D., Petrevska, B., & Limbert, W. (2021). Active sport tourism in Europe: Applying market segmentation model based on human values. *Journal of Hospitality & Tourism Research (Washington, D.C.), 45*(7), 1214–1236. doi:10.1177/1096348020926546

Thaduri, U. R. (2020). Decision Intelligence in Business: A Tool for Quick and Accurate Marketing Analysis. *Asian Business Review, 10*(3), 193–200. doi:10.18034/abr.v10i3.670

Thaichon, P., & Quach, S. (Eds.). (2022). *Artificial Intelligence for Marketing Management.* Taylor & Francis. doi:10.4324/9781003280392

Theodoridis, P. K., & Gkikas, D. C. (2019). How artificial intelligence affects digital marketing. In Strategic Innovative Marketing and Tourism: 7th ICSIMAT, Athenian Riviera, Greece, 2018 (pp. 1319-1327). Springer International Publishing. doi:10.1007/978-3-030-12453-3_151

Thomas, J., Karagoz, P., Ahamed, B., & Vasant, P. (2019). *Deep learning techniques and optimization strategies in big data analytics.* IGI Global.

Thomson, A., Toohey, K., & Darcy, S. (2021). The political economy of mass sport participation legacies from large-scale sport events: A conceptual paper. *Journal of Sport Management, 35*(4), 352–363. doi:10.1123/jsm.2019-0166

Thuita, J., & Njeru, W. (2021). Marketing Information Systems and Competitive Advantage at Consolidated Bank of Kenya Limited. *European Journal of Business and Management Research, 6*(5), 224–227. doi:10.24018/ejbmr.2021.6.5.1077

Tian, H., Presa-Reyes, M., Tao, Y., Wang, T., Pouyanfar, S., Miguel, A., ... Iyengar, S. S. (2021). Data analytics for air travel data: A survey and new perspectives. *ACM Computing Surveys, 54*(8), 1–35.

Tomlinson, A., & Young, C. (Eds.). (2006). *National identity and global sports events: Culture, politics, and spectacle in the Olympics and the football World Cup.* Suny Press.

Tong, L., Yan, W., & Manta, O. (2022). Artificial intelligence influences intelligent automation in tourism: A mediating role of internet of things and environmental, social, and governance investment. *Frontiers in Environmental Science, 10*, 135. doi:10.3389/fenvs.2022.853302

Torres Vega, M., Liaskos, C. K., Abadal, S., Papapetrou, E., Jain, A., Mouhouche, B., Kalem, G., Ergüt, S., Mach, M., Sabol, T., Cabellos-Aparicio, A., Grimm, C., De Turck, F., & Famaey, J. (2020). Immersive Interconnected Virtual and Augmented Reality: A 5G and IoT Perspective. *Journal of Network and Systems Management, 28*(4), 796–826. Advance online publication. doi:10.1007/s10922-020-09545-w

TripAdvisor. (2023). *TripAdvisor Fact Sheet.* TripAdvisor. Available at: https://www.tripadvisor.com/PressCenter-c4-Fact_Sheet.html

Tsaih, R. H., & Hsu, C. C. (2018). *Artificial intelligence in smart tourism: A conceptual framework.* Academic Press.

Tsai, S. P. (2020). Augmented reality enhancing place satisfaction for heritage tourism marketing. *Current Issues in Tourism, 23*(9), 1078–1083. doi:10.1080/13683500.2019.1598950

Tsamados, A., Aggarwal, N., Cowls, J., Morley, J., Roberts, H., Taddeo, M., & Floridi, L. (2021). The ethics of algorithms: key problems and solutions. *Ethics, Governance, and Policies in Artificial Intelligence*, 97-123.

Tscheu, F., & Buhalis, D. (2016). Augmented reality at cultural heritage sites. In A. Inversini & R. Schegg (Eds.), *Information and communication technologies in tourism 2016* (pp. 607–619). Springer. doi:10.1007/978-3-319-28231-2_44

Tsiakis, T. (2015). *Trends and innovations in marketing information systems.* IGI Global. doi:10.4018/978-1-4666-8459-1

Tyagi, A. (2021). *Data Science and Data Analytics: Opportunities and Challenges.* CRC Press. doi:10.1201/9781003111290

Valeri, M. (2023). *Tourism Innovation in the Digital Era: Big Data, AI and Technological Transformation.* Emerald Publishing Limited. doi:10.1108/9781837971664

Vasilopoulou, Ch., Theodorakopoulos, L., & Giotopoulos, K. (2023). Big Data and Consumer Behavior: The Power and Pitfalls of Analytics in the Digital Age. *Technium Social Sciences Journal, 45*(7), 469–480. doi:10.47577/tssj.v45i1.9135

Vehmas, H. (2010). Rationale of active leisure: Understanding sport, tourism and leisure choices in the Finnish society. *Ido Movement for Culture, 10*, 121–127.

Vera, D., Tabesh, P., Velez-Castrillon, S., Kachra, A., & Werner, S. (2024). Improvisational decision making: Context, antecedents, and outcomes. In *The Routledge companion to improvisation in organisations* (pp. 144–163). Routledge.

Verhoef, P. C., Kooge, E., & Walk, N. (2016). *Creating value with big data analytics: Making smarter marketing decisions.* Routledge. doi:10.4324/9781315734750

Viale, R. (2024). Enactive problem-solving: an alternative to the limits of decision making. *Elgar Companion to Herbert Simon*, 198.

Vieira, T., & Simões, D. M. (2024). Virtues of Tribal Behaviour in Sport: The Case of Portuguese Football Brands. *International Journal of Marketing. Communication and New Media, 11*(21), 132–152.

Villaespesa, E., & Álvarez, A. (2020). Visitor journey mapping at the Museo Nacional Thyssen-Bornemisza: Bringing cross-departmental collaboration to build a holistic and integrated visitor experience. *Museum Management and Curatorship*, *35*(2), 125–142. doi:10.1080/09647775.2019.1638821

Villamediana-Pedrosa, J., Vila-Lopez, N., & Küster-Boluda, I. (2020). Predictors of tourist engagement: Travel motives and tourism destination profiles. *Journal of Destination Marketing & Management*, *16*, 100412. doi:10.1016/j.jdmm.2020.100412

Vosgien, T. (2015). *Model-based system engineering enabling design-analysis data integration in digital design environments: application to collaborative aeronautics simulation-based design process and turbojet integration studies* (Doctoral dissertation, Ecole Centrale Paris).

Vu, H. Q., Li, G., Law, R., & Zhang, Y. (2018). Tourist activity analysis by leveraging mobile social media data. *Journal of Travel Research*, *57*(7), 883–898. doi:10.1177/0047287517722232

Walkowiak, S. (2016). *Big Data analytics with R*. Packt Publishing Ltd.

Wamba, S., Gunasekaran, A., Akter, S., Ren, S., Dubey, R., & Childe, S. (2017). Big data analytics and firm performance: Effects of dynamic capabilities. *Journal of Business Research*, *70*, 356–365. doi:10.1016/j.jbusres.2016.08.009

Wang, F., Iyamu, T., Phillips-Wren, G., & Forrest, J. (2023). BDAS-EPM: An Integrated Evolution Process Model for Big Data Analytics Systems. In *Development Methodologies for Big Data Analytics Systems: Plan-driven, Agile, Hybrid, Lightweight Approaches* (pp. 187–203). Springer International Publishing.

Wang, G., Gunasekaran, A., Ngai, E. W., & Papadopoulos, T. (2016). Big data analytics in logistics and supply chain management: Certain investigations for research and applications. *International Journal of Production Economics*, *176*, 98–110. doi:10.1016/j.ijpe.2016.03.014

Wang, J., Zheng, B., & Liu, H. (2021). Satisfying consumers all around: A multidisciplinary view of omnichannel retail. *Industrial Management & Data Systems*, *121*(1), 158–171. doi:10.1108/IMDS-08-2020-0452

Wang, R., Luo, J., & Huang, S. (2020). Developing an artificial intelligence framework for online destination image photos identification. *Journal of Destination Marketing & Management*, *18*, 100512. doi:10.1016/j.jdmm.2020.100512

Watson, R., Berthon, P., Pitt, L., & Zinkhan, G. (2023). *Electronic commerce: The strategic perspective*. Dryden.

Webber, K., & Zheng, H. (2020). *Big data on campus: Data analytics and decision making in higher education*. Johns Hopkins University Press. doi:10.1353/book.78960

Weinstein, A. (2013). *Handbook of market segmentation: Strategic targeting for business and technology firms*. Routledge. doi:10.4324/9780203862483

Winter, M. (2018). Visitor perspectives on commenting in museums. *Museum Management and Curatorship, 33*(5), 484–505. doi:10.1080/09647775.2018.1496354

Wirtz, J., & Lovelock, C. (2021). *Services marketing: People, technology, strategy*. World Scientific. doi:10.1142/y0024

Wixom, B. H., & Todd, P. A. (2005). A Theoretical Integration of User Satisfaction and Technology Acceptance. *Information Systems Research, 16*(1), 85–102. doi:10.1287/isre.1050.0042

Wong, I. A., Ma, J., & Xiong, X. (2020). Touristic experience at a nomadic sporting event: Craving cultural connection, sacredness, authenticity, and nostalgia. *Journal of Hospitality and Tourism Management, 44*, 70–78. doi:10.1016/j.jhtm.2020.05.003

Wong, K. (2016). *Big data analytics in genomics*. Springer. doi:10.1007/978-3-319-41279-5

Woodham, A. (2017). Sport, history, and heritage: Studies in public representation. *International Journal of Heritage Studies, 23*(1), 74–75. doi:10.1080/13527258.2016.1218913

Wörndl, W., Koo, C., & Stienmetz, J. (2021). *Information and Communication Technologies in Tourism 2021: Proceedings of the ENTER 2021 eTourism Conference, January 19–22, 2021*. Springer Nature. 10.1007/978-3-030-65785-7

Xiang, Z., & Fesenmaier, D. (2017). *Analytics in smart tourism design: concepts and methods*. Springer International Publishing Switzerland. doi:10.1007/978-3-319-44263-1

Xin, L., Qiao, G., Shao, Z., Jiang, T., Wen, C., Zhong, Y., & Li, Z. (2023). Understanding continuous sharing behavior of online travel community users: A case of TripAdvisor. *Journal of Tourism and Cultural Change, 21*(3), 328–343. doi:10.1080/14766825.2023.2170239

Yathiraju, N., & Bhatia, B. (2023). Predicting the Future of Heritage Conservation for Sustainable Resource Allocation. *International Journal of Sustainable Development Through AI. ML and IoT, 2*(1), 1–12.

Yoliando, F., Senjaya, E., Christyanawatie, J., & Stevani, N. (2023). A Comparative Study of Artificial Intelligence-Driven Applications in Enhancing Tourist Experience and Compatibility to Indonesia's Tourism Sector. In *Proceedings of the International Conference of Innovation in Media and Visual Design (IMDES 2023)* (Vol. 790, p. 157). Springer Nature. 10.2991/978-2-38476-136-4_14

Yoo, C., Yoon, D., & Park, E. (2018). Tourist motivation: An integral approach to destination choices. *Tourism Review, 73*(2), 169–185. doi:10.1108/TR-04-2017-0085

Zahay, D. (2008). Successful B2B customer database management. *Journal of Business and Industrial Marketing, 23*(4), 264–272. doi:10.1108/08858620810865843

ZareRavasan, A. (2023). Boosting innovation performance through big data analytics: An empirical investigation on the role of firm agility. *Journal of Information Science, 49*(5), 1293–1308. doi:10.1177/01655515211047425

Zarotis, G. (2019). Development of sports tourism. *International Journal of Humanities and Social Science Invention*, *8*(6), 1–7.

Zbuchea, A. (2012). Cultural interests while on holidays: An exploratory investigation. *Journal of Tourism Challenges & Trends*, *5*(2), 53–70.

Zhang, J., & Dong, L. (2021). Image monitoring and management of hot tourism destination based on data mining technology in big data environment. *Microprocessors and Microsystems*, *80*, 103515. doi:10.1016/j.micpro.2020.103515

Zhang, L., Xie, Y., Xidao, L., & Zhang, X. (2018). Multi-source heterogeneous data fusion. In *2018 International conference on artificial intelligence and big data (ICAIBD)* (pp. 47-51). IEEE.

Zhang, Q., Qiu, L., Wu, H., Wang, J., & Luo, H. (2019). Deep learning based dynamic pricing model for hotel revenue management. In *2019 International Conference on Data Mining Workshops (ICDMW)* (pp. 370-375). IEEE. 10.1109/ICDMW.2019.00061

Zierock, B., & Jungblut, A. (2023). Leveraging Prompts for Improving AI-Powered Customer Service Platforms: A Case Study of Chat GPT and Midjourney. *Learning*, *116*, 63–76.

Zikmund, W. G., Babin, B. J., Carr, J. C., & Griffin, M. (2013). *Business Research Methods.* Academic Press.

Zillinger, M. (2008). Germans' tourist behaviour in Sweden. *Tourism (Zagreb)*, *56*(2), 143–158.

Ziska Fields, . (Ed.). (2023). *Human Creativity vs. Machine Creativity: Innovations and Challenges. In Multidisciplinary Approaches in AI, Creativity, Innovation, and Green Collaboration* (pp. 19–28). Global. doi:10.4018/978-1-6684-6366-6.ch002

About the Contributors

Tareq Nael Hashem has been working as a Full Professor in Applied Science at a private university in Jordan since October 2023. He serves as a member of the Dissertation Committee at Westcliff University in the United States. He worked as an Assistant Professor at Philadelphia University for a period of 5 years starting from 2007. He worked as an Associate Professor at Philadelphia University for a duration of 2 years. He later worked as an Associate Professor at Isra University- Jordan for 8 years starting in 2014. He served as the Head of the Marketing Department at Isra University from October 10, 2019, to October 10, 2020. He held the position of Full Professor at Isra University- Jordan from April 7, 2022, to September 15, 2023. The study he conducted encompasses a wide array of subjects, spanning management in diverse industries, digital marketing, marketing information systems, and marketing. He is involved in reviewing, authoring, and editing book projects, and actively contributes to numerous scientific journals and international editorial boards. Furthermore, the researcher possesses practical expertise in the banking sector, having served as a credit officer at the Islamic International Arab Bank, and has also held a marketing manager position in the hotel furnishings industry at Tabarak International Group.

Ahmad Albattat is an Associate Professor in Graduate School of Management, Post Graduate Centre, Management and Science University, Shah Alam, Selangor, Malaysia. He is a Visiting Professor and External Examiner in Medan Academy of Tourism (Akpar Medan). He received PhD in Hospitality Management "Disaster and Emergency Planning and Preparedness" from University Sains Malaysia (USM), Malaysia. He worked as an Assistant Professor, Ammon Applied University College, Amman, Jordan. Senior Lecturer and Research Coordinator in School of Hospitality & Creative Arts, Management and Science University, Shah Alam, Selangor, Malaysia, and Researcher at Sustainable Tourism Research Cluster (STRC), Pulau Pinang, Malaysia. He was working for the Jordanian hospitality industry for 17 years. His teaching and consultancy fields include hospitality management, events management, research methodology, strategic management and final research projects. His research areas include hospitality management, hotel, tourism, events, emergency planning, disaster management, sustainable development goals and human resource. He is an active member of several Scientific and Editorial Board of International journals, reviewer, author and editor for book projects. His latest works have been published in the refereed international journals, conference proceedings, books and book chapters. Option 2 (100 words) Ahmad Albattat is an Associate Professor in Graduate School of Management, Management and Science University, Malaysia. He is a Visiting Professor and External Examiner in Medan Academy of Tourism. He received PhD in Hospitality Management from University Sains Malaysia (USM), Malaysia. His teaching and consultancy fields include hospitality management, events management, research methodology, strategic management and final research projects. His research areas include hospitality management, hotel, tourism, events, emergency planning, disaster management, sustainable development goals and human resource. He is an active member of several Scientific and Editorial Board of International journals, reviewer, author and editor for book projects.

Marco Valeri is Associate Professor of Organizational Behavior, Faculty of Economics, Niccolò Cusano University, Italy. He is Lecture in Applied Organizational Behaviour, Xenophon College, UK. He is Visiting Professor at University of Information Science and Technology (UIST) "St. Paul The Apostle", Macedonia. He is Adjunct Professor at Faculty of Social Sciences and Leisure Management, School of Hospitality, Tourism and Events, Taylor's University, Malaysia. He is Adjunct Professor at Faculty of Economics, Lovely Professional University (LPU), Phagwara, India. He is Associate Researcher in Strategy, Magellan Research Center, School of Management, Iaelyon Business School, Jean Monet University, France. He is Honorary Associate Professor, University of Pannonia, Hungary. Ranked #7 worldwide the most productive family economics scholars according to the ranking published by Texas State University. He's teaching and consultancy fields include strategic management, leadership development, cross-cultural management, international hospitality management. He is member of several Editorial Boards of international tourism journals, reviewer and editor of several handbooks on entrepreneurship, tourism and hospitality management (Emerald Publishing, Springer, Routledge and IGI Global).

Anukrati Sharma is Associate Professor of the Department of Commerce and Management at the University of Kota (A State Govt. University), Rajasthan, India. She is the Director of the Skill Development Centre of the same University. She is also Dean (Honorary) of Tourism and Hospitality at Vishwakarma Skills University, Jaipur (A Govt. State University). She was Head of the Department of Commerce and Management, University of Kota. In 2015, she received a Research

Award from the University Grants Commission (UGC), New Delhi, for her project "Analysis of the Status of Tourism in Hadoti and Shekhawati Region/Circuit (Rajasthan): Opportunities, Challenges, and Future Prospects." She is appointed as the Official Partner of the BRICS (DUT) Funded Project for the years 2022-2024 i.e. (BRICS Research Institute Grant Project Ref: BRI22/1215) titled "Growth and Sustainability of Livelihoods in the BRICS Countries: Knowledge Sharing in Social Justice, Governance, Multilateralism". She is also working on a Major Research Project under Mahatma Gandhi National Council of Rural Education, Ministry of Human Resource Development Government of India. A member of 7 professional bodies, she has attended a number of national and international conferences and presented 45 papers. She has been invited as Keynote, Speaker, Panel member by different countries such as Sri Lanka, Uzbekistan, South Africa, Nepal, Malaysia, Indonesia and Turkey.

* * *

Lalshawala Abdulmannan is a promising Electronics Engineering student currently pursuing her Bachelor's degree at RVCE. With a deep-rooted passion for technology and innovation, Abdul has distinguished himself through academic excellence and his active involvement in various extracurricular activities related to his field of study. From a young age, he was fascinated by electronic devices and their workings, which fueled his decision to embark on a journey in electronics engineering. Since joining Tech University, he has consistently been on the Dean's list, demonstrating his dedication and prowess in subjects ranging from circuit design to digital systems, microelectronics and interdisciplinary subjects. He is an active member of the college Formula Student Electric car Club, where he collaborates with fellow students on projects and participates in competitions. In addition to his coursework and club activities, Abdul has completed internships with leading technology firms, gaining hands-on experience in electronics design and manufacturing processes. These opportunities have allowed him to apply his theoretical knowledge to real-world problems, enhancing learning and professional development. Abdul academic projects often focus on sustainable and energy-efficient technologies. He is currently working as project manager in club, which involves developing a electric formula racing car emphasizing his commitment to green technology and innovation. With his solid academic foundation, practical experience, and passion for electronics engineering, Abdul mannan is poised to make significant contributions to the field of electronics and technology.

Tahreer Abu Hmeidan, a dedicated Digital Marketing Assistant Professor with a Ph.D. from the University of Bedfordshire, UK, focuses her research on the impact of digital marketing on brand equity in Jordanian private hospitals. Currently, as an Assistant Professor at the Applied Science Private University, she merges academic insight with practical experience, drawing from her roles as a Digital Marketing Consultant, Marketing Manager, and Director. Tahreer's commitment to student empowerment is evident through her roles as a Digital Marketing Trainer and Lecturer, where she imparts cutting-edge knowledge and ethical practices, fluently communicating in Arabic and English, and serving as a mentor for aspiring digital marketing leaders.

Bhupender Dighliya has more than ten years of experience in the fields of teaching, research and hotel operation. He has completed his doctorate from Institute of Hotel & Tourism Management, Maharshi Dayanand University, Rohtak - Haryana. He is working as Founding Member of School of Hotel Management, Starex University, Gurugram - Haryana. He has published research paper and book chapter in national and International journals and books. He presented several papers in national and international conferences. He is a dedicated and highly motivated hospitality professional.

Dwijendra Nath Dwivedi is a professional with 20+ years of subject matter expertise creating right value propositions for analytics and AI. He currently heads the EMEA+AP AI and IoT team at SAS, a worldwide frontrunner in AI technology. He is a post-Graduate in Economics from Indira Gandhi Institute of Development and Research and is PHD from crackow university of economics Poland. He has presented his research in more than 20 international conference and published several Scopus indexed paper on AI adoption in many areas. As an author he has contributed to more than 8 books and has more than 25 publications in high impact journals. He conducts AI Value seminars and workshops for the executive audience and for power users.

Heba Allah Gaafar is Professor and Head of Tourism Studies Department, Faculty of Tourism and Hotels, University of Sadat City, Egypt.

Hemant Gupta is Assistant Professor at Alliance University. He holds the Ph.D. degree from NIT Durgapur and Master in Business Management from University of Calcutta and has five years of industrial experience in Pharma and Food sectors. His research interest includes resource management in different sectors, education management and healthcare management.

Sindhu Rajendran is working as an Assistant Professor from the Department of Electronics and Communication Engineering, RV College of Engineering.

Célia Maria Quitério Ramos holds a PhD in Quantitative Methods applied to Economics and Management, in the specialty of Econometrics, by the University of Algarve. Master in Electrotechnical and Computer Engineering by Instituto Superior Técnico. Graduated in Computer Engineering from the University of Coimbra. Also, is an integrated researcher of CinTurs (Research Center for Tourism, Sustainability and Well-Being ().Holds a Professional Diploma in Digital Marketing from Digital Marketing Institute in Dublin, Ireland. She is Coordinator Professor at School for Management, Hospitality and Tourism, also in the UALG, where she lectures computer science, mainly Information Systems, Business Intelligence, Information Systems for Management Support Decision. Celia was the President of the Pedagogical Council, since 2017 until 2021, Director of the degree in Marketing and member of the coordination of the master's degree in Hospitality Management, from September 2015 to October 2019, of the School of Management, Hospitality and Tourism. Areas of research and special interest include tourism information systems, big data, business intelligence, data analytics, smart tourism, sentiment analysis, machine learning, social media marketing, econometric modeling and panel-data models. Célia Ramos has published in the fields of information systems, marketing and tourism, namely, she has authored book chapters, conference papers and journal articles. She is reviewer of many international journals Also, at the level of applied research, she has participated in several funded projects.

Index

V

www.ingramcontent.com/pod-product-compliance
Lightning Source LLC
LaVergne TN
LVHW061541290926
849162LV00004B/875